The Early History of the Lutheran Church in Georgia

The Early History of the Lutheran Church in Georgia

HERMANN WINDE

Russell C. Kleckley, editor and translator

☙PICKWICK *Publications* · Eugene, Oregon

THE EARLY HISTORY OF THE LUTHERAN CHURCH IN GEORGIA

Copyright © 2021 Russell C. Kleckley. All rights reserved. Except for brief quotations in critical publications or reviews, no part of this book may be reproduced in any manner without prior written permission from the publisher. Write: Permissions, Wipf and Stock Publishers, 199 W. 8th Ave., Suite 3, Eugene, OR 97401.

Permission for the use of the images of Johann Martin Boltzius, Anton Leopold von Firmian, Gotthilf August Francke, Samuel Lau, Samuel Urlsperger, and Friedrich Michael Ziegenhagen courtesy of the Francke Foundations, Halle, Germany. Permission for the use of the image of the map of Georgia courtesy of Hargrett Rare Book and Manuscript Library/University of Georgia Libraries.
Scripture quotations are taken from the King James Version unless otherwise noted. Scripture quotations marked (NRSV) come from the New Revised Standard Version Bible, copyright © 1989 National Council of the Churches of Christ in the United States of America. Used by permission. All rights reserved worldwide

Pickwick Publications
An Imprint of Wipf and Stock Publishers
199 W. 8th Ave., Suite 3
Eugene, OR 97401

www.wipfandstock.com

PAPERBACK ISBN: 978-1-7252-7496-9
HARDCOVER ISBN: 978-1-7252-7497-6
EBOOK ISBN: 978-1-7252-7498-3

Cataloguing-in-Publication data:

Names: Winde, Hermann, author. | Kleckley, Russell C., editor and translator.

Title: The early history of the Lutheran church in Georgia / Hermann Winde ; edited and translated by Russell C. Kleckley.

Description: Eugene, OR: Pickwick Publications, 2021. | Includes bibliographical references and index.

Identifiers: ISBN 978-1-7252-7496-9 (paperback). | ISBN 978-1-7252-7497-6 (hardcover). | ISBN 978-1-7252-7498-3 (ebook).

Subjects: LCSH: Lutheran Church—United States—History. | Georgia—Church history. | Ebenezer First Church.

Classification: BX8041 W55 2021 (print). | BX8041 (ebook).

03/24/21

Contents

Editor's Foreword		vii
List of Abbreviations		xi
1	The Sources	1
2	The Historical Background	14
3	The History of the Settlement of the Lutheran Communities	26
4	The Development of the Communities in the Organization of Their Life	112
5	The Pastors of the Communities and Their Theological Position	163
6	The Relationship of the Communities to Other Denominations	207
7	The Lutheran Confessional Identity of the Communities	217
Appendix I: Text of Ebenezer's First Church Constitution		221
Appendix II: Index of the Bibliographically Identifiable Works of the Ebenezer Church Library That Are Mentioned in the Archives		226
Appendix III: Index of the Letter Manuscripts of the Archives of Halle and Tübingen		235
About the Author		241
Bibliography		243
Index of Names		251
Index of Subjects		257
Index of Places		261

Editor's Foreword

THE STORY OF THE early Lutheran church in Georgia is not an isolated tale of an insulated people. The story reaches deep into the history of colonial Georgia where it intertwines with the colony's founding and its struggles to grow and thrive in the decades leading to the American Revolution and beyond. The story also reaches far and wide across the Atlantic Ocean where it is inextricably linked to people and events in Germany, England, and the mountains and valleys of the Austrian Alps. The story begins with a small group of Protestant religious exiles expelled from the territory of Salzburg in the eighteenth century. It passes through the towns and farmlands of southwestern Germany. It is nurtured by the spirit and care of German Lutheran Pietism centered in Halle. It takes a decisive turn through London where it converges with the plan to create a colony to give opportunity to England's poor and protection to England's already established colonies against Spanish forces in Florida.

The story of early Lutheranism in Georgia, then, cannot be told without taking into account the stories of these other places and events, even as it provides a link that connects and illuminates them. The story is not only a chapter in American Lutheran religious history. It is a chapter that adds insight that otherwise would be lost into the social, political, and economic histories of Georgia, colonial America, and the early United States. It is a story that informs our awareness of the critical English-German connection in the eighteenth century, of Halle Pietism and its extensive reach across the globe, and of the Protestant expulsions from the territory of Salzburg in the 1730s, among countless other associations.

In 1960, a young doctoral candidate, Hermann Winde, at the Martin Luther University Halle-Wittenberg, completed a ThD dissertation with the title, "Die Frühgeschichte der Lutherischen Kirche in Georgia," that chronicled that story in its depth as well as its breadth. Earlier works had provided important and useful glimpses into the story of early Lutheranism in Georgia. The most notable and extensive of these efforts, Philip A. Strobel's *The Salzburgers and Their Descendants*, published in 1855, had provided the foundation for later studies for more than a century. Yet as important as Strobel's work had been, it was limited in scope, deficient in available sources, and erroneous in important details. Winde's aim with his dissertation was to produce "a new, comprehensive representation" that outlined "the core of early Lutheranism in Georgia, its theological stance, and piety."[1] Digging deeply in the original sources preserved mainly at the *Missions-archiv* of the Francke Foundations (*Franckesche Stiftungen*) in Halle and the archives at the University of Tübingen, among other places, Winde was able both to expand and correct previous knowledge.

The success of his efforts can be measured by how indispensable his work has become for scholars who have followed him in a variety of fields spanning decades. These include George Fenwick Jones, whose book, *The Salzburger Saga*, has provided the most accessible entry for English-speaking audiences into the story of the Ebenezer community, the settlement created by Georgia's first Lutherans, since the book was first published in 1984. The lasting impact of Winde's dissertation continues to this day, evident in its use in the important 2015 book by James Van Horn Melton, *Religion, Community, and Slavery on the Colonial Frontier*. Between the work of Jones and Melton, a host of other English-language works, including articles for academic journals as well as book length studies, have drawn from Dr. Winde's dissertation.

While many studies over the years have drawn on Winde's work, none have replaced its significance. Much information remains in his study that can be found in no other work of any language. Yet Winde's dissertation remains important not only as a source but as a resource. It provides an introduction to the relevant archival material. It also points to an array of secondary resources from earlier generations of scholarship that remain significant and useful but are often overlooked.

Despite its demonstrated importance and continuing relevance, Winde's dissertation has never been published. It has been available previously only through photocopied exemplars in its original German that are not universally available and not always easy to read. The aim with this translation and edition is to make Winde's important contribution more widely accessible, to scholars and general audiences alike, for those with interests ranging from the story of the Salzburger exiles in Georgia and the Ebenezer community, to the history of Georgia, to early American history

---

1. See p. 12.

more generally, Lutheranism in the American South, and the trans-Atlantic world of the eighteenth century.

This edition revises the format of Dr. Winde's original dissertation but leaves the content intact with only a few minor changes. Where changes or insertions have been made, those alterations are indicated by brackets.

Around 1990, the late Dr. David Noble, Professor of Foreign Language at the University of Vermont and later at Armstrong State University, produced a preliminary, draft translation of Dr. Winde's dissertation that circulated in private hands among a small group of interested readers. I am grateful to Dr. Noble for his work and consulted it on occasion to compare his translation with my own. The translation offered here, however, is a new and original rendering of the text.

I am also grateful to Vince Exley of Marietta, Georgia, a descendant of the Ebenezer community and invaluable resource for all things related to it, who initially suggested this project and facilitated the contact between Dr. Winde and me.

Most of all, I am grateful to Dr. Winde for his work, not only in writing his dissertation on *The Early History of the Lutheran Church in Georgia* but also for his subsequent contributions over the years. Dr. Winde has been a patient and careful partner in this project. His attention to detail, and numerous suggestions and corrections, have greatly improved this translation. It has been a pleasure to work with him in finally making his important work available to a wider audience, both to scholars and to readers with a general interest in the topic, who will continue to benefit from Dr. Winde's scholarship.

Russell C. Kleckley
Minneapolis, Minnesota
June 2020

Abbreviations

ADB	*Allgemeine Deutsche Biographie*. Edited and published by the Historische Commission bei der Königl. Akademie der Wissenschaften. 56 vols. Leipzig: Duncker & Humblot, 1875ff.
B	Boltzius, Johann Martin
Bm	Bergmann, Johann Ernst
Dr	Driessler, Johann Ulrich
E	*Diarium extraordinarium*
EE	Ebenezer
F	Fascicle
Fr	Francke, Gotthilf August
G	Gronau, Israel Christian
J	*Informatoren-Verzeichnis der Franckeschen Stiftungen* (Teacher Index of the Francke Foundations)
L	Lemcke, Hermann Heinrich
M	Muhlenberg, Henry Melchior
R	Rabenhorst, Christian
TK	Tübinger Kapsel
Tr	Triebner, Christoph Friedrich
U	Urlsperger (senior [sen] and junior [jun], as indicated)
UA	Urlsperger, *Americanisches Ackerwerk*
UN	Urlsperger, *Der ausführlichen Nachrichten*
Z	Ziegenhagen, Michael

Abbreviations

( )	In citations, parentheses in original
[ ]	In citations, insertions of the author
< >	In citations, completions to marred passages

Call numbers of the documents of the Missions Archive—Number Letter Number : Number (e.g. 5A10:45)

Call numbers of the Tübingen Archives—Capsule Fascicle: Page

# 1

The Sources

PREVIOUS ACCOUNTS AND THEIR SOURCES

Far removed from the centers of Lutheranism in America, far removed from the mainstream of Protestant emigrants from the archbishopric of Salzburg, and far removed from the grand regions of success of the North American colonists, the Lutheran church in Georgia had its beginning. Even so, it played an essential part in the emergence of American Lutheranism. After the Anglican Church, it had the first organized church presence in Georgia. The first governor of the independent state of Georgia, Johann Adam Treutlen, came from its congregations. It established the first orphanage in America, and the descendants of its first members form the core of Lutheran congregations not only in Georgia but also in South Carolina and Florida. The Lutheran church in Georgia has been conscious of the obligations inherent in this tradition whenever it has borne in mind its own Lutheran character. A wide range of specialized literature testifies to that fact and deserves attention at the outset in order to be able to judge the significance of the material developed here and to chart the path for the undertaking at hand.

The publication and evaluation of the previously known sources for the area of American church history under consideration proceed in three periods that are discernible through specific, characteristic representatives.

1. In keeping with a custom of Pietism and at the explicit instruction of his former superior Gotthilf August Francke, the son of August Hermann Francke, Johann Martin Boltzius, Georgia's first Lutheran pastor, kept an official journal called a *Diarium*, as did his colleagues in Tranquebar in South India, who came from the same school, and as did Henry Melchior Muhlenberg in Pennsylvania.

For the solicitation and encouragement of emigrants for Georgia, a version of this journal was published already a year after the establishment of Lutheran settlements in this colony.[1] But the bulk of it[2] was published from 1735 to 1767 in Augsburg by Samuel Urlsperger and his son Johann August under the titles, "Detailed Reports on the Salzburger Emigrants, Who Settled in America," and, "The American Husbandry of God, or, Reliable Reports Concerning the Condition of the American English in Georgia and the Town of Ebenezer Planted by the Salzburger Emigrants."[3] With these reports 368 letters also were published.[4] Occasionally, the prefaces of the individual "continuations" (*Fortsetzungen*) of this work also are significant sources.

These are, by and large, the most important and comprehensive published sources to date. Their significance will be investigated in what follows.

---

1. "An Extract of the Journals of Mr. Commissary Von Reck, Who Conducted the First Transport of Saltzburgers to Georgia. And of the Reverend Boltzius, One of their Ministers. Giving an Account of their Voyage to, and happy Settlement in that Province" (London: SPCK, 1734), 72 pages. Probably an extract of the time from February 27, 1733 new style (arrival of the Salzburgers in Rotterdam) to July 14, 1734 old style (Von Reck's departure from Ebenezer to London).

2. UN includes November 7, 1733 to December 31, 1743; January 18, 1747 to March 31, 1751. UA includes April 1, 1751 to December 31, 1754; January 1, 1759 to December 31, 1760.

3. *Der ausführlichen Nachrichten Von der Königlich=Groß=Britannischen Colonie Saltzburgischer Emigranten in America*, Samuel Urlsperger, ed. (Halle 1741), Part 1 + Continuations 1–5; Part 1, *Ausführliche Nachricht Von den Saltzburgischen Emigranten, Die sich in America niedergelassen haben*, etc. (Halle 1735); Part 2, Continuations 6–12 of the *Ausführliche Nachricht*, etc. (1746); Part 3, Continuations 13–18, etc. (1752), translated and published in English as *Detailed Reports on the Salzburger Emigrants Who Settled in America*, ed. and trans. George Fenwick Jones, et al., 18 vols. (Athens: University of Georgia Press, 1968–1995). Also, *Americanisches Ackerwerk Gottes oder zuverlässige Nachrichten, den Zustand der americanisch englischen und von salzburgischen Emigranten erbauten Pflanzstadt Ebenezer in Georgien betreffend, aus dorther eingeschickten glaubwürdigen Diarien genommen, und mit Briefen der dasigen Herren Prediger noch weiter bestättiget*, 5 Parts, ed. Samuel Urlsperger and Johann August Urlsperger (Augsburg 1754–1767).

4. Until 1743, including those to Francke; afterwards almost exclusively letters to Urlsperger.

There appeared at the same time, written in the interest of the Trustees of Georgia, a glossed-over depiction of the condition and prospects of the colony[5] and an American response[6] that illuminate the economic performance of Georgia's Lutherans, something of only marginal interest within the bounds of the study at hand. Several letters from the last years of the eighteenth century from the Lutheran pastor Johann Bergmann in Georgia have been included in the series, *Neuere Geschichte der Evangelischen Missions-Anstalten zu Bekehrung der Heiden in Ostindien*.[7]

2. That was the state of affairs when, with the beginning of the nineteenth century, Romanticism, in its various manifestations, also appeared in America. As in Europe, there began to be a feeling of one nation transcending various boundaries, of being settled after turbulent revolutions, and a corresponding discovery of an interest in the history of the nation, the respective states, and each denomination—for the Lutherans, especially since the inspirational year of 1830 [editor's note: the 300th anniversary of the Augsburg Confession]—that was generally, as in Europe, for the most part conservative, orthodox, particular, and confessional, something which did no harm whatsoever to historical research.

The first foundational works, based on the sources already mentioned, appeared for the subject at hand but did not tap any new ones. In 1837, Bancroft wrote his *History of the United States of America*. From 1840 on, the Georgia Historical Society published its

---

5. Anonymous; the actual author is the Secretary of the Trustees, Benjamin Martyn (Binder-Johnson, "Die Haltung der Salzburger in Georgia zur Sklaverei," 191), *An Account shewing the Progress of the Colony of Georgia in America from Its First Establishment* (London, 1741).

6. Patrick Tailfer, *A True and Historical Narrative of the Colony of Georgia* (Charleston, SC, 1741).

7. "Recent History of the Evangelical Missionary Efforts for the Conversion of the Heathen in East India." Printed in the series are:
5B4:1 = April 2, 1799 Bm. original: vol. 5, part 56, 731–33.
5B4:2 = April 3, 1799 Bm. original: vol. 5, part 56, 733–36.
5B4:3 = October 7, 1799 Bm. original: vol. 5, part 56, 736–41.
5B4:5 = January 14, 1800 Bm. original: vol. 5, part 57, 815–16.
Bibliographically unverifiable is the document, Christoph Friedrich Triebner, "Ebenezerische Todes-Thäler, oder Anekdoten einer vier und zwanzigjährigen Amtsführung" (London, between 1786–1793); (Johann Gottlieb Burckhardt, *Kirchen-Geschichte der Deutschen Gemeinden in London nebst historischen Beylagen und Predigten* [Tübingen 1798], 116–17; 5B4:17, 51 = January 26, 1802 Bm. original; 1C34b: 44 = May 4, 1793 Tr. original).

"Collections."[8] Hazelius' *History of the American Lutheran Church* followed in 1846, and one year later the first volume of Stevens' *History of Georgia*.[9] Finally, in 1855, Strobel published his *The Salzburgers and Their Descendants*, a work written with insight and interest, and in doing so made a notable stride forward. Not only was he the first to read more than just the beginning of the thick volumes of the Urlsperger edition,[10] but, since he himself was pastor of the Lutheran congregation in Ebenezer, Georgia, he was able to use the archival materials still extant there after the turmoil of the Revolutionary War: portions of the baptismal, marriage, and death registers, several legal documents pertaining mostly to land transactions, and a number of letters from the period after 1783.

In addition, there were the oral reports, which are not to be underestimated, of the older members of the congregation. His account, undertaken with great diligence, joined with his personal familiarity of the place and the wealth of the material offered by him for the first time in English, awakened in readers the impression that now everything had been said that was to be said, that the work was exhaustive, and whoever wanted to deal with this subject need only to refer to it. And so it happened. Jones,[11] Wolf,[12] Jacobs,[13] Faust,[14] and a whole series of others drew their knowledge from Strobel.[15]

---

8. "Collections of the Georgia Historical Society," vols. I to VI (Savannah, 1840–1904). Apart from the references cited, they contain no new relevant sources.

9. William Bacon Stevens, *A History of Georgia from its First Discovery by Europeans to the Adoption of the Present Constitution in MDCCXVIII*, 2 vols. (1847 and 1859). There also appeared Henry Melchior Muhlenberg, "Journal of a Voyage from Philadelphia to Ebenezer, Georgia, in the Years 1774–1775," trans. J. W. Richards, in *The Evangelical Review* (Gettysburg, January 1850–October 1852).

10. However, he did not work through everything; for example, the entries from Boltzius' *Vita* in UA escaped him.

11. Charles Colcock Jones, *The History of Georgia*, vol. I, *Aboriginal and Colonial Epochs*, and vol. 2, *Revolutionary Epoch* (Boston: Houghton, Mifflin, and Company, 1883).

12. Edmund Jacob Wolf, *The Lutherans in America: A Story of Struggle, Progress, Influence, and Marvelous Growth* (New York and Rostock 1890).

13. Henry Eyster Jacobs, *A History of the Evangelical Lutheran Church in the United States*, the American Church History Series, vol. IV (New York 1893).

14. Albert Bernhardt Faust, *The German Element in the United States with Special Reference to Its Political, Moral, Social, and Educational Influence*, 2nd ed., 2 vols. (New York 1927).

15. It is noteworthy that Gräbner, *Geschichte der Lutherischen Kirche in America*, part I (St. Louis 1892), read for himself UN and UA. With regard to this literature, the quite frequent distortion in American circles of German personal names must be

3. Since there was nothing new to say, interest in the subject[16] also languished until new sources again came to light at the beginning of the twentieth century. Allen Daniel Candler published from 1904, and then from 1908 on, the *Colonial* and *Revolutionary Records of the State of Georgia*, multi-volume collections that made available primarily minutes of the British and American administrative bodies of this colony, together with relevant newspaper articles and correspondence, with the selection determined in keeping with the interests of political and economic history.[17] A whole host of those interested in the topic gladly seized this treasure trove of information and produced a considerable number of studies on specific topics, about which the pages of the *Georgia Historical Quarterly* again and again give ample testimony.[18] Cooper, naturally, in his *Story of Georgia*, also made detailed use of this nearly inexhaustible publication. But it can be recognized from the type of contributions brought together here that, consistent with the nature of the sources, interesting and detailed reports on the political and economic history of the Lutheran settlements in Georgia held pride of place for analysis, since these were almost exclusively the kinds of matters that were negotiated with the English authorities and with which the Lutherans were enmeshed in the fabric of governmental politics. In fact, the previously mentioned articles of the *Georgia Historical Quarterly* deal primarily with this problem,[19] while writings in church history obviously and understandably can profit here only a little and incidentally.

Renewed efforts were undertaken to discover additional sources for the history of Lutherans in Georgia when genealogical interests surfaced in wide circles in the 1920s. Caroline Price Wilson examined

---

noted, leading even to forms such as Boblius (Boltzius) and Irael Clinton Gronder (Israel Christian Gronau). The degree of this carelessness is, as a rule, an appropriate measure of the accuracy of the entire work in question.

16. No one wrote specifically about Georgia; the works that are mentioned are cited only for purposes of completeness.

17. *The Colonial Records of the State of Georgia. Compiled and published under the authority of the legislature by Allen D. Candler*, vols. I–XXV (Atlanta, 1904–1916); *The Revolutionary Records of the State of Georgia. Compiled and published under the authority of the legislature by Allen D. Candler*, 3 vols. (Atlanta 1908).

18. *Georgia Historical Quarterly*, published by the Georgia Historical Society (Savannah 1917–present); for example, Brantley, Corry, Coulter, McKinstry, Newton, Pennington, among others.

19. Corry, "The Houses of Colonial Georgia," 181–201; McKinstry, "Silk Culture in the Colony of Georgia," 225–35; Newton, "The Agricultural Activities of the Salzburgers in Colonial Georgia," 248–63.

court documents of the Effingham County Courthouse (Georgia) and the previously mentioned archival materials available at Ebenezer.[20] After the *Georgia Historical Quarterly* had issued a brief preprint,[21] the English edition of the manuscript, found in the Library of Congress,[22] of Ebenezer's parish register (baptismal, marriage, and death registers) appeared in 1929 through Voigt and Linn.[23]

However, the church history of the Lutherans in Georgia advanced no farther. That nothing surpassed Strobel, despite all efforts in this area, is evident from the new edition of his book in 1953.

SCOPE AND SIGNIFICANCE OF THE ARCHIVAL MATERIAL IN HALLE AND TÜBINGEN

In the course of the examination of the extensive permanent holdings of the Missions Archives (*Missionsarchivs*) of the Francke Foundations in Halle, the archival materials relevant to the Lutheran church in Georgia found there for the investigation at hand were thoroughly studied. Since, as a result of the events of World War II, a portion of these holdings (approximately 1000 pages) came, by way of the state library (*Staatsbibliothek*) in Berlin, into the manuscript division of the library of the University of Tübingen, these materials also have been used in this work. In addition, the *Informatoren-Verzeichnis* of the Francke Foundations was analyzed. This index is a registry with the personal files containing a brief description[24] of everyone who taught in the various institute schools[25] from around 1725 until into the nineteenth century.

Altogether, approximately 7000 handwritten pages were taken into account.[26] Of these, about 4600 pages comprise the correspondence of

20. Wilson, "The Swan of Huss," 372–91.
21. Colquitt, "Records of Ebenezer Church," 97–99, 191–93.
22. Colquitt, "Records of Ebenezer Church," 97.
23. Voigt and Linn, eds., "Ebenezer Record Book," as part of "An Exhibition Commemorating the Settlement of Georgia." Two years later, Linn wrote a doctoral dissertation on the subject, "The Georgia Colony of Salzburgers."
24. According to the following pattern: Residence before arrival in Halle, date of birth, role in the institution with dates; comments on piety, study, method of instruction, school discipline; place and time of entry into first pastoral office. Finally, to complete the personal information for several pastors, available parish books as well as the matriculation register of the University of Halle-Wittenberg were used (specific information at the respective citations).
25. With the exception of the *Paedagogium Regium*.
26. The largest portion of these is compiled in Section 5 of the Missions Archives.

Georgia's Lutheran pastors with the directors of the Francke Foundations.[27] This correspondence includes 154 original letters from Boltzius, numerous outlines of the replies from Halle, with corrections and additions by the directors written in their own hand, occasional copies of American letters to London and Augsburg, copies of letters by the pastors from the early years to relatives or acquaintances in Germany, and also about twenty original letters from members of the American community and intra-European correspondence between Augsburg, Halle, and London.

The collection of these letters in Section 5 of the Missions Archives, beginning in fall 1733, is interrupted by gaps for the years approximately between 1753–1762, and 1768–1782. In both periods of time, disputes arose among Georgia's Lutheran pastors. Destructive wartime events also moved across that region. Consequently, this correspondence was removed in order to protect it from unauthorized eyes. Part of it is found in the Tübingen files; the rest is scattered throughout various sections of the Missions Archives.

The correspondence ends with the letter dated March 17, 1806, the last letter of Pastor Bergmann,[28] something that is possibly connected with the death of Johann August Urlsperger (March 1, 1806), who was one of the supervisors of the emigrants to Georgia. Of the letters, eighty-two (approximately 383 pages) were published in Urlsperger's publications and four (approximately twenty-one pages) in the *Neuere Geschichte der Evangelischen Missions-Anstalten zu Bekehrung der Heiden in Ostindien*.[29] Of the 2351 manuscript pages comprising journals, 2278 were edited by Urlsperger, almost exactly one-third of his output.[30]

The Inspector of the Francke Foundations and Secretary of G. A. Francke, Sebastian Andreas Fabricius, began the collection of this correspondence and deposited the first major items in April 1748 (5D5, 1 = April 19, 1748).

27. They took on average five months; the extremes are three to eight and one-half months.

28. 5B4:45; arrived in Halle on September 1, 1806. [Some years after this dissertation was finished, six additional letters were discovered in the archives of the Francke Foundations. These include an additional, undated letter from 1806 (5B4:46), along with letters from February 27, 1818 (5B4:49); September 7, 1819 (5B4:51); February 22, 1820 (5B4:51); February 28, 1820 (5B4:53); December 16, 1822 (5B4:56)].

29. See above, p. 3, n. 7.

30. 1388 of 3953 pages of printed journals. The greater part, from the hand of a European copyist (the pages are unfolded in quarto format) in the volumes of the series 5B. However, the substantial portion of the journals from Ebenezer or Augsburg arriving in Halle were lost (5A11:30, 130 = July 24, 1745 Fr. draft; 1743 and January 1–12, 1744 were once available but today are completely missing). Moreover, a number of journal "extracts" are available, for the following reasons: The sender of all European and recipient of all American and Indian mail was Ziegenhagen, and later his successor Pasche (5A3:17, 112 = January 8, 1736 B. original), who forwarded the incoming mail

These circumstances will create some reservation regarding our undertaking in anyone knowledgeable about the history of Lutheranism in America, since Tappert's edition of the journals of Muhlenberg[31] has been available for several years. Muhlenberg likewise, and almost at the same time as his colleagues in Georgia, left Halle, and gives in his own accounts seemingly such an impartial and comprehensive report of his activity, including quite a number of letters both received and sent, that there is at first glance hardly anything essential and new to be expected from additional archival material. This raises the question, is the undertaking at hand here worthwhile?

In order to answer the question, the reason and aim of Muhlenberg and Boltzius in keeping a journal first needs to be explored.[32]

1. Muhlenberg wrote his journal because of his pietistic disposition, for which daily self-examination was a requirement. Consequently, no detailed self-criticism can be expected in it, but the outlook is what is decisive.

2. Muhlenberg used the diary for himself as a report on his transactions, finances, conferences, official duties, correspondence, and so on.

---

to Augsburg or Halle. However, the journals, in keeping with Urlsperger's wish, are addressed to him; he wanted to send them to Halle (5A1:21, 100 = December 2, 1733, B. Ps. original). But that proved to be very burdensome for Halle, since the letters arriving here often made reference to events in the journals, which also were not understood. The copies from Augsburg often came after long delay and were not complete; they also had to be solicited (5A3:14, 100 = January 16, 1736 Fr. draft; 5A3:18,120 = May 24, 1736 Fr. draft; 5A7:8, 23 = April 21, 1738 Z. original). For that reason, Gronau in particular prepared, as his time allowed, "Extracts" of the journals for Halle (5A7:2, 3 = January 20, 1738 B. original) that were not compiled separately here but scattered in the correspondence depending on arrival. Through them, Halle was in some measure kept informed, so that the collecting of the complete copies of the journals dropped off. Boltzius also prepared for the SPCK and the Trustees, at their request, an English journal extract that was sent to them in the form of an annual report at the end of each year but was not intended for publication (5A11:23, 84 = December 29, 1744 B. original; UN July 12, 1748; 5B1:7, 30 = December 15, 1748, postscript = December 27, 1748 B. original; UN II, 431 = letter July 21, 1749 B. to U. sen.). None of these are preserved in Halle and Tübingen. The journal manuscripts are of far greater value, as their American originals were not, as with Muhlenberg's journals, partially preserved. In spring 1803 they were "brought to the stores in Charleston as wastepaper and were mockingly skimmed," about which Pastor Bergmann, who reports this, unfortunately did nothing. Also, Strobel reports, "The church records were nearly all destroyed" (*The Salzburgers and Their Descendants*, 207).

31. See Tappert and Doberstein, eds., *The Journals of Henry Melchior Muhlenberg, in Three Volumes.*

32. The following (up to and including point 4) according to Tappert, preface to volume 1 of the edition.

3. The journal served him as a written account for asserting his position in his actions and dealings, especially in the beginning, and to defend against and repudiate attacks, for example, from Zinzendorf or other traveling "preachers."

4. Muhlenberg used his journal as the basis for the reports that he sent at greater intervals to the directors of the Halle Orphan House.

5. If Muhlenberg thought about readers of his journals, he had in mind readers of the original manuscript and the handwritten copies of it.

With Boltzius, and those who occasionally kept the journal in his stead,[33] the situation was fundamentally different. 1. In the instructions from Francke and Urlsperger when he took up his position, Boltzius was obligated to keep an "official journal,"[34] and he followed this order for the entire duration of his activity just as precisely as he also did with his other official duties.[35] With such an approach, the distinctive pietistic character was lost, and it took on a mechanical character. 2. From the beginning, Boltzius was aware that his journal was to be published, as also was the case with the Halle missionaries in Tranquebar[36] whose printed works were recommended to him as a model.[37] Under this circumstance he needed to use discretion, in complete contrast to Muhlenberg. Moreover, publication, as was the case with the "Halle Reports," occurred with the expressed intent to awaken the interest of devout circles in Europe toward the Lutheran communities in Georgia and to encourage them to make various and, if at all possible, not-so-modest donations. Consequently, not only could certain things not appear in the journals, but certain other things had to appear. For

33. Pastors Gronau, Lemcke, or Rabenhorst.

34. 5A1:6, 39; 5A1:10, 54.

35. Yet in his last letter to Francke, "But you have known for some time now, my dearest Herr Doctor, that, because of my headaches, poor vision, and other hindrances, I had to give up the continuation of the official journal kept for so many years with his assistance; and though I should begin with it again several times, from my conscience being pressed due to my sworn instructions, since my Herrn Colleagues were not moved to do it, I nevertheless soon had to break it off again, on account of the reasons mentioned; finally, I, to the complete easing of my conscience, was dispensed from it, first from His Reverence, the most worthy Herr Court Preacher Ziegenhagen, and in the last letter to me from Herr Diacon J. A. Urlsperger" (5B2:22, 90–91 = June 24, 1765 B. original to Fr.).

36. "Der Königl. Dänischen Missionarien aus Ost-Indien eingesandter Ausführlichen Berichten Erster Theil. . . . Vom Ersten ausführlichen Bericht an bis zu dessem zwölfter Continuation mitgetheilet," etc. [First Part of the Submitted Detailed Reports of the Royal Danish Missionaries from East India. . .Imparted from the First Detailed Report to its Twelfth Continuation, etc.] (Halle: Orphan House, 1735).

37. 5A1:10, 54.

the earnest Boltzius, that was somewhat difficult, and so he was taken under wing; the journals were edited, and thoroughly so.[38]

Urlsperger conveyed to Francke the guidelines for the editing:

a. That whenever something appears in the journal that is very detrimental to a person, either omit the passage entirely, or at least the name will be left out.

b. That whenever something appears about the papists, only the harsh expressions, such as "idolatrous," "anti-Christian atrocity," "worldly priests," and so on, should be removed.

c. That whenever passages appear about the usefulness of the private devotional hours, community prayers of faithful readers, and the like, and as stories of praying people are told, they are to be told in such a way that an opponent may not say that these things are made absolutely necessary.

d. That concerning the forgiving of sins, caution should be taken in expressing whether it is important to know the precise time such things occurred, along with other similar things.

e. That it is better to omit the names of authors, at least with several who are held suspect.[39]

Something similar was also said in connection with the editing of the letters.[40] No one will dispute the doubtless justification of such a procedure. But undertaking the dubious pleasure of verifying how this was done leads nonetheless to something that gives pause: this revision was an outright re-working of the material. For example, already radically reworked were the first days of the journey of the first "transport" of the Salzburger emigrants.[41] Later, events of a spiritual,[42] personal,[43] and economic[44] sort were

38. The same was the case with journals from India. See Arno Lehmann, *Es begann in Tranquebar*, 98–99, 144–45.

39. 5A8:1 (undated) U. original to Fr.

40. 5A8:6 = March 2, 1739 U. original.

41. Missing in the printed copy, for example, are the negative reports about Captain Frey and the provisions (for example, January 22, 1734), extensive notes about the Indians (March 19, 1734), and a not insignificant number of days is completely stricken through (Boltzius had reported without exception concerning each day). Entries from the travel journal of von Reck have been incorporated without notation.

42. The prickly matter of the Moravians, for instance, is not mentioned at all.

43. For example, everything concerning the disagreements with Vat, Zwiffler, and Thilo.

44. For example, the crop failures, the delays with the relocation of Ebenezer, and the thoroughly cavalier attitude of Oglethorpe or the Curtius affair.

completely left out. Also, the first reports that came out of Georgia that, with enthusiastic exaggeration, depicted the land as a true paradise were wisely suppressed.[45]

But a distinct glimmer of the unmediated and the personal makes its way through all these augmentations. Indeed, one can plainly see the settlers with their pastors with full energy and fresh courage taking the ax in hand and making an abode for their families.

The editing of the journals was undertaken, in part, by Samuel Urlsperger and also in part by Pastor Johann August Majer, deacon at St. Ulrich's Church in Halle and pastor in Diemetz near Halle.[46] They had much to do, especially in the beginning, until Boltzius again received instructions[47] and noticed after the initial publications how his reports should sound. And so he then, unfortunately, finally conformed accordingly in that he left out of the journal all of the difficulties and events that vexed the community.

When the published reports virtually gleam with reports of uninformative pastoral concerns for several days in a row, then one can be almost certain that again something has happened under wraps. Thus, the thick published journals, for anyone reading long stretches in them, became dull and dry, filled with near endlessly repeating narrations of personal matters, such as birth, illness, and death of members of the community, bound together with pages-long reports about pastoral conversations with the "elderly N. N.," or the "hard-working N.," etc., so that it takes effort to make out events of significance. For that reason, in the secondary literature, only the surface layers, as a rule, have been treated.[48]

The image, then, that one is supposed to and does get of the Ebenezer community from the journals is one of a settlement basking in the sun, slowly but surely moving forward, whose diligent inhabitants enjoy

---

45. Even before their publication, the first reports about the failures in Old Ebenezer had already arrived (5A3:12, 84 = January 15, 1736 Fr. draft).

46. 5B1:29, 126 = September 28, 1750 Fr. draft; 5A11:35, 152 = February 12, 1746 B. original signature in another hand; 5A11:70, 315 = July 24, 1747 B. copy.

47. Moreover, it was pointed out to him (5A1:46, 214).

48. Nevertheless, this also rests essentially with the extraordinary breadth of Boltzius' style, as the manuscripts show. Francke had to admonish him urgently toward brevity, "Also, consider whether you could also compose the journal more briefly; at the very least I must now earnestly consider that in the future only the most important and noteworthy things from it come into print. Because of their extensiveness they do not circulate, and the entire publication from the last installments is still lying there and becoming wastepaper, so that the Orphan House incurs great harm from it" (5A11:30, 131 = July 24, 1745 Fr. draft). Francke advised Boltzius that he should keep a short, print-ready journal and a more detailed journal not intended for publication (5A11:32, 136 = September 8, 1745 Fr. original). But that did not happen.

the well-deserved fruits of their labors without being bothered by any disturbance worth mentioning, and so on. Even Strobel, despite all apparent efforts at a critical assessment, was compelled to adopt this image, since Urlsperger's publications comprised almost his only source for that period, and after him the entire body of literature dependent upon him that rules the field to this very day.

The recently discovered archival material clears up these impressions, since what was not able to appear in the journals made its way to Europe in letters that consequently gain an incomparably higher importance than, for instance, those of Muhlenberg, or even in their postscripts, which were left out in publication or in their public reading,[49] or in enclosures as well as in some secret "supplemental journals" (*Diarium extraordinarium*), from which far-reaching consequences arise.

Because the colonizing success of the Lutherans of Georgia and their contribution to the development of the economy of this state stand in the foreground in the accounts that deal with the subject at hand on the basis of the previously known sources, as already indicated, these matters do not need to be repeated more than is necessary within the bounds of the present theme. They testify to the industriousness of the members of the community and demonstrate, as do many other similar cases, that each settler comprised a constitutive element for the formation of the American economy.

That is worth remembering. Yet the enduring significance of every man and woman as Lutherans who laid the foundation of their church in Georgia does not rest in this fact. For it is no empty symbol that nothing more remains today from their dwellings and widely spread plantations than a stone church. Nonetheless, a history that seeks to outline the core of early Lutheranism in Georgia, its theological stance, and piety has not previously been written. In fact, it could not be written since the known sources were not sufficient. That becomes clear with Strobel whose efforts basically led only to the bland and oft-repeated judgment, "devout piety;" or with Gräbner, who went so far as to depict the pastors as narrow-minded pietists and the members of the community as fanciful believers of dreams.[50]

Such impressions were bound to arise as long as the roots of that initial pietistic direction of the Lutherans in Georgia and their external connections, down to the smallest detail, with their stronghold, the Francke Foundations in Halle, were not thoroughly investigated—they had been alleged for a long time. Regarding these connections, it will become more clear how strongly the Lutheran communities in Georgia, Pennsylvania, Germany,

---

49. For example, 5A2:4 and elsewhere contain stricken and bracketed passages.
50. Gräbner, *Geschichte der Lutherischen Kirche in America*, part I, 151.

England, and even India understood themselves as inseparable parts of the one Lutheran church, that, even with inadequate communication and different political fates, were not alienated from each other, and how this world-wide cohesion held a spiritual as well as an eminently practical significance for all of the parts.

It is by no means the case, then, that only supplements to what is already known are to be sought in the recently discovered material. Rather, fundamentally new realizations emerge that demand a new, comprehensive representation of the time period under investigation. In keeping with this comprehensive account, even apparently "extraneous" events gain a particular illumination. But the emphases of this investigation will not fall where they have previously but will lie where there is something new to say.

2

The Historical Background

THE HISTORICAL SITUATION

For more than a century, England had tried in vain to expand its North American colonies on the east coast farther to the south, since here began the territories that had belonged to Spain since the sixteenth century. Only when its status as a global power began to decline under Charles II and the Asiento Treaty of 1713 also introduced England's successor into American trade did this successor, Great Britain, succeed in establishing itself gradually into these disputed American territories.

On June 19, 1732, a charter appeared that called into existence a society "for establishing the Colony of Georgia in America."[1] It was to be called Georgia, since the king at that time was George II. Georgia, according to the charter, was understood to be "all those lands . . . in that part of South Carolina, which lies from the most northern part of . . . the Savannah, all along the sea coast . . . unto . . . the Altamaha," and to the west "from the heads of the said rivers respectively in direct lines to the South Seas."[2]

In place of the Lords Proprietors, to whom the land legally belonged, there were appointed "Trustees for Establishing the Colony of Georgia in America," to whom the land did not belong and who also received no compensation for their service. In the beginning, they were all "associates" of Dr.

---

1. Printed in Cooper, *The Story of Georgia* I, 115–17.
2. Cooper, *The Story of Georgia* I, 115–17.

Nicholas Bray, the founder of the Society for Promoting Christian Knowledge (SPCK) and the Society for the Propagation of the Gospel in Foreign Parts (SPG). In typical Anglo-Saxon fashion, they joined with the political and commercial purpose of the colony their "philanthropic" efforts to let it become a colony for the "relief of poor subjects made poor by misfortune or want of employment."[3]

These men had the great fortune to have a prudent and ready director of the practical implementation of their plans in Dr. Bray's executor, James Edward Oglethorpe, who understood how to apply effectively the special founding statute that made Georgia into a proper military colony for as long as it took until the Spaniards were subjugated once and for all. Among other things, therefore, holding slaves was forbidden since they posed a factor of uncertainty that could not be afforded on the front. Furthermore, trade with the Indians was not permitted because the Indians often were cheated as a result, which likewise could have severe consequences. In addition, communal farming by the inhabitants of each settlement was desired, and only limited ownership of real estate was allowed in order to keep the population independent, somewhat like the military, from matters of land and property, and so on. Consequently, the colony followed a very specific economic development that was different from that of the other North American colonies, something that cannot be investigated here.[4]

From England's failed attempts at expansion the lesson was now drawn that the settlers themselves would have to help to bring the colony from paper to life and guarantee the continuance of its existence. Procuring these settlers in the quantity needed was now the main objective of the "Trustees." The time period was favorable to them, since precisely in the years in question, the political, economic, and religious situation in Europe led to emigrations of entire portions of populations to an extent never before experienced.

A brief glance for orientation is in order in that regard. After the Thirty Years War, central Europe had still not yet returned to calm. Armies flowed here, there, and in between each other. The France of Louis XIV attempted, unjustly and with force, to construe in its favor the indefinite formulations that the Peace of Westphalia had brought about concerning its border, and the Empire, with its unreliable allies, was able to put up no effective resistance. The emperor was less concerned about the empire than about Spain, and the Turks had approached his door. Wars raged from Gibraltar to the

---

3. Cooper, *The Story of Georgia* I,118; Binder-Johnson, "Die Haltung der Salzburger in Georgia zur Sklaverei," 183–84.

4. On the 20th anniversary of Georgia's founding, the Trustees returned their rights to George II, and Georgia became a royal province directly under the king until the United States was constituted.

Baltic Sea, but the most persistent, and hence most devastating, took place in the regions of southwestern Germany. If Louis XIV could not simply annex the Palatinate, as he had done with Alsace and Lorraine, he at least could attempt to devastate them thoroughly for the protection of his border. Swabia, Württemberg, and the western parts of present-day Austria all the way to Switzerland would likewise enjoy the visit of his troops.

Especially the rural population, which still had not yet at all recovered from the Thirty Years War, was most affected at that time from the turmoil of war. In addition, there came the oppressive burden, especially for those areas, of the splintering of the territories and all of the negative side effects connected with it, not least of all the wish of even the smallest courts to emulate the example of Louis XIV in extravagance. But if that were not enough, some of the territorial lords let themselves be carried away with intolerance in matters of religion, such as the successors of Karl Ludwig of the Palatinate, himself having been prudent on this point, who, guided by Jesuit advisors, proceeded harshly against Lutherans and Reformed. This must have been felt all-the-more severely by those affected, since faith constituted the single possession that remained to them in times of war, hunger, inflation, and plague.

There came, then, what must. Emigration commenced, and in 1708, the powerful peak of this tide appeared. Fourteen thousand refugees, the majority from the Palatinate, sailed down the Rhine via London to America, mainly to Pennsylvania. Fellow sufferers from the other war-plagued parts of southern Germany followed the same route for decades straight in uninterrupted succession and, as in the other areas of North America, their migrations also found asylum in Georgia.[5]

THE EMIGRATION FROM SALZBURG TO GEORGIA

The event that gained the greatest significance for the Lutheran church in Georgia was the final expulsion of Protestants from the archbishopric of Salzburg. Although such actions had occurred here constantly since the Counter Reformation,[6] this final one was certainly the most extensive. There had also been wiser heads among the Salzburg archbishops who had quietly

---

5. Among them, those of interest to us are the Lutherans mostly located in Germany. The Scots, English, French, Italians, and others are not considered here.

6. In 1588, under Archbishop Wolf Dietrich, an expulsion took place; likewise in 1613 in the region of Wagrain, and later, in 1684, disregarding the Peace of Westphalia, the Teffereger and Halleiner (". . . over one thousand . . . ," Jacobs, *The History of the Evangelical Lutheran Church*, 151), who, however, for the most part remained in southern Germany, among them, Joseph Schaitberger (ADB 30, 553–55).

looked the other way from the presence of Protestants in their diocese.[7] When, however, Leopold Anton Freiherr von Firmian was consecrated on October 3, 1727, he, together with Chancellor Hieronymus Christian von Räll, pursued that extremely radical course that, after endless reprisals, attempts of persuasion of the most clumsy sort, threats, imprisonments, and other chicaneries, led to the measures decreed by the Emigration Edict of October 31, 1731;[8] all non-Catholic residents had to leave the land within eight days, those with property one to three months after the disposition by sale of their goods.

Archbishop Leopold Anton Freiherr von Firmian.
Image courtesy of the Francke Foundations.

---

7. For example, Archbishop Paris, during the Thirty Years War until 1653, and Archbishop Franz Anton, 1709–1727. Panse, *Geschichte der Auswanderung*, 16–21, 24–25).

8. Allegedly made necessary by the Salt League (*Salzbund*) of Schwarzach, formed August 5, 1731, portrayed as a conspiracy against the Catholic Church (Panse, *Geschichte der Auswanderung*, 68, 96; Jacobs, *A History of the Evangelical Lutheran Church*, 153; Prinzinger, "Die Ansiedlung der Salzburger," 5).

And so they did, and, in fact, in unexpectedly high numbers[9] that initially poured into the Lutheran areas bordering the archbishopric. Several strands of these also came to Augsburg, where especially Samuel Urlsperger (1665–1772) attended to them with regard to their housing, provisions, and continuing travels. His personal fortunes bound him to the Salzburgers; he descended from a family that the Counter Reformation had driven from Austria-Hungary during the Thirty Years War.

The Reverend Samuel Urlsperger.
Image courtesy of the Francke Foundations.

An amicable relationship with August Hermann Francke remained from two visits to Halle in 1709 and 1712. Between these visits Urlsperger was preacher at the German St. Mary's Church in the Savoy in London, where he became a corresponding member of the SPCK. Dismissed from

---

9. Precise statements regarding the number of the migrating Salzburgers in the course of this expulsion are obviously difficult to make. According to the inquiries of the investigating commission of July 1731, 20,678 professed themselves to be Protestant. Panse, *Geschichte der Auswanderung*, 65. Prinzinger speaks of 22,000 emigrants. Prinzinger, "Die Ansiedlung der Salzburger im Staate Georgien," 5. Cronau tendentiously gives the highest conceivable number of 30,000, as does Strobel. Cronau, *Drei Jahrhunderte deutschen Lebens*, 82; likewise Strobel, *The Salzburgers and Their Descendants*, 43. But there were at least 18,000 before remonstrations were made from the administration to the Archbishop.

the Württemberg court because of his candid preaching, he held office from 1723 in Augsburg as Pastor at St. Anna's Church and Senior of the Evangelical Ministerium. In devoted fashion he lent support for the East India Mission in Tranquebar as well as for the Salzburgers,[10] in whose interests he used his connections to England. Here, wide circles of people took an interest in the fates of the exiles, principally from the five German churches in London at the time, of which the most influential was the "German Court Chapel at St. James."[11]

Two German Lutheran pastors were permanently appointed here. At the time of the Salzburger emigration they were Heinrich Butjenter and Friedrich Michael Ziegenhagen (1694–1776). Like Urlsperger, Ziegenhagen also became a true father to the Salzburgers, because he likewise was a member of the SPCK. Since, on the basis of the already depicted personal connections of this organization with the Trustees of Georgia, the well-being of this colony also lay on its heart.[12]

---

10. 5B3:2, p. 6 (August 30, 1753) B. original; 5A1:6, 36 copy; 5A1:5 copy; Lehmann, *Es begann in Tranquebar*, 164; *ADB* 39, 361–64.

11. Since the time of Prince George of Denmark, the husband of Queen Anne. Burckhardt, *Kirchen-Geschichte der Deutschen Gemeinden in London*, 119–22.

12. The SPCK, until the outbreak of the War of Independence, paid the salaries of Ebenezer's ecclesiastical appointees, that is, two pastors and a teacher, for a total of £ 8083/6/8, apart from various donations in kind. Allen and McClure, *Two Hundred Years*, 390–93.

The Reverend Friedrich Michael Ziegenhagen.
Image courtesy of the Francke Foundations.

At the beginning of 1732,[13] Urlsperger sent to London a report about the Salzburgers with a narrative of their emigration that was published without his knowledge in the July edition of "Gentleman's Magazine"[14] and aroused public attention.[15] Thereupon, the SPCK turned to the Trustees with the question of whether they could not make use of these people. They would like nothing more; in the resolution of their session on December 15, 1732, they agreed and submitted at the same time the stipulations under which the relocation and settlement, initially of 300 Salzburgers, was to take place.[16] They were to receive provisions for one year without cost, additional support in seed, cattle, and farming implements, fifty acres of land per head,

---

13. UN I, 1.

14. Binder-Johnson, "Die Haltung der Salzburger in Georgia zur Sklaverei," 185; Jacobs, *A History of the Evangelical Lutheran Church*, 145, 157; Arnold, *Die Vertreibung der Salzburger Protestanten*, 233–35.

15. UN I, 1; Göcking, *Vollkommene Emigrations-Geschichte* II, 531.

16. Jones, *The History of Georgia* I, 164–66.

ten years tax exemption, the rights of British subjects,[17] and freedom of religious practice. The crossing from Holland to Dover was to be paid by the SPCK; the rest by the Trustees.

Henry Newman, the Secretary of the SPCK, now informed Urlsperger about these decisions as well as about the geographical and other characteristics of Georgia, and conferred to him the authority to assemble an emigration convoy, or transport, as it was called, as well as to appoint a transport leader ("commissioner"), a pastor, and a catechist.[18] Urlsperger made this known in print in 1733,[19] and with that began the gathering together of the first emigrants.

On August 8, 1733, a group of 247 Salzburgers arrived at the city of Memmingen, and after this offer was made appealing to them, forty-two families (equaling seventy-eight persons[20]) accepted. Augsburg was notified, to which the future Americans trekked at the beginning of September.[21]

---

17. 5A1:5, 34 copy; 5A1:7, 40 copy.

18. Göcking, *Vollkommene Emigrations-Geschichte* II, 531; UN I, 2–5. Whoever was willing to go to Georgia was to notify Urlsperger verbally or in writing (5A1:2,16).

19. 5A1:2 (print): "Georgia, Oder: Kurtze Nachricht Von dem Christlichen Vorhaben Der Königlich=Englischen Herren Commissarien Zu Aufrichtung der neuen Colonie Georgia in Süd=Carolina in America, Wie auch Der in London sich befindenden Societaet, So von Fortpflanzung der Erkäntniß Christi den Namen hat, Dreyhundert Protestantische Emigranten nach ermeldtem Georgia aufzunehmen, Ingleichen Von Den guten Conditionen dieser Aufnahme, Und denen Bereits gemachten schönen Anstalten, solche, so aus ihrem Vaterlande um der Religion willen Friedens=Schlußmässig ausgehen, und sich nach Georgia freywillig zu gehen gehöriger Orten angeben, dahin sicher zu bringen, Unter Königl, Groß-Britannischer Majestät Allerhöchst und Hohen Genehmhaltung, Auch auf Verlangen Hoch=ermeldten Königlichen Herren Commissarien Und der Hoch-Löblichen Societaet, Dem Druck überlassen. Franckfurt, Anno 1733." (Georgia, or, Brief Report on the Christian Undertaking of the Royal-English Herr Commissioners for the Establishment of the New Colony of Georgia in South Carolina in America, as Well as of the Society located in London that has the name, Society for Promoting Christian Knowledge, to Assimilate Three Hundred Protestant Emigrants to the Above-Mentioned Georgia; Similarly on the Good Conditions of This Assimilation, and Their Lovely Arrangements Already Made to Bring Safely There Such Who in Keeping with the Peace Settlement Left Their Fatherland for the Sake of Religion to Go of Their Own Free Will to Georgia to the Proper Places Indicated, Under the Most High Royal Great Britain Majesty and High Approval, Also at the Request of the High- Above Mentioned Royal Herr Commissioners And of the Highly-Praised Society, Submitted for Publication. Frankfurt 1733.)

20. Strobel, *The Salzburgers and Their Descendants*, 51.

21. The first group of exiles gathered in Berchtesgaden. Strobel, *The Salzburgers and Their Descendants*, 47. That it happened under von Reck's direction, as Cronau maintains, is not documented anywhere else. Cronau, *Drei Jahrhunderte deutschen Lebens*, 85.

Here, they were very well provided, physically and spiritually,[22] until on October 31, 1733, under the direction of the "commissioner" Baron Philipp Georg Friedrich von Reck,[23] they made way to Rotterdam

In the meantime, Urlsperger had requested from his personal friend, the Director of the Francke Foundations in Halle and corresponding member of the SPCK, Gotthilf August Francke (1696–1769), two clergy for the Salzburgers who likewise were now on the way to Rotterdam; the pastor Johann Martin Boltzius and the catechist Israel Christian Gronau.[24]

Director Gotthilf August Francke.
Image courtesy of the Francke Foundations.

22. They received daily, at the expense of the English Societies, nine, later ten to thirteen kreuzer. In addition, the local residents also provided for them. Daily worship services were held for them; those who could read were given Bibles, catechisms, Arndt's *True Christianity*, and other materials. The children received instruction.

23. Von Reck came from Windhausen near Hannover. Schmidt, *John Wesley* I, 151. He attended lectures under Johann Lorenz von Mosheim, a well-known church historian, in the English-world until the nineteenth century (5D1, 16 = journal December 12, 1733).

24. Since the Halle pastors appointed for the Salzburgers were not able in the short time to come to Augsburg, the Salzburgers were given as a traveling chaplain to Rotterdam the pastoral candidate Schu(h)macher from Ulm. Göcking, *Vollkommene Emigrations-Geschichte* II, 542. On December 1, 1733, Schumacher was released from his offices and returned to his home (5B1, 5 = journal December 1, 1733). Boltzius: "An upright, dear brother of moderate talents" (5A1:20, 94 B original).

The Reverend Johann Martin Boltzius.
Image courtesy of the Francke Foundations.

At the end of November they assembled in Rotterdam, and on the First Sunday in Advent (November 29, 1733), the two clergymen took up their offices, and they preached to the Salzburgers on the "Purisburg," the ship that was to bring them to Georgia.[25] Since it was not yet seaworthy, and also

---

25. UN I, 17; 5D1, 3 = November 29, 1733. The group of Salzburgers was seventy-eight persons, including children, which constitutes forty-one "heads" in the calculation of the cost of passage (5A1:20, 95 B. original; 5D1, 92 = journal March 30, 1734; 5C4:5). Cronau speaks of ninety-one. Cronau, *Drei Jahrhunderte deutschen Lebens*, 82. However, there were only that many after several French and English had arrived in Dover (5C4:5; 5D1 = December 24, 1733). The ship was no man-of-war but a mid-sized ship (5D1, 7 = journal December 6, 1733; 5A1:25, 115: Purrysbourg). With them had arrived from London the schoolteacher Ortmann, sent by the SPCK (5A3:20, 140; Ordmann 5D1 = journal December 16, 1733; Orthmann 5A1:38,169 B. original), with his wife, who was to go along with them to America. He was "a man already on in years" (5A1:20, 95) and up to that point employed as teacher in the so-called Swedish Church (the German Trinity Lutheran Church, Trinity Lane) in London (5A3:20, 140 Z), and could therefore speak German and English (5A1:20, 95; 5A1:25, 115). However, according to Burckhardt, there was no school at this church. Burckhardt, *Kirchen-Geschichte der Deutschen Gemeinden in London*, 106. Perhaps there is confusion with St. Mary's Church in the Savoy, another German church in London, where the situation with the school was rather bad until 1782. Burckhardt, *Kirchen-Geschichte der Deutschen Gemeinden in London*, 91. This would correspond

the weather was not yet favorable enough, the departure was delayed for several days. On December 2, the Salzburgers were finally onboard, and in the following night they departed from Rotterdam with the outgoing tide.[26]

After an unpleasant crossing (twenty days),[27] they were in Dover where the Trustee Captain Coram appeared on December 31, 1733 (new style). He handed over to Boltzius his accreditation letter by which he had been appointed for the Salzburgers "and other German Protestants now going to settle in the said Province of Georgia."[28] On the following day, the Salzburgers were made English citizens by handshake and oath,[29] and on January 8, 1734 (old style) they were again at sea.[30]

After a voyage of almost two months, land was allegedly sighted on March 3, 1734, whereupon the Salzburgers, as they had vowed, sang Luther's

---

with the abilities Ortmann demonstrated in Ebenezer.

26. 5A1:20, 94; 5A1:1, 99; 5D1 = journal December 2/3, 1733. Hazelius writes that the departure took place on November 27th. Hazelius, *History of the American Lutheran Church*, 30. This was the day that the Salzburgers arrived in Rotterdam.

27. They first of all ran aground on sand (they first reached open sea on December 19th), then several became ill because of the very poor provisions (5D1 = journal December 6, 1733; 5A1:28,139 postscript copy); almost everyone became seasick (5D1 = journal December 19, 1733; 5A1:23, 104), the stretch covered on open sea was almost completely in storm, and finally Captain Frey, the ship's captain, was, according to Boltzius' report, a true tyrant (5D1, 31 = journal December 21, 1733 old style) "who loves his dog more than he does a Christian man" (5A1:28,139, postscript B. copy to U.) and declared that "he recognizes preachers as the Devil himself and breaks out in a cold sweat just by seeing one" (5D1 = journal December 5, 1733). In addition, the young Mrs. Ortmann caused "scandal through her free and, for a Christian woman, unbecoming behavior" (5A1:28,137); it continued to be so and, when she was in America, wanted to return (5D1, 74 = journal March 13, 1734).

28. English text; 5D1, 30.

29. Here, Boltzius changes the date of the journal from that of the Gregorian to the Julian calendar of the British Empire. Thursday, December 31st is followed by Friday, December 21, 1733 old style—5D1, 31 = journal December 21, 1733 old style; "At about ten o'clock came Captain Coram as Trustee, along with our ship's Captain Frey and an English merchant. Then the Herr Commissioner read a brief oration in which he extoled the benefactions that had been received and admonished the people to gratitude toward God and the benefactors. And after they all promised obedience with a loud Ja, he read to them regulations composed in German in which were presented to them by the Trustees their future benefits in the land and their obligations. At the bottom of this sheet of parchment many signets were printed. On each of them, the first and last names of the Salzburgers were placed. Finally, they all had to shake hands with the Trustees and touch the signed sheets. At that they were asked whether they intended to obey everything and recognized the signature as their own? Which they all confirmed with Ja."

30. 5D1, 40 = journal January 8, 1734. The voyage proceeded similarly to the first; Boltzius got along better with the captain (5D1, 52 = journal February 7, 1734; 5D1, 55 = journal February 14, 1734).

Te Deum. When the report proved to be a disappointment, they sang the song again two days later when it really was so.[31]

The ship first set anchor in shallow water off the coast. Boltzius, von Reck, and the Captain went by boat to land at Charleston, South Carolina, where they met Oglethorpe who had wanted to sail immediately to England but turned around on their behalf.[32] In the following days they then sailed southwest along the coast to the mouth of the Savannah River, and, after they twice ran aground on sandbanks and were underway again, they reached the harbor of the city of Savannah on Tuesday, March 12, 1734, at about two o'clock in the afternoon.[33] This is the birthday of the Lutheran church in Georgia, and it is still celebrated annually today.[34]

After this "transport," a number of others followed, and although only the second was a "Salzburger transport" with regard to its members, it soon became customary to call all German Lutherans in Georgia "Salzburgers," even when they came from Swabia, Bavaria, Württemberg, Silesia, or other parts of Austria, just as the same thing happened in Pennsylvania with the "Palatines." In Georgia, the Salzburgers were already in the minority with the fourth transport from Germany, so that the title of Strobel's work, strictly speaking, is not exact. Still, it was the Salzburgers who established the first Lutheran congregation in Georgia.

---

31. 5D1, 67.

32. Strobel, *The Salzburgers and Their Descendants*, 59.

33. Hazelius, *History of the American Lutheran Church*, 27, erroneously gives the date of March 11th; Brantley, "The Salzburgers in Georgia," 216, similarly gives the date of March 10th.

34. Rines, *Old Historic Churches of America*, 244.

3

The History of the Settlement of the Lutheran Communities

EBENEZER AND THE ASSOCIATED COMMUNITIES OF ABERCORN, BETHANY, GOSHEN, JOSEPHSTOWN, AND ZION

Mistake in the Selection of the Location

IN ORDER TO ALLOW the new settlers to begin as soon as possible with the construction of their dwellings and the cultivation of their fields, von Reck, with two companions, set out just two days after arriving to choose a favorable location. But he stumbled into a completely impassable area and soon had to turn around.[1] Subsequently, on the following day, a group of eight men struck out: Oglethorpe, Paul Jenys, Esq.,[2] Gronau, the "transport" physician Zwiffler, the Salzburger Gschwandel,[3] and as leader, Tuskenovi, the "supreme military captain" of the chief of the Yamacraw Indians, Tomo-Chichi, along with two other Indians.[4]

---

1. UN I, 84A = journal March 14, 1734, von Reck.
2. "Speaker of the South Carolina House of Assembly." Strobel, *The Salzburgers and Their Descendants*, 62). He had arrived the day before with Oglethorpe from Charleston (UN I, 85A = journal March 15, 1734, von Reck).
3. UN I, 214 = letter March 22, 1734, Zwiffler to Urlsperger.
4. UN I, 85A = journal March 15, 1734, von Reck.

With effort, they worked their way through the primeval forest and landed on the second day of their exploratory trip at a place that seemed suitable to them next to a creek.[5] Here, they fell to their knees, prayed, and sang, "If You But Trust in God to Guide You" (*Wer nur den lieben Gott läßt walten*), and then took the exact markings of the location. After prayer and the hymn, "Amen, that is: It shall be so" (*Amen, das ist: es werde wahr*), the future settlement and the creek were named Ebenezer, at Oglethorpe's suggestion.[6]

Bancroft reports, "They resolved to raise up a column of stone,"[7] which in Strobel reads, "They set up a rock," like Samuel (1 Sam 7:12).[8] This fact is mentioned neither by Urlsperger nor in the manuscripts; on the contrary, one discovers that in this area there was not even a single natural stone there but only sand,[9] so that here is probably the case of the first legend concerning the Lutheran church of Georgia.

When the scouts returned again to Savannah on March 19th, they were full of praise over the favorable condition of the settlement location and the friendliness of the Indians so that Boltzius, immediately on the morning of the following day, celebrated the Lord's Supper for those who were to set forth for the initial clearing of land and building of houses: Gronau, Zwiffler, and eight Salzburgers.[10]

A week later, von Reck set out anew with several people to establish a water connection between the site and the Savannah River by making the Ebenezer Creek passable by boat.[11] This creek, which flows into the Savannah River, was almost standing water with growing and felled trees in it and in which, in contrast to the Savannah River, many alligators lived and killed off the fish, to the dismay of the later settlers.[12] Von Reck's undertaking, however, proved to be so difficult that it was preferable to blaze a path overland through swamps and morasses.[13]

---

5. UN I, 88A = journal March 17, 1734, von Reck.

6. UN I, 212–13 = letter March 22, 1734, Zwiffler to Urlsperger. 5D1, 90 = journal (+UN) March 26, 1734. [*Amen, das ist: es werde wahr*; from the last stanza of the hymn, "Our Father, God, in heav'n above."]

7. First edition, 1837, used by Strobel. Bancroft, *History of the United States of America* II, 566.

8. Strobel, *The Salzburgers and Their Descendants*, 63.

9. For example, 5A2:3,14 = May 6, 1734 B. copy.

10. The rest of the community held their first Lord's Supper in Georgia on the following Sunday (5D1, 89 = journal [+UN] March 24, 1734).

11. UN I, 93A = journal March 27, 1734 von Reck; 5D1, 91 = journal (+UN) March 28, 1734.

12. 5A3:11, 70 = September 1, 1735, B. original.

13. 5D1:32 = journal (+UN) March 31, 1734.

In the meantime, the Salzburgers, their baggage, and their "provisions" were brought by ship first to Abercorn, a small English settlement,[14] from where they gradually moved to Ebenezer where Boltzius arrived with the last settlers on May 7, 1734. He and Gronau occupied here a small house, two quarrelsome non-Salzburger families occupied one,[15] and all the rest occupied a forty-foot long house.[16]

Commissioner von Reck, who now had fulfilled his responsibility, traveled a week later again to Europe, and Boltzius accompanied him as far as Charleston, South Carolina.[17] Land clearing and house building were now the main tasks of the settlers.[18] Oglethorpe had arranged that now a house was to be constructed for each pastor, along with a church, a school, and storehouse for the provisions,[19] for which he sent on loan a carpenter and some black workers, of whom there were perhaps a few dozen in Georgia.[20] A storehouse was built, and then a residence into which one of the troublemaking families simply moved themselves. In the middle of July, the two parsonages were undertaken, but the church and the school were still far out of consideration.

However, for Boltzius, everything proceeded too slowly. He impatiently opined, "Our place does not yet look like a village, much less like a town."[21]

Meanwhile, already underway was the second Salzburger transport,[22] which arrived in Ebenezer around evening on January 1, 1735, and was

14. 5D1, 95 = journal (+UN) April 7, 1734; UN I, 184.

15. These were the disruptive Ortmann and Roth families.

16. 5A1:38, 170 = May 6, 1734 B. original; UN I, 98 = journal April 4, 1734 (von Reck).

17. Boltzius was away from May 14th to June 5th (5D1 under these days).

18. 5A2:5, 22 = May 6, 1734, B. copy.

19. According to Vernon's message to Boltzius (5A3:11, 69 = September 1, 1735, B. original), they received food and cattle from the Trustees free of charge for two years.

20. 5A1:38, 169 = May 6, 1734, B. original.

21. 5A1:49, 191 = July 16, 1734, B. original.

22. The assembly of a second transport was somewhat delayed since the expenses for the first one had exceeded the amount that was planned (5 A 1:37, 166 Z. original). Nevertheless, when an invitation was issued by a published announcement in September 1734 for fifty to sixty Salzburgers (5A1:42, printed handbill), over fifty persons came forward on September 16th and 18th (the deadline was September 20th). In the end, fifty-seven people were assembled (5C4:43, 115, U:54; UN I, 30). Göcking also indicates fifty-seven. Göcking, *Vollkommene Emigrations-Geschichte* II, 555. They received as their traveling chaplain the ministerial candidate Matthäus Friedrich Degmair (UN I, 23). After the end of his activity he wrote again on February 29, 1736, to the Salzburgers in Ebenezer). The trip leader was the Reformed Christian, Johann Vat (5D1, 215 = journal January 13, 1735; 5D1, 142 = journal September 24,

greeted by Boltzius with the words, "May the Lord be praised every day; God places a burden upon us, but He also helps us."²³ In the beginning, things did not go smoothly at all with the provisions for the new settlers until their commissioner Vat energetically intervened for them with Mayor Causton in Savannah.²⁴

In time, the settlers turned to agriculture, since after the expiration of the time for their provisions they would have to sustain themselves. They worked collectively on one piece of land.²⁵ But soon they, who had undertaken it so enthusiastically, experienced a severe disappointment; without fertilization the sandy ground bore practically nothing at all. What Boltzius had heard even before he had been in Ebenezer turned out to be true, "Evil people had made an evil racket about our land, that it is not only almost impossible to make a way to it, but the land itself is sandy and infertile."²⁶ Englanders travelling through likewise noticed the exceptionally bad condition.²⁷

Naturally, this discovery was also very embarrassing before the public, which had expected something great from the progress of Ebenezer as a model case. And so Boltzius at first wrote confidentially to Halle. Francke was of the view that it must certainly be a matter of a decidedly unfavorable

---

1735), a personal friend of Jean-Pierre Purry (5A3:17, 113–14 = January 8, 1736 B. original). Just before their departure from Augsburg, von Reck showed up there and was able to describe to them right away his experiences (5C4:26). By way of Rotterdam, the transport arrived in London during the night of November 3–4, 1734. On the following Sunday, November 7th, a special worship service was held for them in St. Mary's Church in the Savoy, where the pastor of this church, D. Gerdes, and the court chaplain Butjenter administered to them the Lord's Supper. In another worship service the Salzburgers sang for the congregation their "song of exile" (*Exulantenlied*; printed in dialect. Arnold, *Die Vertreibung der Salzburger Protestanten*, 50–52. Schaitberger is the author), which made a great impression on the congregation (UN I, 29). They reached Savannah already on December 30, 1734 (5A3:3a, 18 = February 6, 1735, "We stepped onto land in Savannah on Monday of last year according to the old calendar." December 30, 1734 old style was a Monday. Likewise, 5D1, 208 = journal January 1, 1735; 5A3, 1 = February 6, 1735 B. original). The incorrect dates, UN I, 37, December 27th; Göcking, *Vollkommene Emigrations-Geschichte* II, 555, December 16th; 5C4:56, were taken from London newspapers that often printed inaccurate information (5A3: 4, 25 = March 28, 1735 B. original; December 17th).

23. 5D1, 215 = journal January 13, 1735; 5A3:1, 1 = February 6, 1735 B. original.

24. 5D1, 227–28 = journal (UN partially) January 30, 1735.

25. This manner of working, ordered by Oglethorpe in keeping with the intention of the Trustees, was maintained until the final surveying of the promised fifty acres ("plantations") in summer 1738, although it had already been recognized as impractical in 1736 (5D1, 196 = journal (+UN) June 7, 1736).

26. 5D1, 95 = (UN partially) April 7, 1734. 5A1:49 = probably December 10, 1734.

27. 5D1, 216 = journal (UN) January 13, 1735.

patch, if nothing at all grew on it. With fertilization, surely something must be made of it; perhaps a vegetable garden could be laid out there. But in any case, Boltzius should also notify the Trustees, Ziegenhagen, and Urlsperger about the situation.[28]

The Salzburgers fertilized with wood ash and manure.[29] Yet even though they were so diligent and avid in the gathering of manure from the street and out of the forest, "only that they might make their gardens fertile with it," that Boltzius marveled over it, the result was that European produce did not grow at all. Indigenous produce, for example, corn, grew consistently only on fertilized soil.[30] That was too little.

An additional hardship lay in the fact that all of the provisions had to be carried two to three miles due to a lack of strong horses and wagons.[31] The discouragement of the Salzburgers grew because they saw that the houses had to stand on the soil that was good for farming and the fields lay where, consistent with the soil, only houses should stand.

Surrounding Ebenezer directly on three sides were the so-called swamps, black soil with low reeds where, because of the dampness, even rice could be planted but where the town could not at all spread.[32] The location was a model of poor selection.

The disappointment turned into discontent when the people of the second transport found fertile land very close by: "There is a river on both sides. It only needs to be fenced in above and below so that the wild animals cannot do harm." Yet Causton, brought along by Vat from Savannah, had to prohibit their working of it, since only the Trustees could give them permission.[33]

Francke submitted the letters arriving in Halle regarding the soil conditions to several experts, among them the councilor Cellarius.[34] They were completely bewildered that they even had been able to settle down on

---

28. 5A1, 51, 259, March 11, 1735, Fr. draft; 5A3:2, 9 = May 17, 1735, Fr. draft.

29. 5D1, 161 = journal (+UN) October 13, 1735; 5A3 11, 68–69 = September 1, 1735 B. original.

30. "Watermelons and Indian beans grew the most, whereas with pumpkins, cucumbers, and other garden vegetables things did not quite go as desired. Where it was fertilized, Indian corn grew whereas from wheat, barley, or German grain nothing would grow" (5A3:11, 69 = September 1, 1735 B. original).

31. 5A1:38, 168 = May 6, 1734 B original.; UN June 25, 1734. Gilbert says that the provisions had to be carried from the city of Savannah. Gilbert, "Early History of the Lutheran Church in Georgia," 161. How would that have been possible?

32. 5A3:11, 70 = September 1, 1735 B. original.

33. 5A3:3a, 19.

34. 5A3:12, 85 = January 15, 1736 Fr. draft.

such a place. Where oak trees and the like stand, the soil is good. On the contrary, pine trees and firs grow, as in Mark Brandenburg, even in the very worst soil. Something should grow immediately on freshly cleared land. If it has to be fertilized first, it takes years before a yield comes. Moreover, it is not understandable why they had not settled directly by a river, when they certainly had the choice.[35]

Whether they actually had this choice is now indeed the question, since when the factors that played a role are investigated, it turns out that: 1. Non-English speakers could settle only in a distance six miles from the Savannah River.[36] 2. Oglethorpe was, without a doubt, keen to push the settlement as far as possible into the country and, in fact, the properties of the Uchee Indians already began on the other side of the Ebenezer Creek,[37] so von Reck's note that Oglethorpe had headed out with him "to show me the area and to see which location I would select,"[38] is to be read judiciously. There was, therefore, considering both points, actually only the choice of this place for Ebenezer, and it would have been difficult for von Reck to oppose Oglethorpe's suggestions.

In consideration of these circumstances, Francke, following Boltzius' suggestion, came to the view that it would be best if "a better location and ground would be assigned" to them.[39] With this in mind, he wrote several times to Ziegenhagen so that he would bring the matter forward to Oglethorpe before Oglethorpe sailed again to America.[40] The governor, however, was not readily convinced of the necessity of this measure; with some diligence something could be eked out anywhere. Boltzius recognized what drove him to this stance: "The main obstacle may be that Herr Oglethorpe's reputation might thereby suffer."[41] Nevertheless, Oglethorpe promised Ziegenhagen that he would attend to the Salzburgers, and he sailed to Georgia with their third transport.[42]

---

35. 5A3:2, p. 12 = May 17, 1735 Fr draft.

36. 5D2: 347–48 = *Diarium extraordinarium* ("The Oglethorpe Case") B. copy.

37. 5A3:23, 164 = June 19, 1736 B. original.

38. UN I, 85A = journal March 15, 1734 von Reck.

39. 5A3:2, 14 = May 17, 1735 Fr. draft; 5D1, 162–63 = journal (+UN) October 14, 1735.

40. 5A3:5, 32 = September 26, 1735 Fr. draft; 5A3:8, 53–54 = September 19, 1735 Fr. draft.

41. 5A1:49, 242 = (undated) B. original.

42. Henry Newman, Secretary of the SPCK from 1708–1743, had written again to Augsburg on January 30 and March 18, 1735, to gather an additional emigrant transport. Allen and McClure, *Two Hundred Years*, 387. Yet there were no longer so many Salzburgers, so von Reck, after further inquiry in London, attempted in July to acquire

What now played out must have been unpleasant to the point that Boltzius' report about it counts as the most discontented that he ever wrote.[43] For purposes of public reading or publication, someone from Halle bracketed out over half of the text. Moreover, Boltzius kept a *Diarium extraordinarium* about it.[44] We conclude from both that on Saturday, February 7, 1736, von Reck, who also had returned with the third transport, arrived in Ebenezer and reported that the Trustees and Oglethorpe were in agreement with the assignment of good, alternate land, and for that reason Boltzius was to go with him immediately to Savannah to Oglethorpe, even though the following day was Sunday. In fact, Boltzius reported to Oglethorpe already at nine o'clock in the morning, but the anticipated tension-filled discussion first took place over lunch.

Oglethorpe congenially requested from Boltzius a detailed, written rationale, but also made clear to him in advance that both of the points mentioned above must also be taken into account with regard to the new location. Boltzius respected the treaties with the Indians; he was up in arms over the six-mile distance from the only useful means of transportation, the Savannah River. This stipulation was unbelievably impractical, since there were no Englishmen who would have been able to settle there at all, and in the conditions of the time no town would have been able to thrive that was separated by more than six miles from the main means of transportation by swampy primeval forest.

Boltzius finally persuaded Oglethorpe so that he set out on Monday at midday with him, von Reck, Vat, two officers, and several soldiers for Ebenezer. The settlement and the manner of work of the people pleased him so extraordinarily that he had Boltzius ask them whether they really wanted

---

Moravians from Saxony but did not succeed. Göcking, *Vollkommene Emigrations-Geschichte* II, 559–60. He therefore departed from Regensburg on August 28, 1735, with a group of Austrians; in Augsburg several Salzburgers were added (UN Continuation, 805ff.; 5D2 = journal February 11, 1736; 5A3:27, 199 = October 6, 1736 B. original: "The third transport assembled by Herr von Reck consisting of Salzburgers, Austrians, and several others"). It then traveled the usual way over the Main and Rhine via Rotterdam to London, where the voyage began on October 28, 1735, with 150 people on the "London Merchant" (under Captain John Thomas, UN I, 823ff.). At the same time, the ship the "Simonds" departed, upon which were Oglethorpe, the Wesley brothers with Ingham and Delamotte, twenty-seven Moravians with their bishop David Nitschmann and the pastor Peter Böhler, as well as von Reck's brother. Voigt shows that Wesley traveled with the Moravians and not with the Salzburgers. Voigt, "John Wesley and the Salzburgers," 370–76. On February 16, 1736, new style (= February 5 old style: 5D2 = journal February 7, 1736), both ships landed on Tybee Island at the mouth of the Savannah River.

43. 5A3:23, 162–65 = June 19, 1736 B. original.

44. 5B2, 347–86.

to give up all of this. The answer was unambiguous. He then consented to allow them the development of a good stretch of land between the places designated as "Red Bluff" and "Indian Hut" lying on the Savannah River. But the town should be laid out on a hill two miles from the river on the Ebenezer Creek. He even sketched right away a town plan in Boltzius' house and ordered the surveying of the area. With that, Boltzius objected, the dissolution of the town would already be guaranteed while it was being planned. The people would have to live by their fields to which they then would move individually. Furthermore, they wanted finally to be away from Ebenezer Creek which was especially contaminated at the envisioned location; even dead crocodiles floated around in it. Moreover, no one knew whether there was spring water on the bluff.

In league with von Reck and several "reasonable Salzburgers," Boltzius stayed in Oglethorpe's ear until he finally permitted settling on the Red Bluff, but under the condition that the town was not to be built there until approval to do so was received from the Trustees.[45] There was also the requirement "that houses, huts, the cultivated land, and everything that was nailed down would be left behind."[46] But farming could commence.

The community got its breath back. Oglethorpe conducted the entire affair by the book. But in this example can be seen the effect of leadership conducted by men who sat in far-away England, had never seen the region that they regulated, knew hardly any details about it, and thereby brought the truly active elements to the edge of ruin. Boltzius is to be given great credit for remaining restrained toward those involved. Only in this way could he succeed in the matter, and he showed himself in doing so to be a candid father of his community. But Oglethorpe grumbled vehemently against the settlers even a year later. He held the opinion "that they quit Old Ebenezer without sufficient reason," and "that the land in Old Ebenezer was good and the abandoning of it was almost only obstinacy or willfulness."[47]

A few days later, two twenty by forty-foot huts stood in "New Ebenezer" for the third "Salzburger" transport.[48] Afterwards, in addition to private houses "for the schoolmaster Ortmann and the apothecary Zwiffler," huts were also built for the rest of the community.[49] After Gronau had moved over already on March 28th for the worship service, Boltzius followed on May 24, 1736, as one of the last.

45. 5D2, 40–41 = journal (+UN) February 11, 1736.
46. 5A3:23, 163 = June 19, 1736 B. original.
47. 5A3:42, 277 = February 24, 1737 B. copy.; 5A3:47, 295 = March 1, 1737 Z. copy.
48. 5D2, 45 = journal (+UN) February 16, 1736.
49. 5A3:23, 163 = June 19, 1736 B. original.

In Old Ebenezer, an old woman remained yet for a time, along with a young Salzburger as a cowherd,[50] then, from the summer on, the English Captain Mackentach (McIntosh?) who worked under commission of the Trustees,[51] with his people and some cattle.[52] New Ebenezer bought up this facility in April 1750.[53] The Trustees also settled two Palantine families there[54] who likewise moved away again. Finally, the Trustees even built a sawmill but which the "authorities in Savannah" already a few years later gave to Ebenezer for salvaging after a flood had badly ruined it.[55] Nothing remains from this settlement.

During the difficult time before the relocation of Ebenezer the community was troubled by yet another occurrence about which nothing was published: the "unfriendly and in part unchristian conduct of Herr Vat toward the Salzburgers as well as its preachers."[56] He apparently saw his responsibility as not yet done with the arrival of the second transport in Georgia and fell into conflict with Boltzius in questions of leadership. Unfortunately, it was forgotten to define for him the limit of his duties since it was assumed that he would soon return. Vat now wanted to become mayor in Ebenezer, which in the beginning Boltzius also intended for him. However, he wanted to limit Boltzius and Gronau only to spiritual concerns, and when that did not happen, he became angry. "His greatest annoyance with us [Boltzius and Gronau] comes from this: the people, in all spiritual and material circumstances, take refuge with us and avail themselves to our counsel, which he deplores as contempt for his person and his commission.... Command belonged to him, however, he would occasionally ask us for advice in some cases."[57]

As usual in such disputes over jurisdiction, the occasions for it were without exception trivialities that would not at all have been seen as contentious points with good will on both sides. For example, Schweiger from Ebenezer had dared without Vat's permissions to acquire a wife from Purrysburg, South Carolina.[58] For that reason Vat, despite Causton's instruc-

---

50. 5A3:23, 163 = June 19, 1736 B. original.

51. 5D3 = journal (+UN) July 21, 1737.

52. 5D2, 219 = journal (-UN) July 7, 1736.

53. UN April 2 and 6, 1750; 5B1:37, 150 = June 1750 B. copy. The new place from now on was called simply "Ebenezer."

54. 5A7:2, 13 = January 20, 1738 G. original; 5D7, 8 = January 6, 1741.

55. 5A7:53, 229 = journal (+UN) April 3, 1739a; 5A11:21, 78 = October 29, 1744 B. original; 5A11:29, 98 = February 4, 1744 B. copy.

56. 5A3:20, 138 = July 7, 1736 Z. copy.

57. 5D1, 140 + 144 = journal (-UN) September 24, 1735.

58. Schweiger had quite properly asked Causton, since his wife was the first

tion, gave no provisions to both, having taken over their distribution because Boltzius had wanted to be free from doing so. When Schweiger subsequently received food supplies from Causton, Vat went to him grumbling. But before that he locked up all of the wine intended for the sick and all the provisions in Ebenezer and took the key.[59]

He remained, along with the key, in Savannah for several months with only brief interruptions, a situation that was intolerable for the community.[60] He also established military sentry duty, something that certainly was necessary but excessive in time and expense and through which the men of the community were unduly kept away from their work. Every night and during the worship services six people had to keep watch in a specially constructed watch house and every two hours make rounds through the place.[61]

Vat's desire for giving orders went so far that, after approval for the relocation of Ebenezer had been given, he obtained a document from Oglethorpe that issued all of the relevant agreements in the form of harsh commands to the community. When he read them to the community gathered in the church on Sunday afternoon, February 22, 1736, great confusion arose as a result of this fully superfluous measure,[62] but even more so over the new "orders" it contained:

1. Except for Sundays and holidays, each resident had to work for four hours every morning and evening (they often worked longer on their own).
2. At the new location a hut was to be built for the first carpenters, then a storehouse, and for all the others only two large barracks.
3. The twenty garden plots that lay directly on each side of the town, therefore the ones that were the most convenient, and sixteen in the middle of the town were to be keep free for the use of the Trustees—all completely unnecessary hardships.[63]

Boltzius now had to write extensively again to Oglethorpe. They should be allowed to work as they had been so far in groups of five; without the senseless giving of commands things would go much better. Moreover,

---

non-Salzburger, to move to Ebenezer from South Carolina.

59. 5D1, 16 = journal (-UN) October 15, 1735; 5D1, 176 = journal (-UN) October 22, 1735; 5D1, 181 = journal (-UN) October 25, 1735.

60. 5D1, 194 = journal (-UN) November 6, 1735; 5D2, 14 = journal (-UN), January 16, 1736; 5D2, 50 = journal (-UN) February 16, 1736.

61. 5D1, 143–44 = journal (-UN) September 24, 1735.

62. For example, it was ordered that they were to plow, sow, and harvest the land.

63. 5D2, 55 = journal (-UN), February 22, 1736.

it was now the best time for planting that they did not want to miss by being ordered to build houses, and so on.[64]

In the expectation that Oglethorpe would let reason rule, Vat's commands were generally ignored with the result that he fell into a great rage and continually issued threats, repeatedly stayed away for longer periods, and every time locked the storehouse, from which the community went through extreme inconvenience.[65]

Finally, the expected answer from Oglethorpe arrived: he was in complete agreement with Boltzius' wishes and at the same time turned over to him the entire matter of the provisions.[66] Causton was from then on very accommodating toward him while previously he understandably had sided with the overly-parsimonious Vat.[67] Herr Vat, however, was not at all prepared to turn over to Boltzius the distribution of the provisions. He wanted to have a written instruction from Oglethorpe to him personally, along with similar considerations.[68] This dispute persisted for a while until Vat, together with Oglethorpe, returned to London in October 1736.[69] Only shortly before that did he allow the provisions from Old Ebenezer to be brought to New Ebenezer. Then he attempted to prepare a good departure for himself. After a pause of over a year, he went to church again and also was friendly in other respects to Boltzius until finally, with rifle salvos and hunting horn calls, he left Ebenezer for Savannah.[70]

64. In English, 5D2, 70–74 = journal (-UN) March 1, 1736.

65. 5D2, 110–11 = journal (-UN) March 23, 1736.

66. 5D2, 113 = journal (+UN) March 25, 1736.

67. 5D2, 105 = journal (-UN) March 18, 1736.

68. 5D2, 115ff. = journal (-UN) March 29–30, 1736; 5D2, 130 = journal (-UN) April 13/15, 1736.

69. 5A3:29, 209 = December 8, 1736 Z. copy; 5A3:33, 218 =January 10, 1737 Z. copy.

70. 5D2, 224 = journal (-UN) July 8, 1736; 5D2, 226 = journal (-UN) July 11, 1736; 5D2, 278 = journal (-UN) September 27, 1736; 5D2, 227 = journal (-UN) July 15, 1736. Oglethorpe's itinerary: On February 2, 1733, Oglethorpe arrived in Georgia for the first time. In early spring 1735, he returned to London (5D1, 113 = journal May 7, 1734; Strobel, *The Salzburgers and Their Descendants*, 74). On December 10, 1735, he departed there again (5D2, 206 = journal June 19, 1736; 5A3:8, 53–54 = November 19, 1735 Fr. draft) and arrived at Tybee Island on February 5, 1736 (5D2, 37 = journal [+UN] February 7, 1736). On October 24, 1736, he left Savannah (5A3:29, 209 = December 8, 1736 Z. copy) and after a perilous voyage arrived in London on January 6, 1737 (5A3:33, 218 = January 10, 1737 Z. copy). After the middle of April 1738, he set off again to Georgia (5A7:1, 1 = April 14, 1738 Z. original) where he went on land, this time in Frederica around September 18th (5D4, 268 = journal [+UN] October 2, 1738). On October 10th, he was in Savannah (5D4, 289 = journal [+UN] October 13, 1738) and visited Ebenezer in the middle of July 1739, where he was very favorably impressed (5D6, 13 = journal [+UN] July 18, 1739). Until his promotion to Brigadier General he

Years of Pioneer Work

Various further difficulties lay in the path of the community of Ebenezer. Even though everything had to be started from scratch, the period for provisions ran out on March 29, 1736.[71] What now was taken from the storehouse in Savannah had to be paid for; that meant incurring debts. The third transport had been designated by the Trustees for Frederica, Georgia's southern boundary stronghold,[72] and Gronau was to relocate with them. However, during Oglethorpe's visit to Ebenezer in connection with its relocation, Boltzius declared to him, "We two would not and could not separate from each other," and also that since the members of that third transport, as is to be assumed, had emigrated due to their faith, it certainly would be advisable to bring them likewise to Ebenezer, which in fact is also what happened for the majority of them.[73] However, their entire provisions already had been transported to Frederica so that in the beginning they received nothing at all, and later only very little, in food, cattle, and tools, and even these only with great difficulty.[74] Boltzius cast the blame alternately on Oglethorpe and von Reck, occasionally also on Causton,[75] without recognizing the actual circumstances.

A moving lament by the otherwise very undemanding Gronau indicates just how miserable for a long time the situation of the community then was: "I spoke recently with a young Salzburger who, along with his wife, had been ill for a long time and now had built himself a new hut. He told me in passing what his daily ration had been for a while, namely, in the morning porridge from Indian corn meal (maize), at midday rice and beans cooked together, in the evening several dumplings from boiled rice and Indian corn meal (they have to make these dumplings in this way so that they do not fall apart). All of this they boiled in water and added a little salt; they did not now have fat and meat; her brother for even a longer time had no meat. I was very astonished over this, and especially since I had not detected the least dissatisfaction in them but saw much more that they regretted not at all that they had come here from Germany."[76]

---

remained in Georgia and only left the colony for good on July 8, 1743 (UN July 8, 1743).

71. 5A3:35, 222 = October 27, 1736 B. copy.

72. 5A3:54, 341 = March 17, 1736 Verelst copy.

73. 5D2, 42 = journal (+UN) February 11, 1736.

74. 5D2 ' = journal March 9 and 18 and April 30, 1736; 5A3:23, 164 = June 19, 1736 B. original; 5D3, 8 = journal (+UN) January 17, 1737.

75. 5A3:20, 138 = July 7, 1736 Z.; 5A3:23, 164 = June 19, 1736 B. original; 5A3:27, 199 = October 1736 B. original.

76. 5A3:50, 318 = March 5, 1737 postscript G. original.

According to the terms of settlement, each settler was to be apportioned a house lot (one-eighth acre) in the town, as well as a garden (two acres), and the "plantation" (forty-eight acres) outside of the town. But still in June 1736, the gardens had not been surveyed at all, and the surveyor Jonas, who allegedly had not done this out of laziness, told Oglethorpe that the settlers did not want to accept them as he had surveyed them.[77] Finally, some of them again received poor land while fertile land lay directly alongside.[78] No thought at all could yet be given to the surveying of the plantations. It was even said for a while that there were not to be any individual fields but that all should work one large parcel communally.[79] Through the relocation of Ebenezer the impression partially arose that the Salzburgers were even in the position of consuming provisions for free but not of engaging in profitable agriculture. As a consequence of this ill will that arose against them, they were called upon for tasks of every sort. They were to mark a way by means of signs on trees to Charleston 130 miles away. Von Reck even demanded twenty people for Fort St. George, and no one among the authorities was bothered that Vat was in Savannah with the key for the provisions.

We learn little that is definite about the many and persistent evil rumors that awakened the impression in Ebenezer "as if everything was intended, under good pretense, to let the Salzburgers become genuine beggars so that they would be forced in hunger and extreme indigence to scatter through the entire colony and to submit to the English as servants. They invent a host of untruths, and even though they are refuted many times to the superiors and the matters are presented in their true character and proper circumstances, nonetheless the enemies and slanderers are believed more than our explanation and defense."[80] "I do not at all allow it," Boltzius protested, "and even if I should no longer be preacher in Ebenezer. I am thoroughly tired of all the onerous things that continue to be laid with all flattery and good words on the community, and should the promises made to the people in writing and orally further not be kept, and the Salzburgers are treated not as other English subjects but as slaves, then I do not see how I should and can conduct my office here."[81] All of these things were carefully omitted with the revision of the journal.

Finally, in addition to everything else, Ebenezer and all the surrounding places were struck by a malaria epidemic from around Pentecost 1736. It

77. 5D2, 205 = journal (-UN) June 19, 1736.
78. 5A3:45, 286–87 = December 4, 1736 B. copy.
79. 5A3:23, 162–65 = June 19, 1736 B. original.
80. 5D2, 205 = journal (-UN) June 19, 1736.
81. 5D2, 205 = journal (-UN) June 12, 1736.

embraced such a scope that the journal in September recorded, "I would not know to find four truly healthy men in our community."[82] Ebenezer's small children died with few exceptions,[83] and in October, Gronau concluded, "I now know not a single one, neither among the large nor also among the very smallest who has been spared."[84] Only in December did this epidemic subside[85] only to reappear severely the next year.[86] As a result, the relocation was a hardship.[87]

This time for the Ebenezer community was the hardest in the story of its settlement. Its situation was so wretched that some of the very patient members wanted to go back to Germany or become servants to English settlers.[88] The decisive part of the credit goes to the masterful spiritual guidance and the tough persistence of the settlers that Ebenezer overcame this period and did not disperse again, like, for example, the emigrants led to South Carolina by Jean-Pierre Purry. Never again in the history of Ebenezer did the decisive, community preserving element—the proclamation of the Word of God—prove itself to be so directly empowering.

Then, just when the collapse seemed to be not far away, the change came. Ziegenhagen, to whom the continuous reports from Ebenezer had arrived, had turned to everyone with authority in the matter in order to make clear to them that here an entire community of people willing to work was being abandoned to ruin. He had written to Oglethorpe,[89] to the "comptroller for the Trustees" Vernon,[90] and to Causton.[91] He visited Oglethorpe on February 21, 1737, in London after his return from Georgia,[92] and made it happen that the Trustees, in their session on March 2, 1737,[93] concluded a resolution that was decisive for the well-being of Ebenezer:

1. Extension of the free provisions until the end of September 1737.

2. Immediate surveying of the plantations and exchange of the bad gardens.

82. 5D2, 273 = journal (+UN) September 20, 1736.
83. 5D2, 276 = journal (+UN) September 27, 1736.
84. 5A3: 26, 185 = October 1, 1736 G. original.
85. 5A3:45, 287 = December 4, 1736 B. copy.
86. 5D7, 102 = journal (+UN) March 13, 1741.
87. 5A3:23, 162–65 = June 19, 1736 B. original.
88. 5A3:57, 353–54 = July 29, 1737 B. original.
89. 5A3:40.
90. 5C2:5, 16 = July 5/16, 1745 Z. copy; 5A3:41; von Reck also wrote to him, 5A3:20, 138.
91. 5A3:46.
92. 5A3:42, 276–77 = February 24, 1737 Z. copy.
93. 5A3:47, 295.

3. Approval of provisions and tools for the third transport to the same extent as for the first two.[94]

When Boltzius received news of it on June 8, 1737, he negotiated immediately with Causton,[95] and the ice was now broken. To be sure, it also still took a rather long time until everything came into the desired order; in fact, at first it seemed that hardly anything would change. But the decision for the continued existence of Ebenezer had been made and could be held up to each dawdler. The mountain of difficulties was not overcome until the end of 1737 and beginning of 1738.[96] The sweeping significance of the decree of the Trustees can be shown for the first time from the material treated here, because the previous, unbelievably difficult situation of the community was not known to its full extent.

Now on July 20, 1737, the surveyor Ross, with three settlers,[97] began to survey the plantations which, at Oglethorpe's instruction, were all to lay in a square of four miles per side.[98] But soon Ross disappeared again for a long time and only returned again in September,[99] when things swiftly advanced so that he could report to Boltzius on December 1, 1737, that now a portion of the plantations could be assigned. The next morning, Boltzius held a devotion for this occasion in the worship room, and then the settlers drew for the allocation.[100]

Benjamin Martyn inspected the colony on behalf of the Trustees in the summer of 1738 and visited Ebenezer from June 24th to 26th,[101] during which Boltzius obtained his commitment to advocate for an extension of the plantations along the river in the direction of Abercorn, since not all of the lots of land that had been surveyed to that point were fertile.[102] As a result, four quadrant miles were surveyed on an island formed by the mainstream of the Savannah River with its arm, Abercorn Creek.[103] Finally, in November 1738, all of the plantations, without exception on fertile land,

---

94. Communication to Boltzius by Trustee Verelst, 5A3:54, 341–42 = March 17, 1736 copy, erroneously as 1737.

95. 5D3, 78 = journal (+UN) June 9, 1737.

96. 5A7:2, 3 = January 20, 1738 B. original.

97. 5A3:26, 187 = October 1, 1736 G. original.

98. 5D3, 113 = journal (+UN) July 20, 1737.

99. UN September 3/23, 1737.

100. 5D3, 133 = journal (+UN) December 2, 1737; 5A7:2, 3 = January 20, 1738 B. original.

101. 5D4, 159–60 = journal (+UN) June 24 and 26–27, 1738.

102. 5D4, 161 = journal (+UN) June 26, 1738.

103. 5D4, 263 and 265 = journal (+UN) September 28, 1738.

were surveyed and distributed, and Boltzius, after an inspection tour, wrote to Europe, again satisfied and full of hope for the first time after all of the difficulties.[104]

Yet a new problem emerged: the plantations lay up to six miles away from Ebenezer,[105] and so it was unavoidable that the settlers little by little also built houses and moved there with their families. In the beginning, they erected only small huts for the night and for protection from the rain[106] and returned again to their families for Sundays, until their new fields produced, and they could relinquish the two-acre gardens located next to Ebenezer.[107]

From the summer of 1739, the families then moved out into permanent houses that all stood on the mainland, since the island in the Savannah River was flooded annually.[108] Consequently, Boltzius wondered, since he still did not have a real house,[109] whether he should eventually also move out there, "since then the worship service, the daily prayer hours, and school can be held, by me there and by Herr Gronau here in Ebenezer. For some still are remaining in the town and cultivating near and in it."[110] But Boltzius and Gronau, however, preferred to remain together, as their calls had intended, because the settlers on the plantations were not at all very far away but still lived too far apart from each other to come together in the evening for the prayer hour.[111]

Naturally, the annual yield of the harvest was very decisive for the progress of the community's economy, about which Boltzius had to report each time to the Trustees.[112] Unfortunately, the harvest in the already difficult year of 1737 was bad.[113] Yet in the following years,[114] especially in

104. 5D4, 349–51 = journal (+UN) November 24, 1738; 5A7:40, 172 = journal November 24, 1738 extract; 5A7:49b, 211 = November 25, 1738 B. copy.

105. 5D4, 194 = journal (+UN) July 30, 1738.

106. The first to move out there were Peter Gruber, Thomas Gschwandel, and Ruprecht Kalcher (5A7:40, 170 = journal (+UN) November 18, 1738 draft; Kalcher had to greatly neglect his land because of his duties in the orphanage).

107. 5D4, 360 = journal (+UN) December 2, 1738; UN December 3, 1739; 5A7: 40, 172 = journal (+UN) November 24, 1738 extract; 5A7:53, 225 = journal (+UN) May 10, 1739 extract.

108. 5D6 = journal July/August 1739; 5D4, 265 = journal (+UN) September 28, 1738.

109. 5A7:33, 142 = October 9, 1738 G. original.

110. 5A7:3, 148 = November 4, 1738 B. original.

111. 5D7:40, 174 = November 10, 1738 postscript G.; 5D4, 371–72 journal (+UN) December 10, 1738.

112. 5A9:2, 7 = February 14, B. original.

113. 5A7:3, 6 = January 20, 1738 G. original.

114. 5A7:41, 176 = (1738) Kalcher original; 5A7:50b, 215 = November 1738; 5A7:64a,

1741,[115] they turned out favorably, to the extent that could be expected from the sandy soil. Only in a considerably greater distance from the coast was there truly fertile land in Georgia, on the other side of the tideline.[116]

Now, since the members of the community—increased in December 1741 through the fourth group of immigrants ("Salzburger transport")[117]—had found their permanent residences, work could begin to create a remarkable series of institutions that made evident how strongly pronounced among the first Lutherans was the feeling for communal solidarity, communal work, and communal obligations, not only as a duty of ownership but also as a matter of their character and their responsibilities.

1. At the end of 1737 and the beginning of 1738, the orphanage, felt to be the highest necessity, was founded and soon took on responsibilities beyond those associated with this name[118] and became famous because of its being the first in America.

267–68 = October 30, 1739 B. original; 5A9:8, 35 = journal (+UN) May 24, 1740 extract.

115. 5A10:7, 24 = June 5, 1741 B. original; 5A10:15, 48 = October 14, 1741 B. original.

116. Strobel, *The Salzburgers and Their Descendants*, 66–67.

117. On January 30, 1741, Ziegenhagen reported to Urlsperger that Lutheran and Reformed Alsatians had approached the Trustees and requested acceptance for Georgia. Subsequently, Parliament approved £10,000 for such matters and so there was consent to bring 100 Alsatians, the Lutherans to Ebenezer to the Salzburgers but to settle the Reformed elsewhere. When that was made known, Ziegenhagen wrote, in the already mentioned letter to Urlsperger (5A9:29 = January 30, 1741 Z. copy), that he, without mentioning the Alsatians, might write to the Trustees and request a new Salzburger resettlement initiative. But with unexpected speed, the Trustees already on February 7, 1741, through their Secretary Benjamin Martyn, made a request to Newman, as Secretary of the SPCK, for about fifty Salzburgers for Georgia who should be ready to depart by July 1741 (5A9:23, 96). From Augsburg, Lindau, Memmingen, Ulm, Stuttgart, etc. were now brought together under Commissioner Johann Gottfried von Müllern sixty-one men (UN II, 1205; 5A9:26, 103 = May 11, 1741 U. original) who gathered on June 16, 1741, in Canstatt near Stuttgart where Urlsperger visited them. Traveling along the familiar way, they arrived in London on July 25th new style (UN preface of the 7th Continuation, unpaginated; travel journal of von Müllern and Vigera UN II, 1176–218; 5A9:26 + 30, 139). From here, they departed on September 18th with the "Loyal Judith" (5D8, 598 = journal November 10, 1741: when Boltzius learned of their impeding arrival, he ordered a quantity of rice from the farmer Jonathan Bryan) under Commissioner Johann Friedrich Vigera (he went on August 8, 1743, from Ebenezer to Pennsylvania and was there for a long time a well-regarded teacher: *Nachrichten von den vereinigten Deutschen Evangelisch-Lutherischen Gemeinden in Nord-America*, 109–10; 5A10:19, 70 = May 13, 1742 B. original; 5D9, 5 = journal February 29, 1744) and, after several scares from the Spanish, landed on December 1 off of Port Royal, South Carolina. When from there they had reached Savannah, they met with Boltzius on December 4th.

118. 5A3:57, 354 = July 29, 1737 B. original; 5A7:3, 6–7 = journal (+UN) January 9, 1738 extract.

2. A house was built for Boltzius,[119] and with it a center of the community was created whose importance for the security of the individual community member and upright leadership according to the Word of God remained preserved in the memory of the community long after Boltzius' death.[120]
3. Ebenezer's millworks were built: grain, rice, and sawmills to which, as the first in Georgia, is owed in great part the economic advancement of the community.[121]
4. Sericulture, recommended by the Trustees, was taken on, in which Ebenezer was the most successful among all of Georgia's settlements.[122]
5. Finally, in the summer of 1741, the building of a church in Ebenezer could be undertaken,[123] and a year and a half later one on the plantations.[124]

At Oglethorpe's request, the community even sent a communal letter to Urlsperger in which they called for additional compatriots to come to Georgia.[125] And this flourishing of the place, as soon as acceptable settlement possibilities were granted, occurred at a time when things appeared not at all calm in the rest of Georgia; on October 23, 1739, England had declared war against Spain.[126] As early as the spring of 1739, Boltzius believed that the war already had broken out, which particularly disturbed him because Ebenezer lay neither in the direct of vicinity of Savannah nor of Purrysburg,[127] and with apprehension he tracked the increasing arming of the Spanish[128] as well as the expansion of England, concerning which he

---

119. Boltzius also had owned a house in Old Ebenezer: a living room downstairs and space for worship services and prayer hours upstairs (completed: UN November 8, 1734; Gronau's house: September 20, 1735). In New Ebenezer, each of them at first had a simple cottage (5D2, 175 = journal (+UN) May 15, 1736). 5A5:29, 119 = July 17, 1739 B. original; start of construction of the new house: UN January 2, 1739.

120. When Muhlenberg sought to mediate the Rabenhorst-Triebner dispute, the decisive negotiations intentionally took place there.

121. UN December 5, 1740; 5A9:9, 39 = September 9, 1740 B. original.

122. 5D7, 207 = journal (+UN) April 28, 1741.

123. 5D8, 354 = journal (+UN) July 6, 1741.

124. UN December 10, 1742. An attempt was also made with producing wine (UN February 4, 1742) that even showed some results (UN August 11, 1742) but was given up.

125. 5A7:50b, 217 = November 1738.

126. UN March 14, 1740.

127. 5A3:4, 25 = March 28, 1735 B. original.

128. 5D2, 188 = journal (partially UN) May 27, 1736; 5D3, 17 = journal (+UN) February 10 and 12 1737; 22 = journal (+UN) February 18, 1737; 30 = journal (+UN) March 10, 1737; 5D4, 91 = journal (+UN) April 16, 1738; 94 = journal (+UN) May 18, 1738.

believed that Oglethorpe "had extended the borders of this Georgia so far that the Spanish cannot be content with it."[129] Oglethorpe naturally would have been glad to see that Ebenezer also provided a number of soldiers, but only five men reported, three of them servants, since Boltzius' view was, "Upright people do not let themselves be used in this way but rather one who likes to run around and is pleased with this kind of life."[130]

The fortune of war was then also shifting; reports often came to Ebenezer that naturally were received here with the greatest interest. It was learned, for example, about the badly disciplined troops from Carolina and about the reinforcements that came from England by way of New York.[131]

To be sure, the possibility always had to be considered of falling within the battle zone, and even the possibility of surrendering the place in such a case was considered,[132] but, fortunately, it never came to that. When the situation intensified through the buildup of Spanish troops in 1742 and Frederica was evacuated of civilians, Ebenezer became a place of refuge for many of them.[133] But finally the Spanish were defeated, and in the "Battle of Bloody Marsh" the outcome fell in favor of Georgia.[134] As in other places, a service of thanksgiving was also held in Ebenezer;[135] from then on nothing was to be feared from the Spanish.

Still in the same year (1742), the Ebenezer community had the pleasure of having visit them Pastor Henry (Heinrich) Melchior Muhlenberg who had been chosen by the Francke Foundations in Halle for Pennsylvania and who was on the way there. The Lutheran pastors of Georgia had played a role in the realization of his sending. In the summer of 1734, just when the first Salzburger transport was setting foot in Georgia, the Silesian merchant Daniel Weisiger,[136] a member of the Evangelical congregation in Philadelphia, Pennsylvania, had come to Francke in Halle. With Johann Daniel Schöner and Pastor Johann Christian Schultze, he "had been sent out to gather a collection for the building of several churches and schools in Philadelphia, New Hanover, and Providence," and Weisiger asked Francke "for a capable and

---

129. 5A3:23, 165 = June 19, 1736 B. original.

130. UN April 12, 1740.

131. 5A9:10, 46 = August 5, 1740 B. original.

132. 5A10:39, 140 = (undated) Fr. draft, probably the same as 5A10:38 = April 2, 1743 Fr. draft.

133. 5A10:33, 111 = July 26, 1742 B. original; 5A10:34, 117 = March 27, 1742 Fr. draft; 5A10:37, 129 = April 2, 1743 Fr. draft.

134. On July 7, 1742. UN July 22, 1742.

135. UN August 26, 1742; 5A10:37, 129 = April 2, 1743 Fr. draft; 5D9, 53 = journal (-UN) June 19, 1744.

136. 5A1:45, 201; 5A1:47, 224 Fr. draft; 5A3:3a, 17 = February 6, 1735.

upright preacher and schoolteacher for the aforementioned Evangelical parishes, but in the future, with divine assistance, to seek out and provide more of them, as the aforementioned parishes had a great desire to be supplied with upright preachers."[137] This seemed to be all the more necessary, Francke believed, since their only preacher so far, Schultze, had become almost completely blind, as it was said, due to a dissolute way of life.

Francke wanted to comply with the entreaty, but before doing so he requested information from Boltzius and Gronau about the conditions in Pennsylvania.[138] It was given in detail, though to be sure it reports nothing new. It does show, however, how precisely informed they were.[139] But Francke hesitated, in the manner in which he always was well known, to send anyone, because it was not thoroughly clear to him whether a preacher would be properly received and paid,[140] and he asked Boltzius to go there for himself.[141] But Boltzius did not want to do so without permission from the SPCK. The trip also was not possible for him at that time because of his parish.[142]

137. 5A1:36, 161 Fr. draft = supplement to 5A1:34–35 = July 23, 1734 Fr. draft.; according to 5A1:49, 234.

138. 5A1:36, 162 Fr. draft.

139. There were many Evangelical Lutherans, especially in Germantown, but who lived together with sectarians, especially Quakers, through which much unrest arose. A whole array even converted to the sects for material reasons. In the area near Moly, in the so-called "Great Swamp," lived Caspar "Steber," ordained by Schultze before his departure, who now had a lot of trouble with the community because of his salary. To a great extent, the communities were left to fend for themselves. Still no salary had been arranged for Schultze. Therefore, he acted "like a wild soldier" when the community members did not place enough in the collection plate—because he had ridden their horses to death. In the so-called Great Swamp, school was occasionally taught by a man by the name of Musselbach, whom Schultze was supposed to ordain but hesitated because this man "in Heidelberg had been nothing more than a bridge toll collector and previously had even been Catholic." In the area around New York, there were two Evangelical pastors, and in the Blue Hills resided an elderly, drunken pastor, and afterwards a tailor named van Dehren (= van Dieren. 5A3:4, 26 = March 28, 1735 B. original.; see also *Nachrichten von den vereinigten Deutschen Evangelisch-Lutherischen Gemeinden*, 274) who called himself a pastor and had followers (5A1:49, 234–38 = probably December 10–11, 1734 B).

140. 5A1:51, 256–57 = March 11, 1735 Fr. draft.

141. 5A1:54, 273; 5A3:2, 7.

142. In the meantime, Weisiger also had come to Ebenezer with the second Salzburger transport. After a stay here, (until January 29, 1735) he wanted to report to Francke directly from Philadelphia again (5A1:45, 201; 5A1:47, 224; 5A3:3a, 18 = February 6, 1735 B. copy; 5A3:2, 7). Accompanying Weisiger was the infamous Siron, who made a good impression on Boltzius, but, according to Weisiger's declaration, "had fallen from one sect to another," and, in fact, in Pennsylvania had behaved very offensively (*Nachrichten von den vereinigten Deutschen Evangelisch-Lutherischen Gemeinden*, 57).

He emphatically underscored the requests for a preacher for Pennsylvania.[143] Thus, it was finally decided that Ziegenhagen should ask Francke officially "for a capable subject to be preacher for Philadelphia,"[144] who in fact was found in Muhlenberg.[145] His route led him first to London where Ziegenhagen advised him to go to Ebenezer to have himself instructed about the particular conditions in America.[146] From London, Muhlenberg, with the Salzburger family Kurz[147] that previously had been residing in Holland, went to Georgia and landed in Savannah on Saturday, October 2, 1742, around eight o'clock in the morning.

There, he reported to Colonel Stephens[148] who had him and the Salzburgers accommodated in an inn. Soon, Gronau arrived for the sermon for the next day and took Muhlenberg with him to the house of a member of the congregation with whom the pastors of Ebenezer were accustomed to lodge during their stays in Savannah. After Gronau had conducted the Sunday morning and afternoon worship service, they went on Monday by boat to Ebenezer.

Here, Muhlenberg delivered a silver chalice from Augsburg,[149] preached, and took communion on the following Sunday with the congregation,[150] and departed again on the evening of October 11, 1742, with Boltzius, who was supposed to accompany him to Pennsylvania, by way of Savannah and Port Royal, South Carolina to Charleston.[151] Here, Boltzius turned around on horseback, since no ship was departing to Pennsylvania in the foreseeable future. If he had waited, he would have been hindered in his return until next summer because of the freezing Delaware

---

For his part, Siron characterized Weisiger as an "arch-hypocrite," and his wife "as a very shameful person" (5A3:11, 73 = September 1, 1735 B. original).

143. 5A3:1, 2–3 = February 6, 1735 B. original; 5A3:11, 73 = September 1, 1735 B. original.

144. 5A9:29, 108 = January 1, 1741.

145. 5A10:18, 65–66 = January 12, 1742 Fr. draft.

146. Francke had heard about Zinzendorf's activities in Pennsylvania; Boltzius also had heard that Spangenberg, with whom he had been very severe in Georgia, wanted to settle there (5A3:1, 2 = February 6, 1735 B. original). 5A10:34, 121 = March 27, 1743 Fr. draft; Tappert and Doberstein, *The Journals of Henry Melchior Muhlenberg* I, 22 = journal June 11, 1742 M; 4H1a, 170 = journal October 2, 1742M.

147. A widower with two daughters, married to a widow with one daughter. Tappert and Doberstein, *The Journals of Henry Melchior Muhlenberg* I, 22 = journal June 12, 1742M; 4H1a, 169 = journal October 2, 1742M; UN March 2, 1747.

148. William Stephens (1671–1753); governor of Georgia from 1743–1751.

149. 4H1a, 169–70 = journal October 2, 1742 M.

150. 4H1a, 173 = journal October 10, 1742 M.

151. UN travel journal October 12–29, 1742 B.

River, and he could not leave his congregation alone for so long.¹⁵² The Lutheran pastors of Georgia and Pennsylvania maintained from then on a nearly regular correspondence.¹⁵³

Another visitor to Ebenezer during this time was the German Lutheran pastor Driessler from Frederica, Georgia. He also preached there, and his pronounced affability and friendliness pleased the community so greatly that they collected so much food for him that Boltzius was astounded.¹⁵⁴

How vigorously Ebenezer's economic situation developed in these years¹⁵⁵ is evident in the fact that the orphanage was no longer needed solely as an aid facility and therefore in June 1744 could be turned into a general economic enterprise of the community.¹⁵⁶ Also another event conclusively marks the end of this beginning period: the death of Gronau on January 11, 1745, which was painfully felt in like manner by Boltzius and the community.

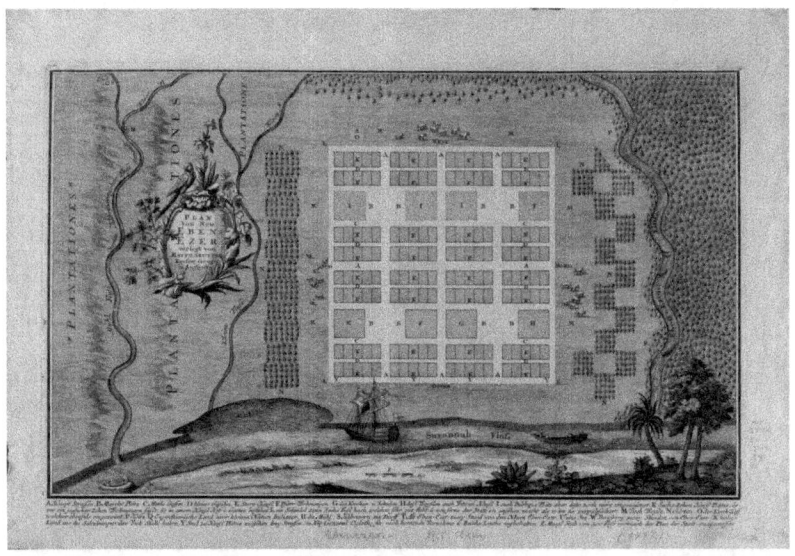

Map of Ebenezer, 1747, by Matthaeus Seutter, as it appeared in the *Ausführliche Nachrichten* (Detailed Reports). Image courtesy of Hargrett Rare Book and Manuscript Library/University of Georgia Libraries.

152. 4H1a, 173 = journal October 11, 1742 M; 5A10:42, 155 = March 9, 1743 B. original.

153. 5A11:11, 35 = January 12, 1744 B. original.

154. 5A1:24, 90 = February 24, 1744 B. original; 5D9, 1 = journal (-UN) February 24, 1744.

155. Despite a livestock epidemic since July 1743; 5A11: 3, 8 (= undated, between July 21 and September 20, 1743) B. original.

156. 5A11:13, 43–44 = June 4, 1744 B. original.

Economic Blossoming

The development of Ebenezer's economy to full bloom and the expansion of the settlement through the establishment of new sites characterize the following time period. Attempts were made to tap new sources of income of the most diverse sort. Boltzius himself submitted to Ziegenhagen[157] and Francke[158] plans for the development of the economy in Georgia:

1. For the boost of lumber export in the face of that in competing Carolina with its slave labor, royal privileges would be required.
2. If trade with Indians would be permitted, its center could be shifted from Charleston to Savannah where the Indians would have to pass through on the way there anyway.
3. Georgia could conduct more cheaply the grain trade of Pennsylvania and New York with the West Indies since it is not as far away.
4. Georgia is especially suited for cattle breeding, in which it also could trade with the West Indies.
5. The Augsburg banker Chrétien von Münch, along with Urlsperger a Georgia Trustee since 1747,[159] could open a shop in Savannah for whites, Indian traders, and Indians.
6. Such a depot for European wares could also be established in Frederica.
7. A direct ship connection from the coast to Ebenezer would bring grain in sufficient quantity for the mills and promote the lumber trade.

But England's main concern was to see the colony strengthened, not economically, but militarily, and so these far-sighted plans were not heeded, to Georgia's disadvantage.

Ebenezer nonetheless developed further. Indeed, at the end of 1747, agriculture was so far along that flour and butter could be delivered regularly to Savannah and soon to other places.[160] But it was soon noticed that the lumber trade was much more profitable,[161] and after the completion of

---

157. 5A11:54 = June 16, 1746 B. extract.

158. 5A11:50, 225–26 = *Diarium extraordinarium* May 1746 B.; UN February 9, 1750; UA May 22, 1751.

159. Along with Samuel Urlsperger, he became a corresponding member of the Trustees in April 1747 (*Einige wenige Umstände von den Personalien Tit. Herrn Samuel Urlspergern, Eines Evangelischen Ministerii zu Augspurg Senioris*, etc., unpaginated [after 1748]).

160. UN December 7, 1747; 5B1:8, 33 = March 28, 1749 B. original.

161. UN February 9, 1750.

a second sawmill in April 1751, it was pursued in full.[162] Silk culture,[163] the production of brandy from peaches,[164] and a complete tannery[165] provided further possibilities for income. Yet to the great chagrin of those involved, the development, despite every effort, could not be called in any way vigorous, as it now actually should have been. Boltzius' observations about it now already have a completely different tone (end of 1751):

1. "No true sustenance can arise among us if there are only nothing but farmers and no townsfolk, craftsmen, and well-to-do people." Accordingly, there were good prospects precisely for the craftsman with some garden land and livestock, since "by law no Negro may learn or practice any craft...."

2. "As long as there are not enough residents in the town [Ebenezer], we can start no such school, as we would wish, for local and outside children." The children from the plantations, because of the great distance, could only come in the mornings for instruction.

3. Without master craftsmen, the entire region remained agricultural, because no possibility was given for the learning of a craft.

4. A larger number of residents would lighten defense, and so on.[166]

162. UA April 27, 1751, June 30, 1752. Unfortunately, they also fell victim to a swindler, named Curtius, who purported to be a pastor's son from Württemberg and told them that he had a wealthy cousin in the lumber trade in New York. Ebenezer produced for him a large batch of lumber. He absconded with it, and there was never any mention of payment. (5A11:37 = February 25, 1746 B., because of postscript to 5A11:36; 5A11:38, 161 = July 19, 1746 Fr. draft; 5A11:61 = journal August 31, 1746 extract).

163. UN May 1, 1747. An extensive representation is rendered according to the work of McKinstry, "Silk Culture in the Colony of Georgia," 225–35. The silk culture of the Salzburgers was their most renowned economic achievement, for which reason all essential reports about it were gladly published by Urlsperger. It need only be mentioned that from Ebenezer, "a small paper full of worm-seeds or small eggs" were sent to the Francke Foundations, which likewise engaged in this cultivation (5A11:52, 238 [postscript to 51] = November 8, 1746 Fr. draft), and it was reported to Georgia that "the worms that came out of it were almost the best and have spun very beautifully," and more sendings were requested (5A11:87, 394 = September 9, 1748 Fr. draft).

164. UN December 5, 1747.

165. UN January 16, 1751. Near the mill, the tanner Neidlinger, with his sons, set up a complete facility: a water-powered tanbark mill with three "stamps" that crushed oak bark to powder; next to it a large workshop with leather pits made out of thick cypress boards. In front of it was a fourteen to sixteen-foot wide and long bridge made of "posts, beams, and boards built in the millstream over the mill weir, on which the leather was prepared." In front of it were two other posts to which the skins were bound for softening, and the canals, that directed the water to the water wheels, served for soaking the skins when they had been taken out of the lime.

166. UA December 7, 1751.

Boltzius therefore foresaw by more than a century the problem of the differing development of America's northern and southern states.

During these years, the question of slavery stirred Georgia's minds. The advantages that neighboring South Carolina had through its cheap labor force were too palpable for the settlers south of the Savannah River to be content in the long run with the Trustees' prohibition of slavery.[167] However, an element of uncertainty was bound up with it: in South Carolina, the men even had to go to church armed because of slave unrest,[168] and at the time of the arrival of the first Salzburgers, a large uprising had just occurred there.[169] Even in Ebenezer opinions were divided. A large part was for the allowance of slaves and at first had to have their minds changed by the doctor and justice of the peace Mayer.[170] The other part of the community, with Boltzius—and finally everyone—dreaded the uncertain circumstances and the burdens of conscience connected with it.[171]

To the argument of the other side,[172] that without slaves nothing was to be accomplished here in this land, the evidence to the contrary, in the shape of Ebenezer together with Boltzius' public stance, was admittedly a thorn in the eye, and it openly stirred up so much hatred against him[173] that he decided that he would now keep silent until the Trustees one day certainly would have to allow slaves,[174] whereupon the opposition would immediately calm down.[175] In fact, the permission for holding slaves in Georgia appeared on July 7, 1749,[176] a first concession to the fact that the military policy of the Trustees in Georgia had been a success but the economic policy a failure.

---

167. There were a couple of African Americans already in Georgia (1 *Diarium extraordinarium* 9:9a, 31 = August 21, 1747 B. extract; 5B1:8, 34 = March 28, 1749 B. original). The following remarks are condensed because the matter already has been extensively treated by Binder-Johnson, "Die Haltung der Salzburger in Georgia zur Sklaverei."

168. UN July 8, 1742.

169. 5D1, 70 = journal March 7, 1734.

170. 5A11:73, 339 = September 10, 1747 L. original.

171. Likewise, in Savannah, Colonel Stephens and Mr. Jones (5D8, 346 = journal July 3, 1741). In Ebenezer, several said that they would rather move again for the sake of serenity (UN April 28, 1749).

172. In Savannah, Captain Robert Williams (5D7, 260 = journal May 29, 1741), Mr. Harris and Habersham (1 *Diarium extraordinarium* 9:a, 31 = August 21, 1747 B. extract).

173. For example, Boltzius only reported to Europe what was positive (UN May 1, 1748). This accusation, as has often been attested here, is not validly maintained; the thoroughly positive character of the publications about Ebenezer is due to those who revised his reports.

174. 5A11:72, 330 = September 7, 1740 B. original.

175. UN III, 519–21 = letter January 4, 1730 B. to U.

176. Jones, *The History of Georgia* I, 442.

Since the "Fathers in Europe" (Francke, Urlsperger, and Ziegenhagen) could not now demand from Ebenezer with a clear conscience that it continue further toward its "material ruin" without slaves, Ziegenhagen attempted to dispel the relevant qualms: the father of every household assumes responsibility for the body and soul of all of those under his care. Therefore, slavery actually is better for the slaves than their earlier way of life, since they would then have, besides assured sustenance, the opportunity to become Christian. Therefore, the much-cited advice of Ziegenhagen goes,[177] "If therefore the need is so great that no other way can be advised, let slaves be held in the faith and for the purpose that they should be led to Christ; thus, such a deed will not be a sin, but it can become a blessing."

The Christian instruction of the slaves laid heavily on Boltzius' heart, for which the German language nevertheless created an obstacle.[178] But the only result was the baptism of children, for whom the slave holders took on the responsibilities of godparents.[179] The following incident is typical. When Boltzius wanted to bless a baptized, dying child in the presence of the non-Christian mother, "she hurriedly lifted it up" in a magical understanding of this act. The next day, the child died. "The heathen mother was very distressed, and because she wished one day to get her child back again, and she had hope for it with the Christian religion, she promised me to let herself be instructed and to accept instruction, which also happened."[180] This inclination, recognized from many African American spirituals, is therefore already discernible in the earliest time of slaves' encounter with Christianity.

To be sure, Ebenezer's slaves, as a consequence of better treatment in comparison to that of other slaveholders, posed few problems to the community.[181] Yet later, Lutheran Pastor Rabenhorst had to concede, "They certainly work with much faithfulness and diligence that I could not so expect from white indentured servants. But they are and remain heathens who carry the name of God in their mouths to please me but do not at all desire Him from their hearts."[182]

---

177. UA April 3, 1751 = letter July 11, 1750 Z. to B. Strobel erroneously ascribes this position to Samuel Urlsperger (Strobel, *The Salzburgers and Their Descendants*, 104).

178. UA May 17 and November 3, 1752.

179. Lawrence surmises that Pastor Zuberbühler of Savannah (Anglican) performed the first baptism of a black resident in Georgia on July 7, 1750. Lawrence, "Religious Education of the Negro in the Colony of Georgia," 51. Boltzius baptized the first black child in Georgia already on March 30, 1747 (UN).

180. UA December 12–13 and 22, 1752.

181. UA February 20 and April 13, 1754, May 3, 1760.

182. 5B2: 65, 233 = February 21, 1736 R. original.

After Gronau's death, Ebenezer became greatly enlarged through several transports of settlers who, in part, founded new sites.

1. In August/September 1745, about eighty Württembergers arrived who, through four years of labor as servants, had to repay the costs advanced by the Trustees for their crossing, as was usual at the time.[183] As also later in such cases, these people mainly were engaged in and around Savannah. When they became free at the end of 1748, they settled near Ebenezer.[184] In February of the following year (1746), Gronau's successor, Pastor Lemcke, arrived.

2. On October 3 and 4, 1749, another transport of sixty-three Germans under the same conditions of transport landed in Savannah, where they were boarded at the expense of the Trustees in Mr. Jones' house. Boltzius, who held a worship service for them on the following Sunday, explained to them that they would have to serve only two years in Savannah, but three years and five months in Ebenezer since the heads of the households there were not as well-off. But most of them nonetheless wanted to move to Ebenezer.

    When they were there, there was nonetheless dissension on that account, until Boltzius admonished them along with their masters to be calm and, as a sign of his good will, distributed to the servants New Testaments and Psalters. Boltzius already had asked the Trustees repeatedly for such people to be used for assistance in the hope by doing so of being able to get by without slaves. However, the white servants fit in poorly in the community. They were unbelieving and disobedient, and through their deviousness caused a lot of trouble for their true-hearted, upright masters. Naturally, they made themselves self-sufficient as soon as possible and established their own plantations. Finally, these who had come over this time were mostly artisans and therefore were of no assistance for farming, and, moreover, the best twenty-one of them were bought free by well-off people in Savannah and kept there.[185]

3. After a long, difficult journey, the first Swabian transport, whose members came from the region around Ulm, reached Savannah at the

---

183. 5C2:5, 16 = July 5, 1745 Z. copy.

184. 5B1:24, 105–6 = November 23, 1748 B. original signature on the letter from another hand.

185. 5B1:22, 99 = November 30, 1749 B. original; 5B1:37, 150 = June 1750 B. copy; 5B1:48, 199 = February 13, 1751 B. original; UN October 8, 10, 12, 16 and December 25, 1749; UN September 18, 1750; UA February 20, 1754.

end of October 1750.[186] Thirty-seven of them moved to Ebenezer.[187] Unfortunately, only some tools were allocated to them by the Trustees, while the immigrants to Carolina also received food and cattle: "It should happen much more here, since this land is to be settled with white people opposite the Spaniards," was Boltzius' view.[188] In contrast to their predecessors, they assimilated well into the community.

4. The second Swabian transport followed. On October 23, 1751, Boltzius met in Savannah two people who arrived in advance: the merchant Kraft[189] and Captain Johann Gerhard Wilhelm von Brahm. Through Urlsperger, the latter had come into contact with the Trustees who, since things were not advancing properly with Georgia, sent him there as General Surveyor, which signified a certain authority of oversight.[190]

On the following day, the ship arrived with the main group. These settlers already had paid for the cost of the voyage in London but were now completely without means. Boltzius preached to them on the text, "Dearly beloved, I beseech you as strangers and pilgrims, abstain from fleshly lusts, which war against the soul; having your conversation honest among the Gentiles: that, whereas they speak against you as evildoers, they may by your good works, which they shall behold, glorify God in the day of visitation" (1 Pet 2:11–12). Moreover, he gained permission to settle them on the "Blue Bluff" across from the Ebenezer Creek where most of them now moved and in doing so founded the place called Bethany.[191] Von Brahm especially took an interest in its success.[192]

---

186. UN November 1, 1750.

187. UN November 1 and 8, 1750.

188. 5B1:46, 188–91 = November 21, 1750 B. original; 5B1:48, 199 = February 13, 1751 B. original.

189. The first husband of Pastor Rabenhorst's wife.

190. Von Brahm (1717–ca. 1799): "An Exhibition Commemorating the Settlement of Georgia 1733–1948" (February 14, 1748–May 12, 1748), 32; 5B4:29, 4 = January 11, 1803 Bm. original. He died sometime earlier at the age of eighty. Von Brahm came from a Catholic family from the Palatinate, fought 1737–1739 against the Turks and returned afterwards to his homeland. Here, he began to preach against superstition; it was not possible on the part of the church to keep him in check, so that he had to be expelled from the territory by a letter of dismissal from the Bishop of Regensburg. Through the influence of Samuel Urlsperger, he converted and came into contact with the Trustees who sent him to Georgia (Mallard, "Liberty County, Georgia," 3; 5B3:41,182 = April 23, 1795 Bm. original).

191. UA October 31, November 1 and 23, December 21, 1751, March 25 and November 27, 1752, April 24, 1754.

192. Gilbert, "Early History of the Lutheran Church in Georgia," 164.

Because of the wide marsh between the new settlement and Ebenezer the connection was somewhat hindered until in the fall of 1755, a bridge with long access dams on both sides was built with great effort.[193] At the very beginning, 100 acres for a school was released; in the beginning of 1756 its construction was undertaken. It was arranged so that it also could serve as a room for worship.[194] But the people in Ebenezer never became very close to the settlers in Bethany. They had not emigrated primarily for reasons of faith, and they had appeared in too great a number to have been integrated into the community already present. Although they raised the smallest gifts in the entire area for the purposes of the church, they insisted upon the same number of worship services as the other neighboring communities of Ebenezer.[195]

One of these, that formed gradually and inconspicuously, was Goshen, which likewise received growth through the second Swabian transport. Named because of the good soil conditions,[196] it originally had been a part of the plantations of Ebenezer but in time had become a self-standing place because it was too far away from Ebenezer. Administratively, it belonged to Savannah.[197] With regard to church life it was closely bound to nearby Abercorn and Josephstown, in the beginning small English and Scottish settlements but which in time, because of the relatively large number of German immigrants, had become predominantly Lutheran communities.[198] Between these places around this time a plantation of 300 acres each for Boltzius and Lemcke was surveyed by governmental order, but because of lack of laborers they were insufficiently utilized, so that those three communities were able to build a church in common from their own means at the end of 1755.[199]

---

193. TK32F11, 1052 = February 17, 1756 B. original.
194. TK32F11,1053.
195. TK32F1b, 105–6 = journal January 16, 1755 M.
196. UN February 26, 1750.
197. UA June 8, 1751.
198. UN I,184; TK32F11,1054–55 = February 17, 1758 B. original.
199. UN I,184; TK32F11,1054–55 = February 17, 1758 B. original.; UN III, 515–19 = letter December 21, 1749 B. to U.

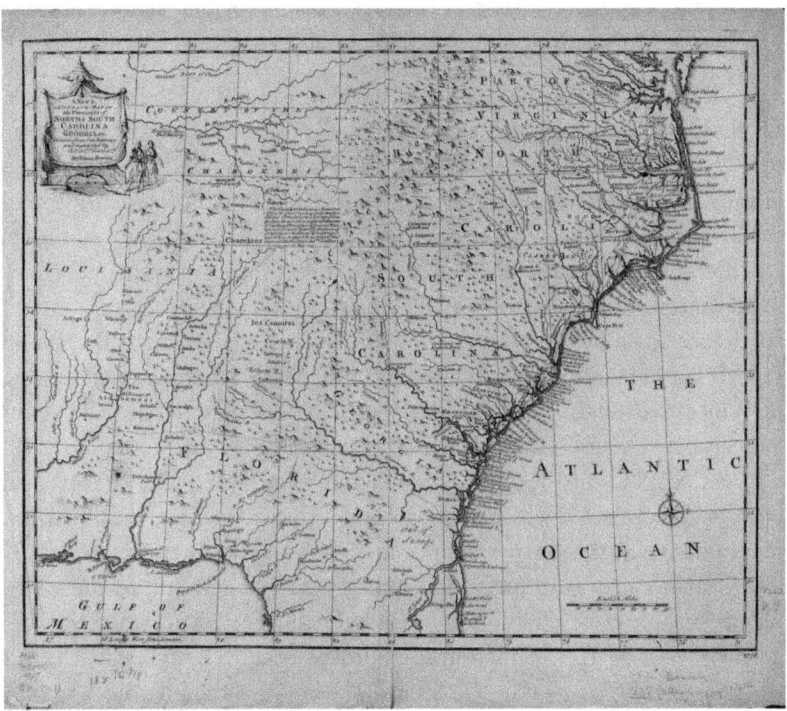

Map indicating the location of Ebenezer, Abercorn, and Josephstown, on the Savannah River north of the town of Savannah. Image courtesy of Hargrett Rare Book and Manuscript Library/University of Georgia Libraries.

Since thus far no pastor lived there, itinerate preachers offered themselves to Boltzius, such as a theology student, Friedrichs, who had studied in Göttingen and Helmstedt, and a forty-year-old candidate of theology named Schäfer. However, Boltzius was very cautious in such matters and preferred not to accept them.[200]

5. The third Swabian transport finally dropped anchor on November 23, 1752, next to Tybee Island in the mouth of the Savannah River. With it came Pastor Johann Siegfried Gerock, appointed for Pennsylvania, with his wife and the "Stückhauptmann" Krauss.[201] No one knew what was to happen with these immigrants, therefore they turned to Boltzius who became considerably indignant over it, "as if I had called

---

200. UN I,184; TK32F11,1054–55 = February 17, 1758 B. original.; UN III, 515–19 = letter December 21, 1749 B. to U. Ebenezer already had been deceived several times.

201. He traveled to Europe with Boltzius' son on June 17, 1753 (UA June 18, 1753).

these people over here and should be their provider," and "as if I had upon me the calling and obligation to fill this colony with people."[202]

All of these settlers were accustomed to expending their last money for the costs of passage and then were in Georgia without any means, so that Ebenezer had to feed them until the next harvest and for that reason already incurred debt. In addition, they had just bought the cattle pen of the Trustees in Old Ebenezer and built the second sawmill, so that there was nothing more left for the new transport. But the immigrants were very unreasonable, called Boltzius a "thief and swindler," and caused constant frictions[203] that still had not been put to rest years later, as Pastor Bergmann reports later about the "devastation and squander of that material blessing that since 1756 has been a constant apple of discord between the Salzburger and Swabian parties." Particular details concerning this are not known.[204]

As chaplain of the third Swabian transport, Pastor Rabenhorst had come to Georgia to become, as envisioned by Urlsperger, the third Lutheran pastor in this area. But since the SPCK paid only two preachers,[205] a larger amount was collected in Germany with which a third preacher's plantation would be established in Georgia and provided with slaves and a white overseer. This plantation soon proved itself to be an establishment of genuinely dubious value. We learn, "The land for the preacher's plantation was given at that time by the council in Savannah to the community, and Herr R [Rabenhorst] was only to confer his name to it," as Boltzius had done for the existing preacher's plantations, Johann Flörl, a member of the community, for the sawmill, and Lemcke for the land for the church and school in Bethany.[206] Yet already during the surveying Rabenhorst took advantage of Lemcke who was supervising, since his private plantation in Goshen directly bordered it.[207]

The administration of the third preacher's plantation was initially taken over by Lemcke, who moved there with his family.[208] But at the turn of the year 1756/57,[209] Rabenhorst "rather willfully and with confidence in his own good talents and skillfulness" took over the administration himself, and when Boltzius, on behalf of Urlsperger, reproached him for it, there were

202. UA October 26–27, 1752.
203. 5B3:41, 181 = April 23, 1795 Bm. original.
204. 5B3:32, 137 = September 7, 1787 Tr. original.
205. UA September 16, 1754.
206. TK32F10, 840 = May 1761 B. original to U. senior.
207. TK32F10, 841 = May 1761 B. original to U. senior.
208. TK32F10, 800 = June 27, 1760 B. original. Enclosure to Fr.
209. TK32F11, 966 = December 1756 B. copy.

such differences that the further common labor of the pastors appeared to be endangered. For that reason, Boltzius considered it advisable for himself "to be free completely from all matters and dealings concerning this plantation and to turn everything over to the discretion and organization of Herr Rabenhorst, who, along with his wise, practical wife,[210] has moved to this plantation, having cultivated his own that lies next to it, and proving to be very active,"[211] which one can imagine. Then, it was only a short step to join his private land, a gift of Urlsperger's, with this plantation and to pay off the investment capital.

When Rabenhorst undertook this in April 1761, Boltzius protested for the last time. After his (Boltzius') death, Lemcke would become the first pastor. Rabenhorst would have to give up the third preacher's plantation and receive the salary of the second pastor. But since all of the good land now had been assigned, no new third preacher's plantation could be laid out if he proceeded as he had proposed. Rabenhorst prevaricated, and since the community elders sided with him,[212] Boltzius let everything run its course,[213] to which Urlsperger also declared his agreement "that from the third preacher's plantation as a public property, a private property now would be made,"[214] and this would also be made legally valid "through governmental confirmation."[215]

The course of events for this matter was played down by Rabenhorst and exaggerated by Pastor Christoph Triebner in a later pastoral dispute. Until now, there has only been groping in the dark for judgment of this matter.

In other points as well, the dealings with Rabenhorst were not very happy. When the last immigrants accused Boltzius and Lemcke of not wanting to support them out of evil intentions, Rabenhorst sided with those insubordinates.[216] Lemcke, who was very unassuming, was regularly pressed against the wall by him. Not only did Rabenhorst bring about Lemcke's removal from the third preacher's plantation and cast him into debt as a result, he was able in other ways to put him at a disadvantage,[217] and even succeeded

---

210. She had "ingratiated herself with Boltzius" (5B4:17, 50 = January 26, 1802 Bm. original).
211. TK32F10, 800 = June 27, 1760 B. original. Supplement to Fr.
212. TK32F10, 836–37 = May 1761 B. original to U. senior.
213. TK32F10, 856 = May 23 1761 Boltzius enclosure to U. senior.
214. 5B2:65, 230 = February 21, 1763 R. original.
215. 5B3:32, 137 = September 7, 1787 Tr. original.
216. 5B3:32, 137 = September 7, 1787 Tr. original.
217. 5B3:30, 128 = August 27, 1787 Bm. original.

in having Boltzius lose faith in Lemcke's good intentions and report negative things about him to Europe. Frau Rabenhorst was said to have contributed primarily to it. Boltzius believed about her husband "that Herr Rabenhorst had no grace, and for the sake of peace said nothing to Herr Rabenhorst."[218] Furthermore, the fact is that Lemcke at this time lived in an unworthy, almost rotted building that stood next to Boltzius' sturdy house.[219]

But with time, it became clear to Boltzius that he had judged Lemcke falsely. He asked him for forgiveness, and soon the earlier, heartfelt relationship between the two was restored again.[220]

The depiction of these and the following awkward circumstances explain why in Urlsperger's publications of the journal the years 1755–1758, and 1761 and following were omitted without explanation. At the same time, they prepare for the judgment concerning Rabenhorst in the later pastors' controversy.

Likewise not to the delight of the Ebenezer community was the conduct of von Brahm. To be sure, he lived in Savannah[221] but nonetheless was active in the establishment of Bethany and also believed that he had to do a few things for Ebenezer, but which awakened the impression there that he had no regard for the existing achievements and viewed them "disdainfully."[222] Around the beginning of 1755 he moved with his family to Charleston, South Carolina, where he conducted the construction of several fortifications.

But in the fall of 1756, he wrote to Boltzius and asked him to arrange with the governor of Georgia for his return. This also took place, and on February 18, 1757, he arrived by land with his family in Ebenezer.[223] Here, he made his accommodations in the massively built storehouse, sent his daughter to Ebenezer's town school,[224] and acquired vast landholdings.[225]

Since about the beginning of 1751, a small citadel had stood in Ebenezer. It was called, "The Name of the Lord," from Proverbs 18:10, "The

---

218. TK32F2, 236 = March 3, 1773 Wertsch extract; 5B4:17, 50 = January 26, 1802 Bm. original.

219. UA July 17, 1753, January 28, 1759.

220. 5B4:17, 50 = January 26, 1802 Bm. original; TK32F10, 799 = June 27, 1760 B. original.

221. UA January 6, 1752.

222. TK32F11, 957 = December 1756 B. copy.

223. TK32F11, 957 = December 1756 B. copy; UA October 15, 1754; TK32F1, 975–76 = journal February 10, 1757 B. original, 1000 = journal February 19, 1757 B. original.

224. UA July 21, 1759.

225. 5D13, 9 = journal August 8, 1763.

name of the Lord is a mighty stronghold."[226] This facility seemed to von Brahm no longer to be adequate for a proper defense, and so he undertook transforming almost the entire location into a fortress. Naturally, that meant a very prolonged burden on the settlers' time, since they had to carry out the construction, and Boltzius complained that "our poor residents of the male gender were weighed down not only with the miserable fortress-building under the direction of Herr von Brahm who came to us here as a test, but that moreover they must conduct strenuous patrols on horseback day and night."[227]

These, however, were absolutely necessary, since a danger arose around the beginning of 1760: the Indians. Their continual attacks on the settlements of white people could only be met with these continuous patrols in which every male settler from sixteen to sixty years of age in Ebenezer and the surrounding area had to participate. Naturally, that brought about considerable loss of work, since twenty men for three-weeks long had to provide this service continually. To be sure, not one single Indian was caught, but the patrols continued until June.[228]

Also during the entire previous time, the Lutherans of that region had had contact with the Indians, since, in fact, until 1751,[229] the Uchee, or Yuchi, Indians, a branch of the Creek Indians, lived to the left of Ebenezer Creek.[230] From there they came occasionally into the white settlements,[231] and understandably they were and remained an item of interest. In letters, journals, and special reports many details about their peculiar clothing, different skin color, and particular lifestyles were narrated. In Halle, there now was great interest for Boltzius and Gronau to begin missionary work among them.[232] That already was stated in the instructions given to them.[233] In correspondence, it was referred to repeatedly,[234] and in view of the small

---

226. UA May 19, 1751.

227. TK32F10, 804 = June 27, 1760 B. original. Enclosure to Fr.

228. UA IV, 119-29 = journal February 1760; UA June 10, 1760, "But he could not get along well with H. B." [Boltzius] and moved to the area of Savannah (5B3:41,182 = April 23, 1795 Bm. original); he always tried to have a good relationship with Ebenezer, but it was not reciprocated by Boltzius (5D13, 9 = journal August 8, 1763).

229. UA summer 1751.

230. In the manuscripts, also written as Ugee, Uitchy, Uitzschy-Indians (5D3, 37 = journal March 28, 1737; 5D8, 515 = journal September 21, 1741; Swanton, *The Indians of the Southeastern United States*, 214).

231. 5A3:17, 114 = January 8, 1736 B. original.

232. 5A1:52, 267 = March 14, 1735 Fr.

233. 5A1:6, 38 point 11; 5A1:10, 52-53, points 5-6.

234. For example, 5A1:52, 267.

community in the beginning, Boltzius also believed that he could spare sufficient time for it.[235]

But that required an understanding of their language; however, no progress was made at all with that. Although Boltzius began several times toward that end,[236] and Francke pointed out to him that the Jesuits and English in the West Indies had succeeded in commencing relationships with them,[237] he nonetheless found no time to set himself energetically to it.[238] Consequently, this mission retreated more and more from his field of view, also not least of all because these people led a *vitam ambulatorium*, so that no work could be done continually with them.[239]

Since trade with Indians was forbidden in Georgia,[240] connections with them were limited to hunters or to families passing through the settlements now and then.[241] The preference was to stay out of their way, due to pilfering and the practice of shooting the freely wandering cattle to get the bells that they wore around their necks.[242]

235. 5A1:33, 149 = March 23, 1740 B. original.

236. He gleaned a few words that Spangenberg copied (5A3:9, 61 = May 17, 1735 B. original; 5D1 = journal July 6 and August 19, 1735) and, Mary Musgrove, playing a large role in this connection (Corry, "Indian Affairs in Georgia, 70, 73 n. 30; Coulter, "Mary Musgrove," 1–30) was supposed to help him, in keeping with Oglethorpe's wish (5D4 = journal August 5, 1738). Also, the English captain of Fort Ogeechy (south of Vernonburg), by the name of Macpherson, had recommended Boltzius to her (5D1, 242 = journal July 6, 1735).

237. 5A1:51, 261 = March 11, 1735 Fr. draft.

238. 5A1:49, 232 = December 10, 1734 B. original; 5A3:17, 114 = January 8, 1736 B. original: "If one of us, in keeping with the will of God and our benefactors, should learn the Indian language, then indeed the regular functions of office in Ebenezer would have to be reduced for him."

239. 5A1: 49, 233.

240. The Indian traders, an important connection everywhere in the American colonies between the white population and the native peoples, were therefore not in Georgia at the time. Only with the arrival of the first Salzburger transport did the husband of Mary Musgrove, in association with Mr. Watson, have dealings with them. The latter was engaged in missionary activity among them in 1741 in the hills on the Mississippi (5A11:71, 325 = July 13, 1747 B. copy). Nonetheless, Oglethorpe immediately banned this trade, since the wares brought to Georgia were to come only to the white settlers (5D1, 70 = journal March 7, 1734), in keeping with the agreement with the Trustees (UN December 12, 1741).

241. Annually, ambassadors of the Indian tribes came to Savannah where they received gifts, with which it was sought to obtain their friendship; on this route they passed through Ebenezer (5D1, 242 = journal July 6, 1735, 246 = journal July 9, 1735, 250 = journal July 11, 1735). Later, Dr. Graham brought the gifts to the settlements of the Upper Creeks, since the Indians had caused unrest in Savannah (UA April 19, 1751).

242. 5A2:3, 14 = May 6, 1734 B. copy; 5D12, 11 = journal January 3, 1744.

During the English-Spanish conflicts, their behavior was viewed with some trepidation[243] to see whether one or the other party had succeeded in securing their favor. However, since England, for good reasons, avoided with painful exactitude grabbing their land, especially with regard to the Creeks, there was peace with them in Ebenezer.[244] Also France's efforts to harness the Nottawegs and Cherokees for its politics was followed with attention.[245] The disturbances, in which the attacks of 1760 were also enmeshed, eventually were settled at the end of October in Savannah at a congress, called by royal decree, of the governors of Georgia, North and South Carolina, and Virginia with Indian chiefs. Old treaties were renewed, and the Creek tribes conveyed a wide stretch of land to the English as a sign of their peaceful intentions, something that greatly calmed the members of the Lutheran settlements as particularly interested parties.[246]

Yet despite these various disturbances, the settlers pursued their economic undertakings with energy and persistence, expanded them, and attained, in part, relatively sufficient prosperity. Ebenezer and its affiliated communities in these years represented, in ecclesial as well as in economic and political respects, an essential factor not to be overlooked in the life of the young colony, something that follows from, among other things, the attention that the "general surveyor" von Brahm bestowed directly to these settlements.

Dissension and War

During this prosperous time of their economic life, events assailed the communities that, in a calamitous interplay, led to the grim ruin of their settlements. It was to Boltzius' benefit that he passed away (he died on November 19, 1765) before the first such moment began to show its effects: the Stamp Act. Although it already had been issued on March 22, 1765, awareness of it

243. 5A3:17, 113 = January 8, 1736 B. original.
244. 5D1, 242 = journal July 6, 1735; 5A2:11, 51 = February 15, 1740.
245. UA July 1, 1751.
246. 5B2:8, 26 = December 30, 1763 postscript L. original. See also Corry, "Indian Affairs in Georgia," 67–81. In the beginning of 1790, Bergmann complained, "No state is so subjugated to the conflicts with the Indians as Georgia" (5B3:38, 169 = January 18, 1790 Bm. original). Yet after a couple of months, he reports calmly, "Peace has been established with the Indians. Congress concluded it a short time ago with their leader Mac Gillivray. He is half white and half Indian" (5B3:39, 173 = August 24, 1790 Bm. original). The relationship of the Lutherans in Georgia with the Indians therefore did not at all correspond to Nebe's assumption that Boltzius and Gronau "certainly . . . would joyfully fulfill their instruction . . . to carry out mission with the Indians" (Nebe, *Die Franckeschen Stiftungen und die Mission*, 9).

first came to Georgia in October of that year, so that here, too, it set minds simmering.[247] Lemcke, the administrator of the parish at the time, stood on the side of the Americans and attempted to bring calm in Ebenezer,[248] which, despite incitements, succeeded after several months, since it was being said that the Stamp Act had been repealed.[249] A little later, however, Lemcke also died (on April 4, 1768), and at the beginning of 1769, Pastor Triebner came to Ebenezer as his successor.

Immediately, a dispute began between him and Rabenhorst that dragged on until the death of Rabenhorst, and, with its factions, embraced all members of the community who were bound with Ebenezer in one form or another. It completely destroyed all community life. But the most dreadful thing was that both pastors carried over the dispute onto the spiritual level and, as a result, created devastation that can only be imagined among the members of the community who were mostly people of a child-like, simple piety. We feel obligated to examine the matter further.

From Triebner's stay in the Halle Orphan House, Francke was familiar with his "self-love" and "inclination to fickleness."[250] Unwisely, Johann August Urlsperger, who now in place of his father had taken over the American affairs, even encouraged Triebner in that regard by giving him money for an "English priest's cassock" to be made in London while Rabenhorst was to buy Boltzius' used Luther frock. He also gave him money to manage for Ebenezer, all of which made Triebner arrogant, but it also apparently meant that Rabenhorst would have to step back. Urlsperger even recommended Triebner to Ziegenhagen as a "pious, learned, quiet, faithful, and peaceful man." But precisely that last description Ziegenhagen could not affirm, since he and Friedrich Wilhelm Pasche[251] came into difficulty because Triebner behaved very discontentedly, even arrogantly, since he allegedly did not receive enough money, as he had been accustomed to from Urlsperger.[252]

When Triebner came to Ebenezer, he moved into a residence in the town while Rabenhorst lived on the third preacher's plantation. Triebner, right from the beginning, wanted to preach only in the town, so that Rabenhorst

---

247. See p. 105.

248. 5B2:29, 115–18 = January 13, 1766 L. original, response to Francke's last letter to Boltzius.

249. 5B2:31, 123 = May 13, 1766 L. original R. original signature on the letter in another hand.

250. 5B2:7, 20 = July 12, 1769 Fr. draft.

251. Since 1751, with Ziegenhagen, 1761 lector of the court chapel, 1767 member of the SPCK (J I, part I, 388), later Ziegenhagen's successor.

252. Ziegenhagen sharply reproached the junior Urlsperger for his poor judgment of human character (5B2:57, 194–96 = December 30, 1768 Z. copy).

preached there only a little; when Triebner preached directly against him, he no longer preached there at all.[253] Instead, he regularly held a worship service every fourteen days at the Zion plantation (this was a place that likewise had formed gradually from the first plantations of Ebenezer).[254] At the same time, an omission traced back to Urlsperger took effect: Rabenhorst had not received an expressed call for Ebenezer but had been sent by Urlsperger "as the travel and ship chaplain of the third Swabian transport and, in case he could remain and settle there, as future standing minister."[255]

Also, the SPCK did not pay his salary, not even when, in his already familiar manner, he suggested to Ziegenhagen after Boltzius' death that he be given the salary of the first minister paid by the SPCK, but that Lemcke, who as the properly appointed and senior minister had taken over the official duties of the first position, should be left in the second position and the income of the third preacher's plantation divided among the two.[256] Urlsperger, however, had sought to clarify this ambiguity. He had specified that Rabenhorst should take over the first position and Triebner the second,[257] and Triebner himself had declared that he had "accepted the second position of an Ebenezer preacher."[258]

Yet that did not suffice: "An awful clamor arose over a banns. Rabenhorst had first published a man's banns in the Zion Church, and Triebner was to publish them a second time in the Jerusalem Church in Ebenezer, which he considered adverse to his honor, since he had been sent by the fathers and the Highly Praised Society."[259] The situation escalated further. Triebner accused Rabenhorst, shortly before Triebner's arrival, of having changed, unilaterally and to the detriment of the community, the administration of the community-owned mills by abolishing, "through the help of the notorious Treutlen and eighteen members of the community, the old trustees [administrative board of the mills] certified by the court, and having himself made sole director of these institutions through a written indenture which they let themselves be induced to sign their names as witness."[260]

253. 5B4:17, 50 = January 26, 1802 Bm. original.
254. TK32F2, 234 = March 19, 1773 R. original.
255. UA I preface (unpaginated); 166–67.
256. The suggestion was rejected (5B4:17, 49 = January 26, 1802 Bm. original).
257. 5B2:55, 186–87 = July 28, 1768 U. original signature on the letter from another hand. However, this does not seem to have been sufficiently known since Muhlenberg, shortly before his trip to Ebenezer in 1774, learned from Heinzelmann that "the first preacher's position there is still vacant" (4C17:9, 157 = journal May 11, 1774 M).
258. 5B2:56, 190–91 = October 25, 1760 Tr. original.
259. 5B4:17, 49 = January 26, 1802 Bm. original.
260. 5B3:36, 152 = July 23, 1788 Tr. original.

The actual state of affairs was as follows: On April 15, 1757, Boltzius turned over in writing the oversight of the mills to Lemcke,[261] who signed over this authorization to Rabenhorst on April 30, 1767.[262] After Lemcke's death, Rabenhorst arranged for the former trustees of the millworks to confer their duties to him, which was legally established in a contract through the signature of those eighteen community members and the official certification of Treutlen, justice of the peace for Bethany and Ebenezer. Thereupon, Rabenhorst dismissed the previous full-time miller who only could be paid with a subsidy from community funds, and leased the mills for thirty-seven pounds annually so that they became profitable for the community.[263] At that time they were in very good structural condition but soon were much neglected, for when Triebner came, "the community was instructed to bear an additional twenty pounds annually for his salary. At this point, Rabenhorst permitted himself something that was unfair; he took thirty pounds for himself as the elder teacher [minister]. The mills suffered great harm as a result."[264]

Triebner, who reported these things to Augsburg, was appointed by Urlsperger in a letter that arrived in May 1770 as the sole trustee of the mills with the instruction "to give his consent to no alteration made by Rabenhorst with the mill and community establishments during the vacancy of the positions of the blessed teachers."[265] In this capacity, he drew up a document right away that was to restore again the earlier status of the administration of the mills, and he attempted each year on Easter Monday, during the election of the community elders, to gain acceptance for this regulation, for the last time in 1773, but in vain.[266]

Here again, the unfortunate role that J. A. Urlsperger played in this controversy between the preachers becomes clear and one of the roots that existed in the controversy becomes evident, that Lutherans everywhere in the New World in each case would have to decide whether they wanted to acknowledge their ties to Europe or their emerging independence.

In Ebenezer, in the meantime, the controversy became extremely acrimonious:

261. 5B2:28, 113 = November 27, 1765 L. original.

262. Strobel, *The Salzburgers and Their Descendants*, 135–38.

263. Already for a long time, they had not been profitable (5D13, 50 = journal (-UA) September 16, 1763). 5B2:60, 207–8 = December 14, 1768 R. original; 5B3:32, 137 = September 7, 1787 Bm. original; 5B3:36, 151–52 = July 23, 1788 Tr. original.

264. 5B4:17, 49 = January 26, 1802 Bm. original.

265. 5B3:36, 151–52 = July 23, 1788 Tr. original.

266. TK32F2, 238 = March 3, 1773 Wertsch extract to Z.

Herr Triebner could not contain himself in public discourses during the worship services from outrageous, gross, stinging speech against Herr Rabenhorst. To be sure, he did not mention him by name, but he gave such descriptions that the children could interpret and construe, and over which his followers smiled happily. And when Herr Pastor Triebner just had explained the pericope about the false prophets, he did it so clearly, described the false prophet so thoroughly on the plantation among the Negroes, etc., that an uprising almost arose in the Jerusalem Church. Different hearers, some crying, some embittered ran out and said that sort of thing had never been heard before in Ebenezer. Herr Triebner's friends, on the contrary, extolled the type of preaching, declaiming with hands and feet, That is a man! He does not mince words! No one has ever before proclaimed the truth in Ebenezer like that! etc. Several of the elders discussed matters among themselves and decided to confront Herr Pastor Triebner and also to ask him at least to refrain from such personal matters and outbursts of physical emotions.... One of these men, who now is probably the oldest of the remaining Salzburgers ... and ... an upright, pious old man[267] but not raised at court nor had been to upper school, was supposed to act as spokesperson. But he had barely stammered out a couple of words when the pastor fell into an astounding furor and became beside himself and forgot that he was a man, someone learned, a philosopher, a Christian, a theologian, a pastor and disciple of Christ, fell into such a state of passion that he cast about crude expressions, and now all those present spoke at the same time in complete seriousness and sought to drown each other out. The shepherd made a fist, and also the sheep, yet they did not make bodily contact.[268]

But Triebner claimed that he had been beaten up by them and to have been sick for a long time afterwards. "In the deplorable dispute with Herr Rabenhorst, Herr Triebner, always let be sung from number 722 in the Glaucha hymnal, 'Peace! Oh peace! Oh peace! Oh divine peace!,' etc. Verse 7: 'The chicks remain by the mother hen; they do not cry and run after the *raven*.' Afterwards, Herr Rabenhorst again came forward, and on Sundays the one preached against the other. It was most vexatious, and already at that time ... all blessing began to depart from Ebenezer."[269]

267. "S. R." = Simon Reiter or Reuter (so Tappert and Doberstein, *The Journals of Henry Melchior Muhlenberg* II).
268. TK32F1b, 74-76 = journal December 30, 1774 M.
269. 5B3:30, 128-29 = August 27, 1787 Bm. original. [Translator's note: italics in

The communities were thoroughly divided into two camps. Already at the end of the year in which Triebner had arrived (1769), Rabenhorst, with several members of his faction, sent a bitter complaint about him to Europe,[270] and on June 17, 1772, a second one followed to Ziegenhagen, signed by Rabenhorst and eleven members of the community.[271] Triebner was not informed about either letter; only at the end of 1772 did he receive from Ziegenhagen an excerpt of the points of complaint that apparently Rabenhorst's partisans earlier had denied making, so that Triebner, on January 14, 1773, made known the names of these eleven members of the community.[272] He also prompted his supporter, the much respected merchant Wertsch, to compose a letter of defense to Ziegenhagen in which this upright man raised a serious accusation against Rabenhorst: "At the time of the late Herr Pastor Boltzius there was always a difference between those who sought God and those who were Christian in word and name only. But when H[err] R[abenhorst] administered the office alone, everyone was called from the pulpit good and pious people, only the crudest Epicureans excepted."

Wertsch reported that he, "on the afternoon of the last thanksgiving festival [March 1772][273] during the prayer as well as during his entire discourse, had sighed and prayed Father, forgive him, for he knows not what he does and what he says.... His sermon at the time was contrary to every spiritual and material good of Ebenezer, full of anger, resentment, and bitterness.... His sermons for the most part have himself, but not Christ and the soul, as their aim."[274]

Further, Triebner, as pastor of the church in Ebenezer, refused communion to Rabenhorst and his supporters since it was customary that it was celebrated only here and not in the churches at the related communities.[275] But Rabenhorst, who received no support from Europe and therefore believed that Triebner was trusted there more than he, allowed himself to be convinced only through the pleas of his supporters not to move to Savannah, through which he had wanted ultimately to prevent the complete division of

---

original. In German, "raven" = "Raben," a clear play on the name Rabenhorst.]

270. 5B3:35, 149 = May 22, 1788 Tr. original.
271. 5B3:36, 158 = July 23, 1788 Tr. original.
272. 5B3:35, 149 = May 22, 1788 Tr. original.
273. See p. 131.
274. TK32F2, 238 = March 3, 1773 Wertsch extract to Z., and 236–37.
275. TK32F2, 234 = March 19, 1773 R. original; 238 = March 3, 1773 Wertsch extract.

the communities.²⁷⁶ But in February 1773, this division nonetheless came to pass, and from then on Rabenhorst no longer came to the church in Ebenezer but remained in Goshen and Zion.²⁷⁷

In the meantime, Muhlenberg in Pennsylvania was charged by the Fathers in Europe to mediate this controversy.²⁷⁸ He sent the young Israel Heinzelmann, the son of his fellow minister in Philadelphia, Pennsylvania,²⁷⁹ to Ebenezer. He came there shortly after this division to be a merchant's apprentice with Johann Adam Treutlen,²⁸⁰ a Rabenhorst partisan, and also to live in his store.²⁸¹ He corresponded regularly with Muhlenberg as well as with Muhlenberg's daughter; naturally, these reports were biased.²⁸²

In one point, however, it was Rabenhorst's party that allowed the split of the communities to take legal form. Triebner writes: in July 1774, "the Rabenhorst party was called together on July 10th to elect churchwardens and vestrymen, which happened according to English custom, in spite of me and the previous elders. This matter was carried out with utter mischief, through advertisements dated on the 5th of July 1774, which were distributed in twelve places in a district of twenty miles, that is, from Goshen to Treutlen's plantation.²⁸³ On the 16th of July, the election was held in the presence of Treutlen as English judge before whom Jenking Davis²⁸⁴ and the young Heinzelmann had to swear that they had been present as two impartial witnesses at the election of the church wardens according to the law of the land."²⁸⁵

Naturally, the previous church elders, from an election in which Triebner had been able to influence the majority, did not give way, and so there

276. TK32F2, 234–35 = March 19, 1773 R. original.

277. 5B3:35, 150 = May 22, 1788 Tr. original.

278. 5B3:35, 149 = May 22, 1788 Tr. original.

279. Born on February 10, 1756, the son of Pastor Johann Dietrich Matthias Heintzelmann in Philadelphia (who had died on February 9, 1756; *Nachrichten von den vereinigten Deutschen Evangelisch-Lutherischen Gemeinden*, 219); died in Ebenezer on September 11, 1774, from the fall from a horse (5B3:35, 149 = May 22, 1788 Tr. original).

280. At the time, justice of the peace and member of the Assembly, later the first governor of the state of Georgia.

281. 5B3:35,148 erroneously states 1783; intended is 1773.

282. 5B3:32, 136 = September 7, 1787 Tr. original.

283. This expanse was nothing remarkable since the communities connected to Ebenezer in fact extended from Bethany, where Treutlen had his plantation, to even beyond Goshen.

284. Medical doctor, Englander, leading member of the Congress party, lived in Ebenezer.

285. 5B3:36, 153 = July 23, 1788 Tr. original.

were now two of these bodies: the "old" church council of Triebner with Johann Caspar Wertsch, Johann Flörl, Christoph Krämer, Matthäus Biddenbach, Johann Paulus, and Paul Müller; and the "new" church council of Rabenhorst with Johann Adam Treutlen, Ulrich Neidlinger, Christian Steiner, Joseph Schubtrein, Samuel Krauss, and Jacob Caspar Waldhauer.[286]

Then came the report that Muhlenberg was on the way to Ebenezer and that on September 8, 1774, he already had reached Charleston, South Carolina.[287] Now the entire community, with both pastors, assembled on Saturday, September 10, 1774, in order yet again to settle the controversy, if possible.[288] Triebner brought up again his old accusations concerning the mills and maintained, moreover, that Rabenhorst also appropriated to himself unlawfully the third preacher's plantation.[289] When it was verified to him that Rabenhorst had done this in agreement with Augsburg, and Triebner was asked to take back his accusations, otherwise he would be banned from the pulpit, he only laughed.[290]

Rabenhorst's faction therefore locked up the church in Ebenezer for the following Sunday,[291] or perhaps not until the next,[292] September 18th. On this day, about an hour before the beginning of the worship service, Treutlen, Jenking Davis, and Johann Nies sat on the pulpit with sabers,[293] and probably did not remain there very quiet and unassuming since when Triebner, as he reports, appeared there with his following, they threatened "murder and homicide if . . . someone approached,"[294] whereupon they

---

286. Repeatedly in the documents, even in Strobel who views this election as a cause of the controversy. Strobel, *The Salzburgers and Their Descendants*, 154–55. But it was only an expression of an actual already long-standing condition and culminating point behind a long series of frictions.

287. 4C17:20, 294 = October 6, 1174 M to Pasche copy.

288. Triebner: The Rabenhort party is of the view that one must for Muhlenberg "alleviate the mediation of the dispute; one of the two teachers must decline" (5D3:36, 153 = July 23, 1788 Tr. original).

289. 5D3:36, 152 and 155 = July 23, 1788 Tr. original.

290. 4C17:2, 294–95 = October 6, 1774 M copy.

291. 5B3:35, 149 = May 22, 1788 Tr. original.

292. According to 5B3:36, 153 = July 23, 1788 Tr. original; it was still open on this Sunday.

293. Triebner: Rabenhorst's "people, who formed a troop of riders" (5B3:36, 153 = July 23, 1788 Tr. original); his followers, for the most part, lived on the plantations and were accustomed to making use of horses because of the great distance from the church. Moreover, because of slave unrest, there was a law that forbade each man, upon a penalty of five shillings, from going to an assembly unarmed (TK32F1b, 79 = journal December 30, 1774 M).

294. 5B3:36, 153–54 = July 23, 1788 Tr. original.

quickly turned around and withdrew to Wertsch's house, and Triebner consoled his crowd "with fitting quotes."[295] In the meantime Rabenhorst's community filled the church and sang triumphantly, "Praise and honor to the highest good."[296] That was the climax.

Rabenhorst's faction now sent Jacob Mack to Charleston to report the latest events to Muhlenberg; yet he remained very restrained and wanted first to hear both sides.[297] On October 28, 1774, he arrived by ship in Savannah, stayed with the Lutheran Stephan Miller,[298] had both pastors come to him, and as a sign that they acknowledged him as competent, had them sign his instructions that had come from Europe for the case at hand. Then, on November 5th, he came to Ebenezer.[299]

Here, at Triebner's suggestion, a face to face discussion was held on November 11th in Boltzius' house among Muhlenberg, Rabenhorst, and Triebner, lasting six hours with the result that Rabenhorst, "with a moved heart and tears forgave [Triebner] for every offense and also asked for forgiveness of his faults."[300] Peace was made and was sealed with a feast in Triebner's house.[301]

However, it soon became apparent that this had been a premature solution: "After several days, the wounds made by the peace began to ache.... It was said by [Rabenhorst's] faction that indeed there may be peace between the two ministers but not between Triebner's and Rabenhorst's factions."[302] Thus ensued almost endless discussions in which both factions turned on each other in a most unworthy manner. They appear devastating when it is realized that they were not able to reconcile the two factions with each other.

Five dates of negotiation are significant.

1. November 22, 1774. Present: Muhlenberg, Rabenhorst, Triebner, and the church elders from both sides. After the drawing up of an itemization of the community property,[303] the accusations against Triebner were treated in five points. According to Triebner's account, he had insisted that witnesses be produced, but that this had not been possible

---

295. TK 32F1b, 79 = journal December 30, 1774 M.
296. 5B3:35, 150 = May 22, 1788 Tr. original.
297. 4C17:20, 295 = October 6, 1774 M copy.
298. Gräbner, *Geschichte der Lutherischen Kirche in America*, part I, 599.
299. 5B3:35, 150 = May 22, 1788 Tr. original.
300. TK 32F1b, 73 = journal December 30, 1774 M.
301. See n. 299.
302. See n. 299.
303. TK32F1b, 66 = journal December 28, 1774 M.

for the accusers, so that they had been "put to shame" and Muhlenberg had apologized.[304] But in truth, Triebner had to acknowledge that "Rabenhorst had not unilaterally made himself supervisor of the mill establishments but had been authorized to do so."[305] Triebner, obviously, construed the peace that had again been made as a backing down of the opposing faction.

2. December 28, 1774, ten o'clock a.m. to three o'clock p.m. Present: The same as the first, in addition to them the trustees of the community's economic undertakings as well as several community members from Bethany. First, the minutes from the previous session, after several objections from Triebner,[306] were signed. Then was considered the church order that Muhlenberg had drafted for the disentanglement and regulation of community affairs. (It will be treated in more detail later.) The community members at Bethany raised a rather vociferous objection against it. Recently, they had had come up on the short end concerning worship services and it appeared now that it would remain so. When the signing of the order threatened to shatter on this point, Muhlenberg went to the extreme. In one hand, he held the inventory list of the community, and if no unity could now be reached, the Fathers in Europe would collect their money invested here (the third preacher's plantation). And then he had already in the other hand a letter to Governor Wright in Savannah with this recommendation. That worked instantly; it was signed.[307]

3. January 12, 1775. Present: the three pastors, the "new" church elders, Johann Flörl, the trustees of the community. The following resolutions were adopted:

   a. In Bethany, a worship service should be held every four weeks by the preacher who lives at the nearest place.
   b. The annual salary of the SPCK of ten pounds for a minister for Ebenezer should be placed in the community chest, out of which all of the ministers will be paid. It was furthermore resolved "that the poor, who could not contribute anything to have their children go to school, should report to the community council" for the purpose of a reduction in fees.

---

304. See p. 69, n. 299.
305. TK32F1b, 61–62 = journal December 28, 1774 M.
306. He had subsequently reconsidered several things.
307. TK32F1b, 61–66 = journal December 28, 1774 M.

c. The church elder Ulrich Neidlinger was named teacher of the town school.

d. Rabenhorst's obligation to the Fathers in Europe, executed on January 2, 1775, concerning the capital that had come to him from the third preacher's plantation was read.

e. Finally, the church order was to be signed by all male members of the community.[308] The final resolution was announced to the community, that is, to all who belonged to Jerusalem Church in Ebenezer and to Bethany, on the following Sunday, January 16, 1775.[309]

4. On Monday, January 1, 1775, Jerusalem Church's bell was rung at ten o'clock a.m., and the community gathered. Rabenhorst was in Savannah on business, but Triebner and Wertsch assisted Muhlenberg. He reported: "I first offered a prayer, and afterwards read slowly and aloud the church and community order, which took over an hour. After that took place, I said, 'Whoever now would like to be a member of the Ebenezer community according to this order and have part in its benefits should sign his name,'" as the participants at the second gathering already had done. Then the people from Bethany asked how the pastor who would serve them would be paid, whereupon Triebner requested only food for himself and his horse. "Thereupon they began to sign their names one after the other, which also took over two hours. I sat nearby on the damp pavement in order to be a witness of every signature. After they all signed, Herr Pastor Triebner concluded with prayer." But, unfortunately, how little the great effort accomplished was evident when immediately afterward the settlers from Bethany came to Muhlenberg and wanted to have worship services for themselves just as often as in the Zion Church. Muhlenberg, however, now referred them to the church council confirmed by the church order.[310]

5. Monday, January 30, 1775, eleven o'clock.[311] Present: same as the second. Here, it became even more starkly evident that the controversy had not at all calmed down. This should have been the concluding gathering, but Triebner started everything over again from the beginning. He bemoaned, blamed, and mistrusted everyone as before. Muhlenberg believed "that such an undaunted temperament was more befitting for a madhouse than for a pastor and example to the flock." It

---

308. TK32F1b, 99–101 = journal January 12, 1775 M.
309. TK32F1b, 103 = journal January 15, 1775 M.
310. TK32F1b, 105–6 = journal January 16, 1775 M.
311. All of the gatherings had taken place in Boltzius' house.

can hardly be held against him if from then on he had no patience with Triebner. The following matters were then concluded:

a. The first copy of the church order, through a comparative reading, was judged to be in accord with the original; the original was placed in the "trustee chest."

b. The minutes of the meetings held by Muhlenberg, written by him in a minutes book, were read.

c. If there should be only one pastor in Ebenezer, then the Sunday worship service should take place in no other church than Jerusalem.

d. Triebner demanded that the church order may not be seen as an idol but must also be able to be changed, whereupon Muhlenberg wrung his hands; only clarifying additions were allowed.

e. At Muhlenberg's recommendation Wertsch was named as "overseer, accounting officer, and treasurer" of the mills; Johannes Flörl, Joseph Schubtrein, and David Steiner as co-overseers and administrators.

f. Rabenhorst, as reported, had arranged for the lease of the mills to a private person, but Triebner wanted them to be administered, as before, "at the community's expense." After it had become clear to everyone—except to Triebner—that the administration at the expense of the community would be too expensive (a miller, overseer, servants, slaves, horses, wagons, etc. were necessary), the mills were leased again to Steiner for five years from January 1, 1775.[312]

On the following Sunday, Muhlenberg gave his farewell sermon in Jerusalem Church on John 20:19, "Peace be with you," and to conclude, the congregation sang, as they did at the time of his departure with Boltzius thirty-two years earlier, "So let us then follow the dear Lord with our cross," and the next day, February 6, 1775, Muhlenberg left Ebenezer again.[313]

In the night between Saturday and Sunday of this week around two o'clock, Ebenezer's bells sounded the alarm: Treutlen and Waldhauer, on Rabenhorst's behalf, forbade Triebner's wife from harvesting mulberry bushes for silkworms on the grounds of the churches and parsonages.[314] To be sure,

---

312. TK32F1b, 124–35 = journal January 30, 1775 M.
313. TK32F1b, 151–56 = journal February 5–6, 1775 M.
314. Rabenhorst as trustee over the churches and parsonages (5B3:35, 150 = May

Mrs. Triebner was in the wrong, since these locations were community property. Nevertheless, it certainly was not necessary to ring the bells in the night to proclaim the prohibition. The controversy continued.

In the same year, Triebner came under suspicion of having had an improper relationship with the younger daughter of Lemcke. The suspicion increased when Triebner refused to appear to defend himself before the community council, which then, on the basis of the church order, suspended him from his office and reported the incident to Urlsperger.[315] When a letter arrived from Ziegenhagen that Wertsch read aloud at the 1775 Christmas Eve service for the "edification" of the community, in which Triebner again was asked to defend himself in this matter before the community, he again declined.[316] To be sure, in November of this year, he had made his innocence credible in a letter to London.[317] In Georgia, though, he did not explain himself further, and also the request of the dying Rabenhorst at the end of 1776 to do so was not successful.[318]

Thus, at this time, there was no Lutheran pastor in office at all in Georgia; in the Ebenezer community, the elder Neidlinger read sermons.[319] The church council turned to Muhlenberg with the plea to assist the community with obtaining a new pastor,[320] and Muhlenberg, with his warm recommendation, forwarded it to Pasche, who had become Ziegenhagen's successor in London.[321] When in the summer of 1777 the Lutheran pastor Christian Streit was sent by Muhlenberg to Charleston, South Carolina, he was able to visit the congregations in Georgia and also preach there.[322] But as for the rest, things were gloomy.

Interwoven with the personal factionalism of the pastors' controversy in those years was a political element that had long been smoldering under cover and now flared up brightly: the opposition between Great Britain's colonial politics and American aspirations for independence. On July 4, 1774, the republican party formed in Savannah with the "Provincial Congress," in

---

22, 1788 Tr. original).

315. 5B4:17, 53 = January 26, 1802 Bm. original.

316. 4H23, 311–14 = journal May 15, 1777 M = letter February 22, 1777 copy, Ebenezer community elders.

317. 4H23, 263 = journal March 20, 1777 M = letter May 6, 1776 Pasche.

318. 4H23, 309 = journal May 15, 1777 M = letter February 20, 1777 Mrs. Rabenhorst.

319. 4H23, 309–10 = journal May 15, 1777 M = letter February 20, 1777 Mrs. Rabenhorst.

320. 4H23, 314 = journal May 15, 1777 M = letter February 22, 1777 copy.

321. 4H23, 347–48 = journal June 12, 1777 M = letter M copy.

322. 5B3: 36, 156 = July 23, 1788 Tr. original; TK32F1a, 32 = September 16, 1780.

which were participating, in addition to Rabenhorst's supporters Treutlen, Waldhauer, and Davis, also Triebner's followers Flörl and Krämer. By contrast, Triebner initiated a resolution for the supporters of the British colonial administration, issued on July 21, 1774, that allegedly was "signed by all residents," yet no one from Rabenhorst's faction was included.[323] As in other places in the United States, also here the fronts were clear before the war for freedom began in 1775. Triebner reports his fortunes himself: "R[abenhorst] preached rebellion, and his faction flourished. On the 3rd of March in 1776, my house was taken from me, and the printing press was set up in it. I paid a fine of forty shillings every month three times."

Then came July 4, 1776, the day of the Declaration of Independence, that also lent new power to the republican element in Georgia. Triebner continues: "On July 7, 1776, I was arrested along with fourteen of my listeners at the order of Colonel Treutlen and led to Goshen, where Colonel Stirk . . . again offered the oath which we took under the following limitation: As far as *Casus Americanus* is right and promotes the good of the Country. Treutlen was not satisfied with this and offered the same [oath] again on July 21st. . . . But my hearers stood steadfastly with me and threw him down the stairs." Later on, when Rabenhorst had died, "Treutlen sought my friendship."[324]

On September 22, 1777, a discussion again took place with Triebner in which they agreed:

1. All false accusations against him should be revoked;
2. the decrees that the Fathers in Europe had conveyed to Triebner should not be further contravened;
3. all unnecessary hostile actions against Triebner should cease.

Moreover, Treutlen planned, in order to promote Ebenezer's wellbeing and to bring about its ecclesiastical independence, to repay all of the European monies invested here, to transfer to the communities, through the republican government, the properties obtained with these monies and from their proceeds to pay the respective pastors—things that should have happened long before.[325]

However, the rest of the supporters of Congress in this region seemed not to be in agreement with such politics of negotiation with a Royalist-inclined pastor, and so the tables turned within a few days. We further read

---

323. TK32F8, 703–4 = January 13, 1779 Tr. original Ebenezer; Strobel, *The Salzburgers and Their Descendants*, 196–97.

324. TK32F8, 704.

325. TK32F2, 240–41 = October 4, 1777 Tr. copy.

what Triebner reported about Treutlen: "Under his administration[326] an act was passed 'for Expulsion [of] internal Enemyes,' that applied to everyone who would not take the abjuration oath. On October 5, 1777, I was led before a committee of twelve men as an enemy of the state, without the slightest evidence. And because I would not take the oath, I was declared a prisoner of war by Speaker John Holzendorff.[327] I waited from time to time for the execution of this declaration from governor and council," but they let him stay on his premises.

At the end of March 1778, Jenking Davis gave him an assignment to go on a spying expedition, which, of course, he did not carry out. For that reason, he now was frequently hunted down and also secretly shot at, and one evening, six drunkards broke into his house, but he escaped through the window. Finally, on May 2, 1778, ten members of Congress surrounded his house. Christian Steiner and Ernst Zittrauer from Ebenezer took him captive and brought him into the house of Daniel Zettler, where Jenking Davis, "with a bare dagger in hand," forced him to swear the oath of abjuration against the English king. In another place, Triebner reported that someone held a drawn sword over him. Both of these frightening expressions probably refer to the unsheathed saber by which one had to swear.[328]

Triebner now lay in wait for his hour of liberation which struck for him on December 29, 1778, when the English occupied Savannah under Colonel Archibald Campbell. In the same night, he broke through to them completely alone, against the tide of republican refugees, among whom were 3000 African Americans, all of whom were hurrying up the Savannah River and on the following day also vacated Ebenezer.[329]

In the night of December 31st, around two o'clock, Triebner met British troops four miles outside Savannah and arranged that also Ebenezer and the surrounding area were occupied by the British.[330] On January 2, 1779, they arrived under the command of Colonel Maitland,[331] and even if, Triebner believed, "some damage occurred with the first incursion of the advance troops, it was in no way proportional to the crimes [of the other

---

326. Treutlen was Governor and member of the Assembly (TK32F2, 240–41 = October 4, 1777 Tr. copy); on March 17, 1777, he was Councilor and Colonel (4H23, 320 = journal May 20, 1777 M).

327. See p. 103.

328. TK32F8, 704-5 = January 13, 1779 Tr. original; Allen and McClure, *Two Hundred Years*, 393–94 = letter March 4, 1799 Tr. to the SPCK.

329. TK32F8, 702.

330. 5B3:35, 150 = May 22, 1788 Tr. original.

331. Jones, *The Dead Towns of Georgia*, 187, cited in Brantley, "The Salzburgers in Georgia," 219.

side]." Moreover, Campbell promised "to provide sufficient restitution for my auditors as friends of the King."

At first, Campbell personally stayed at Ebenezer, and Triebner had the honor to dine with him daily. Of course, Triebner now also preached again in Jerusalem Church without being rehabilitated by the community.[332] But after a while, the English made a hospital out of it.[333] They also broke through the dam at the millworks in order to be able to replenish their supplies by ship all the way to Ebenezer.[334] As a result, the mills were made and remained inoperable.

Then, they established new, extensive redoubts around Ebenezer, and the doctor Jenking Davis, who had fled, relates that Triebner "was appointed a Magistrate and gave Protections and administered the Oath of Allegiance to the Inhabitants. Myself and a few others that had fled to Carolina for Protection, he advised the Officers not to let our Wifes follow us, but to send them to a Plantation about ten miles from Ebenezer in a desert part of the Country, where they were sent to, without any Hopes of seeing their Husbands or Relations! His Actions the whole Time the Brittish kept the Country were more like some Barbarous Savage than a Christian Teacher."[335]

In the course of this year, the 60th Artillery Regiment under General Prevost was stationed here as a standing garrison that consisted for the most part of Germans (Hessians).[336] However, the situation changed again. At the beginning of September 1779, the English had to withdraw to Savannah after they had burned their storehouses in Ebenezer,[337] since on September 12th, American troops that lay three days in Ebenezer arrived here and on September 16th joined with French units outside of Savannah.[338] Under Count Polasky and Count D'Estaing, they then began the famous siege and attempted on October 9, 1779 to take the city by storm, which nonetheless failed. The French sailed away; the Americans streamed by way of Ebenezer to South Carolina,[339] and the English returned.

Things now became very turbulent again, and the communities were severely affected. There was no regular farming, and for that reason there

---

332. TK32F8, 703.
333. 4H24, 19 = journal November 17, 1779 M = letter September 27, 1779 Streit copy.
334. 5B3:32.
335. 4H26, 143 = journal August 8, 1783 M = letter March 18, 1783 Jenking Davis.
336. TK32F7, 628–31 = October 28, 1782 Tr. copy.
337. 4H24, 6 = journal October 29, 1779 M.
338. Since February 6, 1778, the Americans allied with the French against the English; since 1779, Spain also participated in wars on the French side.
339. 4H24, 15–16 = journal November 15, 1779 M.

was a considerable crop shortfall,[340] and within two months, fifty people died from "children's pox."

Triebner attempted to bring the mills again into operation. He bought 150 acres and had built on them, for over 100 pounds, a grain mill by the builder Barnabas Maulsby. However, it seems not to have been in operation for very long, since no mention is made of it after the peace treaty. On April 18, 1781, Triebner's house became the officers' quarters, and in May, a standing "garrison of 200 regular soldiers under the command of the Hessian Major Goebels of Knoblauch's regiment" was again stationed in Ebenezer.[341]

Yet around this time, the republicans on the rest of the continent already had been decisively victorious, and the war actually was already decided in their favor. In fall 1781, they also gathered again in Georgia, in Augusta above Bethany on the Savannah River.[342] On December 8, 1781, the English evacuated Ebenezer for good, and Triebner and the twenty-eight people of his faction considered it advisable to go with them to Savannah.[343]

Several weeks later, on Sunday, December 30, 1781, when the community members just "were about to go to the house of the old potter Georg Gnann[344] to hear a sermon," a troop of cavalry invaded Ebenezer from the area around Bethany and were led by Charles MacCay.[345] They plundered about forty families, beat to death the resident Georg Schiele and an Englishman, and with thumbscrews attempted to glean even more from the already impoverished people. Whoever had not already fled among the English now fled into the "swamps."

But only a few days later (New Year's 1782), the American General Wayne came to Ebenezer and sent that robber captain well-guarded to South Carolina to the main troops "for punishment."[346] Wayne now established himself in Ebenezer with a garrison of 300[347] to 500[348] cavalry and foot soldiers. Colonel Jackson stood with seventy cavalry in Goshen.[349]

---

340. There was drought in the next year.

341. TK32F7, 499–503 = August 22, 1781 Tr. copy; TK32F7, 567–71 = May 5, 1782 Tr. original.

342. 4H25, 7 = journal October 11, 1781 M.

343. 5B3:9, 43 = April 4, 1782 Tr. original.

344. Probably a sermon that was read; Gnann was a church elder.

345. He came from the Ebenezer District. Also spelled McCai, Kai, Coy, Khay.

346. 5B3:9, 43–44 = April 4, 1782 Tr. original.

347. 4H25, 136 = journal July 20, 1782 M.

348. TK32F7, 567–71 = May 5, 1782 Tr. original.

349. 4H25, 93 = journal April 29, 1782 M; TK32F8, 715 = June 1782 Tr. copy.

Around this time (January 1782), Jenking Davis also returned, but found the place in a woeful state. Only two families still lived there. Of all of the residents of the Ebenezer District, more than two-thirds were dead or driven out by the English. The church and houses were heavily damaged.[350] Because of the plundering, extreme food shortages existed so that the soldiers also, in part, had to feed the residents.[351] In May 1782, General Clarke then attempted for the last time to drive the American troops again from Ebenezer, but in vain.[352] Around this time, the republican governor of Georgia, John Martin, issued a proclamation that assured pardon to all former royalists, with a few exceptions: Pastor Triebner, his supporter Jacob Bühler, former tavern keeper in Ebenezer,[353] and David Zübli, farmer in Purrysburg, South Carolina, who was already known as someone hard-hearted.[354] When the English then evacuated Savannah on July 11, 1782, Triebner had to withdraw with them.[355] Thus Georgia, at the end of the war, no longer had any Lutheran pastor at all.

Decline of the Settlements

Ebenezer and its neighboring communities seemed after the war to be completely disbanded. Among the settlers who had fled, a few in fact returned, so that Ebenezer and Goshen could continue to exist. But the other places folded. The disputes between the pastors and their factions, as well as the demoralizing effects of the war, had wrought devastation among the population. A visitor to this area judged, "Ebenezer is no more."[356] And another, "If things are to get better in Georgia, another race of men must arise."[357]

The remaining Lutherans in the period that followed were troubled by several men, mostly only appearing for a short time, who purported to be preachers but were nonetheless somewhat shady figures. Occasionally, Friedrich Gerresheim and Penninger[358] came from Savannah. A swindler

---

350. 4H26, 140–43 = journal August 8, 1783 M = letter March 18, 1783 Jenking Davis.

351. 5B3:9, 44 = April 4, 1782 Tr.

352. 4H25, 135–36 = journal July 20, 1782 M.

353. TK32F7, 499 = August 22, 1781 Tr. copy.

354. See p. 104, 4H25, 135–36; TK32F7, 628–31 = October 28, 1782 Tr. copy.

355. 4H25, 151 = journal August 15, 1782 M; 5B3:32 = September 7, 1787 Tr. original.

356. 5B3: 21, 89 = December 6, 1786 Probst original.

357. 5B3:39, 172 = August 4, 1790 Bm. original.

358. See pp. 96–97.

also was not lacking; in Ebenezer he called himself Adlerstein and earlier had appeared deeper in the country as Pastor Frank.[359] But in Savannah he was uncovered; he was not a pastor at all.[360]

In Ebenezer at the end of February 1783, the members of the community again elected church elders[361] who called the community together on March 2nd, among other reasons, to discuss the resumption of school instruction. Moreover, two days later they wrote to Triebner in St. Augustine, Florida, and asked him to give back the church records that he had taken with him. He responded to them that he had taken the records so that they would not be lost, since the Fathers in Europe would make him responsible for them. In addition, he possessed the unbelievable audacity to explore a return to Ebenezer:

> Can I feel assured of your confidence to live among you in safety and peace as an evangelical Instructor,[362] and that no former dissatisfactions can give rise to new complications and disturbances, but to let old troubles be buried and forgotten. I for my part promise every one in the Parish, that I will assist him, as spiritual adviser in word and deed. Now that the unfortunate dispute has been decided, and we know who is in authority in the land, you can feel assured that I shall recognize, according to the word of God all those who were appointed by the high Powers, as lawful authorities.[363]

The community did not at all take Triebner's return into consideration. For that reason, it was glad to receive a letter from Muhlenberg. For since the connection of Europe with Georgia had been made uncertain, at times even impossible through the war and the strained relationship with Triebner, J. A. Urlsperger and the Director of the Francke Foundations at the time, Gottlieb Anastasius Freylinghausen, had transferred the care for the congregational affairs of Georgia's Lutherans to Muhlenberg who, on February 9, 1779, received an official authorization in that regard.[364]

---

359. Jacob Franck, Evangelical Lutheran pastor in Culpepper, VA (4H23, 371 = journal July 14, 1777 M).

360. 5B4:17, 54 = January 26, 1802 Bm. original.

361. 4H26, 140–43 = journal August 8, 1783 M = letter May 5, 1783 copy.

362. In German, the original was probably "Lehrer," referring in this case to, "pastor."

363. Wilson, "The Swan of Huss," 381–84, translation of the German version available in the Ebenezer church archives, letter April 29, 1783 Tr. original.

364. 4H26, 46 = journal March 14, 1783 M.

The wardens of Ebenezer, Jacob C. Waldhauer and Jenking Davis,[365] answered his current letter and depicted the deplorable condition of the settlement. Although at first they had reckoned—and Muhlenberg also had it in mind—that Friedrich August Conrad Muhlenberg, the second son of the patriarch, would come to Ebenezer,[366] it fell apart, since his brother-in-law, Pastor Schultze in Tulpehocken, Pennsylvania, dissuaded him for the sake of his large family, due to Georgia's unhealthy climate.[367] Moreover, the younger Muhlenberg had just been elected to the "Board of Censors" in Pennsylvania,[368] so that his father knew of no one for Georgia and reported this to Urlsperger.[369] Ebenezer's church wardens also placed their hope on him when at the end of 1783 they wrote a letter to him that expressed emphatically their longing for the Word of God:

> There is still a good seed in Ebenezer, but many have been punished but not humbled through the hard war and other plagues. We have not had a teacher here for a long time. The people run hither and yon and see and hear nothing but wicked examples. Also, young people, boys and girls, have reached marriageable age and have not been confirmed. In a word, a shepherd of souls is lacking. Now you may well think and say that already for fifty years so much good was done for Ebenezer and has gained little fruit. To that we want to say that is true and we are not worthy of it, but we are in need. Try one more time; if we are not worthy of it, do it for the One whom you know well who said that even a cup of cold water should not go unrewarded. . . . Johannes Hangleiter, Caspar Heck, Johannes Miechel, Jacob Genan, Cristoffer Grammer, Nicolaus Shubtrein, Samuel Krauss."[370]

Urlsperger's mind was not closed to this request. To be sure, in the beginning he was of the opinion that Ebenezer should take back Triebner and ask the SPCK to continue to pay his salary.[371] But when these things proved to be impossible, he looked around Germany for suitable candidates

---

365. 4H26, 117 = journal June 18, 1783 M; 140–43 = journal August 8, 1783 M.

366. 4H26, 257–58 = journal January 4, 1784 M = letter August 22, 1783 Waldhauer copy to M.

367. 4H26, 144 = journal August 12, 1783 M.

368. 4H26, 281–97 = journal January 15, 1784 M = letter January 12, 1784 M copy to Waldhauer; *Nachrichten von den vereinigten Deutschen Evangelisch-Lutherischen Gemeinden*, 585.

369. 4H26, 305–7 = journal February 6, 1784 M = letter February 2, 1784 M copy.

370. TK33, 74–76 = November 29, 1783 Ebenezer church wardens original to U. jun.

371. TK32F7, 546–48 = May 14, 1784 U. jun. original; 635b–36 = August/September 1783 U. jun. to Ebenezer church wardens.

with the result that on December 20, 1786, Pastor Johann Ernst Bergmann and the teacher Johann Gotthilf Probst arrived in Ebenezer.[372] Until a short time before, Pastor Christian Eberhard Bernhardt from Württemberg had resided there for about a year. Although without giving proper instruction, he had confirmed the youth, and "on days when the people went for preparation for the Lord's Supper played cards, [and] read novels instead of Holy Scripture. Afterwards, he danced with the young women whom he was supposed to instruct in the Lord's Supper." In the meantime, he had set out for Rowan County, North Carolina.[373]

Soon after the arrival of Bergmann and Probst, a "Charter of Incorporation of the EbenEzer Church and its dependencies" was issued in the House of Assembly in Savannah through the mediation of Chief Justice William Stephens, Esqr., according to which the community of Ebenezer was "confirmed . . . as a German religious society" that received the right that only German would be preached in it and the trustees of the community were authorized to collect the outstanding debts.[374]

The teacher Probst soon played a peculiar role. When Urlsperger had chosen two candidates for Georgia, he followed the precedent of the heyday of Lutheran communities there when two clergy, with effort, had been able to handle the duties of office that arose. But he had not considered that the communities had been much diminished and completely impoverished through the war, so that they could not and also did not want to pay two spiritual workers whom they now also had to pay by themselves,[375] for they had just seen only too well the danger of two factions. If Urlsperger had only informed himself precisely about these circumstances, he certainly would have delayed the sending of the two for as long as Muhlenberg had.

In the hope of soon coming into money again in Ebenezer, Probst had given his assets to his sister in Germany[376] and had set out with excessive enthusiasm. But when he discovered that it was far beyond the reach of Ebenezer's residents ever to appoint an extra schoolmaster, and when he

---

372. TK32F7, 532–36 = November 5, 1784 U. jun. copy to M; p. 669 = June 17, 1789 Probst original; 5B3:22, 93 = January 16, 1787 Probst original.

373. 5B4:17, 54 = January 26, 1802 Bm. original; Bergmann made up the instruction with the already confirmed (5B3:32, 138 = September 7, 1787); *Nachrichten von den vereinigten Deutschen Evangelisch-Lutherischen Gemeinden*, 32; Gräbner, *Geschichte der Lutherischen Kirche in America*, part I, 590; Strobel confuses him completely with Probst. Strobel, *The Salzburgers and Their Descendants*, 222–23.

374. 5B4:2, 5 = April 3, 1799 Bm. original; 5B4:10, 45 = November 23, 1801 Bm. original.

375. 5B3:22, 93–94 = January 16, 1787 Probst original.

376. They amounted to 600 talers (5B3:37, 163 = December 9, 1788 Bm. original.

saw that he was in somewhat unrestrained moral circumstances among them there, he broke out into the kind of lamentation that would be hard to find: "But dearest Herr Inspector,[377] tell me, for God's sake, what offense did I ever do to Herr Doctor Urlsperger that I have been relegated by him into incalculable misery? Indeed, the Herr Doctor should only confer to his enemies the vocations of a schoolteacher to Ebenezer, and he would be avenged, most bitterly avenged."[378]

Nonetheless, he began on Sunday, January 14, 1787, to give instruction with thirty-nine children in a private house, one mile from Ebenezer. At the end of February, there were fifty, some of whom had to go six miles to get to school.[379] If all of the children in question had been able to participate, it would have been about 140.[380] The community also elected Probst as a trustee.[381]

But soon there were differences between him and Bergmann that even spread over the community in the form of factions. They seemed to have to do with disputes over rank and accusations initiated by the schoolmaster.[382] Thereupon the Ebenezer community church council, in its sixth session after the arrival of the two, conveyed to Herr Probst: they had not asked for him from Urlsperger and also could not pay him, upon which Probst burst forth, "I believed that I would die from shock. I now sit here, sigh, wring my hands, weep; in the end, nothing becomes of it."[383] He was given thirty pounds in travel money, and in the beginning of July, he already was in Halle again.[384]

377. Fabricius

378. *Gerecht*; [translator's note: the context suggests that Probst intended to write *gerächt*]. 5B3:22, 93 = January 16, 1787 Probst original.

379. 5B3:23, 97–98 = February 28, 1787 Probst original.

380. 5B3:24, 102 = March 6, 1787 Probst original.

381. 5B3:23, 98 = February 28, 1787 Probst original.

382. Bergmann was supposed to "completely accommodate myself to the regiment of H[err] Probst and alternate preaching with him in Savannah." "He treated me worse than a ragamuffin," Bergmann complained (5B3:30, 129 = August 27, 1787 Bm. original), and further, "We were only together a quarter of a year, but I maintain that the man soon would have put me under the earth," something which to the reader of the letter does not seem unbelievable (5B3:37, 163 = December 9, 1788 Bm. original).

383. 5B3:22, 93 = January 16, 1787 Probst original.

384. 5B3:25, 106 = April 9, 1787 Bm. original; 5B3:27, 115 = July 6, 1787 draft; 5B3:30, 129 = August 27, 1787 Bm. original. In Halle, he nonetheless had to discover to his dismay that his sister returned not a penny of his wealth (5B3:33, 140 = November 16, 1787). Urlsperger took up his cause, and through the mediation of Upper Consistory President von Burgsdorf, he received an appointment in Dresden (5B3:37, 167 = December 9, 1788 Bm. original).

The pastor and the members of the community now again made a serious attempt to elevate Ebenezer. Bergmann held German school,[385] and the community came in large numbers, regularly, and with interest to the worship service.[386] Yet already around 1790, the small group began to disperse again. Part of them moved, obeying their need, to remote plantations that lay up to fifteen miles away from Ebenezer. Another part moved away to avoid the dues for church and school. Moreover, there was the general tendency that "the youth express ... little desire for the German language. They want everything in English. ... The English language is absolutely necessary for advancement. German cannot be maintained because the youth learn neither German writing nor arithmetic, nor will they let themselves be compelled to be taught."[387] This was also the basic tone for the development of the following years.

In 1794, a courthouse as the seat of the judiciary in this region was established in Ebenezer,[388] and the next year, the House of Assembly opened an English school here.[389] Also, on February 18, 1796, Ebenezer became the county seat of Effingham County, but three years later, this was transferred to Springfield. In 1797, the courthouse was moved from Ebenezer,[390] and even the school became an object of great annoyance.[391] Individual prosperity naturally improved with time so that the church capital that the trustees administered grew to $10,000 under the chairmanship of Captain Kogler,[392] and in 1801, a "preacher's and schoolhouse" could be built.[393] Contributing not least of all was the fact that the trustees had sold tracts of land that were no longer being used.[394]

But the settlements dissolved. In 1803 in Ebenezer, there were, along with the church, only three occupied houses and just as many as were unoccupied. The rest of the settlers lived on their plantations where they were deprived of continuous pastoral care.[395] The peculiarity of this pattern of

385. 5B3:37, 165 = December 9, 1788 Bm. original.
386. 5B3:40, 177 = August 24, 1790 Bm. original.
387. 5B3:40, 177 = August 24, 1790 Bm. original.
388. 5B4:2, 5 = April 3, 1799 Bm. original.
389. 5B3:41, 188 = April 23, 1795 Bm. original.
390. 5B4:2, 8
391. See pp. 146–47.
392. 5B4:32, 96 = October 21, 1803 Bm. original.
393. 5B4:10, 46 = November 23, 1801 Bm. original.
394. Approved through the "list of acts Louisville December 1, 1802... N. 9 An act to authorise the Congregation of Eben Ezer to sell certain lands" (5B4:29, 84 = January 11, 1803).
395. For example, 5B3:21.

settlement even later did not lead to the development of closed villages, and today, from everything that at the time belonged to Ebenezer and its communities, only Jerusalem Church still stands. Bergmann's last report from Ebenezer from March 27, 1806, closes by echoing the name of this place: "Thus far has the Lord helped. He will also, according to His mercy, help through the last need."[396]

Excursus:
Church Buildings in Ebenezer and the Related Communities

As everywhere in the beginning stages of Christian communities, so also in Georgia the first Lutheran worship services were held in private houses. In Old Ebenezer, no house of worship stood, even though it was felt to be very necessary.[397] As long as Boltzius still had no parsonage, he held worship and prayer services in the attic in the house of a Salzburger with whom he himself lived at this time.[398] But for the settlers of the second transport, this space did not suffice, so that in 1735 when their commissioner, Vat, had built a guardhouse against eventual attacks by the Indians or the Spanish, the worship services were also relocated there because it was sturdier and roomier. In addition, it was used as a school and slaughterhouse. On holidays, the British flag flew over it on a mast.[399] After the relocation of Ebenezer, Boltzius initially held prayer hours in his own house;[400] otherwise they were, as a rule, in the building previously erected as a storehouse where likewise, along with the worship services, school was also held.[401]

When in the course of 1736 the settlers of the third transport received their own single-family houses, the large communal barracks—the first buildings in New Ebenezer[402]—that had been built for them became free, and one of them was equipped as a church and schoolhouse.[403] But already

---

396. 5B4:45, 142 = March 17, 1806 Bm. original. This is, as far as I am aware, the only time that Bergmann cites the Bible verse that was completely well-worn in Ebenezer's early period. [Some years after this dissertation was finished, six additional letters from Bergmann were found at different places in the archives at Halle: one from 1818, two from 1819, two from 1820, and one from 1820.]

397. 5D1 = journal February 2, 1735.

398. 5D1, 212–13 = journal January 1, 1734; UN September 9, 1734.

399. UN July 9, 1743; UN April 13, 1735; 5D1, 296 = journal August 19, 1735.

400. 5D2 = journal June 13, 1736.

401. 5D2 = journal June 24, 1736.

402. 5A3:34, 220 von Reck copy.

403. 5D2 = journal August 20, 1736.

a year later this hut could barely still be used. The wind blew out the light and there was danger of collapse during a storm.[404] Now Boltzius had to roam around everywhere for a rather long time, because the place for the actual church building in Ebenezer still had not been surveyed,[405] and, in addition, money also was naturally lacking. They went, intermittently, in the kitchen of the house erected for the doctor who was expected,[406] then into the kitchen of the orphanage[407] until the attic was completed as planned.[408] Boltzius held prayer hours and weddings in his house[409] where he had reserved a room entirely for community affairs.[410] However, for the large Sunday worship services, especially on festivals, the old church hut was repaired again and again as necessary.[411]

The construction of a proper church first came again into clear view when in January 1740, George Whitefield came to Georgia for the second time.[412] He brought with him more than fifty-two pounds that he had collected in England,[413] a barrel of iron goods (nails, fittings, etc.),[414] and a bell that, without the clapper, weighed close to forty kilograms.[415] The old church hut was now torn down because of danger of collapse,[416] and at the beginning of the following year, the construction of the church began.[417]

About sixty pounds were available for use, to which Urlsperger also had contributed eleven pounds. And since from Halle had come the advice to count on growth for the church,[418] they had in mind to erect a large, stable building, thirty by forty-five feet. Then later, when the money was there for a stone church, it quickly could be converted to a regular schoolhouse

---

404. 5A7:32a, 140 = October 14, 1737 B. extract; UN November 11, 1739, January 27, 1740.

405. 5D3 = journal February 27, 1737.

406. 5D3 = journal December 24, 1737; 5D4 = journal January 8, 1738; 5A7:2, 3 = January 20, 1738 B. original.

407. 5D4 = journal January 15 and March 29, 1738.

408. 5D3, 138–39 = journal December 10, 1737; 5A7:17, 64 = May 17, 1738 B. copy.

409. 5D6, 10–11 = journal July 16, 1739; 5A9:2, 8 = February 14, 1740 B. original.

410. 5D6, 10–11 = journal July 16, 1739; UN November 17, 1739.

411. 5D3, 147 = journal December 23, 1737; 5A9:2, 8 = February 14, 1740 B. original.

412. UN January 16, 1740.

413. 5A10:2, 7 = April 8, 1741 B. original; 5A9:2, 7 = February 14, 1740 B. original.

414. UN January 16, 1740.

415. Ninety-one English pounds (UN January 25, 1740).

416. UN December 14, 1740.

417. 5A9:25, 113 = February 10, 1741 B. original; 5D7 = journal February 19, 1741.

418. 5A9:2, 7 = February 14, 1740 B. original.

through the installation of two crossing walls, which is why it already was built on the site for the envisioned school. This building was the first house in Georgia serving only for the purpose of a church.[419]

Now, after prayer, the first trees were felled, and on July 14, 1741, the festive laying of the cornerstone took place.[420] For the pastor, it was naturally an occasion of deep reflection when he once noticed that a couple of curious Indians, non-Christians, were helping to build the church just for fun.[421] Soon, on July 24th, under the skillful guidance of the carpenter Kogler, the walls were raised.[422] Then, however, there was a pause because the harvest had to be brought in.[423] But finally, on September 20, 1741 (the 17th Sunday after Trinity), the church could be solemnly consecrated.[424] Coming from Purrysburg, South Carolina, and from the plantations, the people streamed in:

> When men, women, and children had gathered after the signal had been given, we stepped in humility and awe before the face of the Lord and sang standing the hymn, "Come Holy Ghost, Lord God," etc. after which a prayer was offered by my dear colleague [Gronau], and the 24th chapter of Joshua was read, and afterwards two more hymns, namely, "Praise and Honor Be to the Highest Good," etc., and "Greatly Praised Be the Merciful God," etc. were sung, the friendly, helpful heart of the Lord Jesus toward the residents of Ebenezer was explained to the congregation from the gospel appointed for the 17th Sunday after Trinity from Luke 14:1ff., and in doing so we directed our attention I: to several particular items of this friendliness and help of the Lord Jesus granted to us, that as He has blessed us, just as the people in the text, with His gracious presence in the past, so also He will gladly deign to do so in the future, etc., that He also has taken care of our need and will take care of it, that He also has shown to us, as to them, the good and proper way to our salvation and will continue to show it. II: to the obligations to which we are bound through this friendliness and help of the Lord, partly in view toward the founding and leading of Christianity, partly in view

---

419. 5D7, 71–76 = journal February 19–20, 1741, February 20. Ebenezer had the first church in this colony; Savannah and Frederica used secular buildings for worship services.

420. 5D8 = journal July 14, 1741.

421. 5D8, 390 = journal July 21, 1741.

422. 5A10:13, 40 = journal July 25, 1741 extract; 5D8, 398 = journal July 25, 1741.

423. 5D8 = journal September 18, 1741.

424. 5A10:14, 45 = notation Z to journal August 14, 1741 extract; 5D8, 509–10 = journal September 20, 1741.

of the church now being consecrated, that they use it properly in keeping with God's intention. The introit was taken from Psalm 20:6, "We will rejoice in thy salvation, and in the name of our God we will set up our banners." Thus, both in the introit as well as in the sermon itself various particulars of the help and gracious care of the Lord over Ebenezer were stated, for the promotion in us of heartfelt gratitude and praise of God our Lord.[425]

To be sure, the church still lacked the windows,[426] the doors, and the attic,[427] but they managed for the time being with green curtains[428] until these things were added a year later.[429] It was named Jerusalem Church and, as mentioned, was the first church built in Georgia by any denomination.[430]

Yet even in this building the debilitating destruction of the damp climate became evident everywhere. The floor rotted and made the entire church so dilapidated that already in 1751 there was serious consideration about the construction of a brick church; moreover, after the arrival of the Swabian transports it turned out to be too small.[431] It was extensively repaired,[432] yet barely after six years (the end of 1759) things again were just as bad. The floor had rotted again completely and the cramped conditions were unbearable,[433] so that they decided on a thoroughgoing forty-pound repair and expansion that was finished at the end of 1760: "The foundation of the church is completely renovated and the floor has been newly laid, and on the left side a large addition has been properly made so that it now holds many more hearers than previously.... And since the church has been furnished with two wide and high doors opposite of each other, likewise with many large windows, it is cool in the summer, but in the winter, since the doors and windows can be closed, it is not too cold."[434]

---

425. 5D8, 510 = journal September 20, 1741.

426. Probably four, as with the similar (UN February 25, 1742) Zion Church.

427. 5D8, 507 = journal September 18, 1741; UN January 3, 1742.

428. UN January 6, 1742.

429. UN September 11 and November 21, 1742; 5A10:45, 168 = March 9, 1743 B. copy. The entire costs amounted to ninety pounds, twelve shillings, four pence.

430. See p. 86, n. 419. The wooden "Kapelle," built on a foundation of 30,000 bricks in Frederica in 1739 was, first and foremost, a secular building that was put to use, among other things, also for (Anglican) worship services. Corry, "The Houses of Colonial Georgia," 185. The same thing applies to Savannah (see p. 92).

431. UA November 30, 1751.

432. UA January 22 and 28, 1753.

433. UA IV, 109–10 = end of 1759 B.

434. UA June 28, 1760.

But now the community was in the position to erect a sturdy stone church in place of the wooden church requiring constant repair, especially since several people had come with the Swabian transports who could strike the bricks. On September 11, 1764, Boltzius contributed ten pounds to the already existing fund,[435] and after his death, Lemcke, and especially Wertsch, devoted themselves to the new construction. But Wertsch came upon a bricklayer who either did not properly understand his craft or wanted to deceive. He used much sand and too little lime, which naturally did not hold, so that already during the time of construction it looked decrepit. There was even a lawsuit since the money was used up. No new money came in, and the community lost interest.[436]

Finally, however, the church, forty by sixty feet, a simple brick building, was finished, and on March 10, 1770, as the anniversary of the arrival of the first Salzburgers in Georgia was again being observed, the church was festively dedicated as New Jerusalem Church.[437] This church dedication date of the Ebenezer community, a date that is bound even today with the living tradition from the earliest days of the settlement—the "Commemoration and Thanksgiving Festival"—on occasion of the arrival of the first Salzburgers,[438] is herewith for the first time brought to light, a monument in the history of the Lutheran church in Georgia.

Unfortunately, the first thing the new church experienced in its history was the disastrous dispute between Rabenhorst and Triebner, and during the English occupation of Ebenezer in the War of Independence it was used as a hospital and finally even as a stable.[439] Nonetheless, the community, that barely had enough to eat, renovated the badly damaged church again, as it was being said that Muhlenberg's son was coming to Ebenezer as its pastor. Bergmann also cared for it during his time of office and in the fall of 1798 had a new shingled roof made for it.[440] This church is still standing and is in use today. In keeping with its purpose for the community, it was never closed up until Bergmann's time.[441]

---

435. UA November 30, 1751; 5B2:12, 58 = December 31, 1764, B. original.

436. 5B2:60, 209–10 = December 14, 1768 R. original.

437. 5B3:36, 153 = July 23, 1788 Tr. original, in contrary to Gilbert, "Early History of the Lutheran Church in Georgia," 167 and Prinzinger, "Die Ansiedlung der Salzburger im Staate Georgien," 34.

438. See p. 131.

439. Strobel, *The Salzburgers and Their Descendants*, 206–7.

440. 5B4:3, 14 = October 7, 1799 Bm. original.

441. 5B4:33, 92 = February/March 1803 Bm. original.

"New" Jerusalem Church. Photo courtesy of the translator and editor.

On the first plantations surveyed in 1738, regular worship services were held from February 20, 1740, and, as in Ebenezer, they took place also here at first in private houses, especially in the house of Ruprecht Steiner, "the place of public worship on the plantations."[442] Two years later, there then began the construction of their own church that was supposed to be modeled on the example of the "town church."[443] Delays occurred, so that the construction first began on December 6, 1742. Yet after a few days, the walls already were standing, and once again, on the commemoration day of the arrival of the first Salzburgers, March 7, 1743, the first festive worship service was held in it with a sermon on Isaiah 26: 12, "Everything that we accomplish, Lord, You have given to us."[444]

In keeping with the taste of the times, Boltzius named this church "Zion," in order to express its close connection with Jerusalem Church.[445]

---

442. 5D7, 159 = journal April 6, 1741; 5D8, 368 = journal July 13, 1741.

443. UN February 25, 1742.

444. 5A10:44, 164 = March 8, 1743 G. original; 5A10:42, 152 = March 9, 1743 B. original.

445. "We recall with joy the dear words of Ps[alm] 132:13–16, and we report to Your

At the time of its consecration, Zion Church was in the same condition in which Jerusalem Church also was being used,[446] and it cost seventy-three pounds, fourteen shillings, six pence.[447] This disproportionately low price, in comparison to other construction in the colonies at the time, was only possible due to the great amount of voluntary labor of the settlers and their ability to erect this church without outside help.

On the outside, the two churches had no apparent differences, either in material or in the style of construction, from the block houses of the settlers. But the communities took delight in them and rightly so; what community at the time could accomplish the construction of a separate large building to be used only as a church!

At the beginning of 1755, the communities in Goshen, Josephstown, and Abercorn joined together and built a joint church on Boltzius' plantation that lay between the places.[448] In 1759/60, the community at Bethany also completed a small wooden church, and they also had a separate school building.[449]

A Sunday sermon of the pastors of each area was seldom shorter than an hour, therefore the most important furnishings of the churches were a raised pulpit and solid benches that also were constructed for kneeling, like in the "singing hall" of the Francke Foundations in Halle.[450] As in Germany, the men's and women's sides were separated by a middle aisle.[451] Confirmed youth sat to the left and right of the pulpit, and the smaller children in front of it. In addition, there was in the Jerusalem Church and in Zion a separate bench for the pastor and teacher, and another one for young mothers who, after the birth of their children, came to church with their wet nurses for the first time again.[452]

Behind all of these the altar was completely in the background. It was a simple table that stood on a narrow side of the church in Ebenezer between two windows. Above it hung a four by five foot painting of the first Lord's

---

Reverence [Urlsperger, Senior] the dear God Himself has so disposed that the new church on the plantations should receive the lovely name Zion Church, since, conversely, the one in town is to be called Jerusalem Church" (5A10:45, 168 = March 9, 1743 B. copy).

446. Attic, doors, window frames and shutters were still not installed after a year (5D9, 7 = journal March 8, 1744). Altar and benches only first were put in place at the beginning of 1754 (UA January 18, 1754).

447. 5A10:45, 169 = March 9, 1743 B. copy.

448. TK32F11, 1039 = February 16, 1755 B. original.

449. TK32F4, 255 = March 14. 1760 L. original.

450. 5D8, 507 = journal September 18, 1741; prayer was mostly done kneeling.

451. 5D4 = journal November 9, 1738.

452. 5D2 = journal August 20, 1736; UA July 7, 1760.

Supper, a gift from Ziegenhagen.[453] The communities in Ebenezer and Zion commissioned a painter in Charleston to write for both churches in large format the verse, "Rejoice greatly, O daughter of Zion, shout O daughter of Jerusalem; behold, thy King cometh unto thee: he is just, and having salvation" (Zech 9:9).[454]

Another painting from Europe likewise to be hung in one of the churches, raised reservations, and so it was put into Boltzius' study:

> This painting depicts the voyage of the fourth transport. The ship is in full sail on the wild sea. But the eye of God looks upon it, and it is being led from east to west by a rope from His hand reaching out from the bright clouds. At the place where the ship departed as well as the place to where it was to go, that is, Europe and America, are situated on each side four men on their knees with hands raised to God, and it has the appearance as though some were pulling the ship forward and the others helping to push it from behind, both happening through heartfelt, humble, and united prayer. At the hand reaching out of the cloud the words are placed, "My eyes look upon those who fear me." From the mouths of those who are praying go forth these words: 1. "Renew me, O Eternal Light," etc. 2. "May the soul of Christ sanctify me," etc. 3. "May the Lord be praised," etc.[455]

From the Trustees, the first transport already received an altar cloth and a pewter chalice which was later loaned to the Lutheran congregation in Frederica.[456] Similar baptismal vessels arrived later.[457] When Muhlenberg came from Germany, he was able to bring along for Ebenezer a silver, gilded chalice.[458] A large altar Bible already had been sent to them in 1736,[459] and in 1750 they received an additional one.[460]

The bell that Whitefield had brought from Ziegenhagen to Ebenezer was very welcome here, since until then only an instrument had been rung

---

453. UN November 21, 1750.

454. UN September 7, 1743. The painter was named Theus, the brother of the Reformed preacher Christian Theus in Saxe-Gotha (present-day Lexington County, South Carolina). Faust, *The German Element in the United States*, I, 215; (UN December 2, 1741).

455. UN August 17, 1743.

456. 5D1, 22 = journal December 24, 1733 (new style).

457. UN March 19, 1742.

458. UN October 4, 1742.

459. A gift of the President of the Trustees, the Earl of Egmont (5D2 = journal May 1, 1736).

460. 5B1:36, 146 = June 16, 1750.

that, in a storm, for example, could not be heard very far.[461] On Boltzius' house, in which worship services took place at that time,[462] a frame with a small cover was erected on which it was hung, and on January 26, 1740, it was rung for the first time.[463] However, it often happened that the rope broke; then someone laboriously would have to climb up and repair it. For that reason, two strong, thirty-foot-high beams were erected with a roof over it, and for a long time, this was Ebenezer's "bell tower."[464]

Zion Church received already in the fall of the year in which it was completed a small, eight-pound bell from Halle.[465] Both bells hang today in the tower of Jerusalem Church.[466]

THE OTHER LUTHERAN COMMUNITIES

Savannah and the Related Communities of Acton and Vernonburg

In the middle of June 1735, two ships came to Savannah with Lutheran emigrants from the Palatinate,[467] after which another followed at the end of December 1737.[468] Immediately, Ebenezer's pastors looked after them, preached among them every two to four weeks,[469] and administered the sacraments, since through dealings with Mayor Causton regarding "provisions," there was often opportunity for one of them to travel to Savannah. The worship services were held at first "in the open house that was designated to be the church."[470] This "church," that was used by all denominations, was "only nailed together by a few boards and had neither windows nor chancel but only roof and timberwork,"[471] and was a general purpose assembly and administration building. To be sure, a new church was mentioned at the

---

461. UN January 24, 1740; 5A3:45, 288 = December 4, 1736 B. copy. In Goshen, they were called to worship with a horn (UA May 17, 1751).

462. UN March 9 and May 4, 1740; 5A9:11, 47 = journal August 5, 1740 extract.

463. UN January 26, 1740.

464. UN February 24, 1747.

465. 5A10:47 = September 1743 Fr. draft.

466. Brandl, "Ein Besuch in Ebenezer," 159–68.

467. 5D, 258 = journal July 23, 1735.

468. 5D4 = journal January 13 and 18, 1738.

469. 5A7:64a, 268 = October 30, 1739 B. original.

470. 5A3:11, 72 = September 1, 1735. B. original.

471. 5D1 = journal March 14, 1734.

end of 1737, but that was the town hall in which the Anglican and Lutheran worship services, among others, took place.[472]

The spiritual care through Ebenezer's pastors was all the more important for the Lutheran community in Savannah as they were not in the fortunate situation, as was Ebenezer, to be continuously supported by Europe, for which reason they also found the initial difficulties of colonization to be especially burdensome.[473] Eventually, a plan was worked out, in keeping with the particular wish of Oglethorpe, that every four weeks, if not more often,[474] a Lutheran worship service in the German language would be held in Savannah, and mostly by Gronau.[475] Travel costs (rowers) were reimbursed by the congregation.[476] But unfortunately, the result of these preaching trips, which meant a great burden for the pastors, was not what they hoped for, since during the intervening four weeks there was no connection between the pastors and the community members, so that the impressions from the sermons faded away.[477]

Therefore, Boltzius and Gronau decided in fall 1739 to abandon their activity in Savannah[478] and to go there only occasionally to preach,[479] since around this time they also were having extra work from the Zion plantations.[480] Moreover, in Savannah there was unpleasant hostility between the Lutherans and Reformed, not from confessional but from economic and personal reasons.[481] But scarcely had Francke learned about this step when he forcefully advised against it, and in fact, when in the summer of 1743 regular visits resumed again, the condition of the community was no longer so bleak.[482] The time during which no worship service had been held had shown well to the members of the community that they had thrown away something essential. But now they even came from far away for preaching,

---

472. 5D3 = journal December 29, 1737; UN March 7, 1739; UA April 27, 1760; Gilbert, "Early History of the Lutheran Church in Georgia," 165. There were not yet other denominations in Georgia.

473. 5D4 = journal May 5, 1738.

474. Oglethorpe had only counted on a worship service every eight to nine weeks (UA February 9, 1753).

475. UN April 15, 1739, January 13, February 10 and 26, March 13, April 8, 1739; 5A7:58, 246 = July 6, 1739 G. original.

476. UA February 9, 1753.

477. 5A10:12, 36 = July25, 1741 B. copy.

478. 5A7:64a, 268 = October 30, 1739 B. original.

479. 5A10:48, 187–88 = May 4, 1743 B. original.

480. 5A10:2, 6 = April 8, 1741 B. original.

481. 5A10:48, 187–88 = May 4, 1743 B. original.

482. 5A11:2, 5 = July 21, 1743 G. original.

and when Boltzius complained that, in the time between the visits of the pastors, things with the community are like in the parable of the sower,[483] then that is the characterization of a normal community that naturally is not to be compared with Ebenezer, which is an exception.

The Halle pietistic rigor of Boltzius with regard to adiaphora appears in the following notice that is of interest in the history of sports. When he came one afternoon to Savannah, he saw "residents and outsiders at the public market square hitting a ball with shouting and cursing, wasting precious time and giving offense to the youth."[484]

In the summer of 1746, the Anglicans of Savannah planned the building of a church.[485] Ebenezer's mills provided the boards for it,[486] and on Sunday, July 7, 1750, it was consecrated.[487]

In the fall of 1744, an event occurred that was of momentous significance for the Lutheran community of Savannah: the Reformed Pastor Johann Joachim Zübli came from South Carolina to Savannah.[488] He was born on August 27, 1724, in St. Gallen (Switzerland),[489] and probably arrived with his immigrating father, David Zübli,[490] in Purrysburg, South Carolina, on March 25, 1737.[491] He then stayed in various places in South Carolina[492] until the Reformed Palatines from Vernonburg (south of Savannah) asked the Trustees of Georgia in a petition on February 6, 1742, for the appointment of Zübli among them.[493] In October 1744, he came to Georgia[494] and

---

483. 5A11:15, 54 = August 18, 1744 B. original.

484. 5B7, 152 = journal April 2, 1741.

485. 5A11:54, 254 = June 16, 1746 B. extract.

486. 5B1:37, 149 = June 1750 B.

487. UN July 7, 1750.

488. UN October 1, 1750. His biography, up to now, has been incorrectly or only partially correctly written.

489. *Dictionary of American Biography*, XX, 660.

490. See p. 104.

491. 5C4:70 = December 3, 1737.

492. There are contradictory reports about this part of his life. According to Perkins, he stayed in Wando Neck, South Carolina. Perkins, "John Joachim Zubly, Georgia's Conscientious Objector," 313–23. According to *Nachrichten von den vereinigten Deutschen Evangelisch-Lutherischen Gemeinden*, he was the successor of Johann Ulrich Giessendanner in Orangeburg, South Carolina (30). But this note counts on Giessendanner's death around 1737 and overlooks UN June 21, 1741, where he was still active in Orangeburg (likewise 5D3 = journal December 2, 1737; 5D8 = journal June 21, 1741).

493. Perkins, "John Joachim Zubly," 313–23; *Dictionary of American Biography* XX, 660. He was supposed to have been ordained in London on August 19, 1744; however, afterward, it was inaccurately reported that he went immediately to his father in Purrysburg.

494. 5C2:7.

actively served the Reformed German and English speaking congregations in Savannah, Acton, Vernonburg, and Frederica[495] until in 1747 he returned again to the Amelia Township, Orangeburg District, next to Charleston, South Carolina,[496] "as preacher of a Scottish-Independent congregation." Since he was rather ill there, he ordered Halle medicines and books from Ebenezer.[497] Even later he remained a good customer of the Francke Foundations for these articles.[498]

In the fall of 1750, Zübli came for the second time to Georgia and resumed his activity in Savannah.[499] However, he did not remain again for very long since he was not adequately paid,[500] but he went again to Charleston.[501] In 1758, he received a call to the Independent Presbyterian Church in Savannah[502] and returned at the beginning of 1759 for the third time to Savannah with numerous family members, sixteen slaves, and the prospect of a good salary and also served again the German Reformed[503] as well as the places neighboring Savannah.[504]

For the Lutherans of this region his presence meant that regular German worship services took place among them, even if it was Reformed. Thus, they attended these services and believed that they could do without

---

495. 1E9:9b, 33 = August 25, 1747 B extract to Z; UN May 3, 1747; Strobel, *The Salzburgers and Their Descendants*, 118.

496. Inaccurately, Strobel, *The Salzburgers and Their Descendants*, 118–19.

497. 5B1:28, 120 = April 21, 1750 B. original.

498. 5B2:63, 218 = November 18, 1762 B. original; 5B2:1, 1 = December 3, 1763 Fr. draft.

499. UN October 1, 1750.

500. The Trustees expended for him annually the sum of ten pounds (1E9:9b, 33 = August 25, 1747 B. extract). At the beginning of 1746, the former Reformed and now Anglican pastor Zuberbühler had come with Lemcke to Savannah, so that at the time there was little use for Zübli. Ebenezer's pastors now no longer went so often to Savannah for worship services because they did not want to create the impression that they were mixing themselves in his duties; Zübli, however, showed little concern for the Germans.

501. TK32F11, 977 = journal February 11, 1757 B. original.

502. Marjorie Daniel ("John Joachim Zubly," 5) and William Harden, ("Rev. J. J. Zubly's Appeal to the Grand Jury," 161) hold, unaware of the previous history, that Zübli first came to America "about 1758."

503. UA February 6, 1759. The *Dictionary of American Biography* XX, 660, incorrectly states 1760. His father-in-law was the Appenzell "Governor Johann Dobler" (TK32F11, 1028 = February 18, 1755 B. original signature on the letter from another hand), also spelled "Dobbler."

504. UA April 27, 1760. He was highly regarded in this position and received in 1770 the Doctor of Divinity from Princeton College in New Jersey. Nothing appears in the archives about his controversial political activity.

the Lutheran pastors, especially since they had to pay their travel expenses. Also, since 1752, there were no longer any Trustees for Georgia whom Savannah's authorities wanted to please by the punctual payment of these expenses.[505] What unfolded here was the opposite of that which occurred with the Lutheran and Reformed Palatines living together in Charleston; there, the Reformed went over to the Lutherans, because the latter most often had the local pastor.[506]

In Savannah, however, the Lutheran element did not completely merge into the Reformed. Zübli preached here—as before, in the city hall—every second Sunday, and on the intervening Sunday, a small crowd gathered in a private house for edification. The pastors of Ebenezer came to them "as often as desired," or when they had "business" there,[507] until it was arranged that Rabenhorst, who at this time had taken over the itinerate duties, traveled to them only every two months for preaching and every four months for the Lord's Supper.[508] But shortly after Boltzius' death, this also ceased because it did not seem to be much needed.[509] On New Year's Day 1777, Zübli buried Rabenhorst in Ebenezer,[510] and on July 23, 1781, Zübli himself died in Savannah,[511] so that the Lutherans were left to themselves.[512]

As already mentioned, they soon enjoyed the visit of several "preachers" who wandered about the land. In the first half of 1783, the German preacher Friedrich Gerresheim[513] can be found among them. He had previously roamed about in Maryland and Pennsylvania or Virginia[514] and then had been a chaplain with a republican regiment in Virginia.[515] From Savannah, he often preached in Ebenezer and married the daughter of the church elder Waldhauer. However, three days after the wedding, a letter arrived from Pennsylvania or Virginia from his wife from whom he was not yet divorced. He cursed, gambled, drank, attended fights—in Muhlenberg's

---

505. UA February 9, 1753.

506. See pp. 108–109.

507. UA April 27, 1760.

508. UA February 25, 1759; 5D13, 8 = journal August 7, 1763.

509. 5B2:31, 122 = May 13, 1766 L. R.

510. 4H23: pp. 307–9 = journal May 15, 1777 M = letter February 20, 1777 Mrs. R. copy.

511. Jones, *The History of Georgia* II, *The Revolutionary Epoch*, 204.

512. The Reformed received an English-speaking preacher, McCall (5B3:42, 193 = April 20, 1796 Bm. original).

513. Also Frederick Garrisheim (4H26, 140–43 = journal August 8, 1783 M = letter March 18, 1783 Jenking Davis copy), Garrison, Carrison.

514. 4H26, 182–83 = journal September 30, 1783 M.

515. TK32F7, 631–35 = May 27, 1783 Tr. copy.

judgment, "A prodigal son, whom virtuous people would not hire to feed their swine."[516] In Savannah he was dismissed, and from the beginning of November 1783, he laid low in Ebenezer's tavern that belonged to his father-in-law, the church elder.[517] Finally, he moved to Charleston where, while staying with the Lutheran pastor Daser,[518] he "came to a sad end."[519]

After him, the Württemberger Penninger was active in Savannah, who from there likewise ministered to Ebenezer. However, he also was dismissed, "because he got a woman pregnant."[520] Also, the already mentioned preachers Bernhardt and "Adlerstein," as reported, worked occasionally in Savannah.

Yet in all of the confusion, the Lutheran community endured and had its elders and wardens when Pastor Bergmann came to Georgia at the end of 1786.[521] He soon began to preach regularly in German again every four weeks to the Lutherans in Savannah, yet this had to take place in a private house, since the church, unfortunately, had been destroyed by a fire on November 26 and December 6, 1796.[522] Its reconstruction began in fall 1799,[523] and on February 7, 1802, Bergmann, at the request of the "Herren Trustees and elders of the church," gave in it the dedication sermon on the text, "LORD, I have loved the habitation of thy house, and the place where thine honour dwelleth."[524] It lasted, "apart from the prayers before and after the sermon," an hour and a half.[525]

Bergmann's activity, however, did not mean a recovery of the Lutheran character of this community, since he himself had a pronounced inclination toward indifferent and Presbyterian views.[526] He reported pessimistically about the condition of the congregation: "The Savannah German congregation is very small; most have died and the children of German parents are completely depraved."[527] But it must be taken into account

516. 4H26, 183.
517. TK 32F8, 696 = March 18, 1784 Tr. original.
518. See p. 109.
519. 5B4:17, 54 = January 26, 1802 Bm. original.
520. 5B4:17, 54 = January 26, 1802 Bm. original.
521. Strobel, *The Salzburgers and Their Descendants*, 224–25.
522. 5B4:3, 13–14 = October 7, 1799 Bm. original; 5B4:32, 93 = October 21, 1803 Bm. original; 5B4:1, 2 = April 2, 1799 Bm. original; 5B4:2, 8 = April 3, 1799 Bm. original.
523. 5B4:3, 13–14 = October 7, 1799 Bm. original.
524. Ps 26:8.
525. 5B4:20, 65 = April 8, 1802 Bm. original.
526. See pp. 205–206.
527. 5B4:3, 18 = October 7, 1799 Bm. original.

that in the course of time, the German speaking element everywhere was in decline, and for that reason, many Lutherans went over to English speaking denominations since Bergmann preached only in German, and that, moreover, a young person, who had grown up in the confusion of the war and post-war period, had their particular character. Although Pastor Bergmann completely discontinued his preaching trips to Savannah in the first years of the new century, the reorganization of the Lutheran character of this city in 1824 through Pastor S. A. Mealy from Charleston nevertheless shows that the Lutheran element was only under cover and merely needed assembling.[528]

South of Savannah on the "White Bluff" lay the settlement Vernonburg,[529] founded by Germans who mainly came from Zweibrücken in the Palatinate. Boltzius served them with the preaching office, yet there were differences, because Boltzius, pampered through his Salzburger model community, found too much fault with the Vernonburgers. That they were not satisfied with him was evident when he suggested they bring to life a school at their place and offered his help for it: "They appointed a Swiss as schoolmaster who could not properly spell and taught the children such a confession of faith from an old Reformed book that filled me with horror and which this man as well as the elders of the Germans (very defiant and malicious people) justified. From that time on I no longer bothered myself about the school, which also was not desired in the least."

Soon this man died, yet even then the Vernonburgers did not even once accept the ABC books that Boltzius offered to them. Several children were supposed to go to school in Ebenezer, but that was not possible since Gronau about this time already was severely ill, and the instruction could only be properly sustained with effort.[530] But the peculiar attitudes of the Vernonburgers gradually eased, and when Boltzius was once again there to preach at the beginning of May 1747, he could report: "To my joy I perceived that the old residents, among whom I already conducted my office in various years, had set aside their old prejudices and dislike toward me, as though I had been too harsh toward them in my sermons, and now are devoted to me with all the more love."[531] From now on, Lutheran worship services from Ebenezer would be held in Vernonburg every two months.[532] Also, in the beginning of 1757, this community was beset by an itinerate "preacher:"

528. Strobel, *The Salzburgers and Their Descendants*, 240.
529. Named after the comptroller of the Trustees, Vernon.
530. 5A11:15, 55 = August 18, 1744 B. original.
531. UN May 2, 1747.
532. UN December 20, 1749.

"The imposter Carl Rudolf is now wreaking his havoc in Vernonburg as a self-made preacher accepted by some Lutheran and Reformed people. . . . He is a real annoyance."[533]

Between Vernonburg and Savannah lay Acton, likewise a German settlement,[534] that was cared for by Ebenezer in the same way as Vernonburg. On Sunday, after the Lutheran service, Zübli held the Reformed service.[535] Both pastors Boltzius and Zübli dedicated here on April 27, 1760, a newly built joint church for Lutherans and Reformed, for which Ottolenghe[536] in Savannah had gathered the collection. Lutheran services also took place here every two weeks,[537] and "Herr Pastor Zübli gives a sermon here every Wednesday, and every fourteen days he preaches on Sunday morning in this church, in which also the Germans from the neighboring plantations gather."[538]

Frederica

In order to give the necessary military strength to the southern-most point of the English land claims in Georgia against the Spanish, Oglethorpe, on March 8, 1736, had the land surveyed for the fort and town of Frederica on St. Simons Island at the mouth of the Altamaha River and quickly had them built.[539] Settlers of various nationalities, among them also several Palatines and Salzburgers from the third transport, were brought over, a strong garrison was established, and soon more ships called at Frederica than at Savannah; trade increasingly shifted away from Savannah,[540] and it almost seemed in the first years that Frederica should be the capital of the new colony.

Now the Spanish, on whose account all of this had been undertaken, did not long remain idle. The declaration of war followed on October 23,

---

533. TK32F11, 978 = journal February 11, 1757 B. original.
534. UN May 3, 1747.
535. UN May 3, 1747.
536. More detailed information about him than is to be compiled from the archives is given by Lawrence. Lawrence, "Religious Education of the Negro in the Colony of Georgia."
537. UN December 20, 1749.
538. UA April 27, 1760.
539. 4C1:67, 241 = July 30, 1744 Dr. original.
540. UN March 5, 1740; 5A2:11, 51 = February 15, 1740 B. copy; 5A10:15, 46 = October 14, 1741 B. original.

1739,[541] and then became alarmingly evident the vital lack of restraint of the troops and residents who had been thrown together. The Trustees initially summoned to the garrison there the Anglican minister Norris,[542] who was stationed in Savannah, since Whitefield was assigned to Savannah. But Norris only left very unhappily,[543] and his *contra sextum* [translator's note: against the Sixth Commandment] disorderly conduct was not suited for bringing discipline to the population of Frederica.[544]

But since Oglethorpe had had good experiences with the Halle pastors and a considerable number of Germans lived in Frederica, he asked Boltzius from Savannah on November 3, 1739, for a pastor from Halle.[545] The request was relayed, and on December 22, 1743, the Lutheran pastor Johann Ulrich Driessler entered Frederica[546] with a troop of Scottish soldiers and the Anglican pastor Bosomworth.[547]

He described his first impressions in the following report: "The town and fort are laid out regularly and in quarters, and one has to wonder that in so short of a time such large forests on which the place stands could be cleared and filled with so many houses.... At the four corners, large towers have been placed. Toward the east stands the gate at a small wall, toward the south the forest is left for protection and ventilation, toward the north is the camp or barracks of the soldiers, and toward the west we have the ocean by which the storehouses have been nicely built."[548] In this town, Driessler discovered sixty-two German speaking Lutherans.[549] Among them he now developed a very active work. His parsonage had on the ground floor a parlor, furnished with a stone floor, in which all of the worship services and

---

541. UN March 14, 1740.

542. UN May 23, 1739.

543. 5D6, 29 = journal July 31, 1739.

544. 5A10:2, 6 = April 8, 1741 B. original. The activity in Frederica of Charles Wesley, the brother of John Wesley, also was only of short duration. He had come with his older brother to Georgia (5D2 = journal June 11/19, 1736) and was employed in Frederica as Oglethorpe's *Secretarius* (5A3:29, 208) and also tended to the Lutheran community as much as possible. Jacobs, *History of the Evangelical Lutheran Church*, 184. Soon, however, he had a falling out with his superior and left the colony. Cooper, *The Story of Georgia* I, 274.

545. 5A7:64b, 271 and 274 = journal November 3 and 10, 1739 extract.

546. 4C1:67, 234 and 250 = July 30, 1744 Dr. original.

547. 4C1:67, 227 = July 30, 1744 Dr. original.

548. 4C1:67, 241.

549. 5D9, 1 = journal February 24, 1744; 5A11:24, 90 = February 24, 1744 B. original. Also Reformed, Swiss, and Württembergers lived there: 4C1:67, 246 = July 30, 1744 Dr. original, and 249, 4C1:71, 273–74 = April 10, 1745 letter Dr. copy.

classes were held; it was likewise his study. The private residence was in the half-floor above it.⁵⁵⁰

Moreover, the spiritual care of the Anglicans soon also came to Driessler. Apparently, Norris had again been removed, since Bosomworth had been called to Frederica. Yet things did not go much better with him since his behavior also aroused much offense.⁵⁵¹ In the summer of 1744, Driessler married him to the half-Indian Mary Musgrove who became famous in Georgia's history,⁵⁵² and soon they both moved to his and her plantations near Savanah so that he only seldom came to Frederica, where from among the approximately 1000 English, only about twenty attended his worship services. Therefore, the commander of Frederica, Major Horton, asked Driessler in writing⁵⁵³ soon after his arrival to take over also the English worship service and official acts, which is also what happened.⁵⁵⁴ Even when the Anglican pastor Zuberbühler arrived with Lemcke in Frederica on January 22, 1746, nothing changed in that regard, since Zuberbühler went to Savannah, and Bosomworth, who for some time had completely vanished, conducted his office neither in Savannah nor in Frederica. Therefore Driessler, at Major Horton's request, also continued to function as the Anglican pastor from Frederica, with a one-time interruption of a quarter year.⁵⁵⁵

In addition, he still had multiple sideline activities. He wrote, among other things, a "Church History in Frederica"⁵⁵⁶ that, unfortunately, has not been preserved, and translated the Lord's Prayer and several Bible passages into the language of the Cherokee Indians living around Frederica.⁵⁵⁷ Every week, he traveled twice to the plantations, some of which were thirty miles away, whose settlers would need to come to Frederica already on Saturdays for the Sunday worship service,⁵⁵⁸ until at the turn of the year 1744/45 a hut was erected halfway in between where he could instruct the children from the plantations.⁵⁵⁹

550. 4C1:67, 241 = July 30, 1744 Dr. original.
551. 5D9 = journal April 29, 1744; 5D12 = journal January 18, 1745; 5B1:24, 105 = November 23, 1748 B. original signature on the letter by another hand.
552. 4C1:67, 250 = July 30, 1744 Dr. original; UN July 28, 1749.
553. 4C1:76, 301 = February 17, 1746 Dr. copy.
554. 4C1:69, 258-59 = January 28, 1745 Dr. original.
555. 4C1:76, 295-301 = February 17, 1746 Dr. copy.
556. 4C1:67, 247 = July 30, 1744 Dr. original.
557. With a helper, probably Mary Musgrove (4C1:76, 302 = February 17, 1746 Dr. copy).
558. 4C1:71, 273 = April 10, 1745 Dr. original.
559. 4C1:69, 260 = January 28, 1745 Dr. original.

Life in this border and military town was indescribably turbulent. One day, when Driessler sat quietly in his room at the window, a shot suddenly flew by close to his head, and he received permanent scars on his face from the glass shards;[560] someone had only wanted to clean his musket. Another time, on Wednesday in Holy Week,[561] just when his wife lay very sick, the "bomb house" in the immediate vicinity sprang into the air with a terrifying noise: "We thought nothing else than that the world was going under,"[562] he reported. And even Boltzius realized, "He has great joy from the adults and children in his small congregation, but when he only looks out the window or hears what goes by on the street, he has great sorrow because of the great sins and disorders."[563]

These demoralizing circumstances and unhealthy climate contributed to the fact that Driessler died already in 1746.

In the following year, Frederica greatly declined, since it had fulfilled its purpose as an outpost. Many Germans moved away,[564] and a new commander, Colonel Heron, who was not known to Ebenezer, assumed duty. For a short time (1747), the Reformed pastor Zübli served here,[565] but he held no worship service in German.[566] In the summer of 1749, Colonel Heron sent two ships full of discharged soldiers to England,[567] went himself to Charleston at the end of the year,[568] and in 1751, Frederica was again abandoned to the forest.[569] The Lutherans had moved north, in part also to the area of Ebenezer.[570]

---

560. 4C1:67, 230 = July 30, 1744 Dr. original.

561. On March 21, 1744. According to Cooper, on March 22, 1743. Cooper, *The Story of Georgia* I, 255; at least the year is incorrect.

562. 4C1:67, 230

563. 5A11:23, 87 = December 29, 1744 B. original.

564. 1E9:9a, 32 = August 21, 1747 B. extract.

565. Hazelius, *History of the American Lutheran Church*, 101; Cooper, *The Story of Georgia* I, 447; Strobel, *The Salzburgers and Their Descendants*, 118.

566. Bittinger, *The Germans in Colonial Times*, 147.

567. UN July 3, 1749.

568. UN December 4, 1749.

569. Strobel, *The Salzburgers and Their Descendants*, 119.

570. UN September 26, 1750: the former soldier Dods and his wife. A few Palatines still lived in 1789 in the area around Frederica (1C30a:3 = January 12, 1789 Bm. original).

CONGREGATIONS IN SOUTH CAROLINA UNDER THE CARE OF GEORGIA

Purrysburg

About six miles from Ebenezer, on the opposite side of the Savannah River, lay the village of Purrysburg. It arose from the initiative of Jean Pierre Purry,[571] who came from Neuchatel and from 1732 brought there several ships with emigrants.[572] Most of them were Reformed Swiss whose number increased several years later through Reformed from Appenzell,[573] but three Lutheran families also were there already in spring 1734, and several more lived in the surrounding area.[574] For each emigrant group of 100 men, Purry received 400 pounds paid out by the English authorities and likely engaged in his enterprise mainly for this reason.[575] After the crossing, the settlers were left on their own and had to struggle with considerable difficulties.[576]

In American historical scholarship, Purrysburg is an example of a community of settlers disdainfully left in the lurch by the recruiter. Already before the first Lutherans came to Georgia, the ecclesiastical affairs here had been taken over by the justice of the peace, a Lutheran from the area around Berlin who was a former royal Prussian valet named Johann Holtzendorff,[577] who read from a postil on Sundays to his brethren in the faith.[578] He was replaced in 1735 by Schönmannsgruber, who also taught school for a while but already the next year moved to Pennsylvania.[579]

When Ebenezer then was founded, a close personal and spiritual relationship developed between the two places. There were intermarriages, several children from Purrysburg almost always attended the school in Ebenezer,[580] and, finally, people who wanted to get ahead relocated entirely

---

571. 5D1 = journal December 28, 1733 (new style).

572. Jacobs, *History of the Evangelical Lutheran Church*, 150.

573. 5A9:8, 36 = journal May 29, 1740 extract.

574. 5D1, 85 = journal March 19, 1734; 5D3, 121 = journal November 17, 1737.

575. More particular details in Bittinger, *The Germans in Colonial Times*, 121–23.

576. 5A3:6, 42 = March 28, 1735 G. original.

577. TK32F8, 704 = January 13, 1779 Tr. original.

578. 5D1, 85 = journal March 19, 1734; 5A3:58, 364; 5A9:8, 36 = journal May 25–26, 1740 extract.

579. Also Schmansgruber. 5D1 = journal September 3–4, and December 10, 1735; 5D2, 146 = journal April 26, 1736, 156 = journal May 3, 1736; 5A3:22, 150–51 = August 31, 1736.

580. 5D3, 48 = journal April 17, 1737. They mostly lived in the orphanage, occasionally also with families (5D4, 33 = journal February 10, 1738).

to Ebenezer, and these, understandably, were mostly very useful people. There were, for example, the brothers Ambrosius and Johann Jacob Zübli[581] from St. Gallen. Their older brother, David Zübli, the father of the Reformed pastor, arrived in Purrysburg after them on March 25, 1737[582] and had had the good fortune to inherit a plantation from a widow moving to Georgia.[583] But his brothers saw nothing from this blessing, and since they already had worked there occasionally since the founding of New Ebenezer,[584] they moved for good at the beginning of 1738 to this community[585] where they received "some assistance in their great poverty in which their brother in Purrisburg had rather unmercifully let them flounder."[586]

One of them was used as a "Preceptor,"[587] but since the spring of 1741, they both worked for daily wages in Savannah.[588] However Jacob, the younger brother, had an unstable disposition.[589] He went to Pastor Brunnholz at the Lutheran congregation in Germantown, Pennsylvania, and taught school there until the summer of 1747. Then he gave it up and wanted to learn to paint, but he died suddenly and left behind a pregnant, indolent wife.[590]

Another person who soon relocated to Ebenezer was the Lutheran "Master Theobald Kieffer from Purrysburg."[591] He wanted to move there already in August 1735,[592] however that did not come about so quickly due to the authorities, and so he remained where he was as a herdsman and planter but regularly attended the worship service at Ebenezer with his sons[593] and meanwhile looked after the ecclesiastical affairs of the Lutherans in Purrysburg.[594] In order to be closer to the teaching and worship services at Ebenezer, he undertook the effort to resettle and exchanged his land near Purrysburg with a plot upriver so that he now lived directly across from Ebenezer on the other side of the Savannah River. At the beginning of 1737 he

---

581. Also Zubli, Zubly, Züblin, Zieblin, Ziebely.
582. 5C4:70 = December 3, 1737.
583. 5B3:1, 2 and 1b, 2–3 = October 10, 1737 draft David Zübli.
584. 5D2:62 = journal February 25, 1736.
585. 5D4 = journal February 7, 1738.
586. 5A7:17, 66 = May 17, 1738 B. copy.
587. 5A7:721 = February 14, 1738 B. original.
588. 5D8, 459 = journal August 15, 1741.
589. 5D4, 54 = journal March 9, 1738.
590. UN May 20, 1748.
591. He consistently appears with this title and name of town.
592. 5D1 = journal August 6, 1735.
593. UN October 1, 1737.
594. 5A7:40, 174 = December 9, 1738 postscript G.

built the first cottage here.[595] However, this land was immersed almost to the height of a person from the spring flood, and only the roof was to be seen of the cottage in which, fortunately, his family did not yet live.[596] But that also happened from time to time to the settlers of Ebenezer. Later, his family and the families of his sons moved completely to Ebenezer, and Theobald Kieffer became here justice of the peace, captain of a militia company, and member of the House of Representatives of the General Assembly in Savannah, all voluntary.[597] Also, through his diligence he rendered outstanding service to Ebenezer. He was "an upright and faithful friend" of Boltzius, with whom he was about the same age.

When the Stamp Act became known in Georgia in fall 1765 and Boltzius admonished compliance, the rebellious element would have all too gladly contradicted him by force. But they did not dare it; instead they attacked his friend Kieffer. He was so badly beaten "in Savannah by wild rabble-rousers because of this matter that he soon died. It was actually meant for Boltzius."[598] His sons, quite worldly Americans not averse to a good spot of drink, signed the church order of Muhlenberg in 1775.[599]

A descendant of the upright Master Kieffer was the Reverend Ephraim Kieffer who, in a time of great need was appointed as pastor without theological study, diligently took care of the Lutherans around Ebenezer from 1849–1851.[600]

Ebenezer's ecclesiastical relationships also developed just as actively with the Lutheran families of Purrysburg as with Savannah. Boltzius and Gronau often went there with a fast, small boat that belonged to the community,[601] from time to time administered the Lord's Supper,[602] and were summoned for baptisms[603] and marriages.[604] But more often the Purrysburgers came to Ebenezer, and also to Zion, and almost without exception, several of them were there for all festivals, communion Sundays, and also regular Sundays.[605] That did not change even when in November

---

595. 5D3 = journal March 26, 1737.
596. 5D3 = journal March 7, 1737.
597. UA May 5, 1760.
598. 5B4:17, 50 = January 26, 1802 Bm. original.
599. Strobel, *The Salzburgers and Their Descendants*, 181.
600. Strobel, *The Salzburgers and Their Descendants*, 181.
601. UN August 11, 1734; 5D1 = journal September 30, 1735.
602. For example, UN December 4 and 7, 1734; 5D3 = journal February 2, 1737.
603. UN June 8, 1734, November 13, 1741.
604. UN June 9, 1735.
605. 5D2 = journal April 25 and November 7, 1736; 5D4 = journal May 21, 1738;

1734, Purry brought with him the French Reformed pastor Chiffelle,[606] who indeed held French and German worship services on alternating Sundays, yet he spoke no German and therefore on ordinary Sundays he read aloud the German translation of the Book of Common Prayer and a German sermon on festival Sundays.[607]

At Boltzius' instigation, in fall 1735 a school was established in Purrysburg on a trial basis which Holtzendorff was to conduct for two pounds per quarter.[608] His successor, as mentioned, was Schönmannsgruber, and after his departure, it was tried with the elderly Unselt,[609] but he was not really able to do it any longer, and the distances to the school were, in the long run, too far for the children, and so the matter was put completely to rest in the summer of 1737.[610]

But then, at the end of 1738, the Moravian pastor Peter Böhler[611] reported to Master Kieffer and offered to teach and preach without pay. He was accepted, and Gronau offered him his support. But even though he had given assurance of being Lutheran,[612] he and the Moravian Schulius, with whom together he gave instruction, did not use at all Luther's Small Catechism but only "a small hymnal printed in Amsterdam."[613] But their activity also came to an end already again in 1740. Schulius died from a fever on July 24, 1739, despite being treated by the physician Thilo from Ebenezer,[614] and Böhler went to the Moravians in Pennsylvania. He believed that he would be more useful there, since "H[err] Whitefield wants to establish a Negro school there; perhaps he wants to be the schoolmaster, since he could accomplish nothing in South Carolina."[615]

For a time, Purrysburg even had its own German Reformed pastor: the elderly Swiss Zoberbiller.[616] The Swiss emigrants from Appenzell who

---

UN March 14, 1742.

606. UN November 22, 1734; Gronau performed his marriage ceremony: 5D4, 8 = journal February 5, 1738.

607. 5D3, 121 = journal November 17, 1737.

608. 5D1 = journal September 3–4, 1735.

609. His family moved to Ebenezer after his death.

610. 5A3:57, 358–59 = July 29, 1737 B. original.

611. See p. 211.

612. 5A7:40, 174 = December 9, 1738 postscript G.

613. An excerpt from the hymnal of the Moravian Brethren (5A7:53, 226 = journal May 13, 1739 extract).

614. 5D6, 31 = journal July 1739.

615. 5A9:8, 36a and 37 = journal May 29, 1740 extract.

616. In contrast to his son Bartholomäus Zuberbühler, his name is consistently written this way in the archives. (The name of the son in the English literature:

arrived in South Carolina in the spring of 1737 had taken him[617] on in Rotterdam as their chaplain and obtained for him from London the "episcopal confirmation." But then they did not want him any longer, and when the Appenzellers went to Purrysburg,[618] Zoberbiller set off to New Windsor and Savannahtown[619] (upstream on the Savannah River in South Carolina). His wife died here on June 27, 1737, a daughter eight days later, and soon afterwards yet another,[620] so that in May 1738 he moved to Purrysburg where his third daughter lived.[621] Here, he delivered rather appealing sermons but, unfortunately, died already in November 1738.[622] His son, the Reformed theology student Bartholomäus Zuberbühler,[623] was already in America before his father in 1736. He had wanted to return right away to Germany when he heard about the imminent arrival of the Swiss.[624] He therefore remained and directed the surveying of the envisioned settlement of New Windsor next to Savannahtown, South Carolina.[625]

After the death of his father, he preached for a while in Purrysburg and at the end of 1739 went, at Oglethorpe's wish, to Pallachocolas, South Carolina, as preacher and reader.[626] Ebenezer's pastors were asked to support him and to give reports about him.[627] But probably in September 1741, Zuberbühler asked Oglethorpe for appointment as Reformed minister in Savannah, and Oglethorpe inquired about him from Boltzius who wrote that he was too little acquainted with him, but he did not write that Zuberbühler,

---

Zouberbuhler; Gräbner, *Geschichte der Lutherischen Kirche in America*," part I, 567: Zauberbühler). He was related to the Helffenstein family living in Ebenezer (5A9:8, 36 = journal May 29, 1740 extract).

617. With his wife and three daughters.

618. 5D3, 54-55 = journal April 29, 1737.

619. Gräbner incorrectly states, "Savannah." Gräbner, *Geschichte der Lutherischen Kirche in America*, part I, 567.

620. 5D4, 172 = journal July 11, 1737; 5A9:8, 36 = journal May 29, 1740 extract.

621. 5D4, 129 = journal May 21-22, 1738.

622. 5A7:40, 174 = December 9, 1738 postscript G. original; 5D4, 371 = journal December 9, 1738. The two sons of his third daughter went to school in Ebenezer. When her husband had died, she was soon married again by the justice of the peace in Purrysburg, Captain Lindner (5A9:8, 36 = journal May 29, 1740 extract; 5D8, 417 = journal July 31, 1741). The name of her new husband is unknown.

623. See pp. 106-107, n. 616.; various spellings in accordance with the archives. Also used are the forms Zoberbüller and Zoberbieler.

624. 5D2, 52 = journal February 19, 1736.

625. 5D4, 129 = journal May 21-22, 1738.

626. Oglethorpe's private property near the border with Georgia, occupied with several Swiss from New Windsor.

627. 5A7:64b, 271 = journal November 3, 1739 extract.

in his view, understood the preaching office as a means of making money.[628] The Trustees of Georgia spoke up for his appointment; he went to England and was ordained as an Anglican pastor on November 11, 1745.[629] Together with Pastor Lemcke, he returned to Georgia where he landed on January 22, 1746, off of Frederica,[630] and from then on resided in Savannah. He died in mid-December 1766.[631]

Not until the summer of 1759 did Purrysburg again receive a Reformed, German-French pastor, Abraham Immer,[632] who came from the Swiss canton of Bern. The close relationships between Purrysburg and Ebenezer that had existed in the early years of both settlements already had noticeably faded around this time, since after the migrations of the Germans to Georgia and the German Reformed Appenzellers to New Windsor, South Carolina, the French Reformed element in Purrysburg became more and more decisive.[633]

Charleston

When the first Salzburgers landed in Charleston in March 1734, they found already a number of Lutherans, among them even two Palatines, who either were emigrants from 1709 and later who scattered to the south or came from Purry's transports.[634] Boltzius preached and celebrated the Lord's Supper with them. As already mentioned, there were also here numerous Reformed who mostly attended the Lutheran worship service since they had no pastor of their own, but the Lutheran congregation was somehow, but continuously, provided with pastors, even if sometimes poorly.

---

628. 5D8, 519-20 = journal September 26, 1741, 596-97 = journal November 9, 1741. At the end of February 1743, he attempted, fraudulently, with fake powers of attorney and shady companions, to oust the preacher Giessendanner from Orangeburg but did not succeed. Gräbner, *Geschichte der Lutherischen Kirche in America,*" part I, 567-68.

629. Cooper states that his ordination took place on November 1st, not November 11th. Cooper, *The Story of Georgia* I, 277 n. 1. Lawrence, states that the ordination took place on November 11th. Lawrence, "Religious Education of the Negro in the Colony of Georgia," 501, n. 11.

630. 4C1:76, 295 = February 17, 1746 Dr. copy; 5D11, 21.

631. Lawrence, "Religious Education of the Negro in the Colony of Georgia," 50.

632. At the end of 1760, he visited Boltzius in Ebenezer who was very impressed by his erudition and his affable manner (UA December 2, 1760).

633. UN June 20, 1742.

634. 5D10 = travel journal May 26, 1734 B; probably resident here since Queen Anne's grant in South Carolina.

The further care of Charleston by Ebenezer's pastors, as with Savannah, was bound to travel for official business that, however, occurred much more sporadically here.

In the early years, Gronau was sometimes there for the worship service that he held in a private residence. However, he was always glad when he could return to quiet Ebenezer.[635] Here, it was quickly noticed that regular visits to Charleston could not be undertaken because of the great distance of 130 miles. The connection practically went dormant, and when Boltzius once again went there in 1753, he found no organized Lutheran congregation.[636] In the archival material nothing is discovered again before 1774 when the "German Lutheran St. John's Church and Congregation in and about Charlestown in South Carolina," officially founded in the meantime, did not turn toward Ebenezer, since Rabenhorst and Triebner were causing havoc there, but to Muhlenberg in Pennsylvania to obtain a Lutheran pastor.

It is discovered in doing so that in June 1767, the Lutheran pastor Johann Severin Hahnbaum had come to Charleston, but "only lived a couple of years; during his illness a young student, by the name of [Friedrich] Daser, from Württemberg, came here without testimony and credentials."[637] With the approval of the congregational elders he became vicar and married Hahnbaum's daughter. When her father died, Daser was engaged as preacher for three years, but he conducted himself so negligently that the well-to-do in the congregation wanted to be rid of him, but the others wanted to retain him. Finally, he wanted to travel to London to have himself ordained by the Lord-Bishop, and there was certainly joy that he was going.

Then he noticed that he did not have any money for it and wanted to stay, whereupon the congregation turned to Muhlenberg for help. He drafted for them a long letter of request in English from the congregational elders to Pasche in London for a Lutheran pastor, in which his salary was fixed, and it was stipulated that he should relate to Pennsylvania but not to Georgia.[638] But Europe sent no one, so that in 1777, Muhlenberg sent to Charleston Pastor Christian Streit who had been envisioned possibly for Ebenezer. He was born in Easton, Pennsylvania, into the large family of the city council member and elder of the Bedminster community L. Streit. He understood English better than German and was a respected pastor in the town of his

---

635. 5A3:6, 42 = March 8, 1735 B. original; 5A3:56, 347 = August 29, 1737 G. copy.

636. Gräbner, *Geschichte der Lutherischen Kirche in America,*" part I, 572.

637. Gräbner, *Geschichte der Lutherischen Kirche in America,*" part I, 574; Daser came from Swabia.

638. 4C17:20, 295–97 = October 6 and October 22, 1774 M copy to Pasche. Friedrich Wilhelm Pasche, 1728–July 11, 1792 (J I, 88).

birth. In 1773, he applied for a position in Germantown, Pennsylvania, but was declined[639] and remained in Easton[640] until later summer 1776. Since he was unmarried,[641] he moved at the end of August 1776 to Virginia to take over a position as chaplain with the 8th Regiment stationed there, for which Muhlenberg issued to him a letter of accreditation.[642] On April 19, 1777, he appeared again with Muhlenberg, and shortly thereafter went to Charleston to the Lutheran congregation. Here, he was duly installed in 1778.[643] But the events of war drove him away again. In fact, Charleston had become republican on May 12, 1780, but in July 1782, he was again with Muhlenberg in Pennsylvania[644] and went to the town of New Hanover.[645]

Now the congregation in Charleston resorted again to Daser,[646] but his stay, for reasons already known, was not long, so that the congregation now put into effect the plan that already had been formulated before Streit's arrival:[647] they called again the elderly pastor Johann Nikolaus Martin, who already at one time had been a pastor in Charleston from November 1763[648] but in the meantime had been living in the country. Probst, who met him in Charleston in December 1786, reported about him that he "is a true disgrace on the office and Christianity, for he is wild, insolent, and never sober."[649] But anyone familiar with Probst's lamenting style, and keeping in mind the impression that the American post-war affairs must have made on a newly arriving European, will rightly understand this judgment.

639. 4C17:9, 99,106,128 journal spring 1774 M referring to events of the preceding year.

640. The place is also written as "Eastton."

641. 4C17:9, 123.

642. 4H23, 133 = journal August 23, 1776 M.

643. TK32F1a, 32 = September 16, 1780 M; copy of the original from October 31, 1778. Triebner reports that Muhlenberg had promised to Rabenhorst's party in 1777 to send a preacher to Ebenezer and even in the same year recommended Streit who had been called from Charleston "by the eminent Ebenezer community council." But, apparently, he did not assume his office here (5B3:35, 148 = May 22, 1788 Tr. original).

644. 4H26, 71–72 = journal April 9,10,11, 1783 M; 4H24, 162 = journal June 12, 1780 M. Moreover, there had been differences in Charleston between Streit and Daser (5B3:21, 90 = December 6, 1786 Probst).

645. 4H25, 122 = journal June 23, 1782 M.

646. 5B4:17, 54 = January 26, 1802 Bm. original.

647. 4C17:20, 295 = October 6, 1774 M. copy.

648. Gräbner, *Geschichte der Lutherischen Kirche in America*, part I, 574. He was an educated bookbinder (4C17:20, 295). As a strict republican, he declined to pray for the King; consequently, he was dismissed and dispossessed of his property (Qualben, *The Lutheran Church in Colonial* America, 267).

649. 5B3:21, 89 = December 6, 1786 Probst original.

The Lutheran church in Georgia owes much thanks to the congregation in Charleston, since it was its pastor, Dr. John Bachman, who came to Georgia after Pastor Bergmann's death in 1824 and, with a strong hand, preserved the remnant of the devastated communities from collapse.[650]

---

650. Strobel, *The Salzburgers and Their Descendants*, 252.

4

The Development of the Communities in the Organization of Their Life

CONSTITUTION AND REGULATION

The Legal Status

DURING THE TIME UNDER consideration, there were in Georgia four legal forms of the Lutheran communities that, in part, differentiated themselves in their importance from the forms with the same name in other colonies or states of North America. First, in the beginning of community-building there is the type of settlement with a partial or predominantly Lutheran population. One such "community" comprised all Lutheran residents; it possessed no organizational form, and therefore also featured no legal entity and stood in no relationship with an ecclesiastical umbrella organization such as a synod. As in other regions of the United States, especially at the beginning of the great "westward movement" in the first third of the nineteenth century, these "congregations" in Georgia were visited—not regularly—by itinerate clergy, and congregants came from far off.

In Georgia, however, Lutheran communities of this type remained for only a short time in this loose relationship, often scarcely for a year, since they developed into the second type: they elected congregational wardens, and in doing so gave themselves an initial organizational form. As a rule, they also established their own school and even built a small church, all, however, without recording their members in a list. Communities of this type in Georgia were, for example, Abercorn, Acton, Josephstown, Savannah, and Vernonburg, but these also did not last for very long.

The third type represented a further stage, a partial or completely Lutheran settlement with its own pastor (and elected community representatives), yet with only the partial character of a legal entity. For example, if the state were to give land, then this land must be assigned to a designated person representing the community.[1] With this type of community a distinction is to be made with regard to the payment of the pastor and the expenses of the community between

> a. such as those whose pastor was to be paid by a "patron," as was envisioned in Frederica with Oglethorpe,
>
> b. such as those that started with regular payments from Europe but additionally with voluntary yet consistent contributions in the form of church taxes (to which type Ebenezer belonged until the end of English rule), and
>
> c. such as those that themselves defrayed all expenses, even the pastors' salaries, through fixed contributions, as was the case in Savannah, where the Lutherans also contributed to the salary of Zübli, and in Ebenezer immediately after the Revolutionary War.

Finally, there follows the fourth, the type of an incorporated Lutheran congregation with the full rights of a legal entity. Only in this stage was a congregation "established." For Georgia, this is known from the archival material only to be the case for the German Lutheran community of Ebenezer that, after the arrival of Bergmann, was confirmed by the government in Georgia in a "Charter of Incorporation of the Eben Ezer Church and its dependencies" as a German religious society.[2] The interesting reason for this late date will be discussed later.

Compared to the other states of North America there were, therefore, fully valid congregations in Georgia only after the war. However, this paradox already makes clear that the standard terms for this set of issues have another content, as has been said, for Georgia and its particular situation. If one were to transpose them from the other states, one could speak of a "Lutheran Church" here only from 1860, since in this year the founding of an actual synod happened. Yet that would not be justified, since in the time frame treated here, the cooperative work of the Lutheran pastors (also with

---

1. In Ebenezer, for example, Boltzius, Lemcke, and Johann Flörl.
2. 5B4:10, 45 = November 23, 1801 Bm. Original.

Driessler) could not have been closer, even in a "synod." In addition, the pastors active in the Ebenezer District regularly held a conventicle every week that was a synod except in name. A purely legalistic understanding of the word "church" in our context would therefore do justice neither to the Lutheran concept of church nor to the actual state of affairs.

The Lutheran congregations in and around Ebenezer and their pastors[3] represent yet another peculiarity within the framework of the Lutheran church in the United States: they were under the Anglican Church. That is, before Samuel Urlsperger began to gather the first emigrants, he obtained the assurance that they, even if they would be subjects of Great Britain, could retain their Lutheran confession. Even more remarkable was the case with their pastors: they were Lutheran clergy employed and paid by the SPCK. A similar case existed with the clergy at the German court chapel in London who likewise as Lutherans were under the Anglican bishop of London who appointed and confirmed them. The SPCK, the governing authority of the Lutheran pastors of Georgia, nonetheless never approached them with any spiritual or legal instruction in the time under consideration. The only connection consisted in the fact that the pastors sent in annual reports, and the SPCK paid the salaries of the pastors, as well as in the beginning they intervened with the Trustees concerning Ebenezer's economic interests. Therefore, the Lutheran pastors were in no way servants of the Anglican Church since they were not, as was Zuberbühler, ordained by a bishop, but a point had been made in Germany that they were to be ordained by a Lutheran consistory before their sending.

In Georgia, not much was understood about these provisional relationships. It was seen that the pastors received Anglican salary, they wore Anglican vestments,[4] and Driessler even held Anglican worship services. Thus, to outsiders, the Lutheran congregations largely seemed to be Anglican ones that only had the privileges of certain special rites and the use of the German language. Along with the fact that, except for the Anglican Church, no other religious community in the English possessions could be "established," this explains why, from this unsettled situation, the actively working Lutheran congregations were not officially "established" until the end of British rule in Georgia.

The lack of a legal determination became evident again in real estate transactions. When the New Jerusalem Church was built, the church elder Wertsch addressed a petition to the colonial government in Savannah to give to the community the land upon which this church and the two parsonages

---

3. With the exception of Rabenhorst and Bergmann, and probably also of Driessler.
4. With the exception of Rabenhorst; see also p. 196.

stood, buildings that belonged to the community. The request was granted, but to the great astonishment of the members of the community it was stated in the deed of donation that the buildings and land in question are "granted to the jurisdiction of the Church of Engeland [sic]"[5] and to the Ebenezer community, "according to the rights and ceremonies of the Church of Engelland [sic],"[6] but not to the "Congregation in and about Eben Ezer according to the Augustan Confession and Liturgy,"[7] as had been wished, or "for the holding of evangelical Lutheran worship services by missionaries from the Revered Society in London according to the Augsburg confession of faith."[8]

Oversight or intentional? Muhlenberg, who made the effort to have this passage corrected, discovered during his stay in Savannah from the "President of the Royal Council, Esq. Habersham,"[9] that there actually had been inclinations in Savannah to annex Ebenezer to the Anglican Church so that the disastrous conflict between Rabenhorst and Triebner could have been mediated by a constituted authority.[10]

Little favorable light in this connection falls on Rabenhorst who, at the dedication of the church, tried to persuade Triebner "concerning the great utility and better appearance among the English if we would merge or join with them," and Triebner believed that Rabenhorst had brought about the misunderstanding of the grant.[11] Triebner deserves the credit, regardless of his motives, for averting this acute danger of the Anglicanization of the Lutheran congregation. Only new legislation after 1783, when the Anglican Church was no longer the state church in Georgia, brought final clarity to this imprecisely formulated legal situation.

In this connection, we must also take a look at the legal side of the relationship of Georgia's Lutheran communities to the "Fathers" in Halle and Augsburg. An already lingering malady in the congregations of Ebenezer and its neighboring locations was that they were regarded until the War of Independence as mission stations of the SPCK. Even more calamitous was that they also fell into financial debt with Germany. In the beginning, Urlsperger had only the right granted to him by the SPCK to appoint a pastor for Georgia (Ebenezer or Frederica) for each new instance. When the work

5. TK32F1b, 148 = journal February 4, 1775 M.
6. 5B3:36, 153 = July 23, 1788 Tr. original.
7. TK32F1b, 148.
8. 5B3:36, 153–54.
9. TK32F1b, 168 = journal February 10, 1775 M.
10. TK32F1b, 168–69 = journal February 10, 1775 M.
11. 5B3:36, 152–53 = July 23, 1788 Tr. original.

became too great in the area under the care of Ebenezer, he sent there, at his own initiative, Rabenhorst, whose salary he secured through proceeds from a fund collected by him with which the third preacher's plantation was established. The fund remained under the proprietorship of Urlsperger so that the communities were made dependent on him. But it is to be noted to their credit that there was no lack of effort to free themselves from this paternalism. Rabenhorst, as well as Treutlen, tried repeatedly to repay to Germany the capital of the third preacher's plantation and to transfer the establishment to the community property of Ebenezer, as well as to arrange its income in such a way that all of the pastors could be paid from it and forgo the pay from the SPCK.

However, these efforts were persistently thwarted by Triebner. They signaled, allegedly, a malicious detachment from the "Fathers" in Europe and amounted to an alteration in the relationships on the basis of which he was called. Such conduct naturally led the short-sighted younger Urlsperger again and again to Triebner's side, which he knew only too well. It is characteristic of Muhlenberg's foresightedness that during his attempts to mediate the pastors' dispute he uttered not a syllable on these questions. His expected position would have created much resentment toward him from the Fathers in Europe.

One of the worst consequences of that dependence was that there was no way for Ebenezer to refuse to accept Triebner's call. Here, the negative consequence can be noticed that the Directors of the Francke Foundations in Halle had no rights in connection with Ebenezer but only an advisory voice. The unrest with Triebner as well as with Probst would then have been able to be avoided since Halle was not in agreement with the appointment of both because their character already was known there. Nonetheless, there arose from the unencumbered nature of this relationship a much closer connection between the pastors of Ebenezer and Frederica with Halle than with Augsburg. Moreover, in Georgia the always most eagerly anticipated medicines and books were received from Halle but demands for payment of debt from Augsburg. For that reason, once Ebenezer's community board of directors had received Bergmann from Urlsperger, it was no longer interested in a further connection with the Senior from Augsburg.[12]

While insufficient foresight in these questions caused much harm here, attempts at the emancipation of the communities were clearly and effectually in Ebenezer's church constitutions, which are to be considered in the following.

---

12. 5B4:17, 51 = January 26, 1802 Bm. original.

The Church Constitution

The unity of church and state was familiar to Georgia's first Lutherans both from Germany and from England. Several particular problems resulted from it. In every settlement where the Lutheran element prevailed, "secular affairs" also had to be taken on. This was naturally the case in Ebenezer, but also in the plantations around Zion Church, in Bethany, Goshen, Abercorn, and Vernonburg.[13] Since here, with few exceptions, church community and settlement community coincided, all of their regulatory entities had a two-sided function, all the way up to the pastors, which of course most evidently and consequentially had an impact in Ebenezer.

Boltzius, and after him foremost Rabenhorst, had to exercise along with their spiritual office the full functions of a mayor and of the economic leader of the community enterprises. That meant not only a detrimental burden of time but most of all a not unforeseeable danger to the impartiality of the conduct of their office, not to mention clearly potential misuses of the spiritual office. It went so far that Oglethorpe offered to remove from Ebenezer all of the people who were out of favor with the pastors. Only the highly sensitive conscience of a Boltzius could resist this in the long run. But even here things did not unfold without malicious gossip, and one man who could not deal at all with the joining of both offices was Rabenhorst. Every possible negative side of the binding of church and state was played out in miniature in Ebenezer. As already has become clear in numerous examples, Boltzius from the beginning looked after the economic affairs of his community. Yet after a quarter year it was already necessary that he regularly discussed these matters with the men of Ebenezer. For the first time on June 14, 1734, he had them meet for a "conference" and kept a "conference book."[14] This meeting from then on was held each week, mostly on Friday at midday.[15] Francke, who was informed about it, emphatically approved, since there was no other secular authority in Ebenezer.[16]

There soon emerged from this body, when Commissioner Vat organized the community watch, four men who were elected by the community. They had to take over the local watch and to help Boltzius with the temporal and spiritual governance of the community, for which purpose the ongoing weekly conference served.[17]

---

13. Frederica had an English town commandant, and the seat of government was in Savannah.
14. UN June 14, 1734.
15. 5D4, 64 = March 17, 1738.
16. 5A1:52, 264 = March 14, 1735.
17. 5D3 = journal February 19, 1737.

Naturally, however, all directives and undertakings came from Boltzius, and he realized very soon that he sat between two chairs in these functions. Already in the summer of 1737, he endeavored to rid himself of secular matters since the dissatisfaction and the resulting malicious gossip of several people had a disruptive impact on his spiritual duty.[18] However, the opposite happened. Oglethorpe issued to him and Gronau a power of attorney to exercise the judiciary in Ebenezer and in the areas belonging to it;[19] that is, they were justices of the peace,[20] although Boltzius had to handle the work. He had to attend to everything, be it surveying, home construction, obtaining provisions, the sale of crops, raw silk, or boards as well as for the construction of the mills, and so on. He was thoroughly aware of the danger connected with this, and he had repeatedly asked in London for an extra mayor for Ebenezer, who, however, could not also be paid, and so the situation remained as it was.

Certainly, it would not have been easy to find someone who could have gotten along so well with Boltzius as the unassuming Gronau. Gronau had managed the money for the church and orphanage, and so after his death, Boltzius' range of duties had increased to the point that he recommended the surgeon Mayer as "justice of the peace and administrator of external matters." On December 15, 1747, at a gathering of the residents in the Zion Church, he entered his office,[21] for which the community paid him with wood and grain,[22] until he was confirmed in September 1748 as justice of the peace by the Trustees with a parchment power of attorney.[23]

But there were also too many inconveniences connected with it for him, not least of all, the constant trips to Savannah. On May 2, 1750, he resigned from the office, and so it fell anew to Boltzius[24] who considered a new arrangement. Fourteen days later, on May 25, 1750, he reported, "I had the whole community [which naturally involved the men] meet together. . . . I divided all of the residents in and next to the town and on the plantations into seven districts or quarters, and in each district I appointed a supervisor, under the customary English name of tithingman. . . . They will confer from time to time with their people in their particular districts over

---

18. 5D3 = journal June 4, 1737.
19. UN March 7, 1739.
20. 1E9:9a, 32 = August 21, 1737 B. extract.
21. Oversight over the mills and the sale of lumber.
22. UN December 15, 1747.
23. They even paid him 20 pounds for it (UN September 30, 1748). Other justices of the peace were Johann Flörl, Theobald Kieffer, and Pastor Rabernhorst.
24. UN May 2, 1750.

secular things and the improvement of their sustenance, and I, in turn, with them."[25] Boltzius already did that at a time when the civil government had not thought at all about the division of districts.

If the direction in secular administration came from the English example, it did as well in the ecclesiastical. As in the Anglican Church, the election was held on Easter Monday for the vestry with church wardens, also called trustees (elders) and deacons, or church and community supervisors, were named. Both bodies, together with the pastors, formed the church council (*Kirchenrat*), in which the older of the pastors presided.[26]

Specific properties, such as the mills or the glebe land, were handed over to the trustees for administration, while the office of the deacon found its establishment in a particular charter: the church constitution. Strobel reports the following concerning it:

> It was required of the pastors and each member of the congregation to subscribe to the "Augsburg Confession" and the "Symbolical Books," and to submit to a code of regulations drawn up by the Rev. Samuel Urlsperger of Augsburg, Rev. Frederick M. Zeigenhagen [sic] of London, and Rev. Gotthelf [sic] Augustus Francke of Halle. These regulations were prepared in 1733, and continued in force, with some few alterations, (which were made principally by Dr. Muhlenberg, in 1774,) until 1843.[27]

Indeed, the pastors pledged themselves in accordance with their calls to the Augsburg Confession and the other confessional writings, but there is no mention about a signing of these books by the members of the community. It is not at all evident from the sources under consideration whether a copy of the confessional writings was even available to them. There has now been found in the archives a German version of that "code of regulations," the first Lutheran church order of Georgia, the wording of which is added to this investigation as Appendix I.[28]

Several things are to be noted, also in comparison of this text with the English translation rendered by Strobel.

1. Instead of the preamble, in the case of Strobel,[29] the manuscript features the introductory sentence: "In the good judgment of the vestrymen, or

25. UN May 25, 1750; 5B1:37, 152.
26. TK32F1b, 58 = journal December 24, 1774 Muhlenberg.
27. Strobel, *The Salzburgers and Their Descendants*, 93.
28. TK32F11, 1043 a.b.c.–1044; in Strobel in English. Strobel, *The Salzburgers and Their Descendants*, 94–99.
29. Text: "In the name of God: The fundamental constitution, articles, and rules upon which a German Evangelical Lutheran congregation was formally established,

of the duly elected church elders (*Kirchen Vorsteher*), the following is made known to the Christian community." Church elders were elected at the earliest in 1735/36. But they could only be designated with the English term several years later when the community members, some of whom in the beginning could not read at all and therefore were cheated with paper money,[30] had become somewhat accustomed to English. There can therefore be no mention of the implementation of the church constitution in 1733. At the same time, the authorship of the "Fathers in Europe" is made doubtful by the introductory sentence of the manuscript.

2. Two sentences of the fourth part, second paragraph, originally stood in the manuscript in the reverse order. The Strobel text emerges from cross-outs, footnotes, and changes in wording.[31] It involves an insertion in a quotation of the London church order that takes account of Ebenezer's special circumstances and whose placement was carefully considered by the drafter, that is, by the writer.

3. In place of Strobel's concluding sentence that is missing in the manuscript,[32] it is stated here: "In the first gathering of the congregation, it must be stipulated, among other things, whether the church elders, on the Sundays when Holy Communion is administered, wish to abide with the collection and gathering of offering as intended in no. 9, or, as has been customary until now, namely, that each person places his gift in the box that has been placed." The practice "that each time at the administration of the Lord's Supper the bowls would be placed at both church doors" for the collection first arose in 1753.[33] The sentence further shows that the church constitution only began to be discussed around this time.

---

upon the basis of the Holy Bible, our Augsburg Confession, (and the other Symbolical Books,) since the year 1733, in and about Ebenezer, in His Great Britannic Majesty's province of Georgia; and which were unanimously approved, confirmed, and unalterably determined upon, under hand and seal, by the reverend founders, viz. Messrs. Samuel Urlsperger, Frederick Michael Zeigenhagen, Gotthelf Augustus Francké, most worthy members of the venerable society in England, instituted for the promotion of the knowledge of Christ; together with the first ministers, elders, deacons, and regular church members, His Great Britannic Protestant Majesty's faithful subjects." Strobel, *The Salzburgers and Their Descendants*, 94.

30. UN May 17, 1735.

31. Originally, "Mäβiges Schul Geld," now "einiges Schul Geld."

32. "to these establishments may God, who is a God of order, add his heavenly grace, for the sake of Jesus Christ! Amen."

33. UA July 1753.

The Development of the Communities in the Organization of Their Life

4. The place of the undated manuscript in the fascicle that is often informative even if, of course, not absolutely certain, indicates the year 1755. That is not to be rejected out of hand since at that time affairs in Ebenezer had developed so far and had become so much looser in comparison to those of the beginning period that they required legal definition, and only after Georgia had become a royal province in 1752 were several legal regulations made in Ebenezer.[34] The preamble reproduced by Strobel also alludes to this time with the formulation: "His Great Britannic Majesty's Province of Georgia;" the Trustees are no longer mentioned. With the date of church constitution being determined for this time, it becomes evident why not the slightest mention of it occurs in the correspondence of those years. It was the time of the friction between Boltzius, Lemcke, and Rabenhorst. The entire correspondence of these years was withdrawn in Halle and has not been completely preserved.

After these clarifications, the Strobel preamble is understood thusly: The church constitution does not originate from 1733 but only from the period around 1755. It was not composed by Francke, Urlsperger, and Ziegenhagen but by Ebenezer's church council; that means in the actual state of things, by Boltzius. But since the community already to this point had these three men to thank for much advice, they sent it to Europe for review, and the "Fathers" "endorsed it, confirmed it, and adopted it unalterably... with signature and seal."[35] And so arises out of what has been said the sensational realization that we have before us in this discovered manuscript originating from Boltzius' own hand the German original of Georgia's first Lutheran church constitution.

In the material that has been dealt with there is to be found, unfortunately, no copy of the church constitution that Muhlenberg drafted and introduced in Ebenezer in 1775, although he, as did Boltzius previously, sent a copy to Europe for evaluation. Also, in America, the constitution that was in force until 1843, and which was still available to Strobel, has been lost, so that one is dependent upon its English "extract" translation.[36] Accordingly, no repetition of its content is required here. It should only be noted that Muhlenberg probably left it intact and inserted it as the first part in his church constitution.[37] The necessity of the church tax that is exten-

---

34. For example, the determination of the glebe lands, the establishment of the third preacher's plantation.

35. Strobel, *The Salzburgers and Their Descendants*, 94, Preamble.

36. Strobel, *The Salzburgers and Their Descendants*, 167–79.

37. Strobel's supposition: "It has been stated that this was the original discipline,

sively established in it, the manner of paying the pastors, and the various duties of the deacon were only briefly, if generally, indicated in the part that, according to Strobel, originated with Muhlenberg. It is important to note further that it was first possible for the Ebenezer community, on the basis of the Muhlenberg church constitution, to remove Triebner from his office.[38] Previously, he had been unimpeachably appointed by the SPCK.

It may seem remarkable that the church constitutions otherwise made no appearance at all in the life of the community. But this shows precisely that they had fulfilled their purpose. On the basis of their stipulations, many things in the community ran well and quietly,[39] and it was also the case here as with every good church order; it is only noticed when it is not there.

The Finances

As already reported, the SPCK paid the salaries for two pastors, as long as Georgia was British. However, these were so small—fifty pounds[40] for the first pastor and thirty pounds for the second per year—that they could not get by, especially since all those in question had large families. Urlsperger's efforts for salary increases remained unsuccessful,[41] and so they relied on charitable gifts from Europe that, to be sure, came in a certain measure and, all together, constituted many times over what the SPCK raised, but upon which one could not count. While the community, therefore, was not burdened with the pastors' salaries during the colonial period, they nonetheless in time had considerable expenses for an entire array of their facilities which no longer could be defrayed from the more sparingly flowing gifts from Europe, so the communities were called upon for free-will offerings, but they would not be sufficient.

For that reason, the church constitution stipulated that community members, through their signature, should obligate themselves for the payment of a regular, assured contribution; non-payment meant expulsion from the community. But even this was not adequate, because the amount

---

subsequently amended by Dr. Muhlenberg in 1774. It is impossible to state to what extent it was altered, but that Dr. Muhlenberg made some additions to it, and changed several of the articles, cannot be questioned." *The Salzburgers and Their Descendants*, 99–100.

38. Until they, in keeping with the church constitution, had requested and received further counsel from Europe (when he had fallen under suspicion of adultery).

39. The church tax, the dismissal of Triebner, pastoral care of the various communities, elections, and so on.

40. About 830 goldmark.

41. 5A1:31.

of the contribution was left open. For that reason, Ebenezer's seven church elders and the two in Bethany gathered at the beginning of July 1760 and "resolved, that all hearers retain their own pews [in the church] and choose others that please them, and also design and have them specially adapted, for which they might pay the carpenter and give a donation to the church. However, all of this uncoerced. These pews, after the passing of the owner, go to the church, and the relatives or others who subsequently wish to occupy them, must redeem them with a small gratuity."[42]

There was an additional source of income: the occasional services. "What the Englanders pay for them (usually) ten schillings or less, are entered in my community account and are used for exigency in the community. On the other hand, what our residents pay for weddings, baptisms, and funerals (which is only a little) is placed in the church treasury, in which also comes the offering from the communicants every six weeks, and each time does not amount to an entire Pf. Sterling."[43] But from Rabenhorst we hear the well-worn song, when they are supposed to give something, "it is unbelievably difficult, even among those who are well off in their sustenance; the money is always scarce even among those who have sufficient valuables."[44]

During the war, nothing at all came in,[45] and afterwards nothing much at first could be expected from the impoverished people, yet along with the salary for Bergmann contributions for the church and school were also raised.[46] How the situation of the church treasury fundamentally improved, among other ways through the sale of landholdings that were no longer needed, has already been explained.

WORSHIP SERVICES AND ORGANIZATIONS

The Worship Services

According to general usage in Germany, the usual Protestant Sunday worship service at the time was the preaching service; communion services were exceptional. It was also treated in this way by the pastors of Ebenezer

---

42. UA July 7, 1760.
43. 5D13, 40 = journal September 5, 1763.
44. 5B2:60, 209.
45. 5B3:9 and 11.
46. In Ebenezer, the tuition amounted to one dollar quarterly, while in Savannah it cost six to eight dollars (5B4:1 8, 57 = April 7, 1802). 5B3:40 = August 24, 1790.

and Frederica who took care of Georgia's other Lutheran congregations, so that even here a common depiction is possible.

The order of these worship services was imaginably simple. It would not always begin with a hymn but often with an extemporaneous prayer (called prayer "from the heart") of the pastor, during which he and the congregation kneeled. If it began with the prayer, the hymn now followed, otherwise, the *lectio biblica*, a longer section of Scripture, one or two chapters, that was read aloud and that needed to have no connection at all with regard to the content of the sermon or to the character of the Sunday. In keeping with an old Lutheran custom, the story of the destruction of Jerusalem was read aloud annually on the 10th Sunday after Trinity.[47] Afterwards, one or two hymns were sung in a row, naturally without organ, and then followed the sermon that needed to have a proper length; one to one and a half hours was the rule. In the worship service on Sunday morning, the sermon was always preached on the gospel for that Sunday, as was the case with the great model for Georgia's congregations; the German court chapel in London.[48]

During Boltzius' time, it was the custom in the Jerusalem Church in Ebenezer that the members of the congregation brought their Bibles and during the sermon looked up passages that the pastor mentioned in order to retain them better. Moreover, it was customary to give to the congregants at the "end of the discourse such biblical verses to take home in which they might have, as it were, in a nutshell the material that had been treated."[49]

At a not precisely fixed point in the worship service, the school children, who sat together, would recite a psalm or sing hymns not yet known to the congregation that they had learned in the previous week. This custom was practiced frequently, not only on festivals, and was very well received, since through it the congregation, despite the lack of an actual, implemented liturgy, quite actively participated in the worship service. If something of that kind did not take place, the announcements followed the sermon after the hymn and prayer: the date of the next Lord's Supper was announced, cases of church discipline were reported, the first attendance of church for women who had given birth was commemorated, the settlement of a dispute between community members was made known,[50] or, on New Year's Day, the statistics from the previous year were read aloud.[51] The men's side

---

47. Probably from the Augsburg Agenda (5D2 = journal August 29, 1736).
48. UN November 30, 1735; Burckhardt, *Kirchen-Geschichte der Deutschen Gemeinden in London*, 51–52.
49. UN May 26, 1735.
50. UN December 6, 1739.
51. UN January 1, 1743.

of the church made a worthy impression during the entire worship service: due to the danger of a sudden attack, they sat there with sabers, pistols, flintlocks, and daggers—by order of the government officials.

This form of worship service was, under Boltzius, understood for a long time to be in a process of development, as is indicated by the fact that the parts were not in a completely rigid order. How they finally appeared is shown by Muhlenberg's church constitution of 1775 that stipulated that the Sunday worship service should be further retained unaltered in the form introduced by Boltzius.[52] After the introit prayer, in keeping with the German court chapel in London, the teacher delivered the *lectio biblica*, then, after a congregational hymn, the epistle or the gospel for the Sunday was read, and, after another hymn, an extemporaneous prayer of the pastor was said with the Lord's Prayer following. Thereupon, after the reading of the text, the sermon followed, concluding with a prayer, at which was prayed the general prayer of the church, in keeping with the aforementioned agenda with a second Lord's Prayer. The announcements with the votum from the pulpit, hymn, and benediction comprised the conclusion.

Pastor Bergmann did not follow this order at all: "Regarding liturgy, we know nothing here," he wrote.[53] At the beginning he prayed while kneeling an extemporaneous prayer "from the heart," whereupon the only hymn of this worship service was sung, after which an impromptu prayer again followed while standing. Instead of the epistle or gospel, he then read "an entire chapter from the Holy Scripture from which also the text [for the sermon] is taken,"[54] that would then be given: "When the sermon is ended, several things are announced, occasionally noteworthy events in the Kingdom of God are read aloud, after which we fall again on our knees. Here, however, each has his freedom" to pray kneeling or sitting.[55] This diminished form, that is contrary to every Lutheran practice and barely involves the participation of the congregation, may have occurred to Bergmann through his close contacts with Presbyterians and Baptists and thereby naturally corresponded to his theological stance, which will be described later.

Beside the form of worship service already depicted that goes back to Boltzius, there were two additional forms of the worship service without the administration of the Lord's Supper that were regularly held. The first was the catechetical or repetition hour that took place on Sunday afternoon

52. Strobel, *The Salzburgers and Their Descendants*, 75–76.
53. 5B4:34, 98 = February 7, 1804 Bm. original.
54. 5B4:9, 38 = April 25, 1800 Bm. original.
55. 5B3:42, 190 = April 20, 1796 Bm. original.

at five o'clock.[56] In it, either a sermon was preached informally (at times conversationally) on the Sunday epistle, but most often Luther's Small Catechism was treated in instructional style with the congregation, especially with the youth.[57] However, in Lent, the passion story was treated, or the sermon that was heard in the morning was "catechetically" repeated, that is, discussed in depth with the listeners.[58]

The pedagogical principle of repetition was especially fostered in Ebenezer's dependent communities, and Boltzius wrote concerning it in his journal: "We think very highly of repetition at our place, and thus it happens that every time in the church and school we complete only small amounts, and spend several weeks on one chapter, history, . . . hymn, etc."[59] No indication appears that this method had become boring to the community.

The other regularly practiced form of proclamation was the weekday sermon, which also was used in Germany. When possible, it took place in the middle of the week, which meant that only communities in the immediate vicinity of Ebenezer could come to take enjoyment in them. These also enjoyed great popularity and in no way diminished the central place of the Sunday worship service for the life of the community.

The multiplicity of the worship services held in Georgia's Lutheran congregations before the War of Independence are grouped as follows:

1. Jerusalem Church at Ebenezer. As long as it was the only Lutheran church, worship services took place three times on Sundays;[60] since the beginning of 1740 until the disruption of the war two times, a morning preaching worship service and an afternoon catechization. Every Thursday was the weekly preaching service that Boltzius held himself for as long as he was able.[61] Bergmann also held worship services twice on Sundays.[62]

2. Zion Church on the plantations. From the founding of the plantations until long after Boltzius' death the worship service was held on every other Sunday and on the second day of the three great festivals,[63] alternatively held by Boltzius and Gronau, and then Lemcke, later

---

56. UN April 27, 1740.

57. 5D3, 5 = journal January 9, 1737.

58. 5A7:53, 226 = journal May 14, 1739 extract; 5A7:64b, 271 = journal November 4, 1739 extract.

59. UN July 27, 1748.

60. 5D4 = journal (+UN) December 10, 1738.

61. UA June 13, 1759.

62. 5B4:2, 6 = April 3, 1799 Bm. original.

63. UN April 9, 1740; 5A9:8, 36 = journal May 25–26, 1740 extract.

by Rabenhorst.[64] In 1741, edification hours took place on Tuesdays and Fridays,[65] and instead in 1746 a weekday preaching service on Tuesday,[66] later moved to Wednesday and for a long time was held by Boltzius, and, after his death, by Rabenhorst.[67]

3. Goshen. In 1759, Rabenhorst held here a weekly preaching service every second Wednesday and continued it until after Boltzius' death, since he lived here.[68] When the conflict with Triebner arose, Rabenhorst additionally held a preaching service every Sunday until shortly before Muhlenberg's arrival.

4. Bethany. Since this location was not far from Ebenezer and, in addition, was soon connected with it by a bridge, the community members there needed no extra Sunday worship service but could go to the Jerusalem Church. Instead, they had a weekly preaching service every Wednesday, at first held alternatively by Lemcke and Rabenhorst, and later only by Lemcke.[69] However, the community also wanted to have its own Sunday worship service, and with Muhlenberg's visit in 1775 they were promised one that was to take place every four weeks.

5. Savannah. When one of Ebenezer's pastors was here, which happened more often in the beginning, and later every four weeks where a worship service was held at eight o'clock and one o'clock, then the Anglican worship service took place there in the same building at ten o'clock and three o'clock.[70] The midday worship service was most often cloaked in the form of a catechetical lesson. Gronau, and afterwards Rabenhorst, most often provided the service. Bergmann also, when he was in Savannah, held worship services twice.

6. Vernonburg. Lutheran worship services took place here every two months, held by Gronau, Boltzius, or Rabenhorst.

7. Acton. The same as in Vernonburg.

8. Frederica. The preaching worship service was on Sunday mornings; in the afternoons was the "children's instruction" in which the sermon

---

64. 5B2:31, 122 = May 13, 1766 LR.
65. 5A10:2, 6 = April 8, 1741 B. original; 5A10:45, 169.
66. 5A11:56, 252 = August 5, 1746 B. original.
67. UA June 13, 1759.
68. UA June 13, 1759.
69. TK32F4, 255 = March 14, 1760 L. original; 5D13, 2 = journal August 2, 1763; UA June 13, 1759; UA IV, 109.
70. UN August 2, 1742.

was not repeated or reviewed but a type of children's service or Sunday school was held by Pastor Driessler who was very gifted in catechization and in which a subject prepared during the week was summarily treated. The repetition hour of the sermon was put off until the evening. There was no weekday sermon; instead there was a midweek prayer hour.[71]

The communities celebrated the Lord's Supper with deeper reverence and greater care, every six weeks in Ebenezer,[72] and every other month in Savannah.[73] The coming celebration was announced, in the beginning one Sunday and later two Sundays in advance, and whoever wanted to take part in it remained after the worship service in the church where they were registered for it with the pastor who read the names at the conclusion on the intermediate Sunday for possible objection on the part of the community members or for mutual forgiveness.[74]

This was a practice of church discipline that was treated very rigorously by Boltzius and Triebner, less so by Rabenhorst, since with the numerous pastoral conversations taking place in the ensuing days it often happened that one or the other who had given notice of participation would not be allowed to the Lord's Supper this time by the pastor and later by the authorized church council. There was, for example, one who had been away for three months for work, and it had been discovered that he had behaved wantonly there; another had stolen, and, in turn another had gotten drunk without showing remorse. If such people had evidently improved themselves, they would be admitted the next time; not being admitted did not mean expulsion from the community.

Besides these individual conversations, a preparatory sermon took place in the week before the communion service for those who wanted to commune, or, when there were too many, the preparation took place in groups. Boltzius reported, "This midday I had with me the unmarried people from the community ... who wanted to go to the table of the Lord to speak briefly with them from the Word of the Lord, to sing, and to pray.

---

71. 4C1:67, 244 = July 30, 1744 Dr. original.

72. UN March 16, 1735, November 19, 1747.

73. 5B1:24, 105 = November 13, 1748 B. original signature on the letter in another hand. It was customary in the Ebenezer District to hold communion only in Jerusalem Church, so that the Rabenhorst party, when Triebner resided in Ebenezer, did not commune. If communion was to be held in Savannah, the pastors traveled there already a few days in advance in order to conduct careful "preparation" (5D4 = journal April 4, 1738; UN May 3, 1739).

74. 5D3 = journal (+UN) February 19, 1737; 5D4, 41 = journal April 3, 1737.

This evening . . . the married people and widows are coming to me for this purpose."[75]

There was no private confession in Ebenezer and in the communities under the care of its pastors;[76] the preparation and the celebration of the Lord's Supper were carried out according to the liturgy "as is customary in the court chapel in London."[77]

Pastor Bergmann described his practice: "A preparatory sermon is held on Saturday. Before the administration of the Lord's Supper a prayer is given, then several passages from the last words of the Lord, then the Words of Institution of the Lord's Supper, then those who are coming for it are briefly admonished to contemplate the high worth of this holy institution. But I cannot regard it as good that there is singing during the distribution of the blessed bread and wine; it would be better if it happened after the administration. When the hymn has ended, a psalm of praise and thanks is read, then there is prayer; after this, those who have received the Supper are again encouraged to live for Christ, and it is ended with the blessing of the Lord. The elders of the community must now have careful oversight that a wicked member does not sneak in."[78] And from 1799, he reported: "The number of communicants is now very small. When I came to Ebenezer, the number every six weeks was seventy to eighty; now barely ten to twelve, sometimes only six to seven, because it is no longer tolerated that after partaking one continues to live so disorderly, as was the case previously."[79] Contributing to this lamentable outcome, since German was less and less understood, was also certainly the fact that Bergmann was not to be moved to conduct the worship service in the English language. Even already in 1787 from far away Halle it was suggested to him to give the sermon in English.[80] However, since he did not act on it, he had to look on as a portion of the community members drifted to English speaking denominations.

The Occasional Services

The special confessional status of the communities bound to Ebenezer shows itself most clearly in that here two worship books were used, a Lutheran

75. UN April 6, 1737.
76. 5B4:29, 87 = January 11, 1803, Bm. original.
77. 5D1, 84.
78. 5B4:29, 87.
79. 5B4:2, 10 = April 3, 1799 Bm. original.
80. 5B3:33, 141 = November 16, 1787.

one and an Anglican one. In keeping with his instruction,[81] Boltzius had himself thoroughly briefed in Dover by the court chaplain Butjenter over the use of the worship book of the German court chapel in London,[82] of which he also received a copy.[83] It was a German translation of the Book of Common Prayer.[84] The administration of the sacraments complied with it; baptism was performed in the presence of the congregation.[85] However at Bergmann's time, there were no longer any godparents.[86] Also, the preparation for the Lord's Supper and the Lord's Supper itself, as already mentioned, was arranged according to this order.[87] In the beginning, Boltzius rigidly adhered to the London worship book that no foreigner could marry an English couple[88]—otherwise, he would have been able to perform the marriage for the famous Mary Musgrove who had asked him to do it—however, from around the 1760s on he also regularly baptized and married English people.[89]

Urlsperger had had delivered to Boltzius through the chaplain of the first Salzburger transport, Schumacher, a Lutheran "Augsburg Church Worship Book."[90] The rest of the occasional services in Georgia were arranged according to its forms: confirmation of emergency baptisms in the public worship service,[91] marriages,[92] and probably also the reading of the history of the destruction of Jerusalem.[93]

But, moreover, Georgia's Lutheran congregations had several particular usages and customs for which there was no formula in either of the two worship books and that, in part, originated from the old homeland of

81. 5A1:10, 58 point 20.

82. 5D1, 22 = journal December 24, 1733 new style.

83. UN May 26, 1735, February 20, 1741.

84. *Nachrichten von den vereinigten Deutschen Evangelisch-Lutherischen Gemeinden*, 23; Jacobs, *A History of the Evangelical Lutheran Church*, 143; see also *Das allgemeine Gebet-Buch* (Appendix II, no. 2).

85. 5D2 = journal May 27, 1736; UN August 21, 1737; 5D4 = journal January 8, 1738.

86. 5B4:2, 10 = April 3, 1799 Bm. original.

87. 5D1, 84–86 = journal March 19–20, 1734; Burckhardt, *Kirchen-Geschichte der Deutschen Gemeinden in London*, 47–48. When Prince Frederick of Wales married a princess from Gotha in June 1736, a petition for them was also inserted for them in the intercessory prayer in Ebenezer.

88. Burckhardt, *Kirchen-Geschichte der Deutschen Gemeinden in London*, 49; 5D3 = journal (+UN) March 12, 1737.

89. 5B2:9, 33–34 = December 31, 1763 B. original.

90. 5A1:20, 95 B. original.

91. 5D2 = journal (+UN) January 18, 1736; 5D4 = journal (+UN) July 11, 1738; UN February 24 and March 13, 1735.

92. UN November 13, 1734.

93. 5D2 = journal (+UN) August 29, 1736; UA August 11, 1751.

Salzburg but in part represented original creations of the communities in Georgia. At the top of the list to be named here is the already mentioned "Commemoration and Thanksgiving Festival" at which the members of the community remembered annually on the day of the arrival of the first Salzburger transport their own safe voyage and all of the help that they had experienced in the difficult years of the settlement, as was practiced in varied forms by several groups of settlers in America and also as the original understanding of "Thanksgiving Day" of the United States amalgamated these traditions.[94] The first Salzburgers had pledged the annual celebration during their voyage,[95] and they have kept, with their descendants, this vow faithfully to the present day.[96] Though the exact arrival date had been March 12, 1734, the celebration does not always take place on this day but on another convenient day close to this date, even on a weekday but not, as Strobel indicates, on Reminiscere Sunday.[97] One or two festival worship services with thanksgiving prayers and hymns were held on the occasion, and the sermon was on, for example, the text, "It is of the Lord's mercies that we are not consumed, because His compassions fails not. They are new every morning; great is Thy faithfulness" (Lam 3:22–23).[98]

Another particular feature in Ebenezer's community life in which the members openly participated was the annual harvest sermon, mostly conducted by Boltzius, that also could fall on weekdays.[99] The date was determined by the conclusion of the work on the harvest; the range of the dates was between September 21st and November 20th.[100] Boltzius once treated the special destinies of the community with the words, "When thou hast eaten and art full, then thou shalt bless the Lord thy God for the good land which He hath given thee" (Deut 8:10).[101] Even Pastor Bergmann held the harvest sermon.

One custom that had a particular face in the communities in the early period was the first return to church of women after childbirth, which the

94. Annually, on the last Thursday in November.
95. 5D1, 65–66 = journal March 3, 1734.
96. Rines, *Old Historic Churches of America*, 244.
97. Strobel, *The Salzburgers and Their Descendants*, 9. Only in 1734 had March 10th old style been the Reminiscere Sunday.
98. 5D3 = journal (+UN) March 12, 1737; UN March 9, 1737: "We are accustomed, on such commemoration and thanksgiving festival, to remind gladly our hearers as much as possible of the spiritual and material benefactions that God the Lord has so abundantly showed to us from the beginning in this land of our pilgrimage."
99. UA November 14, 1751: Thursday.
100. UN September 21, 1747, November 20, 1750.
101. UN September 21, 1747.

young mothers were accustomed to observe with their children and midwives six weeks after their return.

Especially in the beginning, the mortality among the newborn was shockingly high; of the thirty-nine children who were born until the end of 1738, not fewer than twenty-seven died shortly after birth,[102] and with the coming of almost every child there were complications of fever. However, the mother and child were out of danger around the time of the return to church (baptisms were a few days after birth). On that point, we cite the following report from the journal: "A wife held her return to church with her small child, for which we . . . conducted it in the following way: On the Sunday when it takes place, it is announced to the congregation, and they are asked to remain together after the worship service has concluded so that there can be communal prayer over mother and child. The new mother with her small child steps to the front of the table, and the preacher reads to her four points that are appropriate for her circumstances, such as

1. What she and her child have received as special spiritual and material benefactions from the fatherly hand of God.
2. That God requires for it nothing other than heartfelt gratitude in word and deed.
3. What is the duty of an upright mother toward her small child.
4. That for the exercise of such duty she has need of the earnest use of the means of salvation, and especially of prayer. Thereupon, public prayer is offered for her and the blessing is pronounced."[103]

If a settler had built a new house, he asked one of the pastors to dedicate it with the word of God. This happened very often,[104] since quite a few who in the beginning had lived in Ebenezer in time moved to their plantations. The head of the house invited a few friends,[105] a hymn was sung, and Boltzius, for example, spoke on this occasion mostly about one of the commandments.[106]

But the buildings belonging to the community also were dedicated in this way, such as, for example, the second sawmill. On a Sunday, the community gathered at the mill and sang the hymn, "My Hope Stands

---

102. 5D4 = journal December 13, 1738.

103. 5D1, 278–79 = journal August 11, 1735 copy = UN August 10, 1735. Completed text of the address: 5D4 = journal October 8, 1738.

104. For example, 5D4 = journal February 6, 1738; 5D8 = journal October 1, 1741; UN March 13, 1742, March 21, 1743; UA March 27, 1751, July 2, 1752.

105. UN November 17, 1742.

106. UA December 2, 1751.

Fast Upon the Living God."[107] Then, Boltzius gave an oration on the text, "Every creature of God is good, and nothing to be refused, if it be received with thanksgiving; for it is sanctified through the word of God and prayer" (1 Tim 4:4–5). He explained in addition,

1. The reason we recognize and esteem it [the mill].
2. How we should properly use it. We have to regard it as a creature of God, and indeed as a good creature that was sent only from the good God and which . . . should come to the good of the community. The proper use of it is also indicated to us in that we received it as a good creature of God with thanksgiving and consecrate it now and in the future through the word of God and prayer.

"Because I am otherwise accustomed to use the duties of life according to the Ten Commandments from the blessed Wirth's Confession and Book at the dedications of our new houses, I read finally the seventh duty after the second commandment. Afterwards, the congregation sang the verse, 'The Lord is never parted from his people,' and, 'So come before his face.'"[108] The mill and the first trial sawings then were viewed.[109]

Also with burials there were several particular features in Ebenezer. Boltzius learned to his great astonishment that in the Salzburg territory only women who died in childbirth were buried in coffins. In keeping with ancient custom, all other bodies were dressed, laid on a board and wrapped with a blanket to be carried to the grave. This practice was therefore also retained in Ebenezer.[110] Boltzius reported how things further proceeded in this regard:

1. The signal for the burial is given with our little bell.
2. Such a time for it is generally chosen when the hearers have left their work so that all whose circumstances permit it can attend the burial.
3. When our school children and several people have gathered at the place where the body is, a funeral hymn is sung and then a passage is read from the Bible that especially deals with death.
4. Our schoolchildren with the schoolmaster walk behind the pallbearers, and behind these are the rest who are escorting the body. Nothing is

---

107. Freylinghausen: *Geist=reiches Gesang-Buch* (Appendix II, no. 39), volume I, number 307.
108. "Praise and honor be to the highest good," verse 9.
109. UA April 27, 1751.
110. 5D1, 100 = journal April 13, 1734.

sung underway, but as soon as the corpse has been buried, we sing together, "Now let us bury the body," etc.

5. After the burial, a brief awakening to the Word of God from the heart is read to the persons assembled, and then concluded with prayer and several verses from a hymn.[111]

Even at Pastor Bergmann's time, the burials were accompanied by the schoolchildren.[112]

The Assemblies

It already has become clear that Georgia's Lutheran pastors transferred very precisely, in part down to the smallest details, the arrangements and practices familiar to them from the European homeland to Georgia and reconstructed them there. As is generally known, this is a characteristic of all of America's Lutheran churches and, moreover, a feature of immigrant communities all over the world. For the initial period of the Lutheran church in Georgia this means that the pastors brought with them the theological direction of the place where they had received their theological training, and also the forms of this direction—Pietism of a Halle character—in Germany. The Orphan House in Halle was for them a model in such a way that a church history of these communities in Georgia cannot be written without a detailed consideration of the circumstances in Halle at that time. This point has only so far been hinted in the relevant literature, occasionally expressed only with a single sentence, but never investigated or presented with the needed comprehensiveness.

The institution most often mentioned in connection with Pietism in Germany was the conventicle, private or house meetings in which pietistic religiosity was cultivated by small circles of the converted, independent from the life of the constituted ecclesiastical communities. One sang the very extensive number of new chorales, prayed, most often kneeling, "from the heart," read edifying material, for example, biographies, reports from the spread of the pietistic movement or other pietistic circles, institutions, and endeavors, and, not least of all, practiced an extensive reading of Holy Scripture—all of this by no means necessarily in the presence of a clergyman.

Such private gatherings also took place in the early years of the settlement of Georgia, in Ebenezer, Savannah, and on the plantations around Zion

---

111. UN March 14, 1735.
112. 5B4:2, 6 = April 3, 1799 Bm. original.

Church and elsewhere. There was no particular house for it,[113] but people went to houses of members of the community or to Boltzius' house.[114] These gatherings took place in the evenings, were scheduled for no particular day, were not publicly announced (but not in order to keep them secret) and had no specified membership. Sometimes the members of the community met with each other; sometimes they invited a pastor to come, and sometimes Boltzius himself organized a meeting. There would be read, for example, a biography of Luther,[115] passages from the Bible,[116] or even the New Testament progressively.[117]

Taken as a whole, however, these private gatherings were nothing essential in the life of the community, since the situation in Ebenezer was not like that under which these gatherings arose in the Lutheran regions of Germany and had come to spread. That is, there was here no circle of the pious in the midst of nominal Christians but whoever lived at that time in Ebenezer (with a few exceptions) was also a true church-goer. Even when this situation shifted through extensive immigrations, the private gatherings were not taken up anew; in the meantime, in keeping with the actual ideal situation of the community, other arrangements took over the functions that otherwise were assigned to the conventicles. These arrangements were intended for the entire community and were visited by it almost with zeal; they will now be described. Thus, this phenomenon that had caused much strife in Germany became a blessing in Ebenezer and, by many visitors, an admired calling card of the community.

The Evening Prayer Hours

Already on the ship of the first Salzburgers and after their settlement in Ebenezer devotions, called prayer hours, were held in the mornings and in the evenings after supper.[118] After a while, the morning prayer hours were discontinued because this time was too inconvenient for the farmers. But the evening prayer hours, that lasted about a full half hour,[119] enjoyed all the greater popularity. Even the people from the plantations came to Ebenezer

---

113. 5D2 = journal November 6, 1736.
114. UN May 1, 1737, October 1, 1739.
115. UN May 1, 1737.
116. For example, John 14–17: UN December 12, 1739.
117. UN October 1, 1739.
118. Between five o'clock and six o'clock p.m. (5D12, 25 = journal March 3, 1745). 5D1, 44 = journal January 21, 1734; 5A1:33, 149 = March 23, 1734 B. original.
119. 5D2, 10–11 = journal January 13, 1736.

for it whenever they could. The prayer hours most often took place in the church and in fact, as in Halle, by candlelight, although that was rather expensive.[120] In Savannah, whenever a pastor resided there, they took place in the house of Mr. Altherr from St. Gallen, who likewise donated the expensive candles for it.[121] There was no fixed order for it. However, as with the pietistic private gatherings that dropped off in time, there was much and long praying "from the heart" by the pastor while kneeling. Boltzius once confessed that this form of prayer was a genuine necessity for him, since in doing so he did not need to think of an ending.

Such prayers, naturally, have not been passed down to us in their exact wording, yet we learn from many individual reports that they were from the same piety as the hymns that are yet to be discussed. Compared to the standards of the time, they were remarkably free from mystical notions, especially those of marriage. In Ebenezer it was also customary to bring before God in true simplistic manner all economic and financial concerns, and there were certainly plenty of these concerns, particularly in the early years; consequently, the appeal of these early prayer hours in the community is understandable.

Also, as in the conventicles, an in-depth reading of the Bible was customary. After a beginning was made with individual sections, they committed themselves from the middle of April 1736 to the continuous reading of the Old Testament.[122] With the principle practiced here of using small segments, only slow progress could be made, and after seven years had passed, they were only comparing the books of 1 Kings and 1 Chronicles with each other.[123] In this way, together with the custom of looking up passages during the sermon, there developed a thoroughly admirable knowledge of the Bible for the participants. The connections of the people of Israel living under the guidance of God with the fate of the Salzburgers, who had emigrated on account of their faith, allowed these readings to become a great benefit for the community.

In turn, in keeping with the model of the private gatherings in Germany, edifying histories also were read in Ebenezer's evening prayer hours. In part, they certainly had a purely edifying character and came from books out of Ebenezer's extensive church library, that is still to be discussed. They gladly contemplated the biographies of important personalities of the Pietist movement: Anton Wilhelm Böhme (Ziegenhagen's predecessor), Abbott

---

120. 5A10:40, 145–46 = January 7, 1743 B. original.
121. UN June 5, 1750.
122. 5D3 = journal (+UN) April 16, 1737.
123. UN May 27, 1743.

J. J. Breithaupt, Johann Anastasius Freylinghausen, Provost Porst, Joseph Schaitberger, Spener, and so on. Or they read from the treasure of August Hermann Francke's writings and from postils. Much material for such purposes was also compiled in magazine-like series that were owned and used in Ebenezer, for example, "Closter-Bergische Sammlung Nützlicher Materien Zur Erbauung im Wahren Christenthum" (Berg Cloister Collection of Useful Material for Edification in True Christianity), or "Sammlung Auserlesener Materien zum Bau des Reichs Gottes" (Collection of Selected Materials for the Building of the Kingdom of God).[124]

But on the other hand, these readings had an informational character, something that is not mentioned in the journals. They replaced the newspaper, radio, and television of our day, and, again, provided a basis for encouraging the community to active participation.[125] Here, the Salzburgers learned what had become of their brethren in the faith who had moved to east Prussia. Through the mediation of Halle, they even stood with them in an exchange of correspondence that stretched out over several years.[126] Here was further followed[127] with great interest the continuations of "Der Königl. Dänischen Missionarien aus Ost-Indien eingesandter Ausführlichen Berichten" (The Detailed Reports Sent by the Royal Danish Missionaries from East India).[128] They learned from missionaries who had been sent to Tranquebar and took an animated part in their activity, since there were also in Georgia similar non-Christians of color. They could put to use their experiences with tropical illnesses. They gazed at the familiar picture of the first indigenous pastor, Aaron.[129] Indeed, the community collected from its own initiative a sum of money for the "Malabars."[130]

However, the letters that arrived in Ebenezer from London and Augsburg, but especially from Halle, occupied a very special place. When these letters, that are extant in part in outline, are read, then it is recognized that they really had been written by "fathers" of Georgia's communities. It was not only the material help and counsel that was bound with them that made

124. See Appendix II, nos. 17 and 79.

125. For example, 5A3:49, 311 = March 1, 1737 B. original; 5A7:18, 73 = January 1, 1738 B. copy; 5A7:53, 230 = journal May 9, 1739 extract; 5B2:66, 236 = September 30, 1763 B. original.

126. 5D9 II, 28–81 copy; a number of letters from Salzburgers who had emigrated to East Prussia (Rastenburg) to their compatriots in Ebenezer.

127. 5A9:9, 41 = September 9, 1740 B. original; 5A11:56, 252 = August 5, 1746 B. original; UN May 17, 1740.

128. See Appendix II, no. 10.

129. Lehmann, *Es begann in Tranquebar*, 253.

130. 5D8, 287 = journal June 6, 1741.

these letters so valuable to the communities, but also—and especially—the certainty taken from them that their senders had an interest in the community members and their concerns and had not become weary of encouraging them and praying for them. The following notation from Boltzius shows how intensive was the occupation with these messages: "Much of the good received from these letters is entered in the journals, but far from what God has bestowed to us. We also have become, with diligence, sparing with it, because we are concerned that several readers of our journals might not be pleased when they notice that we occupy ourselves so long in the prayer hours with the letters. It is very dear to the members of our community when we do not rush, and bring every point close to their hearts and repeat them catechetically in the next prayer hour."[131]

As was the case for Boltzius in his exposed location, so were the letters also more valuable than material donations for Driessler in his lonely post. But after Boltzius' death, Timotheus Lemcke, the son of the pastor, complained, "Not the least bit of news from our dear fathers and benefactors has been communicated to the community and also to me, which is very strange to them, since they were accustomed in the past to be continually gladdened from it."[132]

The Hymn Hours

Pietism had created an abundance of new hymns that corresponded to its needs, about which the Freylinghausen hymnbook[133] already gives conclusive information. Its texts encompass in broad sweeps every variety from the healthy internalization of the life of faith to the insipid accumulation of empty or ill-considered images, and often neither the melodies nor the rhythms coincide with the content of the respective hymns. In the same way that these hymns at first were partially spread in Germany through the conventicles before they made their way into the congregational worship services, so they also were learned in similar fashion in Ebenezer. The musically-inclined Boltzius, for whom this matter lay especially close to heart, reported himself how he proceeded in doing so: "Many in our community have great pleasure in the new, and mostly unfamiliar, hymns in our hymnbook, although indeed we already have taught various ones to the community through the children with whom we learn them in school. Yet since the adults who had a good trained voice have been dismissed from

---

131. 5A11:24, 88 = February 24, 1744 B. original.
132. 5B2: 61, 214–15 = November 1, 1768 Timotheus Lemcke copy.
133. See Appendix II, no. 39.

school, it no longer goes on so well in this way. Therefore, I decided to spend an hour on Sundays after the catechization for the learning of the unfamiliar melodies, for which today, in the name of God, a beginning was made. Only the women, among them such who possess some ability, sing aloud; but the men and children sing softly along with them."[134]

That caught on, and from it developed the community's hymn hours that, as a rule, were held about twice weekly in the winter in connection with the evening prayer hours.[135] They lasted about three-quarters of an hour so that participation was possible for all. Similar hymn hours were also arranged in the Halle Orphan House, and there, too, they followed this model. However, in the hymn hours in Ebenezer they were not just mechanically learned, as in the citation above; the main goal here also was edification. For that reason, candles likewise were lit, and the people took the hymns to heart, not only outwardly.

At the same time, the hymns of the Freylinghausen hymnbook that they most often sung is interesting and characteristic of the pietistic direction of the first Lutherans in Georgia. The journals name an abundance of hymns (about twenty per year). Most of them can be found under the following headings of this hymnbook: the mystery of the cross, death and resurrection, the joyfulness of faith, Christian life and Christian conduct, divine providence and governance, human misery and perdition, true contrition and conversion, true and false Christianity. The following groups are not at all represented or only in limited number: on Jesus and his manifold names and offices, on chastity, on love for Jesus, on the surrender of the heart to God, on spiritual marriage, on the high nobility of the faithful, on the hidden life of the faithful, on heaven and the heavenly Jerusalem.

As is to be expected, in the frequency of the hymn writers the time period of Pietism comes first, followed by the time period of the Counter Reformation; only at a great distance after that appears the Reformation, and almost nothing is represented from the time period of the Thirty Years War.

The expected and resultant fruit of the hymn hours was that the community members tapped the abundance of the Protestant treasury of hymns. But soon they also availed themselves to polyphonic hymns,[136] and even truly artful compositions.[137] When, therefore, the Palantine immigrants ar-

---

134. 5D4 = journal June 18, 1738; 5A11:10, 31 = December 21, 1743 B. original.

135. 5D8 = journal November 8, 1741; UN December 21, 1743.

136. For four voices (UN December 25–26 and 30, 1739).

137. UN January 27, 1740. They also corrected hymns that were erroneously learned (5D7 = journal January 18, 1741).

rived, it seemed to the people of Ebenezer and its neighboring areas that their compatriots in the faith could not sing any of the hymns;[138] the pastors soon tried to help them.

EDUCATION

The Schools

As did many other Lutheran communities in America, also Ebenezer and the villages joined to it, such as Frederica, maintained their own schools that certainly were, in regard to finances, perennial problem children for the community treasury yet significant for the Lutherans of Georgia, indeed, even for those of South Carolina, far beyond its immediate parish. Despite many adverse circumstances, the instruction was conducted and supervised throughout with interest. The considerable result is shown by the numerous letters, preserved in the original, written by members of the community, simple farmers, and that, of course, are not orthographically flawless but are written in a style that is impressive.[139] The example of Governor Treutlen, who enjoyed only Ebenezer's education (with some private instructional hours with Boltzius), is likewise to be recalled.

To be sure, here also the outward conditions were pioneer-like and very simple when Gronau, in keeping with his call and instruction,[140] began teaching on May 15, 1734. Especially in winter, when it was cold even in Georgia and there was no heated room, he had to move with the children from one private house to another.[141] There were no blackboards.[142] When therefore the number of students had grown through the arrival of the second transport, instruction was held in Boltzius' house where the worship services also took place.[143]

After the relocation of the settlement, they had to find accommodation in the temporary first storehouse, again in the room for the worship services. But there was no large table there, and so there could be no instruction in

138. 5D4 = journal January 18, 1738.

139. See p. 80.

140. 5A1, 38; 5A1:7, 41. In keeping with Urlsperger's instruction, Boltzius, the administrator of the pastoral office, had the "main oversight" over the schools—following the German example (5A1:8, 43).

141. UN June 25, 1734.

142. They did not come until UN February 19, 1735.

143. 5D1, 232–33 = journal February 2, 1735. The connection between church and school everywhere in America was unique to German Lutherans; for example, it was foreign to the Anglicans (5B4:3, 14 = October 7, 1799 Bm. original).

writing.[144] As soon as the guardhouse was finished, they moved there, since it could be heated.[145] In the summer, instruction could be held only in the mornings because of the great heat,[146] and there was a pause in the winter because of the cold.[147] When, then, Jerusalem Church had been built, the instruction was moved there,[148] or they went to one of the parsonages,[149] and in the winter to the orphanage.[150] Only at the end of June 1750 had things come so far that a separate schoolhouse, built onto a building of the orphanage, was constructed with an official residence for Kalcher on one side and on the other side a large hall that also was used for the raising of silkworms.[151]

On the plantations at Zion Church instruction as well as the worship services took place at first in Ruprecht Steiner's house,[152] and after that in the kitchen of the Salzburger Krause.[153] When the church was built in 1743, it was also used for the school, but in the winter, it had to give way to the heatable private houses of Steiner and Brandner.[154] At the end of November 1747, construction began on a schoolhouse[155] that was dedicated in April 12, 1748.[156] The settlers in Bethany also built for themselves their own schoolhouse.[157]

The number of school children and their attendance were as modest as the initial outward circumstances. In New Ebenezer, it began with fourteen school children.[158] They were often sick,[159] even all of them during the malaria epidemic of 1736 so that school was canceled completely

---

144. 5D2 = journal June 24, 1736.
145. 5D1, 296 = journal August 19, 1735; 5D2 = journal November 22, 1736.
146. 5D3 = journal July 2, 1737.
147. UN January 5, 1739.
148. UN January 18, 1742.
149. 5A10:45, 160 = March 9, 1743.
150. UN March 23, 1747.
151. UN March 30, 1750; 5B1:37, 150–51 = June 1750 B. copy.
152. 5D8, 583 = journal October 31, 1741.
153. UN November 30, 1742.
154. UN March 23 and December 2, 1747.
155. UN November 22, 1747.
156. UN April 12, 1748.
157. TK32F4, 255 = March 14, 1760 L. original; TK32F8, 674–75 = September 27, 1771.
158. 5D2 = journal May 9, 1736.
159. UN September–October 1734.

for a long time.[160] During the harvest time there was also not much that could be done. The bigger children had to help with the grain and so on,[161] and the smaller ones had to pick beans.[162] When, then, in the course of the establishment of the plantations most of the families moved away from Ebenezer, the school there also became very small.[163] However, a steady stream of German children from the surrounding area came to it, especially from Purrysburg.[164] These children were boarded either privately or in the orphanage.[165] In 1771, the number of all students in Ebenezer, Zion, and Bethany came to more than 100.

Notwithstanding all of the difficulties, the school program developed steadily and smoothly. In Ebenezer, the children very soon were divided into two classes; the younger ones learned reading with Ortmann,[166] and the older ones learned writing and arithmetic with Gronau. In the mornings and afternoons, they had a joint hour of catechetical instruction with Gronau, four hours daily altogether.[167] The boys who already could read had to work during the instruction in this subject and the girls had to learn knitting.[168] Already in 1737, Boltzius began to administer regular instruction in English,[169] which after a few years his young English servant Bishop continued,[170] and from the summer of 1741, it was even taken over by an extra English teacher named Henry Hamilton.[171]

When the newly established school operation at Zion Church created a genuine burden for the teaching personnel, the instruction of reading and writing in Ebenezer was handed over to Ortmann. However, because of his inadequate abilities he was let go in 1743,[172] and the surgeon Mayer took over his responsibilities, two to three hours daily.[173] But since he was

160. 5D2 = journal September 11, 1736.
161. 5D4 = journal September 14, 1738.
162. 5A7:33, 143 = October 9, 1738 G. original.
163. UN July 16, 1742.
164. For example, 5D2 = journal January 28, 1736; 5D3 = journal April 17, 1737.
165. 5D2 = journal January 28, 1736.
166. (5D3 = journal May 2, 1737). Even that was only possible after the children had been brought over the worst (5A1:49, 232 = not dated, probably December 10–11, 1734).
167. UN February 19 and March 17, 1735, July 16, 1742; 5D2 = journal February 22, 1736.
168. UN April 11, 1735.
169. 5D3, 36 = journal March 25, 1737; 5D3 = journal (+UN) May 3, 1737.
170. UN January 3, 1740.
171. His wife was named Regina Charlotte (5D7 = journal (+UN) June 1, 1741).
172. 5A11:23, 85–86 = December 29, 1744 B. original.
173. UN September 16, 1743; 5A11:23, 85.

often ill, he gave up teaching completely at the beginning of May 1747, so that Lemcke, since Gronau had died, had the school operation completely alone.[174] To be sure, Mayer's brother was appointed on June 1, 1747,[175] but not much became of it, and the school continued to be left to Lemcke.

Francke's instruction directed the care of the plantations at Zion Church: they looked around "among the Salzburgers themselves whether someone could be found among them who could be used as a schoolteacher,"[176] with the result that initially Ruprecht Steiner, and later Johann Georg Kocher, taught reading and writing,[177] while Boltzius took over the religious instruction.[178] In November 1749, Kocher was replaced by Wertsch who got along well with the children and gave instruction for three hours daily in writing and reading.[179] The Salzburger Martin Lackner followed him from March to October 1753,[180] until in fall 1755 Rabenhorst followed,[181] and afterwards Lucas Geiger on the plantations,[182] the doctor Thilo in Ebenezer,[183] Johann

---

174. UN April 22 and May 27, 1747.

175. UN May 27 and June 2, 1747; 5B1: 2, 11 = July 19, 1748 B. original. He was still active.

176. 5A1:10, 51–52 Fr. draft.

177. 5A10:54, 211 = not dated (ca. 1743) Kocher original; UN February 7, 1742, November 9 and 23, 1742. There was little satisfaction with Kocher. He became smug and finally even "a blasphemer" (TK33, 41 = journal April 18 (1759) copy).

178. UN July 16, 1742.

179. UN November 8 and 17, 1749.

180. UA March 26 and October 30, 1753.

181. UA October 30, 1753; TK 32F10, 874 = January 15, 1756 B. original.

182. UA October 30, 1753; TK 32F10, 874 = January 15, 1756 B. original. "Since the previous schoolteachers left, we have had for three months in the town and plantation schools faithful co-workers in Messrs. Thilo and Lucas Geiger" (who was trained by the former teacher in the *Paedagogio regio*, M. Geiger who died in Memmingen).

183. UA October 30, 1753; TK 32F10, 874 = January 15, 1756 B. original. The schoolteacher Lucas Geiger lived on the plantations at Zion Church (TK32F11, 968 = December 1756 B. copy). Boltzius reports concerning the school children: "In the catechetical hours they are instructed fundamentally and clearly by my worthy Herren colleagues Lemcke and Rabenhorst in the principal matters of the Christian religion from the catechism, Bible verses, and the order of salvation in the manner as it occurs in the German schools of the Halle Orphan House. According to this method, our two schoolteachers, Herr Thilo and Lucas Geiger, also must comply exactly in introducing the catechism and biblical verses in reading, writing, etc." (TK32F11, 1050 = February 17, 1756 B. original).

Adam Treutlen from October 1758 to spring 1759,[184] after him Johann Martin Paulitsch and Neidlinger until September 1763.[185]

When they ceased their activity, "Johann Adam Treutlen, who with an advance from a merchant started a business at our place in wet and dry goods, offered" to give instruction in Ebenezer daily for six hours in German and in English, under the condition of being able to cancel the instruction for business reasons. Boltzius was not happy to have anything to do with him since, already during Treutlen's first teaching appointment, he had become acquainted with his "arrogant, wise-above-all and incorrigible disposition that cannot be told or instructed about anything."[186]

There was even a female teacher, the "school mistress Heckin," who took up her office in 1764.[187] In 1763, there was an additional teacher in Bethany and in Goshen.[188] In December 1765, Ebenezer acquired the law student Doerbaum who instructed Timotheus Lemcke in Latin and took over the sale of medicines and books from Halle.[189] But he seems not to have lived in Ebenezer for very long; nothing more is heard about him. In 1771, Timotheus Lemcke taught reading and writing to the satisfaction of everyone.[190] As a rule, instruction in religion was given by the pastors.

---

184. "Johan Adam Treutlen (until now the town schoolteacher) has proved himself to be, as in his previous life so also during the time in which he taught school, a headstrong and fickle person whom I have tolerated with much patience and leniency." About fourteen days earlier, he was to have contractually taken over again the school for a year, but before that he went "to Savannah to the merchants with whose goods he was dealing here." They believed that it would not be good if, along with his business, he also taught school, and so he left Ebenezer without giving notice (TK33, 41 = journal April 18, 1759 B. copy).

185. 5B2:9, 35 = December 31, 1763 B. original.

186. UA April 20 and June 6, 1759; 5D13, 49 = journal September 16, 1763.

187. 5B2:12, 56 = December 31, 1764 B. original.

188. 5D13, 30 = journal August 28, 1763.

189. 5B2:4, 12 = September 25, 1766 Fr. draft; 5B2:29, 117–18 = January 13, 1766 L. original: "He served in Germany as private tutor with various gentlemen for their children, and also was in London eighteen years ago, and heard and spoke with His Reverence, the dear Herr Court Preacher Ziegenhagen. Most recently he was with the Prussian ambassador in Regensburg, Herr von Platho, from whom he also has a reference, and as he afterward came to Würtemberg [sic], the University of Tübingen also gave him one. Finally, at the advice of a Reformed pastor, he traveled to Pennsylvania, but there was nothing for him there. Then, he came to Charles-Town and wished to return again." However, because there was a travel ban between England and its American colonies, due to the unrest concerning the Stamp Act, he remained for the time being here. "His father was a pastor in in the Hanau area" (5B2:29, 117–18).

190. TK32F8, 674–75 = September 27, 1771 Tr. original.

Since among the adults who came to Georgia there were naturally also some who were illiterate,[191] a special instruction in reading and writing was scheduled for them[192] during the midday meal.[193] It enjoyed keen interest since the readings, mainly from edifying texts, played an important role in the community and formed an important part of their expression of piety. It often happened that the adults sat between the school children and took part in the instruction, even when they already could read and write.[194]

The Lutheran community in Frederica also could enjoy meticulous instruction when Pastor Driessler was active there. We take from his fully packed weekly plan: Mondays and Thursdays, "Nine o'clock to eleven o'clock, the little children who are not needed for any work come from the town. They are not divided into classes so that, as in the Orphan House [in Halle], they have the same books and activities. They learn spelling, reading, and always a Bible verse that I teach in catechetical fashion. From twelve o'clock to three o'clock, since because of the heat no one works, and all the people are accustomed to sleeping, come

1. again these little children from the town.
2. A number from the plantations.
3. A number of adults: they learn spelling, reading, a Bible passage, words of Luther [the Catechism] that I reach in catechetical fashion.

Praise God! Now we have come so far that they read, look things up, etc. Evenings from seven o'clock to nine o'clock the single adults come again. Praise God! They write and do arithmetic in some of the evenings; in the others, the passage is taught catechetically, which we will discuss next Sunday in the instruction for the children in the afternoon." Tuesday and Friday: "Nine o'clock to eleven o'clock, the little ones come again to the town. A part of the Catechism is learned by heart, taught catechetically, and the hymn that we will sing on Sunday is presented to them and sung every day 10,000 times. God be eternally praised. They have learned the VI. main part, as well as many Bible passages and many hymns, perfectly. Midday at twelve o'clock I go to the plantations. I teach, so that the little children who, because of the heat and the long distance, cannot come here, will not be neglected. I examine the adults and then sing with the adults the hymn for the next Sunday. I conduct at the same time a visit of home and heart. God be eternally

---

191. 5A1:28, 137 = December 22, 1733 new style.
192. 5D2 = journal January 22, 1736.
193. From two o'clock to three o'clock p.m. (UN May 5, 1742).
194. 5D3 = journal (+UN) January 25, 1737.

praised! Things are going quite well. The evening instruction is the same as on Monday and Thursday."[195] Unfortunately, this prolific work came too soon to an end through Driessler's early death.

When the spiritual care of the community members in and around Ebenezer was underway again after the turmoil of the War of Independence, the efforts with school were also undertaken again. However, severe controversies arose from the altered relationship of the German and English-speaking residents. When the school was founded in 1795, the House of Assembly appointed George Fisher as teacher. He was a native of the county of Yorkshire in England and previously had conducted school on an island next to Savannah and later in Purrysburg, yet both times with the result that no one was unhappy to see him leave. In Purrysburg, he squandered the wealth that he brought from his wife. He was, moreover, a "free spirit" and a follower of Thomas Paine. Yet he showed himself in Ebenezer to be reasonably agreeable and friendly among several of the commissioners supervising him and with the annual salary of forty pounds during his probationary year. He taught reading, writing, and arithmetic for a tuition of two to three talers per quarter, for orphans for free, so that Bergmann, after the expiration of this probationary year, approved his permanent appointment.[196]

However, other aspects appeared in the teacher's behavior. He forbade the children from attending the German worship services and insulted the Germans horrifically so that Bergmann had no one to confirm in 1797. Since this could not continue, Bergmann announced to the congregation after the morning worship service on January 24, 1797, that now he would report these incidents to Europe. The community recommended to him to begin again the German school that already had existed under Probst, but Bergmann feared even worse friction from such a course of action.

On the second following Sunday, Fisher himself appeared, with the justice of the peace Mattheus Rahn, at the morning worship service, and when Bergmann left the pulpit after the sermon, they fell upon him, as he wrote, and had with them English schoolchildren who were to testify that Fisher had not forbidden them from the German worship service, and, moreover, they "both bellowed like the most senseless and coarsest people." Naturally, Bergmann rejected these "witnesses," reproached Fisher that the freedom of religious practice applied to everyone, and expelled the judge Rahn from the congregation, whereupon the Baptists likewise excommunicated the surveyor and judge from Ebenezer, William Gardner, who also had participated in this matter. The good relationship that Bergmann had

---

195. 4C1:67, 244 = July 30, 1744 Dr. original.
196. 5B3:42, 193 = April 20, 1796 Bm. original.

with the Baptist community finally led a Baptist commissioner to bring about Fisher's dismissal for September 1797.

However, Fisher still lived in a house next to Bergmann until Christmas, and so, naturally, all sorts of things went on: "At the Christmas service, the schoolmaster contrived to have English people stand outside the church, beating on the window shutters with heavy clubs in order to disturb the worship service; then, this evil man wanted to coax the people in Ebenezer to turn over their houses to him for a Christmas dance," but he did not succeed. This was his glorious exit.[197]

The successor to this purely English school was a German-English school[198] that was already founded on March 27, 1797, in which reading, writing, arithmetic, and reading of the Bible was conducted in both languages.[199] Bergmann taught in it with energetic interest, and, from around 1800, Gottlieb Ernst, a former student of Triebner, with success.[200] In fact, the good influence of this regular schooling soon became noticeable.[201] On New Year's Day 1803, the church vestrymen brought to Bergmann a school constitution that after a few alterations was introduced.[202]

Confirmation Instruction

The children who were to be confirmed around the age of fourteen first had to take part in preparatory or confirmation instruction that was conducted by the pastors, most often four hours every week.[203] During that time, Luther's Small Catechism was mainly treated, making use of its Bible passages that were compiled and learned.[204] In addition, Freylinghausen's *Ordnung des Heyls* (Order of Salvation) and *Compendium oder Kurtzer Begriff der*

---

197. 5B4:2, 5–7 = April 3, 1799 Bm. original.

198. 5B4:43, 134 = 134 = April 22, 1805 Bm. original.

199. 5B4:2, 7.

200. 5B4:7, 28 = April 22, 1800 Bm. original; 5B4:45, 141 = March 17, 1805 Bm. original.

201. "The youth lately have markedly increased" (5B4:10, 40 = November 23, 1801 Bm. original).

202. 5B4:36, 105 (= part 2 from 5B4:29) = January 11, 1803 Bm. original.

203. UA May 7 and June 4, 1751; B. on the plantations, L. in Ebenezer: TK32F10, 793 = March 26, 1761 B. copy; B. in Ebenezer: TK 32F10, 875 = January 15, 1756 B. original.

204. UA May 7, 1751. The instruction in the school also took place using the Small Catechism. 5A11:69, 312 = July 24, 1747.

gantzen Christlichen Lehre (Compendium or Brief Summary of the Entire Christian Doctrine) were frequently used.[205]

Boltzius only pronounced admission to confirmation when it was clear to him that the child in question had understood what the Christian faith was about and had signified its acceptance.[206] The experience of conversion was not a condition, yet it was the case that confirmands, who were inspired more intensively to contemplation over matters of faith through the instruction, arrived at a special awareness of their general sinfulness, and then most came to Boltzius in tears. But such children were not thereupon confirmed as a matter of course, but it had to be apparent from their conduct that it had not been a flash in the pan. It happened often enough not to cause a stir that children just a year from their confirmation were placed back and participated in further instruction.[207]

The confirmation itself did not take place at a specified date. It took place once in March,[208] the end of May,[209] also in August,[210] occasionally on Good Friday,[211] at Pentecost,[212] or at Christmas,[213] even on a Saturday.[214] About the rite of confirmation (*Actus Confirmationis*), Boltzius reported:

> 1. It would be announced to the community a day or two in advance that several children would be confirmed, and such an important undertaking is being commended to the community for prayer. 2. Instead of the regular sermon, the children are being examined publicly over several important points of faith, and they must verify all points with selected passages of Holy Scripture without having to look them up in the Bible. Time usually does not allow for the catechism to be recited, which also is not at all necessary since they otherwise recite it in the afternoons between the first and second hymns of the Sunday. The entire examination is directed toward the edification of the entire community. 3. The children who have been examined

---

205. 5D1, 323 = journal August 27, 1735.
206. 5D3, 66 = journal May 19, 1737.
207. For example, 5D4 = journal (+UN) December 6, 1738.
208. 5D4 = journal March 30, 1738.
209. 5D3 = journal May 22, 1737.
210. 5D1 = journal August 17, 1735.
211. UN April 1, 1743; 5D9 = journal March 23, 1744.
212. UN June 7, 1747.
213. UN December 22, 1739.
214. "On the coming Saturday before Quasimodo Sunday, twelve children will be confirmed and consecrated in the confessional service" (TK32F10, 793 = March 26, 1761 B. copy).

step closer to the communion table and are addressed in the following way: "In Christ, dearly beloved children, you have the intention today to go with the congregation for the first time to the table of the Lord, to which end you have been instructed up to now from the divine Word according to the grace that God has granted, and for this important intention have been prepared with many earnest admonitions and heartfelt prayer." The indication then follows that according to their baptismal certificates or reliable witnesses they have been baptized, and "he that believeth and is baptized shall be saved" (Mk 16:16). In baptism, the godparents promised on behalf of the baptized child to renounce the devil and all his ways and to surrender oneself to God. But they have thrown away this baptismal grace and through repentance they should renew the baptismal covenant: "If this is also the case with you, that you heartily confess and repent your sins and falling back from baptismal grace, and, as repentant sinners, heartily yearn for the forgiveness of your sins and the grace of God in Christ, then confess publicly with your mouth." Response, "Yes." Thus, in this way each renews his baptismal covenant in the presence of the entire congregation, namely, "I, (the name is stated), renew herewith, etc.; I believe in God the Father, etc." Then follows a prayer that takes up these thoughts, the Lord's Prayer, and a blessing.[215]

The first communion followed immediately.[216]

The Church Library

Already on May 26, 1738, Boltzius reported the establishment of a "church library,"[217] the holdings of which Appendix II of this study gives an impression. Because most of the books had been selected by Francke or Urlsperger and sent to Georgia, we find here mainly works of the Halle Pietism school, among which edifying literature predominates, in keeping with the purpose of the library for the community. In fact, postils were in great use in the community. However, there was one book that, after the Bible, was most beloved by everyone: Arndt's *True Christianity*.[218]

---

215. UN December 23, 1739.
216. 5D3, 66 = journal May 19, 1737.
217. 5D4 = journal May 26, 1738.
218. For example, UN October 7, 1739; 5A11:2, 6 = July 21, 1743 G. original.

In general, there was quite a bit of reading done in Georgia's first Lutheran communities,[219] and the reading of these edifying texts, during the evenings in the family circle or on the sickbed, shaped the writing style of the community members, as their letters show, as well as their piety. Just like the "Evangelical Magazine" edited by Schmucker and Helmuth, the first Lutheran periodical of America,[220] this literature also contained a considerable number of reports about the last hours of pious men and women and depicted in ever-recurring expressions the joy with which they met death. In these images, many pious people in Georgia's Lutheran communities patterned their conduct in the face of death, and the numerous reports about it in the journals proclaim that many passed away with a hymn or a Bible verse or a brief prayer of help on their lips.

But the library was a great benefit not only for Ebenezer and the surrounding places. Even Savannah and the neighboring settlements were supplied regularly with books, especially Bibles, New Testaments, and ABC books,[221] and again and again one learned in Ebenezer about compatriots in the faith, also Reformed Germans, from places too far away to be visited by a pastor. The books especially reached into South Carolina, for example, Congaree (Saxe-Gotha), Halifax, New Windsor, Orangeburg, Pallachocolas, Savannahtown, and other places were kept in mind.[222]

Besides the spiritual literature, there was also in the library a series of medical works that gained importance, especially at a time when, far and wide, no doctor was available. Boltzius learned much from them, and from them Timotheus Lemcke acquired his entire medical training with which he provided great service to the community. Also found here was a foundational work on mill construction with numerous illustrations, a gift from Samuel Urlsperger.[223]

In the secondary literature there is a quote passed on from a letter of von Brahm, according to which there are said to have been books available in thirteen different languages in the church library.[224] From the archival material, which gives rather abundant information about the books, only titles in German, English, and Latin are known. If the other titles also had been represented, they had no importance for the library, since no one in

---

219. 5D4 = journal May 28, 1738.

220. Wentz, *A Basic History of Lutheranism in America*, 91.

221. 5D4 = journal February 2, 1738.

222. UN April 25, 1750; see also *Nachrichten von den vereinigten Deutschen Evangelisch-Lutherischen Gemeinden*, 67.

223. 5B2:28, 113 = November 27, 1765 L. original signature in another hand; see also Appendix II, no. 93.

224. Cooper, *The Story of Georgia* I, 284.

these communities understood Aramaic, Coptic, or Syriac. According to some incorrect information given by Johann Gotthilf Probst, Ebenezer's church library was destroyed by fire during the War of Independence.[225] However, a considerable part of its holdings could be traced bibliographically from the Halle manuscripts. On this basis, most of these books could be found in the library of Lutheran Theological Southern Seminary in Columbia, South Carolina, by its librarian, William Richard Fritz in cooperation with Raymond E. Davis (of Savannah).

DIACONAL ACTIVITY

The Orphanage

Halle Pietism also made its influence felt through an establishment whose name had resounded far and wide: the orphanage, the first in the United States. Establishments of this sort had arisen everywhere in Germany, both as concrete representations for the practical results of the devout expressions of Pietism as well as the consequences of the distinctive pedagogical interests of this trend. Such institutions were known to Boltzius from Halle, the explicit example also for Ebenezer,[226] and from Thommendorf in Silesia.[227] And because there already were orphans in Ebenezer who could only be sustained and raised with effort by other families in the community, Boltzius proposed the construction of an orphanage already in December 1734.[228] Accordingly, it can only be maintained that this was not the original purpose of the facility if the intention is to shift the pride of place to the Englishman Whitefield and his Bethesda Orphan Home.[229] From the sources, such an assertion is not attested.

Already before such a building could be constructed, nine orphans since 1737 lived under the supervision of the Salzburger Ruprecht Kalcher in the hut that had been built for the doctor who had been expected,[230] and from about the first half of 1737, the community had taken in an orphan

---

225. 5B3:21 = December 6, 1786.

226. 5A7:34, 149 = November 4, 1738 B. original. Orphans from the Francke Foundations wrote to orphans in Ebenezer: 5A10:3, 9 = May 13, 1741 B. original; 5D7, 241 = journal May 20, 1741.

227. See also pp. 165–66.

228. 5A1:49, 233 = undated (probably December 10–11, 1734) B. original.

229. Corry, "The Houses of Colonial Georgia," 187–88.

230. 5A7:3, 6 = January 20, 1738 G. original; UN September 9, 1737.

boy from Purrysburg and an English girl who had wandered in.[231] After a long time had passed because of a lack of money, and, in the meantime, Ebenezer had been relocated, Francke also approved the plan that had been submitted to him,[232] and on November 14, 1737, the foundation stone was laid. Sixteen men of the community who were to carry out the construction were gathered, and Boltzius spoke on Matthew 25:34–36 ("for I was hungry and you gave me food").[233] On January 9, 1738,[234] the facility was ready.[235] It comprised six buildings: an orphanage (thirty by forty-five feet) with three living rooms and three bedrooms, built with the fifty pounds that Urlsperger had sent,[236] a building for the kitchen with a pantry, a cattle stable that anticipated future growth, a pig pen with a hen house in the floor above it, an outhouse, and a hut for milling,[237] baking, and washing. The next day, in place of the evening prayer hour, the dedication took place with Luke 11:49–52,[238] and then the facility was occupied.

The Kalcher couple were the house parents.[239] From everything that is reported about Kalcher, it is seen that he must have been a very simple person but of superb character. He signed an original letter to Halle: "Ruprecht Kalcher, orphan father in Ebenezer."[240] And that he truly was.[241] Also moving in were the Schweighoffer widow, the Salzburger Herzog,[242] three orphan boys and eight orphan girls from Ebenezer, to which also soon came in addition four boys and four girls from Purrysburg.[243] Boltzius held morning devotions with them,[244] and a book was kept over the conduct of the children.[245]

231. 5A3:57, 359 = July 29, 1737 B. original.

232. 5A1:51, 255 = March 11, 1735 Fr. draft.

233. 5A7:33, 143 = journal November 14, 1737 extract. [Translator's note: Mt 25:35 comes from the New Revised Standard Version.]

234. 5D4 = journal January 9, 1738; 5A7:3, 6–7 = journal January 9, 1738 extract.

235. 5A7:12, 39 = May 8, 1738 Fr. draft: "I myself could not suppose that you would achieve it so soon."

236. 5A7:3, 6 = January 20, 1738 G. original.

237. Until this time, there was only a hand mill.

238. 5D4 = journal January 10, 1736; 5A7: 3, 8 = journal January 10, 1738 draft.

239. Ruprecht and Margaretha, Salzburgers from the second transport.

240. 5A10:23, 81 = January 30, 1742 Kalcher original.

241. In 1742 and following, Vigera assisted him since he was overburdened with his supervision and his own plantation (5A10:37, 130 = April 2, 1743 Fr. draft).

242. 5A7:3, 7.

243. 5A9:9, 40 = September 9, 1740 B. original.

244. 5A7:33, 143 = journal November 14, 1737 extract.

245. 5D4 = journal August 9, 1738.

The Development of the Communities in the Organization of Their Life

In the time that followed, the establishment of the orphanage proved increasingly to be more of an institution that was in a position to help needy persons in the community.[246] Mothers could give birth here, children of single mothers were raised here until they were at the point where they could help at home,[247] and the Salzburger Riedelsperger spent a seventeen-week long illness here.[248]

The institutions were continuously enlarged. A barn was added,[249] and after a short time, yet a second one;[250] in 1740, even several auxiliary buildings.[251]

In time, however, the orphans grew up and were distributed as servants among the families of the place. New ones were not added, and so it was that in 1744, there were no more occupants in the original sense. For that reason, the facility was completely converted into what it already partially had become, an economic enterprise of the community. The orphanage (it continued to keep this name) owned horses and Ebenezer's first plow;[252] also in the beginning the only corn hand mill. The raising of silkworms was first conducted here to a larger extent,[253] and from here the millworks and other things as well were brought to life and undertaken.[254]

But Kalcher, because of these numerous duties, had to neglect his own farm, and so it was decided, "He should remain here with his family, continue farming with the horses and continue the silk production, feed himself and his family in this way with the work of his hands and keep everything that belonged to the orphanage in good order."[255]

As the orphanage always had adapted itself to the current needs of the community and served it—be it even with the only alarm bell available in Ebenezer[256]—it fulfilled in a similar way the function of a church "community house" in which regular instruction, the prayer hour, and even sometimes the worship service could take place. In doing so it showed the practical character of its builders: at this time, it was more needed and more

---

246. UN December 15, 1739.
247. UN February 2, 1740.
248. 5A11:4, 12 = August 7, 1743 Riedelsperger original.
249. 5D6 = journal August 13, 1739.
250. UN July 19, 1740.
251. UN December 15, 1740.
252. 5A9:8, 35 = journal May 24, 1740 extract; 5D8, 851 = journal October 30, 1741.
253. 5A11:13, 43 = June 4, 1744 B. original.
254. 5D9 = journal May 22, 1744.
255. 5A11:13, 44.
256. 5D6, 18 = journal July 20, 1739.

useful than a church that, of course, could have been built with the money that was spent.

Health Care

The prominent status that Ebenezer occupied among Georgia's settlements was decidedly based on the fact that here, almost constantly, the position of a doctor, in part from the Francke Foundations, was filled. Moreover, Ebenezer continuously obtained from the Halle Orphan House the famous medicines that stood in high regard and in good use in the entire world,[257] and even in Georgia bestowed help far beyond Ebenezer all the way into South Carolina. Their value was elevated even higher here because of the heat that was especially difficult for Europeans to endure,[258] since one sickness never ceased to cause them difficulty: malaria. When a new transport of immigrants reached the colony, it fell victim to it without exception,[259] and even later the settlers did not remain untouched by the constantly recurring attacks. At the time, they did not yet attempt treating it properly with quinine, which later on became indispensable,[260] so they actually had no remedy at all.[261] Often, diarrhea and dysentery-like illnesses occurred, sometimes immediately after the end of the voyage,[262] and sometimes as a result of the very drafty wooden huts.[263] From Halle, they received the copy of a medical assessment that had been prepared for Tranquebar.[264]

One very strange illness that appeared again and again was the uncontrollable desire of children up to the age of thirteen to eat all sorts of dirt, especially soil, sand, clay and also charcoal, leaves, and paper, and even tobacco. No prohibitions and sufficient supply of other foods helped. If they continued to eat such things, they became sick, and, as it was even noted

---

257. See Lehmann, "Hallesche Mediziner und Medizinen," 117–32.

258. Bittinger, "The coast country of South Carolina was by this time ascertained to be—save in exceptional places—malarious, and impossible for the continued residence of white men." Bittinger, *The Germans in Colonial Times*, 123.

259. 5D2 = journal March 25, 1736; 5A10:40, 144 = January 7, 1743 B. original.

260. 5D3, 114 = journal July 22, 1737; 5A10:55, 215 = November 15, 1743 Fr. draft.

261. 5A2:3, 12 = May 6, 1734 B. original: "Also in this hot land, because of a lack of beer, they like many hot drinks, such as brandy, punch, and flip, which they prepare from water, brandy, sugar, and lemon."

262. 5D1, 219 = journal January 16, 1735.

263. 5A1:44, 191 = February 16, 1734; UN July 23 and following, and August 18, 1734, April 1, 1735.

264. 5A1:45, 202.

several times, "died from eating dirt."²⁶⁵ Nothing was known to help against this disease.

Concerning the already mentioned shockingly high infant mortality of the early years, Boltzius wrote in 1748, "If our dear residents in Old and New Ebenezer had kept their children from the first years of our arrival, the first of them already would be thirteen to fourteen years old, and therefore would be a great help to their worn out parents who cannot obtain servants here.... Schweiger already has had seven children in this land, of whom he has none left except a single three-year-old little son who is also sickly."²⁶⁶

It is easy to appreciate how much the Halle medicines always were desired in these circumstances. This point was missing in almost none of the regular letters of the years after the coarsest development of the settlement and it remained until the time after the war, since whole stacks of order forms, even from farmers who did not belong to Lutheran communities, were sent to Halle. The medicines arrived, were sold in Ebenezer, and the amount of these contributions was deducted from the contributions that arrived in Halle for Ebenezer.

If things had gone according to the plans for the Ebenezer community, then they would have set up already in 1743 a hospital in a house in Old Ebenezer for residents and outsiders. But this building belonged to the Trustees who did not hand it over, even though it stood empty, until it had fallen down and the remnants could be salvaged.²⁶⁷ The sick in Georgia's communities experienced the most proficient care of the time through Ebenezer's doctors who extended their medical visits all the way to Purrysburg.

Johann Andreas Zwiffler,²⁶⁸ who came from Hungary,²⁶⁹ had been given to the first Salzburger transport as their doctor,²⁷⁰ a "quiet and polite person."²⁷¹ It seemed at first that he would establish a good relationship with the life of the settlers. In the beginning he cooked for the bachelors Boltzius and Gronau.²⁷² On Christmas Eve 1734, he married a "person

---

265. UN July 19, 1747; TK33, 58 = journal May 17, 1759; UA June 20, 1760.

266. UN January 7, 1748.

267. 5A11:3, 9–10 = undated (between July 21 and September 20, 1743) B. original; 5A11:21, 78 = October 29, 1744 B. original.

268. UN I, 213; *Nachrichten von den vereinigten Deutschen Evangelisch-Lutherischen Gemeinden*, 297, has, incorrectly, "Daniel."

269. 5D3 = journal March 7, 1737.

270. 5A1:20; 5D1 = journal November 27, 1733.

271. 5D1 = journal December 15, 1733.

272. 5A1:38, 169 = May 6, 1734.

who joined him from Germany,"[273] and Boltzius noted, "Herr Zwiffler, along with his wife, so far have brought to light clear evidence of their upright conversion."[274] In Old Ebenezer they lived on the second floor of the storehouse; in New Ebenezer they received an extra hut, and he was tirelessly active in the community.[275]

However, he was only an apothecary; in "surgery," therefore he was little or not at all versed in cupping, bloodletting, and so on.[276] He prescribed rather radical treatments, and since the people for that reason sometimes did not keep precisely to his instructions, he vehemently bellowed one day that if things remained as they were, he would do nothing more, "rather, the devil should fetch him."[277] Boltzius was appalled over this. He believed that Zwiffler had to be brought to remorse over his impudence, but Zwiffler, however, did not accept, and so resentment remained between the two.

That Boltzius understood something about medicine, and that he knew it, seems not to have been an advantage here, since he believed that Zwiffler was making "too much fuss about his ability."[278] Moreover, Zwiffler wanted to have an appropriate salary and not to live only as a settler from the gifts of the SPCK,[279] but Ziegenhagen did not know where he would get the money for it. When Zwiffler's wife died on October 6, 1736,[280] there was nothing to keep him in Ebenezer. He had in mind obtaining permission from Oglethorpe to return,[281] and on March 7, 1737, he actually did depart after he had left behind several written medicinal instructions.[282] Later, news of him came that he did not return to Europe but had remained in Philadelphia, Pennsylvania,[283] where he joined with the Moravians and died in June 1749.[284]

Christian Ernst Thilo, his successor in Ebenezer, was to be the most difficult case in Boltzius' occupation of leading people. When Ziegenhagen

---

273. 5D1 = journal December 24, 1734; her name was Anna Regina (UN October 6, 1736).

274. 5A3:4, 24 = March 28, 1735 B. original.

275. 5D2, 170–71 = journal May 13, 1736.

276. 5D1, 134 = journal September 18, 1735.

277. 5D1, 132 = journal September 18, 1735.

278. 5D2, 383.

279. 5A3:20, 139 = July 7, 1736.

280. UN October 6, 1736.

281. 5D2 = journal October 31, 1736; 5A3:27, 201 = October 6, 1736 B. original.

282. 5D3, 29 = journal March 7, 1737.

283. 5A3:61, 384.

284. *Nachrichten von den vereinigten Deutschen Evangelisch-Lutherischen Gemeinden*, 297.

The Development of the Communities in the Organization of Their Life

became aware of Zwiffler's intention to leave Georgia and Boltzius' related request for a successor, he first directed an unofficial inquiry concerning it to Francke but immediately conveyed to him that, as things now stood with Oglethorpe and the Trustees, he harbored little hope for a salary.[285] Francke's response read that he had found someone named Thilo from among the students of the medical professor Juncker who understood something about "surgery" and was prepared to go to Georgia, even without the prospect of a fixed salary.[286] Thilo had distinguished himself among his fellow students during his three-year study of medicine in Halle through his vivacious nature. However, he then became suddenly quiet,[287] and was for two years the supervisor at the Orphan House infirmary in the surgery unit under Professor Juncker.[288] According to an assessment report of his supervisor he had become a "hypochondriac"[289] who preached to his patients in the consultations.[290] Also living in Halle were both of his sisters "who recognized and admired his prophetic and apostolic gift,"[291] and in whose home he played all sorts of music with his beautiful bass and violin,[292] and probably something more happened there.[293] If the doctor in Ebenezer would have had the prospect of a regular salary, the choice in Halle would hardly have fallen to him.

After several delays,[294] Thilo traveled from Halle[295] and was in London on October 1, 1737 (new style).[296] Ziegenhagen took him along to the weekly meeting of the Trustees where he was granted free "provisions" for three years,[297] yet he seems to have behaved rather awkwardly there.[298] On

285. 5A3:36, 227 = January 27, 1737 Z. original.

286. 5A3:37, 230–32 = February 21, 1737 Fr. draft.

287. 5A5:16, 58.

288. 5A5:15, 55; 5A5:16; 5A5:38, 252.

289. Hypochondria at that time was viewed not as something pertaining to various diseases but as a disease in its own right.

290. 5A5:16; 5A3:53, 336 = November 7, 1737 Fr. draft.

291. 5A7:39, 167 = December 6, 1738 B. original.

292. UN December 25–26, 1739; 5A5:16, 58.

293. "But in Halle there were a couple of women whom he remembers in prayer and otherwise as his dearest friends, but whose names he did not want to tell me" (5A5:19, 74b).

294. 5A3:43, 281 = March 2, 1737 Z.

295. 5A5:10, 45 = October 3, 1737.

296. 5A5:10, 45 = September 22/October 3, 1737; 5A5:13, 50; 5A6:3, 5 = September 23, 1737 Z. original.

297. 5A5:14, 53.

298. 5A3:61, 386 = October 13, 1737 Z. original.

October 12, 1737 (old style), he departed from England,[299] and after a voyage without any storms worthy of mention, he arrived on January 13, 1738, unexpected and greeted with great joy in Ebenezer[300] where he moved into the handsome residence next to the orphanage that long since had been built for the doctor.[301]

However, appalling reports from Boltzius soon reached Halle over his unbelievable behavior. He made thoroughly unreasonable demands, for example, that completely insignificant letters that had been sent be recovered by any means, even though he did not know at all what was in them. When Boltzius refused, Thilo behaved appallingly. He, Thilo, would have to bear the wrath of God, and so on. He went home, and when Boltzius followed him, Thilo sat at the table, had taken off his shoes, wiped them inside and out with a cloth and murmured, "I have walked in the shoes in which I bore the wrath. The wrath is tucked inside them; I must wipe it out," whereupon Boltzius clapped his hands together.[302] With the determination that God wanted it so, he explained all of his senseless dealings. For example, he once had already put powder in the spoon to give it to someone who was sick when he put it away again since God allegedly intended something else.[303]

With such behavior, there was naturally no more talk of trust in him from the patients. Also, to the annoyance of the community, he did not go to any worship service or prayer hour,[304] since he accused the community of idolatry with the preachers.[305] They were completely at a loss. In addition to that, Thilo had continuous relationships with young women and girls from the community whom he visited during the time of the worship services or evening prayer hours or even later[306] and caused terrific chaos until finally, three trustees of the community complained to Boltzius in due form.[307]

In the official journals, there was not even a hint at all of this, but Boltzius kept a *Diarium extraordinarium*[308] and complained in letters to Francke who, along with Zieganhagen, considered whether Thilo should

299. 5A5:12, 48.

300. 5D4, 14 = journal January 13, 1738; 5A7:2, 2; 5A7:3, 6; 5A5:19, 74 = February 27, 1738 B. copy.

301. 5D4 = journal January 17, 1738; 5A3:57, 356 = July 29, 1737 B. original.

302. 5A5:19, 73 = February 27, 1738.

303. 5A7:22, 91 = August 25, 1738 B. copy.

304. 5A5: 19, 73–74.

305. 5A5:23, 84 B. copy.

306. 5A5:27, 108–9.

307. 5A5:27, 109–10.

308. 5A5:27 = DE.

be terminated.[309] But Ziegenhagen was of the opinion that Francke should write to Thilo that if he did not improve himself, then he (Francke) "himself would make application to the Trustees for his dismissal and removal."[310] Francke conveyed this to Thilo in a letter that was alarmingly severe for the style of the time.[311]

Thilo, however, had felt the coming storm, and, in the meantime, had married. After preliminary, almost endless quarreling and great disorder, and a wedding date canceled by "divine initiative," and so on, Boltzius married him on July 17, 1739, to the young Reformed woman Friederica Helffenstein.[312] Subsequently, his behavior somewhat improved so that people were willing to give him another try.[313] But he continued to stay away from the worship service which, in a place with circumstances like Ebenezer at the time, must have caused great offense: Also, he continued to conduct his duties badly and unreliably,[314] did not cease keeping the community in tension with his inspirations, and so it remained until he died on July 25, 1765.[315]

Johann Ludwig Mayer, on the other hand, provided great service to Ebenezer. In view of the dismal circumstances with Thilo, he, a surgeon but not a practicing doctor, was received with enthusiasm when he arrived in Ebenezer with the fourth transport at the beginning of 1742.[316] He already had seen much of the world and most recently had been living with his wife in Memmingen.[317] Already after a few weeks, we hear Boltzius: "The surgeon H. Mayer is very active and makes every effort to be useful to the people of our place without interfering with the office of Herr Thilo."[318] He and not Thilo was, in practice, the actual doctor in Ebenezer. Moreover, he was unceasingly active in the life of the community, so far as his health permitted, as repeatedly indicated. Boltzius acknowledged, "I consider it a special sign of the providence of the Heavenly Father over me and our

---

309. 5A7:42, 183 = May 27, 1739 Fr. draft.

310. 5A7:47, 196 = June 4, 1739 Fr. draft.

311. 5A5:28 = June 4, 1739 Fr. draft.

312. 5D6, 12. Text: Matthew 5:1–12.

313. 5A5:32; 5A7:64a, 269 = October 30, 1739 B. original.

314. 5A10:32, 116 = September 4, 1742 B. original; 5A10:40, 147 = January 7, 1743 B. original; 5B1:5, 18 = January 11, 1748; 5B1:7, 26 = December 15, 1748.

315. 5B2:23, 94 = September 6, 1765 B. copy.

316. UN II, preface to the seventhth continuation; UN January 6, 1742. The spelling of his name is not consistent. Here, the most frequent form has been chosen.

317. UN III, 434–36.

318. 5A10:17, 56 = March 13, 1742 B. original.

community that he sent us this upright man."³¹⁹ He died probably in the fall of 1763.³²⁰ Afterwards, Timotheus Lemcke and Jenking Davis took care of the sick of Ebenezer and other places as well as they could.³²¹

Donations from Europe

For as long as Georgia was a British colony, the Lutheran communities required support from Europe that was channeled directly to Ebenezer and, through this community, to the others. The reasons for it already have been included several times in earlier chapters of this investigation. What remained decisive were the economic limitations decreed from England that, without exception, pointed the settlers to farming or to trades that produced raw materials (the production of raw silk or indigo), the profits from which were set at the will of the motherland who alone had the right of purchase. The lumber trade, which matched the natural conditions of Georgia and had its promising prospects with the West Indies, was forbidden, and finally, continuing farming on the alluvial sands of the mouth of the Savannah was almost the most misguided thing that could be done.

It was also the case for Ebenezer that the first German settlers, lacking any experience in the conditions of the soil and climate, at first attempted the planting of German crops and grains that in large part did not thrive before they came to the knowledge of what best grew here, and even then, despite truly remarkable industry, they brought forth no real prosperity. In this difficult situation, there constantly came into Ebenezer, especially from Halle and Augsburg but also from London, gifts of money and goods that mainly had been raised by readers of the journals published by Urlsperger and that by far exceeded in scope the charitable gifts of the SPCK.³²²

In the beginning, along with the medicines that were constantly sent, these were composed especially of gifts in linen and household utensils that meant an incomparable help for the settlers. Fortunately, among the numerous shipments, only a single trunk was lost,³²³ and two trunks that were designated for the missionaries of the Halle-Danish mission in India

---

319. 5A11:23, 85 = December 29, 1744 B. original.

320. 5B2:9, 36 and 38 = December 31, 1763 B. original.

321. With Davis, probably meant here is the English medical doctor who already was active in Ebenezer before fall 1770 (TK32F8, 675–76 = September 27, 1771 Tr. original). He died in fall 1788 (5B3:39, 176 = August 24, 1790 Bm. original).

322. 5B1:16, 69 = May 12, 1749 B. original.

323. 5D5, 2–27.

The Development of the Communities in the Organization of Their Life 161

erroneously reached Ebenezer where, naturally, their contents also could be put to good use.[324]

Since, in time, those items that in the beginning were exceedingly rare in Georgia were also for sale here, the monetary remittances from Europe stepped into the foreground. Cash was not always sent, since losses through exchange and the fluctuating rate of the pound sterling had to be taken into account.[325] For that reason, the method already mentioned was soon used where the money coming in from Germany was directed to the Francke Foundations from where extensive shipments of medicines and books were compiled from orders or according to discretion. These articles were sold in Ebenezer, and the proceeds, to the extent that were not designated for a particular purpose, supplied Ebenezer's "poverty chest"[326] that was in great demand each time a new group of immigrants arrived.[327]

But because the sale of these items soon developed into a regular business, it was seen to be necessary in Ebenezer to set up a standing establishment for these goods that was administered in part by Mayer but mainly by Wertsch. In doing so, he became for the Lutheran communities an important middleman to such an extent that Pastor Bergmann, from the accounts of the community members who dealt with him, concluded that he should be called the actual father of Ebenezer.[328]

Concerning his life, it is reported that Johann Caspar Wertsch came from Ansbach and learned the trades of baker and miller. When he arrived in Georgia with a group of immigrants on October 3, 1749,[329] the teacher on the plantations, the weaver Kocher, had just resigned his office, and Boltzius had to take over his work.[330] But it was soon noticed that Wertsch's good schooling was to be put to better use than for menial service. Teaching reading and writing for three hours daily at the school on the plantations was handed over to him. From Boltzius, he received written instructions for it and two, later six pounds salary annually from European donations, from which he paid his redemption, that is, the costs laid out for his voyage that had to be reimbursed.[331] He proved to be extraordinarily satisfactory.

324. 5D6, 2–3 = journal February 8, 1740 extract.

325. 5C2:1, 2.

326. 5D1, 102 = journal April 16, 1734. It was established with the bequest of the Salzburger Lackner.

327. 5D2 = journal April 30, 1736; 5A3:23, 164–65 = June 19, 1736 B. original.

328. 5B3:30, 127 = August 27, 1787 Bm. original.

329. See p. 52. UN November 17, 1749; UA May 9, 1751, February 8, 1753.

330. UN November 8, 1749.

331. UN November 17 and December 6, 1749; UA June 9, 1752, February 8, 1753.

After the end of this activity in 1753, he was appointed as "shop keeper" in the store that sold the goods coming from Halle and along with them the products of the community's own agricultural undertakings.[332] On March 14, 1758,[333] he married Gronau's elder daughter, Hanna Elisabeth, and now he wanted, understandably, "to be not only the administrator but the owner of this business." He bought it and paid for it in four years.[334] Mention already has been made of his role in the pastors' controversy. He had only one daughter, named Hanna,[335] and died at the end of 1779; his wife already had died earlier.[336] After his death, he was said to have wandered around as a ghost and conducted his business just as he had done in life.[337]

---

332. TK32F11, 1075 = March 3, 1755 B. original signature in another hand; 5B2:9, 27 = December 30, 1763 B. original; 5D13, 50 = journal (–UA) September 16, 1763.

333. Strobel, *The Salzburgers and Their Descendants*, 311.

334. 5D13, 50.

335. Born August 22, 1770 (5B3:35, 147 = May 22, 1788 Tr. original). She had a richly diverse life. After the death of her father, her uncle, Pastor Triebner, took her in and fled with her from Ebenezer in the face of Continental Army troops to the island of New Providence in the Bahamas (5B3:30, 127 = August 27, 1787 Bm. original). She was supposed to have remained there until the completion of her eighteenth year (that is, until she had come of age, as long as Triebner retained the records of her inheritance 5B3:32, 138 = September 7, 1787 Tr. original). But because of her inheritance she returned somewhat early (in 1788) to Ebenezer (5B3:35, 147) and married in this same year Hergen Herson (born 1764), who came from the area of Oldenburg. He came directly from London where he probably had spoken with Triebner (5B4:43, 132 = April 22, 1805 Bm. original). He was a Freemason, demanded payment for debts that already had been paid to Wertsch, simply appropriated to himself the orphanage property that belonged to the community, devastated fields with horses, and in other ways brought Ebenezer into disrepute. He died in 1797 from the complications of an ax blow inflicted on him by one of his slaves (5B4:2, 8–9 = April 3, 1799 Bm. original). He ran through the assets of his wife and incurred debts as well. (5B4:3, 16 = October 7, 1799 Bm. original). His widow soon married the calmer Christopher Hudson, who lived twenty-seven miles from Ebenezer in the direction of Augusta. He "was a quiet man yet he also sought his own interest.... He was no open despiser of the Word, but there was also no proof to indicate that he was a Christian," was Bergmann's judgment (5B4:17, 53 = January 26, 1802). They had one daughter who already died in 1804 (5B4:43, 132 = April 22, 1805 Bm. original). Hudson also died suddenly in 1799. His widow soon again married, to Johann Martin Daescher (John Martin Dasher, the oldest son of the father of the same name 5B4:17, 53) who lived five miles from Ebenezer. However, she again had misfortune: he died on September 24, 1804 (5B4:41, 120). Whether the former Fräulein Wertsch entered into further marriages escapes our knowledge, since the archives terminate shortly thereafter.

336. TK32F8, 693 = March 18, 1784 Tr. original.

337. 5B4:17, 49 = January 26, 1802 Bm. original.

5

The Pastors of the Communities and Their Theological Position

JOHANN MARTIN BOLTZIUS

"Hans Mertin"[1] Boltzius was born on December 15, 1703, in the town of Forst (Lower Lusatia) into a long-established, middle class family that for generations had been clothmakers. Along with an older brother[2] and two younger sisters,[3] he spent his childhood with parents who were certainly

---

1. So reads the entry in the baptismal register of the Evangelical (Lutheran) church in Forst. In this area there is much forest [*Forst*] with some farmland on sandy soil, similar to Georgia's coastal area. Boltzius often mentions (for example, UN September 13, 1739) that agricultural knowledge came very handy for him, yet that is likely not so much the case, since he was not able to evaluate the situation at Old Ebenezer properly. His father (Martin) and his grandfather (Johann), whose names he bore, and all three godfathers (baptism on December 17th) were clothmakers, at the time in Forst the most common occupation, to which the town owed its importance (the information about the family relationships is taken, unless otherwise noted, from the baptism, marriage, and death registers of the Evangelical church in Forst).

2. Whose name was not identified since Boltzius' parents married outside of Forst, perhaps in the hometown of his mother, and the oldest son was probably born there. He did not reside in Forst and became a "journeyman shoemaker." He also wanted to come to America, but Pastor Boltzius put no stock in it since, "He was good for nothing" (5A3:37, 359 = July 29, 1737 B. original).

3. Catharina and Maria Elisabeth. He seems to have been especially close with Catharina, the elder of the two.

devout, but not pietistically-minded in a pronounced way.[4] Because they wanted him to be educated, he went to school, first in Forst and Guben where he was raised in a spirit similar to that in his parents' house.[5]

However, that would change when, around 1723, he attended a *Gymnasium* in Berlin.[6] Here, he learned "to distinguish quite well light from darkness."[7] Friedrich Korte from Köpenick, who was the same age, became his friend there.[8] Afterwards, he received the desired possibility for study that was bound in a peculiar way to the world-wide connections of the Francke Foundations in Halle. Boltzius' uncle, Senior Pastor Johann Müller,[9] who had received a theological education financed through the recommendation of the father of the famous Halle physician Christian Friedrich Richter, had been sent by August Hermann Francke in 1703 as teacher to Russia where around 1711 he became the confessor for Princess Charlotte Christine of Braunschweig-Wolfenbüttel, the wife of Alexei Petrovich, who was the son of Peter the Great.[10]

After her death on October 21, 1715, he returned to Berlin where Provost Porst took a special interest in him and recommended him to his pietistic friend, the County Commissioner von Burgsdorf,[11] on whose estates in Leppehne, in the county of Soldin (Brandenburg), he was appointed to a position. Since von Burgsdorf himself lived in Lübben (Lower Lusatia)

---

4. When he wanted to move to the University of Halle, Catharina, out of concern for his further development in this atmosphere, became even "melancholic for a time" (UA June 22, 1759). Father: Martin Boltzius (Bolzius, seldom Poltzius; never Bolze or otherwise), born February 18, 1676, as son of the citizen and clothmaker in Forst, Johannes Bolzius and his wife Elisabeth, née Panse (baptismal register of the Forst Evangelical church, 1676), died October 1, 1733 (death register of the Forst Evangelical church, 1733). Mother: Eva Rosina, née Müller (UA June 22, 1759), born end of December 1675 outside of Forst, died January 20, 1739 (death register of the Forst Evangelical church, 1739). A fifth child of the Boltzius parents named Sigismund lived only ten months (death register of the Forst Evangelical church, August 20, 1716).

5. 5B1:45, 186 = August 21, 1750 B. original.

6. 5B1:45, 186 = August 21, 1750 B. original.

7. UA June 22, 1759. Possibly, he met Provost Forst here. In connection with his studies, Boltzius visited the worship service of the Berlin synagogue (5A2:12, 56 B. copy). His landlord was a Herr Koch (5A2:10, 47 = May 24, 1734 B. copy).

8. He also lived with him later in Halle; in 1730, Korte became a pastor in Lithuania (5B1:28, 123 = April 21, 1750 B. original; J I, 33) and died already before 1750 (5B1:29, 128 = September 28, 1750 Fr. draft).

9. A brother of his mother, with whose son Boltzius corresponded (5A1:35, 5A2:5).

10. Imprecisely by Eduard Winter, who did not pursue a cited diary note of A. H. Francke dated August 7, 1716. Winter, *Halle als Ausgangspunkt der deutschen Russlandkunde,* 70.

11. UA June 22, 1759.

The Pastors of the Communities and Their Theological Position

where the consistory for Forst was located, belonging to Electoral Saxony, Pastor Müller procured for his nephew a stipend of 100 talers for four years of theological study,[12] to which von Burgsdorf attached the stipulation that Boltzius would study in Halle.

Despite the initial reservations of his relatives and teachers,[13] Boltzius set out and arrived in Halle at the Francke Foundations on Easter 1727,[14] and matriculated in the theological faculty on May 7th of the same year.[15] Here, he encountered and heard the three pillars of Halle Pietism, Professors Paul Anton, Joachim Justus Breithaupt, and August Hermann Francke,[16] and, as he himself narrates, complied with the instructions from Francke's program of study, *"Idea studiosi Theologiae,* or the Portrait of an Assiduous Theological Student, How He Should Prepare Himself Properly for the Use and Service of the Lord and for Every Good Work,"[17] and participated in the students' devotions for edification. Although during his time in school he, according to his own report, succumbed to vain, human scholarship and "was led astray" from his "actual purpose,"[18] he now experienced his conversion, in the manner of the Franckean model.[19] Just as he already had been sickly during his stay in Berlin,[20] he was thoroughly so here and had to take a "trip for his health to his homeland."[21] While doing so, he visited Herrnhut and met Zinzendorf.[22]

Presumably on this trip he had an experience that was significant for him in several respects with regard to his later position: he visited the pietistically-inclined pastor Daniel Gottlieb Mäderjan[23] in Thommendorf, County Bunzlau (Silesia).[24] At the time, this place lay directly on the border with Silesia on Saxon-Lusatian territory, and for that reason his church was a refuge church for the Protestants from Bunzlau and the surrounding

---

12. 5A3:11, 63 B. original.
13. UA June 22, 1759; 5B1:45, 186 = August 21, 1750 B. original.
14. UA November 24, 1760.
15. Matrikel der Universität Halle-Wittenberg (1690–1730).
16. UN November 16, 1749; TK32F11, 1046 = February 7, 1756 B. original.
17. UA June 8, 1759; see also Appendix II, no. 26.
18. 5A3:27, 200 = October 6, 1736 B. original.
19. 5B1:16, 68 = May 12, 1749 B. original.
20. 5A2:10, 45 and 47 = May 24, 1734 B. copy.
21. UA April 3, 1759.
22. 5A1:43, 188 = October 8, 1734; 5A1:46, 208; 5A3:11, 71 B. original.
23. He became assistant here in 1725, died on April 6. Rademacher, *Predigergeschichte der Kirchenkreise Bunzlau I und II*, 24.
24. 5A7:53, 227 = journal May 14, 1739a; UN June 19, 1735.

area who were living beyond the border. There, Protestant worship had been banned, since, according to the Peace of Westphalia, almost all of Silesia had fallen under the sovereignty of the Catholic Ferdinand III of Bohemia. The influx of the pilgrims to these village churches of refuge became so strong that, at many of them, one or even several assisting pastoral positions had to be created, and extensive expansions of the churches became necessary, also in Thommandorf. Mäderjan was the assistant, and a "Bunzlau gallery" was put in the church.[25]

In 1727, following the Halle model, there were established here, through the patron Count Erdmann von Promnitz, orphanages and schools,[26] for which the inspector was the pastor-administrator. All these things made a powerful impression on the young Boltzius and prepared in him a particular understanding of the fate of the Protestant Salzburgers. In addition, Silesian Pietism, in the figure of Pastor Mäderjan, seems to have had an enduring influence on him, something that is to be explored later. From his post in America Boltzius recalled his stay several times.[27]

In 1730, Boltzius became the Vice Inspector of the *Latina* of the Francke Foundations.[28] He had supervision of the free time of the students in several dormitories and over their school work, to ensure that they went to bed punctually, so on. For doing so he received his housing,[29] wood, light, and board free of charge and could further pursue his studies[30] which he ended in 1731 as planned. After that, as a *Candidatus SS. Ministerii* (candidate for holy ministry), he occasionally substituted for Deacon Majer at St. Ulrich's Church in Halle[31] and, with his pronounced musical ability, was co-founder of the *Collegium Musicum* of the Francke Foundations.[32]

---

25. In the eastern wall of the church cemetery, a "Bunzlau Gate" was opened up. The occasional services of the Bunzlauers for the period from 1653–1741 are recorded in the Thommendorf Church books, etc. (according to the statements of Superintendents Karl Paeschke, Niesky, and Walther Seimert of Bad Langensalza who worked in the archives of the Thommendorf Church before 1945).

26. Eberlein, *Schlesische Kirchengeschichte*, 97; Geißler, *Als Der Wohl=Ehrwürdiger und Wohlgelahrte HERR George Geißler*.

27. For example, 5A7:53, 227; UN June 19, 1735.

28. 5A1:5; 5A1:14, 68.

29. In the house of the students.

30. The Inspectors stood in a looser relationship to the Foundations than did the *Informatoren* (teachers); for that reason, they are not recorded in any special register from which important information for Boltzius could be drawn.

31. UN September 7, 1739.

32. 5A3:12, 91–92. The *Collegium* functioned vocally and instrumentally. Boltzius mastered the general bass (UN March 12, 1740), played the piano (5D1, 6 = journal December 2, 1733), and with love took responsibility in Ebenezer for the community

From this temporary holding position,³³ he received in 1733 the call as pastor to Georgia.

On August 31st and September 3rd, Samuel Urlsperger had addressed to the London agencies several questions concerning filling the office of pastors for the Salzburgers. He received the following answer: "The first question is: Whether these people, their children, and descendants shall have and retain the free confession of the Lutheran religion along with a pastor and catechetist? Answer: The establishment of the colony of Georgia is grounded on freedom of conscience. Concerning the pastor, the Salzburger emigrants should be treated in the same way as are the colonists of the English Church whose pastors are provided by the Lord Commissioners and are to be maintained for so long until the colonists are in position to supply for them the necessary support."³⁴

With that, Urlsperger quickly looked around for suitable men. At first, he offered the positions to two candidates³⁵ about whom it became known that they were adherents of Zinzendorf,³⁶ whereupon they were quickly disregarded.³⁷ Finally, on November 1, 1733, Boltzius and Gronau received from the Director of the Francke Foundations, G. A. Francke, and Inspector Mischke,³⁸ their certificates of call³⁹ that were ceremoniously presented.⁴⁰ In them, Boltzius was obligated to instruct his future congregation in the writings of the prophets, the evangelists, and apostles according to the Unaltered

---

singing, for which he himself prepared polyphonic verses and rehearsed them (5D1 = journal February 9, 1735; 5D4 = journal June 18, 1738).

33. These were not at all "lucrative and honourable positions" that he and Gronau held here, as Strobel believes. Strobel, *The Salzburgers and Their Descendants*, 55.

34. 5C4:15 = September 7, 1733, is a copy of the original to U. sen., since on page 63 is mentioned the power of attorney that the Lords Commissioners (Trustees) had in mind to convey to him, and later they also did this.

35. One of them was Stephan Carl Siebeth from Osterburg (Altmark), born in 1709, since 1729 in the Francke Foundations, since April 1730 in Jena (J I, 28) (5A1:4, 33 = undated), in which "H. Siebeth and I . . . here in Jena" declared themselves prepared to accept the calls for America. The sender is not indicated, but is perhaps the other candidate, possibly named Liberkühn, whose name was recorded on the page in another hand.

36. That is, they probably belonged to the "awakening" circles in Jena that were connected with Spangenberg.

37. 5A3:4, 29 = April 1, 1735 postscript B. original.

38. 5D1, 66; presented by Pastor Majer.

39. Drafted by Urlsperger, copies 5A1:5 and 7 = October 31, 1733.

40. 5B3:5, 17 = November 3, 1753 B. original: Celebration of twenty-year anniversary of his time in office. If Boltzius had not accepted the call, Friedrich Christian Hahn would have been called (5D1, 29 = journal December 30, 1733 new style): born in 1709, in the Francke Foundations since 1728, in London since 1731 at one of the German churches in London (J I, 7).

Augsburg Confession, the Apology, and "other things." The determination of the salary was also not forgotten.[41]

Since the Salzburgers with whom he was to travel to America were already underway to Rotterdam and the Trustees wanted to have them in Georgia as soon as possible, the departure of Boltzius and Gronau had to take place as quickly as possible.[42] They were now properly equipped as missionaries.[43] They also received from Francke and Urlsperger written instructions for the journey and the conduct of their offices[44] and departed already on November 7, 1733,[45] from Halle to Wernigerode where they were to be ordained, as had all missionaries setting out from Halle since 1731. There was no legal reason for the choice of this place, but decisive was the close relationship that existed between the pietistic Duke Christian Ernst von Stolberg-Wernigerode, along with his wife Sophie Charlotte,[46] and the Halle Orphan House.[47] There, because Francke urged it,[48] the two candidates were examined at once on November 10th by the "highly praised ducal Stolberg consistory,"[49] and already on the following day, on Wednesday, November 11, 1733, during the weekly service[50] in the pal-

---

41. 5A1, 35 = October 31, 1733 U. copy. Although his future time of service was not limited according to his call, one counted on only a few years. But after two years, it was clear to Boltzius, they he would remain with the community for good (5A3:11, 75 = September 1, 1735 B. original).

42. For that reason, Boltzius would not have been able to bid farewell to his mother (5A1:26).

43. 5A1:9, 45–49. They received footmuffs lined with fur, a medicine chest, seventy talers in cash, and other things. Altogether, their sending cost the Francke Foundations 200 talers. Twenty ABC books, fifteen Small Catechisms, and twenty to thirty copies of Freylinghausen's *Ordnung des Heyls* were sent later.

44. 5A1:6 and 8 U. copy. Here, the confessional writings are named: The Unaltered Augsburg Confession, Apology, Smalcald Articles, the main symbols (creeds), Large and Small Catechisms. 5A1:10 and 12 Fr. draft. It was explained to him how they should conduct themselves at the post, customs, inns, voyage to England, carriages, with seasickness, and so on.

45. UN November 7, 1731.

46. 5A1:15–16.

47. Falke, *Lebensbilder aus dem Hause Stolberg-Wernigerode*, 74, 85–90; *Nachrichten von den vereinigten Deutschen Evangelisch-Lutherischen Gemeinden*, 6–7; Förstemann, *Graf Christian Ernst zu Stolberg-Wernigerode*, 56; Reichel, "Die Enststehung einer Zinzendorf feindlichen Partei in Halle und Wernigerode," 549–92.

48. 5A1:15, 76.

49. 5A1:6, 36.

50. 5A1:15, 75 = November 10, 1733 Sophie Charlotte original signature in another hand.

ace chapel, they were ordained by the Court Chaplain Samuel Lau.[51] He preached on Isaiah 54:3–5,[52] and Court Deacon Seydelitz, Pastor Ziegler from Ilsenburg, Giese, and Deacon Zachariae assisted.[53] At the ordination there was a renewed commitment to the Lutheran confessional writings.[54]

Court Chaplain Samuel Lau.
Image courtesy of the Francke Foundations.

Already on the next day, they traveled farther and arrived in Rotterdam on November 25th.[55] Their stay here had been prepared in the best way possible from Halle. They had been provided with several letters of

51. He also examined them.
52. 5A1:16, 79; 5D8 = journal August 1, 1741.
53. 5A1:15–16.
54. The ordination took place, even though Duke Christian Ernst was absent but was on a trip home from a visit with his cousin, King Christian VI, in Copenhagen. Reichel, "Die Enststehung einer Zinzendorf feindlichen Partei in Halle und Wernigerode," 556–59. He was expected any day (5A1:15).
55. 5A1:17, 82; 5C4:14, 58.

recommendation,[56] and thought had even been given to providing them again with money here.[57] Just two days later, the Salzburgers arrived, and on the 1st Sunday of Advent (November 29, 1733), Boltzius and Gronau began their office.[58]

After successfully recovering from the voyage, keeping house along with their pastoral duties was a genuine burden for the two bachelors, and so on August 5, 1735, Boltzius married the Salzburger Gertraud Kraher, who was about seventeen years old.[59] She was born sometime around the end of 1718 to the beginning of 1719 in the region of Salzburg.[60] When the expulsion of the Protestants began, her Catholic father remained in the land with several underaged children—the youngest was half-a-year old. The mother[61] emigrated[62] with her daughters Catharine[63] and Gertraud[64] and came to Georgia with the first Salzburg transport.[65] The Boltzius couple had four children; Samuel Leberecht,[66] Gotthilf Israel,[67] Catharina

---

56. 5A1:9, 13, 17, 22.

57. That did not go completely smoothly, since Boynd, who was supposed to give them twenty ducats charged to Halle's account (5A1:19, 93), had recently been defrauded and first wanted to make inquiry to Halle (5A1:17, 84; 5D1, 1 = journal November 26, 1733). Boltzius and Gronau came into some difficulty until, after Francke's reply (5A1:19, 93), the money was paid out on December 1st (5A1:21).

58. UN I, 17.

59. 5A3:11, 75 = September 1, 1735 B. original; UN I, 2307. The spelling "Kroher," which is widely given in the secondary literature, is only very seldom documented and originated from the deep pronunciation of the vowel in the Salzburger dialect.

60. 5B1:19, 86 = July 28, 1749 B. original: "She is now thirty-years old;" 5B1:28, 122 = April 21, 1750 B. original: "about 31 years old;" 5B1:41, 168 = September 14, 1750 B. original: "She is about thirty-two-years old."

61. Barbara Kraher née Rohrmoser, born 1696. Died November 16, 1735, in Ebenezer (5D1, 205 = journal November 16, 1735; UN I, 2311; 5A3:22, 151–52 = August 31, 1736 Fr. draft).

62. 5A1:50, 245–46; 5D1, 206 = journal November 16, 1735.

63. Who later became Mrs. Gronau.

64. Possibly also with a third. Gronau reported that his wife emigrated "along with her mother and two sisters" (5A1:50, 245–46), but this can also be a mental error, since a third sister never appears.

65. Frau Boltzius, since her first childbirth, was constantly sick; anything else about her is hardly reported (5D1:19, 85–86 = July 28, 1749 B. original).

66. Born January 2, 1737 (UN October 31, 1750), died October 31, 1750 (5B1:42, 171–72 = November 5, 1750 B. original).

67. Born November 22, 1739 (UN for the date, UN III, 519 = letter December 21, 1749 B. to U.), died August 13, 1774 (J II, 56).

Maria,[68] and Christiana Elisabeth.[69] The two sons were the special pride of the parents,[70] and their foundational education lay close to the heart of their father.[71] In summer 1748, Francke offered to Boltzius to send them to Halle for their further education; he would assume the costs.[72] Boltzius accepted, even if with a heavy heart.

The travel date was set already for Christmas 1750,[73] when the parents received a heavy blow. Within one week, Samuel Leberecht and Christiana Elisabeth died.[74] Their death was so close to Boltzius that not he, but Lemcke, buried them.[75] But Gotthilf Israel was still too little to make the trip to Germany alone; he remained with his parents for another two years until Captain Krauß came to Ebenezer with the third Swabian transport on behalf of von Münch to set in motion his endeavors (plantations and trade). On June 17, 1753, Gotthilf Israel bid farewell to the community and departed with Krauß. His father accompanied him to Savannah,[76] and then they sailed[77] to London where Krauß brought the fourteen-year-old to Court Chaplain Albinus who further conveyed him to Halle.[78]

68. Born July 27, 1741 (5D8, 407 = journal July 27, 1741), died 1777/78 (5B3:22, 95 = January 16, 1787 Probst original).

69. Born before 1744 (5A11:23, 86 = December 20, 1744 B. original), died November 6, 1750 (5B1:42, 174 November 6, 1750 postscript B. original).

70. Samuel Leberecht "has a gentle nature, but it, unfortunately! *ad utrumque flexibilis*. The little one is tougher and more defiant, and needs more sternness, but he can keep up with his brother fairly well in learning, even though he is three years younger" (5B1:2, 12 = July 19, 1748 postscript B. original).

71. Boltzius greatly regretted not being able to teach them himself, due to a lack of time (5A11:50, 219 = *Diarium extraordinarium* May 1746 B. original), but he nonetheless gave them private instruction in Latin and geography (5A11:59, 273 = October 9, 1746 Samuel Leberecht original). In 1747, Lemcke took over their instruction in the school and in private hours (1E9:9a, 31 = August 21, 1747 B. extract) but was replaced in the private instruction in the same year by Thilo, from whom they received instruction, along with the previous subjects of Latin and geography, also in singing (5A11:72, 336 = September 23, 1747 B. original). However, this effort had to be broken off already after ¾ year because of the teacher's "laxity in discipline," and from then on Boltzius and Lemcke divided the private instruction that the boys received along with regular school (5B1:2, 6–7 = July 18, 1748 B. original).

72. 5A11:81, 369 = July 12, 1748 Fr. draft.

73. 5B1:45, 184 = August 21, 1750 B. original.

74. Both died from strophulus, together with severe cramps and respiratory distress (5B1:42, 171–74 = November 5–6, 1750 B. original; UN October 31 and November 6, 1750).

75. He preached on Wisdom 4:14 and 5:16–17. (UN November 1 and 7, 1750).

76. UA June 18, 1753.

77. It was planned by way of Charleston and Pennsylvania.

78. 5B3:6, 23–24 = June 4, 1753 B. original. When he then arrived in Halle (the

In the following years, his father Boltzius became very frail. It especially hindered his work that his left eye was unusable from fall 1753 and became covered with a membrane.[79] From the weary style of his diaries and letters it becomes apparent how much his energy diminished in the last years of his life, and for that reason, it would have made him and Lemcke very glad if the young Boltzius would have become his father's successor.[80] When Pastors Krug and Voigt went to Pennsylvania at the beginning of 1764,[81] Gotthilf Israel would have preferred to come along in order to be closer to his parents. Urlsperger also already had his appointment to Ebenezer in sight. However, Francke believed that G. I. Boltzius was not yet firm enough in his faith and also had not yet acquired the necessary self-denial to take over such a position. Nevertheless, if Urlsperger still intended to send him to Ebenezer, it certainly would be advisable to do so while his father was still living.[82]

However, in the last months of his life, the elderly Boltzius was alarmingly clear that from the first generation of those who had emigrated because of their faith, almost no one was alive any more, and that the young

---

Orphan House provided for him housing, wood, light, bed, instruction, and books, all together thirty-six talers, sixteen groschen annually; Ziegenhagen bore the rest, fourteen talers annually [4C8:28, 131–32 = March 6, 1755 Fr. draft]), he had to overcome the pox (4C8:22, 105 = June 3, 1755 Fr. draft) and was further instructed in the Foundations (J II, 56). However, it unfortunately soon became apparent that he became in many respects a problem child for his supervisors, and Francke had this to criticize about him: "On one hand self-love and conceit, and on the other hand a strong inclination to make things pleasant for himself" (5B2:3, 6 = September 3, 1765 Fr. draft). Such reports understandably caused his father deep concern, and since he did not, if possible, want his ill wife to know about it, he bore the weight even more heavily (5B2:14, 74 = September 20, 1764 B. original). In October 1757, G. I. Boltzius began theological study, in August of the following year became a teacher at the girls' school, and in April 1760 at the Latin school (evaluation of his teaching activity: "He seems to have fear of God, has lovely study habits and is diligent; his delivery is good and is well mannered, has a Christian regimen," J II, 56). In the same year, he also gave his first sermon in St. Ulrich's Church in Halle, where his father also had preached, on Psalm 37:4–5. (UA IV, 285 = December 1760 B.). In April of the following year, he visited Urlsperger in Augsburg who would have liked to have kept him as a private teacher in the area, but Francke preferred to have him in the Orphan House (5B2:64, 226 = February 19, 1763 B. original signature in another hand) and after his return in October, promoted him to teacher in the *Paedagogium Regium* (J II, 56; 5B3:2, 6 = September 3, 1765 Fr. draft) which made his father very happy (5B2:63, 221 = November 18, 1762 B. original).

79. 5B3:3; detailed history of his illnesses by Thilo for Halle. 5B3:7; UA March 18, 1754.

80. 5B2:12, 62 = December 31, 1764 B. original.

81. *Nachrichten von den vereinigten Deutschen Evangelisch-Lutherischen Gemeinden in Nord-America*, 428.

82. 5B2:17, 81–82. = April 13, 1765 Fr. draft to U. sen.

generation, while they certainly listened to preaching, did little to take it to heart, so that he wanted to spare his son from this difficult post. He thought that perhaps he could go to Pennsylvania.[83]

But before the matter could develop further, Boltzius died on November 19, 1765, at six o'clock in the morning.[84] The last letter written by him has been preserved, his farewell letter to Ziegenhagen that he wrote, already in a scarcely legible handwriting but still with complete mental clarity, fourteen days before his death.[85] On the day after his death, he was buried by Rabenhorst in the Jerusalem Church cemetery. Rabenhorst preached on the texts, "He hath made him to be sin for us, who knew no sin; that we might be made the righteousness of God in him" (2 Cor 5:21), and "This is a faithful saying, and worthy of all acceptation, that Christ Jesus came into the world to save sinners" (1 Tim1:15).[86] Already during the middle of the nineteenth century, Pastor Boltzius' grave was no longer identifiable;[87] today, a monument stands near the church for him and his fellow pastor Gronau.[88]

83. 5B2:22, 92–93 = June 24, 1765 B. original. TK32F11, 1015–1016 = journal March 12, 1757 B. copy. At this thanksgiving festival, Boltzius preached on Psalm 7:12–14: "Not only the condition of times but also the perilous condition of very many of my first hearers has given me the opportunity for such needed material, for which certainly I can apply with complete right (although as far as I am concerned, in weakness) Jeremiah 25:3; I have now preached diligently to you for twenty-three years, but you never wanted to listen."

84. With fever and tortuous pain (5B2:27, 107 = November 21, 1765 R. original, who wrote this letter to Francke as Boltzius' last instruction; 5B2:28, 111 = November 27, 1765 L. original).

85. 5B2:25, 100–105 = November 5, 1765 B. original.

86. 5B2:27, 107.

87. Hazelius, *History of the American Lutheran Church*, 100. Hazelius' comment dates from 1841.

88. Brantley, "The Salzburgers in Georgia," 224. Because of his death, Boltzius was spared from learning that his son, up until September 3, 1765, had incurred altogether 200 talers in debt, and his father was most politely asked how he had in mind to pay it, in a letter that his dismayed widow now received (5B2:3, 6 = September 3, 1765 Fr. draft), but also could not reimburse this sum since she only further received the salary of her husband for one half year (5B2:31, 120 = May 13, 1766 LR). There is nothing to ascertain about her further lot. The daughter, Catharina Maria, somewhat challenged mentally, lived with Pastor Triebner (5B3:22, 95 = January 16, 1787 Probst original). Gotthilf Israel Boltzius became an assistant of the Evangelical Ministerium in Halle, and there also *diaconus* (second pastor in rank) at the Market Church (the Church of Our Dear Lady) and three years later, *archidiaconus* there. When he died in this office on August 13, 1774 after a long illness (J II, 56), he left behind his second wife (1D9:45), a three-year-old daughter Henriette (1D9:46; Probst knew her; 5B3:22, 95), and 880 talers in debt, the repayment for which his scanty household effects were not remotely sufficient (1D9:45–46.; 1D13:44 = March 14, 1774 B. younger to Consistory Counselor Jetzke at the Market Church: "to be opened after my passing").

Boltzius, the first Lutheran pastor in Georgia, imparted to his community through his activity a direction of piety that endured long after his death. Already from the material presented here so far has been made clear the leading role that belonged to him in all areas of life for the community, obviously first regarding its piety, so that an investigation of his own theological stance is indispensable for understanding it. The intensity of his influence was especially evident when later the community was confronted with doctrinal positions of other pastors that deviated from this general line in not unessential points, and the reactions of the community to it highlights distinctively the development of the theological directions within early Lutheranism in Georgia.

It does not need to be emphasized that a man like Boltzius, who underwent his education at that time in Halle and during his entire life cultivated the closest contact with his theological teachers, felt obligated to their theological stance as closely as possible. On that point, previous scholarship is united, and it diligently conveys this fact, yet—apart from a few exceptions[89]—without closer explanations. But precisely such explanations are required, because only these show his dependence on that theological position, and because it must further be taken into account that precisely the Halle theology of those years went through a very intense development in which the peak times of the individual directions are easily isolated. However, the influence of those directions in wider spheres are to be seen not consecutively in time but to a great extent in a juxtaposition that, not least of all, is to be ascribed to the commonalities of Pietism and Enlightenment.

When Boltzius matriculated in Halle on May 7, 1727, it was only four weeks before the death of August Hermann Francke (June 8, 1727), and during his study, Boltzius also experienced the death of the two other pillars of the first generation of academic Pietism in Halle: Paul Anton (1730) and J. J. Breithaupt (1732).[90] In addition, it is also a commonplace that with the passing of Francke, Pietism already had crossed over its highpoint. Thus, Boltzius underwent his education in the pathway of the second Halle generation, and, with all of its peculiarities, it remained definitive for him throughout his life. An exemplary model can even be seen in him for the theological training of Halle Pietism for the second generation that took on the responsibility of preserving the legacy of the founder down to the subtle details, so anxiously conservative and, accordingly, so lacking in independence, as only less distinguished followers can prove themselves to be.

89. Schmidt, "Die Anfange der Kirchenbildung bei den Salzburgern in Georgia," 21–40; Gräbner, *Geschichte der Lutherischen Kirche in America*, part I, 150–52; both in need of correction, as will be explained in the following.

90. Also, the London court chaplain Böhme had died in 1722.

Here in Halle, Boltzius now became acquainted with the principle of a consistent biblicism that would become normative for his entire activity.[91] In doing so, in his proclamation he bound the talent of applying constantly the word of the Scripture to the respective situation, not only of the individual but also of the community with their deeply felt difficulties as settlers.[92] In Halle, he further learned in the dogmatics of his revered and often-cited abbot Breithaupt[93] to distinguish between fundamental doctrines of the first and second order, a critical, indeed dangerous moment for the history of the Lutheran church in Georgia that is still to be described.

In Halle, Boltzius also experienced as prescribed his conversion, and the dawning state of grace was for him, and despite every required *tentatio* heeded by him, a possession that was unalterable and inalienable for him. He also held strongly to it with his congregation in America. In keeping with the Halle model, his preaching at first was also admonition to conversion,[94] whereby Boltzius, in the case of contrition, between the two Halle possibilities of *contritio legalis* and *evangelica* characteristically favored the latter.[95] The bitter suffering of Jesus for the sins of people was a beloved subject of many evening prayer hours, even beyond Lent. Further in keeping with Francke's instruction, those awaiting conversion[96] had to experience remorse over their entire sinful nature, and so resounded Boltzius' preaching.

However, it is interesting to observe that the members of the community in a very considerable number again and again understood this as something to be felt for concrete, individual sins.[97] In this connection, it is of interest how Schmidt judged the relationship between Boltzius and Commissioner von Reck. While he believed at first after reading the publications of Urlsperger that he should be regarded as a serious and responsible travel

---

91. 5D1, 56 = journal (+UN) February 14, 1734.

92. See, for the example, the speech for the dedication of the mills, see pp. 132–33.

93. 5D2, 35 = journal February 4, 1736. See also Ritschl, *Geschichte des Pietismus in der lutherischen Kirche*, 399–400.

94. UN September 28, 1750; the community complained that Boltzius preaches too severely. The Vernonburgers had the same complaint about him.

95. 5D1, 66: "Where there are such hungry and faithful hearers you may well preach the gospel."

96. TK32F10, 902 = July 27, 1756 B. original signature in another hand.

97. Many communications regarding pastoral conversations give awareness of it (UA/A). Such a concept of sinful nature was too abstract for the community members, and it testifies to their probity when, for example, they came to Boltzius in great scruples of conscience because of the misappropriation of small amounts of money or because of minor cheating among each other, who then was not sparing in consolation with reference to the work of Christ.

escort,[98] serious doubt about it came to him after a quick look in the Halle archives.[99] While he had assumed differences with Boltzius were attributable to von Reck's unfavorable characteristics,[100] a closer investigation of the records prompted the suggestion that Boltzius met a man in von Reck who did not come from the Halle nest and consequently could be a grave danger for the newly founded settlement. Von Reck was, namely, a student of Mosheim in Helmstedt,[101] a fact that Boltzius viewed negatively—indeed, theologically simplistic (as was his position toward Georgia's Moravians), but intuitively so. It was decisive for him that Mosheim viewed the problematic conversion as not at all necessary for salvation. In fact, Boltzius only formed a better opinion of von Reck when clear signs of remorse became visible in him, which happened rather soon.[102]

In the main features of his pedagogical activity, Boltzius was also a faithful student of his Halle teachers. That became apparent in his on-going instruction in the schools, but especially when the entire rearing of several children was entrusted to him through Ebenezer's orphanage. Obedience and reverence for parents and superiors, diligence that did not tolerate any useless fiddling away of time, and love of the truth were, as in Halle, also his principles that he sought to implant in the children.[103]

If Boltzius shows himself to this point as an almost dependent copyist of the theological model established by Francke, then there are also with him several deviations from that line, even if they are detectable only with a keen ear. These can be reduced to a common denominator: the selection of hymns in the sources of his time, naturally chosen mainly by him, that were sung in worship services, evening prayer hours, and hymn hours, leaving out such hymns that contained harsh forms of expression. There is no surprise regarding mystical texts in keeping with the Halle example, but even with the penitential hymns such were not used that approached coarse tastelessness or shallowness.[104] Furthermore, as already mentioned, Boltzius, in his

---

98. Schmidt, "Die Anfänge der Kirchenbildung bei den Salzburgern in Georgia," 26–27.

99. Schmidt, "Das hallische Waisenhaus und England im 18. Jahrhundert," 38–55. Schmidt investigated only the early years of the Halle archives and even these only for his special concern, John Wesley.

100. 5D1, 2 = journal November 28, 1733: "The Herr Commissioner is very superficial and vain."

101. 5D1, 16 = journal December 12, 1733.

102. 5A1:38, 167–68; 5D1 = journal April 10, 1734.

103. See also Ahrbeck, *Über die Erziehungs—und Unterrichtsreform A. H. Franckes und ihre Grundlagen,* 77–93; here, 85–86.

104. In his letters, there appears only once or twice in the early years the designation

admonition to contrition, preferred the *contritio evangelica* to that more rigorous approach. The dream conversions in Ebenezer and elsewhere described by Gräbner[105] represent in the extensive literature (Urlsperger) and in the sources actually individual cases, so that it is incomprehensible how Gräbner, working from this plentitude of cases, could have sought out those singular, albeit extreme events and elevated them as a general feature. Seen as a whole, the expressions of communal piety, despite every emphasis of feeling, adhere to a soberness that is refreshing for the time. Even if there is frequent mention of tears and sighs, this was for the time by far no sign of a "truly unhealthy style," as Gräbner believes.

Boltzius also deviated from the example of Francke in an additional point in that, in the administration of Ebenezer's orphanage, he did not exercise the overly stringent discipline of the Halle institutions but, with some leniency, gave room for youthful needs for moving around, even if under the strict guidance of his authority. He repeatedly mentions just in this connection how important for his instructional activity had been the writing of the Thommendorf pastor Mäderjan, *Instruction for Salvation*.[106] As this text and the other evidence shows,[107] the Silesian forms of Pietism had been thoroughly free from extremes, so that Mäderjan, whose activity, as mentioned, made a strong impression on Boltzius, also may have had a lasting influence on him in this more moderate position. The characteristics mentioned stand out more clearly from his usual attitude, since he otherwise shows the entire image of the imprint of Halle Pietism, something that also pertains to the practical side of his office.

We have seen him already moving in this path in the various provisions of church discipline, admission to the Lord's Supper, the methods of instruction, devotional gatherings, the establishment of the orphanage, and so on. Even in the question of adiaphora, a particularly acute question in Halle, he conformed completely with his teachers. He was averse to every game,[108] not at all to mention drinking. Dancing was never mentioned; conversation over non-spiritual matters was detested, marriages were celebrated modestly, and, finally, in all of the multitude of Boltzius' written pieces that have been preserved, there is not a single joke to be found, indeed, not once the tendency to a harmless smirk—something that, for example, makes the reading of Muhlenberg's journals so refreshing. Only

---

"dead dog" as an expression of his sinful nature.

105. Gräbner, *Geschichte der Lutherischen Kirche in America*, part I, 151–52.
106. 5A7:53, 227; UN June 19, 1735. See also Appendix II, no. 69.
107. Eberlein, *Schlesische Kirchengeschichte*, 97.
108. See also p. 94.

in edifying matters did Boltzius have his edifying joy. It may be that this has to do with his disposition; yet it is striking that this characteristic found its place mainly in the journals, less in the letters where he could write more informally.

Finally, a fact must be mentioned that seems strange to a casual observer, that Pastor Boltzius simply looked after everything that came up in connection with the colonization of the communities around Ebenezer in their economic endeavors. He did this following Urlsperger's instruction that had been delivered to him upon departure, in which he had been exhorted to the "exercise of an active and evangelical Christianity in faith and good works."[109] As a result, he nevertheless fell into a position that justifiably gave occasion to his colleagues and followers for divergent judgments. With Gronau, he always got along brilliantly, and Gronau looked upon him with esteem, even reverence. When Boltzius was away once on official business, Gronau found the responsibilities that fell to him as too difficult for him, and not only because they were unfamiliar. He recognized Boltzius as the greater of the two to whom he gladly saw take over authority.[110]

The first person, who was more closely acquainted with these circumstances as a late arrival—the physician Thilo, whose judgment nevertheless does not count for much—was immediately indignant over the idolatry that the community carried on with its pastors,[111] and Bergmann reported in 1787, certainly not without something of an envious sideways glance, "No minister in America had the power that Herr Boltzius had;"[112] he had kept completely under his thumb Gronau's successor Lemcke, even though he was his brother-in-law. Moreover, he claimed that things for a long time were not as sunny in Ebenezer as Boltzius always had depicted them, and that Boltzius had been too gullible and had let himself be deceived by manipulative people regarding their alleged piety.[113]

There may be some truth in all of that. It does not necessarily occur to a person of a straightforward nature in a position of leadership that he also causes offense. But those who accuse him of such things do not consider that Boltzius himself had been sharply conscious of this danger and, in order to steer clear of these misunderstandings, urgently and repeatedly requested in London and Halle that he be relieved of the burden of secular matters; however, things remained as they were.

109. 5A1:6, 38 U. copy.
110. For example, UN May 18, 1734.
111. He means Boltzius; he got along better with Gronau.
112. 5B3:30, 82.
113. 5B3:30, 127 = August 27, 1787 Bm. original.

The lack of independence, however, in which the community was held through Boltzius' personality, had to have a corresponding effect after his death. There is hardly a justification, though, for seeing the ground for the subsequent radical decline of Ebenezer as already having been laid by him. Eight years later from his earlier assessment, in fact, we hear Bergmann make a somewhat more objective judgment: "In the wretched destruction that ensued after his passing from time he certainly played no part."[114]

But the enduring merit of this man exists in one point, and far above all other circumstances, this merit remains for a long time in the awareness of the communities and has finally spun around him an almost legendary glow; that is the love that goes deep into the heart with which this shepherd took care of his flock, with which he took upon himself their many needs great and small and truly was weighed heavily by them, of which only a fraction fills the copious sources, and the magnitude certainly was not at all appreciated by those to whom it applied even if, old and young, they looked up to him in true filial reverence.

ISRAEL CHRISTIAN GRONAU

As the thirteenth of fourteen children, Israel Christian Gronau was baptized on March 11, 1714, in Kroppenstedt, Oschersleben County (Saxony-Anhalt).[115] His father, Heinrich Gronau, was deacon at the Lutheran church of this place.[116] His mother, Anna Margaretha née Lange, came from Kroppenstedt; her grandfather had been a deacon here.[117]

At the time, Kroppenstedt was a respectable city whose wall with three towers is still preserved today. It possessed market rights and its own judiciary, as a column in front of the almost imposing city hall indicates, in front of which a royal guard was posted for that reason until 1901.[118] The pre-

---

114. 5B3:41, 181 = April 23, 1795 Bm. original.

115. Baptismal register of the Lutheran church in Kroppenstedt; in keeping with the custom of the time, the baptism followed one or two days after birth.

116. Born in 1684, in 1687 organist in Kroppenstedt, in 1699 rector of the school there, in 1705 *diaconus* (second pastor in rank). On September 3, 1724, he suffered a stroke that hindered the further conduct of his office. Buried on April 27, 1731 (marriage register of Lutheran church in Kroppenstedt, 1688; death register, of the Lutheran church in Kroppenstedt, 1731).

117. Her grandfather was *diaconus* (second pastor in rank) Schnelle, her father was Andreas Lange. She herself: Anna Margaretha née Lange, born 1673, married October 23, 1688, died August 3, 1744 (marriage register of the Lutheran church in Kroppenstedt, 1688; death register of the Lutheran church in Kroppenstedt, 1744).

118. According to reports of local residents.

Reformation gothic hall church was richly decorated; its nave aisles were widened around 1600 in the style of the time, and in the sacristy there was a private door for the deacon who through it had only a short way across the street to his house, a massive stone structure. Here, and in the school, lying in a triangle with the church and diaconia, the little Israel Christian Gronau spent his childhood until he went to neighboring Halberstadt, at the time only a little larger, for his further education.[119] Here, he perhaps lived in the house of his godfather, Pastor Lic. Clauder, at St. Paul's church.[120]

On April 16, 1729, he matriculated in the theological faculty in Halle[121] and lived at the Francke Foundations where he taught at the girls' school[122] from October of the following year, about which his personal files report: "Heartily fears God, is rather studious, somewhat timorous in speaking: keeps the children in rather good order."[123] Again, a year later, he was preceptor of the orphan boys,[124] and in 1732, he was chosen by Francke as traveling preacher to a contingent of Salzburgers who moved from Halle to East Prussia.[125] After his return, it was intended to send him as pastor to the Salzburgers in Lithuania, but that came to nothing, and shortly thereafter he received the call to the Salzburgers in the completely opposite direction,[126] and, in fact, as assistant pastor and catechist.[127]

As was the case with Boltzius, detailed instructions were given to him,[128] and under the charge of his more resolute colleague, he reached his congregation and finally Ebenezer. Here, already on October 1, 1734, he was married by Boltzius to Catharine Kraher,[129] during which Boltzius preached on John 10:27–29.[130] Almost apologetically, Gronau reported his decision to Francke: "I certainly would not have decided upon this change, since I never have had an inclination to the state of marriage, unless external circumstance had not required it of me [he means his poor living

---

119. 5D12, 18 = journal January 13, 1745.
120. Baptismal register of the Lutheran church in Kroppenstedt, 1710.
121. Matrikel der Universität Halle-Wittenberg 1690–1730.
122. 5A1:7, 40.
123. J I, 47.
124. J I, 47; 5A1:14, 60.
125. 5A1:14, 68; 5C4:93.
126. 5D12, 18 = journal January 13, 1745.
127. 5A1:7, 40–41.
128. 5A1:8, 42–44.
129. Her sister later married Boltzius. Catharine, born ca. 1716 (according to the information on the age for her sister), died before February 1777 (4H23, 309 = journal May 15, 1777 M = letter February 20, 1777 Mrs. R. copy).
130. 5A1:50, 247.

conditions] and recognized the will of God. . . . She also would not have done it because she also had no desire toward marriage, unless, after further consideration and diligent prayer, she had not seen more clearly that it was the will of her Father in heaven."[131]

In spite of all of that, they were soon gladdened by three children: Catharina,[132] Hanna Elisabeth,[133] and Friderica Maria,[134] among whom, unfortunately, the first died already in infancy. The father Gronau was almost always sickly since the malaria epidemic of 1736.[135] His condition deteriorated when he once at the beginning of 1743 had to preach in Savannah in a drafty room, from which he caught such a severe cold that he never could be rid of it,[136] and Boltzius often had to take over the work by himself.[137] Even two longer sojourns in Whitefield's orphanage, Bethesda, where there was healthier sea air than in Ebenezer, did not help.[138] At the beginning of December 1744, he could no longer get out of bed.[139] Typhus set in,[140] and he felt his end approaching. On January 9, 1745, he took communion,[141] afterwards fell into a feverish delusion, and on January 11, 1745, after ten o'clock in the evening, calmly passed away with the words, "Come, Lord Jesus, amen, amen, amen."[142] Boltzius buried him the following Sunday (January 13, 1745), and the surgeon Mayer read John 11:1–45.[143] Frau Gronau soon married her husband's successor, Pastor Lemcke. The elder

---

131. 5A1:50, 246.

132. Born in summer 1736 (5A3:26, 186 = October 1, 1736 B. original), died at the end of 1736 (5A3:50, 317 = January 7, 1737 G. original).

133. Born September 11, 1738 (5A7:32, 139 = October 5, 1738 B. original), died between 1770 (5B3:32, 138 = September 7, 1787 Tr. original) and 1779 (4H26, 124, since her husband, Wertsch died, but Triebner was to administer his estate).

134. Born in the middle of 1743 (5A11:28, 122–23 = January 19, 1745), died after spring 1784 (TK32F8, 687 = March 18, 1784 Tr. original) but before the middle of 1788 (5B3:36, 154 = July 23, 1788 Tr. original).

135. For example, 5A10:17, 54 = March 13, 1742 B. original.

136. 5A11:27, 111 = January 14, 1745 B. copy.

137. 5A11:13, 42 = June 4, 1744 B. original.

138. 5A11:14, 47 = August 9, 1744 B. original; 5D9, 80 = journal September 3, 1744.

139. 5A11:23, 86 = December 29, 1744 B. original.

140. 5A11:27, 111 = January 14, 1745 B. copy.

141. 5D12, 15 = journal January 9, 1745.

142. 5A11:27, 111.

143. 5D12, 19 = journal January 13, 1745. Annually, on the first Sunday after Epiphany, Boltzius, in the sermon, remembered Gronau to the congregation (TK32F11, 1049 = February 17, 1756 B. original). Pastor Driessler also, when he learned about his passing, gave a memorial sermon for him in his community.

daughter, Hanna Elisabeth, became the wife of Johann Caspar Wertsch, and the younger Friderica Maria became the wife of Pastor Triebner.

Gronau was destined always to stand behind Boltzius, which complied with his disposition, as he himself writes, "I also usually follow him gladly and let myself be guided by him because I see that he possesses much wisdom from God and intends to treat me uprightly, but I am still far too simple. I am writing this circumstance only so that Your Reverence [Ziegenhagen] might see how we two treat each other."[144] And from Boltzius we hear, "My worthy colleague Herr Gronau . . . works with me in one spirit and with united energies with young and old. May God be praised for the benefaction of our close collegial friendship!"[145]

Gronau's death meant for Boltzius a genuine loss, since he did not have such a great understanding with any of his other brothers in office. Their conformity in theological insight contributed not insignificantly to this friendship. Gronau also had experienced in Halle his conversion that was a consequence of attending the hymn hours in the Francke Foundations.[146] These hymn hours distinguished themselves from those in Ebenezer in that they represented the central devotional services of the Institutions at which, to be sure, singing took place, but not primarily. Many of the young theologians at the time owed their conversion to them.

Since nothing essential appears in the journals concerning Gronau's theological position, his letters to Francke are of greater importance. From them is learned that Gronau exerted great effort to keep pace with the activity of his brother in office, but he quickly noticed that he was not in a position to do so, and a deep despondency and dejection took hold of him. We read: "My Worthy Herr Professor, things are not well with me. In all matters, I am a wretched person. There is nothing well with me. No one else could believe how things really are; I am no use for anything at all."[147]

This differs from the tirades typical for the time, such as, "I am a miserable worm and dead dog," and the like, and testifies to the upright and reflective character of this man. That is confirmed by the fact that Gronau, during the entire period being reported, addressed to the Halle professors the only theological question from Georgia. For its part, however, it gives shameful testimony of the "scholarliness" of the Halle Pietistic theology. The question is, how is the line, "may such a kiss reconcile God" in Breithaupt's

---

144. 5A3:56, 347 = August 29, 1737 G. copy to Z.
145. 5A9:10, 46 = August 5, 1740 B. original.
146. 5A10:21, 74–75 = January 22, 1742 G. original.
147. 5A3:58, 365–66 = June 9, 1737 G. original.

hymn, "O, Son of God from Eternity," to be understood,[148] and Francke responded with a long exposition.[149]

In Ebenezer, Gronau conscientiously performed many necessary smaller tasks that were not apparent to anyone. The bookkeeping for the construction of the church kept by him and the administration of the orphanage money was always impeccably in order.[150] The popularity that this sympathetic man always enjoyed in his quiet, modest way showed itself with his death: the community extolled him for always being ready to give spiritual encouragement to everyone he met,[151] and the critical Francke writes "of the faithfulness, humility, pure mind, and gentle conscience of the late man."[152]

JOHANN ULRICH DRIESSLER

The future pastor of Frederica was born on August 14, 1692.[153] He, too, spent his student years in Halle,[154] where August Hermann Francke made a powerful impression upon him and also supported him[155] materially as well as through a teaching position in the Orphan House.[156] After the end of his studies, he was pastor in Gröningen near Crailsheim (Württemberg),[157] where he was removed from his office "out of pure envy."[158] The superior who was responsible for him, Baron von Crailsheim,[159] issued a decree on August 24, 1741, to remove Driessler from the parsonage and the venue. Afterwards, on September 19, 1741, when the bailiffs moved in, the congregation stood in front of their pastor and signaled to the gentlemen to withdraw. As a result, von Crailsheim had to summon armed troops from Ansbach who then expelled Driessler on December 2, 1741, with great fanfare.[160] He found ref-

148. 5A10:31, 108 = March 21, 1742 G. original.
149. 5A10:38 = April 2, 1743 Fr. draft.
150. 5D12, 22 = journal January 17, 1745.
151. 5D12, 22 = journal January 17, 1745.
152. 5A11:29, 124 = July 9, 1745 Fr. draft.
153. 4C1:61, 204 = August 28, 1743 Dr. original; 4C1:69, 262 = January 28, 1745 Dr. original.
154. 4C1:52, 174 = June 6, 1743 Dr. original.
155. 4C1:72, 277 = April 17, 1745 Dr. original.
156. J does not extend that far.
157. 4C1:7, 19–26 = September 21, 1742 Dr. original.
158. 4C1:22, 72 = November 17, 1742 Fr. draft.
159. Also Creylsheim, Creylβheim (4C1:12, 43).
160. 4C1:7, 19–26 = September 21, 1742 Dr. original.

uge with his wife in Schwäbisch Hall, first in the house of the notary Chur,[161] then with the needle maker and merchant Schwarz.[162]

On January 28, 1742, he offered his service to Francke[163] who, however, declined him. In the same spring, Driessler received a letter from two men from Pennsylvania in which they requested several pastors and made promises regarding salary. Driessler sent this letter to Halle and inquired whether it was to be believed and whether he could be one of those for whom they were looking. But Francke did not know the people, regarded the promises as uncertain, and gave notice that only Ziegenhagen was authorized to issue calls for Pennsylvania; he had requested only one pastor who, "after much effort," had been found in Muhlenberg, and he already had departed.[164] However, already at the beginning of May 1740, Francke had received Oglethorpe's request for a Lutheran pastor for Frederica;[165] why did he not think about Driessler for it? At the time when Ziegenhagen had transmitted Oglethorpe's letter to him, Francke had his eye on a certain Schach, who up until that time had been an instructor at Pastor Majer's house.[166] He was to have departed right away, but then news reached Europe about the conditions in Frederica that were said to be so confused and morally loose[167] that Schach's departure was delayed until things finally fell apart.[168] But the matter was very important to Oglethorpe. On July 17, 1741, he urged Boltzius once more[169] and asked the Trustees to pay for the journey of one pastor from Halle to Georgia; otherwise, he would take on the expenses himself,[170] and Boltzius reported this to Halle. Unfortunately, however, there was nothing in particular to report about Frederica,[171] so that Francke, who always greatly procrastinated over things of this sort,[172] did nothing about Driessler's offer that was made about this time.

161. 4C1:2, 7 = February 8, 1742 Dr. original.
162. 4C1:4, 13 = August 29, 1742 Fr. draft.
163. 4C1:2, 7–8.
164. 4C1:3, 11–12, May 5, 1742 Fr. draft.
165. 5A9:1, 1 = January 5, 1740 B. original; 5A7:66, 283 = May 4, 1740.
166. 5A9:5, 15.
167. 5A10:12, 36 = July 25, 1741 B. copy.
168. 5A10:20, 72–73.
169. 5A10:13, 40–41 = July 17, 1741 Oglethorpe copy = 4C1:37, 124.
170. 4C1:37a, 125 = July 17, 1741 Oglethorpe copy to Verelst.
171. 5A10:12, 36.
172. Francke similarly delayed before the sending of Muhlenberg.

Meanwhile in Georgia, Vigera, the commissioner of the fourth Salzburger transport, made an exploratory tour of Frederica,[173] and likely on the basis of his report, Francke finally decided on September 12, 1742, to offer the position to Driessler,[174] who naturally accepted it immediately.[175] He was now to go by water to Rotterdam, if possibly before winter, for which Francke would in the meantime pay. With joy, Driessler immediately went to Augsburg, held there a very edifying trial sermon on October 17, 1742, and subsequently gave to Urlsperger his unequivocal assurance that he in no way had any ambitions that resembled those of Zinzendorf.[176] With the explicit guarantee of the call for Frederica, he returned to Schwäbisch Hall, learned English, auctioned off his furniture,[177] and, at the request of the city council, preached on Sunday, November 18, 1742, in the main church among such a throng that it was said, "No one can recall that such an indescribable crowd of people had been in the church."[178]

Yet to his great sorrow, matters did not immediately go forward, since Francke had been commissioned by Oglethorpe with responsibility for the call, and Francke had heard in the meantime that the Spaniards had occupied all of Georgia.[179] For that reason, he only issued the call, at Urlsperger's urging, after more than a quarter year.[180] But then the next obstacle was in the way. It was learned that Oglethorpe, denigrated by antagonists, had to come to Europe and defend himself, so that Urlsperger now advised Driessler to look for another position.[181] That must have been all the more bitter to Driessler since shortly beforehand he had turned down two offers from Germany.[182] Yet because the obstacles seemed never to cease, Driessler now lost his patience. On July 29, 1743, he travelled by coach with his wife and eighteen-year-old maid[183] from Schwäbisch Hall to Heilbronn; from there by ship via Mannheim and Mainz[184] to Düsseldorf. Here, he en-

173. 5A10:19, 70 = April 13, 1742 B. original.
174. 4C1:5, 72–73 = September 12, 1742 Fr. draft; 5A10:20, 72–73 = November 12, 1742 Fr. draft.
175. 4C1:7, 19–26 = September 21, 1742 Dr. original.
176. 4C1:18, 56–57 = October 18, 1742 U. senior.
177. 4C1:19, 63–64 = November 7, 1742 Dr. original.
178. 4C1:12, 38–39 = November 22, 1742 Dr. copy.
179. 4C1:14, 48 = October 8, 1742 Fr. draft.
180. 4C1:29 = January 21, 1743 U, original signature in another hand; on March 7, 1743: 4C1:35, 120–21 Fr. draft.
181. 4C1:49, 165 = May 10, 1743 U. copy.
182. 4C1:54, 180 = June 1, 1743 Fr. draft.
183. 4C1:18, 56–57 = October 18, 1742 U. original; perhaps the granddaughter.
184. He preached in Mannheim. 4C1:59, 195 = August 6, 1743 Dr. original.

countered the misfortune that his ferry boat overturned. His wife was immediately pulled out, but he had to swim for a rather long time until he also was pulled to shore. A severe shock, a head wound, and a considerable loss of luggage were the results of this incident.

On August 21, he reached Rotterdam, where three days later he continued to London with the Catherine Sloep under Captain Rowlathon,[185] and finally, on December 22, 1743—it could have been a year and a half earlier—he arrived in Frederica.[186] At this outpost, Driessler was greatly strengthened by his connections with Ebenezer and Halle. Soon after his arrival in Georgia, he made a visit to Ebenezer,[187] and the community there gave Frederica a communion chalice to use.[188]

Oglethorpe had wished for Driessler to be placed under Pastor Boltzius,[189] and so the two communities maintained a connection through a continuous exchange of letters.[190] Driessler also reported his experiences to Francke, and, for that matter, in truly exhausting detail. For example, one letter had been written on twenty-four, tightly written pages, a total of 1000 and more lines;[191] a treasure trove for us, a torment for Francke who had to respond to them. But he also let Driessler know that all too well. He answered curtly and briefly and often did not go into the content at all but only acknowledged joyfully that Driessler was still alive. In doing so, he did not consider at all how important for Driessler must be this connection with Europe and especially with Halle, his spiritual home, and apparently did not agree to respond to Driessler's request to convey to him, as he had for Boltzius and Gronau, some suggestions for the conduct of his office.[192]

As already reported, Driessler displayed vigorous activity. His lively style[193] gave him quick access to his hearers, as was the case with his visit in Ebenezer and his sermons in Germany, so that even in Schwäbisch Hall the envy of his colleagues had begun to awaken. In contrast to the deliberative and somewhat didactic character of Ebenezer's first pastors, his more cheerful style was felt to be pleasant and relaxed. If his style of pastoral praxis is

---

185. 4C1:60, 197–200 = August 22, 1743 Dr. copy.

186. 4C1:67, 227 = July 30, 1744 Dr. original.

187. 5D9, 1 = journal February 24, 1744; 5A11:24, 90 = February 24, 1744.

188. UN February 1, 1747.

189. 5A11:30, 126 = July 24, 1745 Fr. draft.

190. 4C1:67, 242 = July 30, 1744 Dr. original; 5A11:63, 289 = May 16, 1747 B. original.

191. 4C1:67 = July 30, 1744 Dr. original.

192. 4C1:68, 253 = April 3, 1745 Fr. draft.

193. 5A11:23, 87 = December 29, 1744 B. original.

compared with that of Boltzius, Driessler was less active in home visitation and much more with his greatest interest in catechization, and it is uplifting to hear when he acknowledges, "This school work is my rest, catechization my element and my greatest prize when I see that it is blessed."[194] He labored in it often up to the edge of his strength, so that Francke had to admonish him that above all of his work, he should also "preserve enough time for himself."[195]

That certainly would have been necessary, since Driessler suffered from "stones"[196] and was greatly weakened by the hot climate. He had to limit his teaching[197] and unfortunately died already in 1746.[198]

HERMANN HEINRICH LEMCKE

When Boltzius reported Gronau's death to Senior Urlsperger, he requested at the same time a successor for him, however with the comment that he himself "would not be the first pastor but rather, as God wills, the assistant and catechist. For I am too weak for the first position and would rather stand under a superior."[199] Then, when the SPCK also learned about Gronau's death, they officially asked Urlsperger to provide a successor, and the Trustees offered to pay for the voyage.[200] Urlsperger relayed the matter to Halle where Francke chose the candidate in theology Hermann Heinrich Lemcke,[201] who at the time was barely twenty-five years old.

He was born in 1720[202] in Fischbeck in County Schaumburg as the son of the schoolteacher there,[203] but came already as a child to the Halle Orphan House, and with that was the first of the pastors sent to Georgia who also

---

194. 4C1:67, 244 = July 30, 1744 Dr. original.

195. 4C1:68, 253 = April 3, 1745 Fr. draft.

196. 4C1:69, 261 = January 28, 1745 Fr. draft.

197. 5A11:21, 81 = October 29, 1744 B. original.

198. Last preserved letter: 4C1:77 = February 17, 1746 Dr. original; UN February 1, 1747, his wife returned the chalice. His wife, who also was constantly sick, moved to be with her granddaughter (see also p. 185, n. 183) who had married a Reformed Swiss merchant during Driessler's lifetime (UN February 1 and October 3, 1747).

199. 5A11:27, 114–15 = January 14, 1745 B. copy.

200. 5C2:1 = June 25, 1745. He was supposed to come as soon as possible, since the ship with the first transport with servants was supposed to depart from England to Georgia in August 1745 (5C2:5).

201. 5A11:42, 178 L. original and 5A11:53, 244 L. original where the name is spelled "Lemke," otherwise, Lemcke.

202. J I, 283; 5C2:16, 38.

203. 5C2:21; a brother, A. C. Lemcke, is mentioned 5B2:61, 215.

had received his schooling here.[204] In 1742, he began his theological study in Halle, and in January of the following year became a teacher "in the German boys' school." G. A. Francke formed the judgment about him, "He has a fear of God but is somewhat lazy, average in his studies, but quite good in speaking and discipline."[205] In 1745, he became *Inspector vicarius mensarum Orphanotrophei*,[206] and in the summer was designated as the *Adjunctus Pastoris and Catechet* for the communities in Georgia, contrary to Boltzius' wish.[207] Due to the brevity of time, the proper call through Urlsperger was only sent to him in Georgia.[208] On August 13, 1745, he already departed from Halle[209] to Wernigerode where on the following day he was examined on original sin in the presence of Count Christian Ernst, and on August 15th was ordained by Court Chaplain Lau, as Boltzius and Gronau had been.[210] One day later, he continued on via Minden,[211] and things were arranged so that Lemcke could stay on August 18th in Fischbeck with his parents who knew nothing about his commission.[212]

He then went to London via Amsterdam and Rotterdam,[213] and on November 21, 1745 (new style), he began the voyage from Gosport (south England) on board the "Judith" under Captain Walther Quarme.[214] Traveling with him was Pastor Zuberbühler, who had just come from London from his ordination. Lemcke could learn from him right away some things about his new area of labor. They landed on January 22, 1746 (old style) off Frederica,[215] from which Lemcke sailed with the boat of commander Major Horton to Savannah,[216] and on Friday, February 7, 1746, arrived in

---

204. 5C2:9 = August 12, 1745; 5C2:16, 38.

205. J I, 283.

206. J I, 283, 5C2:16, 38.

207. 5C2:9 = August 12, 1745.

208. 5C2:18, 53–55; UN III, 202; 5C2:20: Not a single confessional writing is mentioned in it.

209. 5C2:12.

210. 5A11:44, 185 = probably February 28, 1746 L. copy; 5D11, 1–2.

211. 5D11, 16.

212. 5C2:21.

213. From September 3 to October 25, 1745 new style in London (5D11, 5; 5C2:26).

214. 5A11:32a, 138 = December 22, 1745 Fr. draft.

215. After 10 weeks, 3 days. 4C1:76, 295 = February 17, 1746 Dr. copy.

216. 5A11:35, 149 = February 12, 1746 L.

Ebenezer.²¹⁷ On the following Sunday, he gave his introductory sermon, and on the Monday afterwards began to teach in the school.²¹⁸

As was most practical under the given circumstances, and also as was desired by Francke and Urlsperger,²¹⁹ Lemcke soon subsequently married Gronau's widow,²²⁰ thereby freeing the European authorities from her additional care. In doing so, Lemcke also got back the favor of his superiors which he had almost squandered through a travel diary that he had kept in a peculiar, rather careless way.²²¹ To the two surviving children of Gronau were now added two daughters²²² and a son named Timotheus²²³ who showed considerable abilities and soon became a genuine support for his frequently sickly father.²²⁴ He taught in Ebenezer's school, and he acquired medical knowledge with the help of his father from the books of the church library and of the physician Thilo that enabled him, after Mayer's departure and Thilo's death, to practice as a surgeon.²²⁵

Around the time of Boltzius' death, Lemcke's health increasingly worsened,²²⁶ so that from time to time he could not tend to his office. Rabenhorst reported concerning his end, "His last illness began with pains in his right side, fever, and headaches, but varied so that neither he himself nor his family, along with me, suspected his end this time. . . . He was too weak to say anything in particular except to cry out, 'My God, my God, come.'" On Easter Monday, April 4, 1768, he died "shortly after four o'clock in the

---

217. 5A11:45, 148 = February 4, 1746 B.; 5A11:40, 170 = February 22, 1746 L. original.

218. 5A11:35, 149–50.

219. 5A11:38, 163 = July 28, 1746 Fr. draft to B.

220. 5A11:53, 242 = May 13, 1746 L. original; 244 = Z notation.

221. 5D11. When it had arrived in Europe, while Lemcke was still onboard the ship, Francke had sent to him in Ebenezer a rather strict letter admonishing him to humility, orderliness, and obedience toward Boltzius (5A11:32a = December 22, 1745 Fr. draft).

222. The older, born in 1747, died in 1802 in Ebenezer as Mrs. Herson (therefore her husband was probably related to Hergen Herson), was very sickly (5B4:29, 87 = January 11, 1803 Bm.). The younger, born December 1748 (5B1:24, 107 = November 23, 1748 B. original signature in another hand), died in Ebenezer before 1802 (5B4:29, 87), did not marry. Triebner later came under suspicion of having an illicit affair with her.

223. Probably born soon after his sisters (TK32F8, 674–75 = September 27, 1771 Tr. original erroneously states 1742), died before February 1777 (4H23, 309).

224. 5B2:33, 126; 5A11:62, 287 = March 13, 1747 B. original.

225. 5B2:28, 112 = 1765; 5B3:13.

226. 5B2:19, 87 = undated (April 12, 1765) R. original.

morning" and was buried on the following day by Rabenhorst with the text, Isaiah 45:15.[227] His wife survived him by only a few years.[228]

Like Gronau, Lemcke also stood in the shadow of Boltzius' personality, and later that of Rabenhorst. It is regrettable that because of Rabenhorst's profit-seeking, Boltzius for a time did not have a good opinion of Lemcke, whereupon, however, a heartfelt reconciliation soon followed, since Lemcke was a modest, calm, and perhaps somewhat awkward person who did not make much of himself.[229] Yet he had a wide range of interests and was proficient in music, architecture, and medicine,[230] but especially in botany. Several times, he assembled herbaria for the cabinet of curiosities (*Naturalien-Kabinett*) of the Halle Orphan House,[231] and also once in a while forwarded "oddities from the kingdom of nature" that he, in part, had collected with the surgeon Mayer.[232]

Moreover, he was "a great friend of children,"[233] something that made him much beloved in his teaching. In the proclamation of the Word, he was as precise and careful as probably no other of his colleagues in Georgia, who probably also followed August Hermann Francke in this point as their model, since Lemcke, who otherwise was very reserved, spoke his opinion openly in this regard and, one might also think, with intentional emphasis:

> I saw today an unshakable attentiveness in my hearers, to which, as I already have noticed several times, many things contribute when God's Word is delivered rather clearly, simply and emphatically, and in good order, provided that the teacher has prepared well in advance or that he indeed must be very well versed in divine truths and stands in the required frame of mind. Today, I dealt with waiting on the coming of Christ in judgment. In order to be able to help with retention, I make not only divisions, but also several, though fewer, subdivisions. I explain the sentences with a few words, and I add the application right away so that I can stop when the time does not permit me to express

---

227. 5B2:59, 200–203 = April 6, 1768 R. original. He did not die in 1772/1773 as Gilbert assumes. Gilbert, "Early History of the Lutheran Church in Georgia," 167. Hazelius' desired clarity over his end (*History of the American Lutheran Church*, 101) can be given from the archives.

228. 4H23, 309 = journal May 15, 1777 M = letter February 20, 1777 Mrs. R. copy was written after her death.

229. 5A11:32a, 138; 5B2:40, 146 = March 27, 1766 Fr. draft.

230. 5B3:30, 128 = August 27, 1787 Bm. original.

231. 5B1:14, 61; 15, 64–65; 49, 205; 5A11:39, 167 = July 21, 1746.

232. 5B1:35, 140 = November 5, 1750; 5A11:39, 167 = July 21, 1746 Fr. draft.

233. 5B1:2, 7 = July 18, 1748 B. original.

everything. But when the sentences relate very closely to each other, and I know that I save enough time for the application, I wait for it until the last. From such an arrangement I have the benefit of being able to look through at my sermon from beginning to end and it eases the delivery for me.[234]

Pastor Bergmann confirmed the same point: "His delivery was not as lively as that of Herr Boltzius. But he preached soundly, as I have seen from the manuscripts that he left behind; he brought no extraneous matters into the pulpit, like Boltzius, Rabenhorst, and Triebner did."[235] That also corresponds with the rest of Lemcke's disposition. But the community certainly had an ear for his style of preaching, since he was regarded by it with "love and esteem as an upright preacher,"[236] even if he did not outwardly make much of an appearance.

CHRISTIAN RABENHORST

When from 1750 the Swabian transports considerably increased Ebenezer's residents, it also became clear in Germany that the two pastors, Boltzius and Lemcke, were not capable of the additional work. When, therefore, the third transport was put together in 1752, the members asked Urlsperger to give them a traveling chaplain who also, if possible, could remain with them. Urlsperger made the request accordingly to Halle which recommended two candidates, from whom the younger, Christian Rabenhorst, would accept the call.[237]

He was born on July 7, 1728,[238] in Pagenköpp (Eastern Pomerania) as the son of the teacher there, Christian Rabenhorst, and his wife, née Oldemann. He had three sisters, all of whom survived him.[239] When he was about twelve years old, his mother died, and his father moved to Blumberg near Stargard (Mecklenburg), where he again accepted a teaching post. Shortly thereafter the pastor there died, and succeeding him was Pastor

---

234. UA December 9, 1753 L.

235. 5B3:30, 128.

236. 5B2:40, 146 = March 27, 1766 Fr. draft.

237. UA I preface (unpaginated).

238. 5B3:36, 153 = July 23, 1788 Tr. original; J I, 432; UA I, 166 on July 27.

239. 1. Maria Hoppe née Rabenhorst, wife of the Sexton Ernst Gottlieb Hoppe in Daber (Eastern Pommerania). He died on July 1, 1776. They had five sons (TK32F7, 613 = August 29, 1778). 2. Mrs. Neumann née Rabenhorst was a widow in 1799 (5B4:4, 22 = November 1799) in Berlin (TK32F2, 208 = January 13, 1781 Freylinghausen). 3. The name of the third sister was not known in Halle (TK32F2, 208).

Rautenberg, who up to that point had been Inspector at the Latin School of the Halle Orphan House.[240] He gave instruction in Latin to the young Rabenhorst, and in August 1744, brought him, a sixteen-year-old, to Halle,[241] where especially G. A. Freylinghausen interceded for him,[242] as he expected no great sum of money from home.

From this time of schooling at the Orphan House, Rabenhorst reports: "Since I had become tired after my initial fear of God, had neglected prayer, and had strayed, and it was made known to you [Freylinghausen], and you said in my presence to dear Inspector Mauritius in the Inspectors' room, 'Our Rabenhorst is no longer his old self,' and, accordingly, I now was mindful that I had lost your favor, I now was instantly moved and made the resolution as I went downstairs, to be all the more devout to God who sees all things."[243]

By all misfortune, several hundred talers that were to be used to finance his studies were stolen at night during this time from his father. Consequently, at the conclusion of his schooling around the turn of the year between 1749 and 1750, he came to Silesia as the house teacher for the family of Count Bogatzky.[244] However, already in April 1750, he appeared again in Halle for theological study. In addition, he functioned from the next year on as teacher at the boys' school of the Francke Foundations, later also in the upper class of the Latin school for the disciplines of Religion and Latin as well as supervisor for the orphans.[245]

The choice as pastor for Ebenezer fell to him at the recommendation of Pastor Majer at St. Ulrich's Church in Halle.[246] Francke was not in agreement with it, since Rabenhorst was thought to be narcissistic and selfish.[247] Nevertheless, no more thought was paid to it, and Rabenhorst received his call on June 6, 1752,[248] started out from Halle, and reached Augsburg on

---

240. There was also an orphanage in Stargard that had a relationship with the Halle Orphan House (TK32F2, 217 = May 5, 1759 R.).

241. UA I, 166–67.

242. He also had Francke to thank for providing for him, without cost, instruction, maintenance, and books (TK32F2, 214).

243. TK32F2, 228–29 = March 19, 1773 R. original.

244. Probably the brother of Carl Heinrich von Bogatzky who had been living in the Halle Orphan House since 1746. His father had died between 1718 and 1721. Bogatzky: *Lebenslauf, vom ihm selbst beschrieben,* 91–94, 229.

245. UA I, 166–67; J I, 432: "He had a good fear of God, was diligent, had an exquisitely flowing delivery, and also well disciplined."

246. 5B4:17, 49 = January 26, 1802 Bm. original.

247. He held this view for a long time (5B2:40, 146–47).

248. UA June 6, 1754.

July 24, 1752. Four days later, he preached in the main church there, St. Anna's,[249] on the call to mission (Mk 16:15–16) and was ordained immediately afterwards by Samuel Urlsperger and the rest of the ecclesiastical "ministerium" at Augsburg.[250]

The transport, with its pastor, approached Tybee Island on November 23, 1752, and anchored there. On December 16th, Rabenhorst arrived in Ebenezer where he delivered his first sermon on December 24th.[251] However, when Boltzius heard about the arrival of a third pastor for Ebenezer, he was not very pleased by it and did not quite understand the necessity of this measure taken by Urlsperger. Only when he noticed the alleviation that this third position meant for him did he become of a different mind.[252]

Rabenhorst's salary, as reported earlier, was secured through the establishment of the third preacher's plantation. Moreover, Urlsperger (senior) suggested that Rabenhorst could have his midday meal with the merchant Kraft. However, before this suggestion could come into effect in Georgia, Kraft had died and Rabenhorst had married his wife.[253] She was born Anna Barbara Brant,[254] who had relatives in Ravensberg (Mecklenburg).[255] She had first married the merchant David Kraft[256] who had arrived in Ebenezer at the end of October 1751 with the second Swabian transport and there, in Mayer's house that actually had been built as a store, kept a "shop and merchandise."[257]

Through this marriage with this widow Kraft, Rabenhorst received a share of her not inconsiderable property (also plantations), and because he was known as slightly egotistical, but she was extremely frugal if not even greedy,[258] this estate, together with his preacher's plantation, was a great temptation for him; the salary level for Boltzius and Lemcke was fixed, but his income depended on his industriousness that he quickly developed, not always to the satisfaction of the community and his colleagues. Bergmann was told about him, "He was a dear and pleasant man in company,

---

249. Urlsperger was the pastor there.
250. See also p. 63.
251. UA December 16 and 24, 1752.
252. UA II, 353 = letter February 9, 1753 B. to U.; 5B1:50, 207 = August 4, 1753.
253. Married on February 22, 1753, by Boltzius, using Isaiah 61:10 as the text (UA February 20–21, 1753). They had no children,
254. 5B4:19, 60 = January 15, 1775 R. copy.
255. TK32F2, 208 = January 13, 1781 Freylinghausen draft.
256. Also spelled Craft, 5B4:19, 60 = January 15, 1775 R. copy.
257. UA July 6, 1752. This marriage also was childless.
258. 5B4:3, 17 = October 7, 1799 Bm. original.

but self-interest cannot be denied about him." Moreover, when he preached outside of the community, he allowed himself, at the instigation of his wife, to receive money for it from the congregation, something that greatly infuriated the people and Boltzius, since, after all, he owned such a profitable plantation. "In trade and commerce he indeed dealt honestly; he was certainly very precise about all things, but he paid everyone properly.... Now and then he gave something to poor people, but he had to do it secretly, because he otherwise would scarcely have a quiet hour in his house."[259] After her death, Frau Rabenhorst was said to have wandered about at night in the moonlight as a white woman and to have looked for her buried money.[260]

Since Rabenhorst lived not in Ebenezer but in Goshen, and also was the healthiest among the three pastors, he looked after the surrounding areas, however, he also came down with tuberculosis[261] and chronic intestinal trouble that became especially noticeable in his later years.[262] On his birthday in 1774, his old slave women attempted to poison him,[263] which his adversary Triebner viewed as divine judgment. Muhlenberg, however, could not make up his mind about that[264] since, according to another version, while the old woman was grinding coffee, "some poison fell into the coffee grinder out of paper that lay on a shelf above. Rabenhorst and his wife drank from it and vomited." But fourteen days later, the poor slave woman, with Treutlen's collaboration, was burned alive.[265]

From September 1776, Rabenhorst could no longer preach, and at the end of the year, his end also had come. He had the 8th chapter of Romans read to him, especially from verse 28 to 30, and afterwards to the end of the 39th. In spite of his weakness, he was always vivacious and also remained so until his end, and with folded hands and clear mind, after singing twice the hymn, "'May the soul of Christ sanctify me, etc.,' gently and blissfully" departed on December 30, 1776, his wife reported. On January 2, 1777, he was buried in the cemetery of Zion Church by Pastor Zübli, using the text Isaiah 57:1.[266]

259. 5B4:17, 50 = January 26, 1802 Bm. original.
260. 5B4:17, 49. She died before January 1781 (TK32F2, 209 = January 16, 1781 Freylinghausen draft).
261. 4C17:29, 327 = March 27/29, 1775 M. copy.
262. 4H23, 309.
263. 5B3:36, 100.
264. TK32F1b, 53 = journal December 24, 1774 M.
265. 5B4:17, 48.
266. 4H23, 307-9 = journal May 15, 1777 M = letter February 20, 1777 Mrs. R. copy; 5B4:17, 48.

With him, a new theological direction entered Georgia's young Lutheran church. He also had studied in Halle, had the benefit of his schooling in the Orphan House, and afterwards visited the local university. However, in comparison to Boltzius' time of study, things here were now completely different. It was the time of the impact of Wolff and Baumgarten, and then again, the time when the Orphan House received new energy through the presence of Bogatzky (since 1746). A widespread awakening of the students took place that was not driven by the administration (1746), and Bogatzky held heavily attended student devotional hours and raised the demand as it had been previously with regard to theological study: conversion at the expense of scholarship. Which of the two sides was the stronger influence on Rabenhorst can already be recognized from his "conversion experience" on the steps of the Orphan House. One looks here in vain for the penitential struggle demanded by Francke, both father and son, but established in its place the resolution deliberately made to turn oneself decisively to God.

It follows the same line when later Boltzius expressed the opinion about him that he "has no grace,"[267] and when Rabenhorst received greater latitude after Boltzius' death, numerous reports soon reached Europe concerning his negligent and freehanded handling of church discipline and admission to the Lord's Supper, as already noted.[268] For example, he found nothing offensive about a young man who dressed as a woman, occasionally even undermined Triebner's efforts at church discipline,[269] and allowed people who "lived in open sin" to come to communion.[270] In doing so, he greatly scandalized a part of the community members.

Concerning the judgment that he put himself in the middle of his sermons,[271] there is Triebner's observation: his sermons were "lovely, historical, but they were lacking soul, that is the Holy Spirit who chastises, teaches rightly, admonishes, and consoles,"[272] which matches Boltzius' view. If Muhlenberg had the highest praise for Rabenhorst and in doing so used Francke's terms, "Oration, meditation, tentation have made him an orthodox theologian in the true sense,"[273] then not too much weight should be put on it since, unfortunately, various signs indicate that Rabenhorst, together

---

267. TK32F2, 236 = March 3, 1773 Wertsch extract to Z.
268. See p. 66.
269. TK32F8, 723–24 = October 6, 1770 Tr. extract to U. junior.
270. TK32F2, 237 = March 3, 1773.
271. See p. 66.
272. TK32F8, 725 = October 6, 1770.
273. TK32F1b, 153 = journal February 5, 1775 M.

with his wife, sought to make Muhlenberg biased[274] through special acts of friendship[275] and a variety of gifts, and through him to stand in a light that had to be favorable in Europe. The indicated "orthodoxy" is, moreover, not at all a counterargument against his having been influenced by Baumgarten.[276] Even the fact that he, in all of his worship services, appeared in regular clothes, like the "Dissenters," without Anglican vestments,[277] and, being indifferent to the confession and tradition of his Lutheran church, wanted to move Triebner to a merger with the Anglican Church because it would be beneficial to the community, points in this direction.[278]

All in all, it is no wonder that Rabenhorst became the rallying point of those who just as easily ignored changes in secular government just as much as they did changes in Rabenhorst's preaching compared to that of his predecessors.

CHRISTOPH FRIEDRICH TRIEBNER

When in the year of Boltzius' death (1765) the eighty-year-old Samuel Urlsperger stepped down from his office, his son, Johann August Urlsperger (1726–December 1, 1806), also took over the official duties regarding Georgia,[279] although he only succeeded him officially when his father died in 1772.[280] He now began to arrange for a successor for Boltzius. The

274. That, nonetheless, had no consequences for his judgment of Triebner. Muhlenberg also treated him with emphatic impartiality, even when in time he admittedly could no longer have any appreciation for his ideas.

275. Even in this connection she was praised by Muhlenberg (TK32F1b, 153 = journal February 5, 1775 M.).

276. Also a further note of Muhlenberg is to be heard with care when Rabenhorst's overall attitude is kept in mind: "When there was unrest over the Stamp Act that was to be introduced, His Execellency [the governor of Georgia] wrote to H. R. [Herr Rabenhorst] and asked if he would teach his hearers that the matter would be very useful and advantageous for them, etc. H. R. [Herr Rabenhort] then answered: he would prefer to keep his impudence away from what was not in keeping with his office, etc. He taught his hears about penitence, faith, and godliness, and when that went off well, then they would also be faithful subjects" (TK32F1b, 157–58 = journal February 6, 1775 M).

277. 5B2:25, 103 = November 5, 1765 B. original.

278. See p. 115.

279. 5B2:2, 4 = September 3, 1765 Fr. draft; 5B2:35, 134 = April 11, 1766 U. junior original.

280. ADB 39, 355–61. In 1775, he founded the *Gesellschaft zur Beförderung des thätigen Christenthums* (Society for the Promotion of Active Christianity), and in 1780, the *Christenthums-Gesellschaft* (Christian Society), the predecessor of the *Basler Missionsgesellschaft* (Basel Missions Society) (*Nachrichten von den vereinigten Deutschen Evangelisch-Lutherischen Gemeinden*, 26).

matter was brought to Ziegenhagen[281] who also induced the SPCK to ask him officially to replace the position through Urlsperger and the Francke Foundations.[282] At the time, however, there was no one to be found from the Francke Foundations,[283] and therefore the Urlspergers, both father and son, at first suggested a Württemberger[284] who, however, declined it.[285] Then there was an attempt to fill it with the Salzburger theological candidate Schwer, who at the time also was in Württemberg. Thought was also given to the very capable Court Chaplain Reitz of the Count Reuss-Plauen at Obergreiz, but from whom they hardly expected acceptance.[286] Finally, Mauer and Triebner were available to be chosen, but Francke was not agreeable to either; Mauer was "somewhat grim and phlegmatic," and "Herr Triebner has always seemed to me to be somewhat arrogant, egotistical, and unstable, . . . so that I do not have the heart to recommend him for Ebenezer."[287]

Francke knew Triebner so well because he already had been at the Halle Orphan House. Born in 1740 in Pössneck (Thuringia),[288] he became a teacher in Greiz in 1760. His territorial lord, Count Heinrich XI of Reuss-Plauen at Obergreiz,[289] whose house already had been amenable to Pietism under August Hermann Francke,[290] made it possible for him to study theology, which he began in Halle in July 1764. However, at the beginning of the following year he transferred to Leipzig where the Enlightenment philological exegete Ernesti set the tone of the faculty's spirit, something with which Triebner did not agree. Already in September, therefore, he returned, "because he did not improve himself there as he thought he would." Along with his studies, he now taught at the girls' school of the Francke Foundations[291] and received here a noticeable influence on his faith position.[292] In

---

281. 5B2:33, 126 = March 9, 1766 U. senior and junior copy to Z.
282. 5B2:58 = September 9, 1766 Broughton (Secretary of the SPCK) to Z.
283. 5B2:40, 147-48 = March 27, 1766 Fr. draft.
284. 5B2:33.
285. 5B2:35, 132 = April 11, 1766 U. junior original.
286. 5B2:37, 136 = May 26, 1766 U. junior copy; p. 136b: "Schwehr."
287. 5B2:42, 155 = September 8, 1767 Fr. draft, 156.
288. J II, 124.
289. Triebner, *Die Beschaffenheit eines Menschen*, 3.
290. See Appendix II, no. 27; 5D3 = journal May 1, 1737.
291. Evaluation: "There is a true foundation there, only much self-love rules there. Study habits are poor, but the delivery is rather fine, discipline is paternal" (J II, 124).
292. 5B2:6, 15 = July 6, 1769 Fr. draft; 5B2:49, 173-74 = April 8, 1763 Reitz copy; "since he left Halle, he has become much poorer in spirit."

August 1768, he returned again to Greiz[293] and received a position at the orphanage there.[294]

Therefore, because Francke was not in agreement over him, he recommended Kleiminger, "a son of a Salzburger emigrant who lives in Heylbronn, is studying here at the university and teaching at the Orphan House." Francke originally wanted him for Tranquebar, but perhaps a better place for him would be in America with his Salzburg compatriots.[295] But Kleiminger did not want to go, and since there was no one else—there should have been long enough to anticipate Boltzius' approaching death and actually to have been able to discuss the question of his successor; in the meantime, Lemcke also died—the decision fell to Triebner, and with it occurred for Georgia's Lutheran communities the gravest mistake of their history.

In order to alleviate somewhat Francke's reservations, Urlsperger asked the Senior Pastor Bürckmann in Nuremberg for an expert assessment of Triebner. In doing so, Bürckmann commissioned Triebner's superior, the very same Court Chaplain Reitz, who without a doubt had knowledge that he himself had been in consideration for Georgia, and since he understandably did not want to leave his good position, he assessed Triebner as charitably as possible.[296] Triebner, therefore, was appointed by Urlsperger as pastor for Ebenezer,[297] and, in fact, "in the position of H. Lemcke,"[298] whereby it remained overlooked that up until now this had been the second position in rank, but after Boltzius' death the first position, though not confirmed as such by Europe.

His ordination took place on October 12, 1768, in Augsburg.[299] From November 23rd to December 12th he caused trouble for Ziegenhagen in London,[300] and subsequently started the great journey[301] with Pastors Helmuth and Johann Friedrich Schmidt who were destined for Pennsylvania.[302] Soon after his arrival in Ebenezer (1769),[303] he married the

---

293. J II, 124.
294. 5B2:46, 169 = June 13, 1768 Fr. draft.
295. 5B2:42, 157.
296. 5B2:49, 173–74.
297. 5B2:7.
298. 5B2:50, 178 = November 8, 1768 Fr. draft.
299. In residence from September 12, 1768 to October 27 (5B2:57). 5B2:56, 191.
300. 5B2:57, 194 = December 30, 1768 Z. copy.
301. 5B2:50, 178 = November 8, 1768 Fr. draft.
302. *Nachrichten von den vereinigten Deutschen Evangelisch-Lutherischen Gemeinden in Nord-America*, 43.
303. 5B3:32, 137 = September 7, 1787 Tr. original.

The Pastors of the Communities and Their Theological Position 199

twenty-six-year-old Friderica Maria Gronau,[304] whereupon four children arrived; the first lived only eight days.[305] Then followed a daughter[306] and two sons, Christoph Friedrich[307] and Timotheus Traugott.[308]

With this entire family and his niece Hanna Wertsch, Triebner, when the British troops evacuated Ebenezer on December 8, 1781, fled to Savannah,[309] which the English also left on July 11, 1782,[310] so that he had to leave with them, as he did previously. The refugees remained for several weeks on board a ship off of Tybee Island in the mouth of the Savannah River until at the beginning of August they landed in St. Augustine, Florida, where there was an artillery officer who, "three years ago, under General Prevost, has been in Ebenezer" and in Triebner's house, and took in him and his family.[311] Here he learned that he was counted among those "who on pain of death must not return" to Georgia[312]—an order that remained in force until around 1801.[313]

He reported about his activity here: "Since the 60th Regiment, which three years ago was stationed in Ebenezer, comprises the garrison here, and a large part of it is German, I was asked by many of them to give a sermon on Sundays in the German language, which I carried out after receiving permission; thus, I preached to them from the 10th Sunday after Trinity to the 22nd, confirmed three young people, and baptized several children; I also had seventy communicants on the 22nd Sunday after Trinity." However, he declined the position of a Lutheran field chaplain that was offered to him

---

304. Gilbert, "Early History of the Lutheran Church in Georgia," 168. TK32F8, 675 = September 27, 1771 Tr. original.

305. In fall 1770 (TK32F8, 675–76).

306. Born 1773 (1C34b:63 = June 12, 1793 Tr. original).

307. Born 1776 (1C34b:63). He was married to a woman who did not understand any German (5B4:41, 121 = December 3, 1804 Bm. original) and lived in Savannah as a merchant after the War of Independence (5B4:45, 141 = March 17, 1806 Bm. original). Bergmann buried his second son in Ebenezer according to the English rite because of his wife (5B4:41, 121).

308. TK32F7, 628–31 = October 28, 1782 Tr. copy. Born around the turn of the year 1777/78 (1C34b:63 = June 12, 1793 Tr. original).

309. 5B3:32; Allen and McClure, *Two Hundred Years*, 394; 5B3:9 = April 4, 1782 Tr. original (according to 5B3:10, 47 to Pasche).

310. *Encyclopedia Americana* XII, 489.

311. TK32F7, 628–31 = October 28, 1782 Tr. copy.

312. 4H26, 129 = journal July 14, 1783 M; Allen and McClure, *Two Hundred Years*, 394–95.

313. His son asked Bergmann for a signature so that the elder Triebner "could again be pardoned and become an American citizen" (5D4:17, 53 = January 26, 1802 Bm. original).

by Colonel Borbeck of the Hessian Knoblauch Regiment since it seemed too uncertain with regard to his family.[314]

When the Hessian regiment was then to be redeployed to New York and Nova Scotia, Triebner did not go there since he had heard about the rough climate, but went with his family[315] on December 22, 1783, on board the "Commerce" from St. Augustine[316] to the Bahamian island New Providence where he settled in the town of Nassau. Here, he preached regularly on Sunday mornings and in the afternoon, a mile away. Once, even sixty slaves came to him in the evening with their black pastor and had him deliver a sermon to them.[317]

However, Triebner also did not stay here long; Hannah Wertsch, and probably also his son Christoph Friedrich remained here,[318] but he himself with the rest of his family returned to London where they arrived in July 1786. Here, Triebner became pastor at the German St. Mary's Church in the Savoy[319] and over the coming years sent to Germany wordy letters of defense over his conduct in Ebenezer. He seemed now almost even to have arrived at a mellower view with regard to the justification of the War of Independence.[320] After about ten years, he was called to Kingston near Hull,[321] from where in the summer of 1802, he visited the Francke Foundations and his former advocate, Pastor Reitz, who was now in Etzdorf near Rosswein (Saxony). In Halle, allegedly little was discussed about Ebenezer.[322] Triebner died in England in 1818.[323]

Triebner also had studied in Halle (1764–1766) and also was decisively stamped there, only not in the same direction as Rabenhorst, which his quick return from Leipzig already indicates. For all of the influence of Professors Wolff, Baumgarten, or Semler on the wide circle of students, the Director of the Francke Foundations, Gotthilf August Francke (d. 1769), who was still teaching, may not be forgotten. Bogatzky (d. 1774) also was still active, and to Professor Johann Georg Knapp (1705–1771) with whom

314. TK32F7, 628–31= October 28, 1782 Tr. copy.

315. His wife was pregnant.

316. The journey was dangerous. He took forty-nine barrels of luggage with him that contained, in part, cheaply purchased food products that he wanted to sell more expensively but some were lost.

317. TK32F8, 677–88 = March 18, 1784 Tr. original.

318. 5B3:26, 112 = May 8, 1787 Tr. copy.

319. 5B3:26, 112.

320. 5B2:26, 82c.

321. 5B4:3, 16 = October 7, 1799 Bm. original; 5B4:7, 29 = April 22, 1800 Bm. original.

322. 5B4:27 (unpaginated) = November 15, 1802.

323. Strobel, *The Salzburgers and Their Descendants*, 209.

Triebner studied[324] and who was revered by many students, he owed enduring impressions. That he already had established this direction before his studies is recognized from the title of his paper that he published on the occasion of his departure from Greiz to Halle, *Die Beschaffenheit eines Menschen vor, in, und nach seiner Bekehrung* (The State of a Person Before, During, and After His Conversion).[325] Moreover, it is significant that the pietistic Urlspergers always maintained a closer relationship to him than to Rabenhorst. Therefore, the strange realization arises that Triebner was more indebted to the theological direction of G. A. Francke than was Rabenhorst who studied there fifteen years before him. This example indicates for its part that late Pietism also represented even at this time quite a considerable factor in Halle's theological life.

In his activity in Georgia, Triebner also remained true to himself. Even his opponents in Ebenezer gave him "the testimony that he preached the Word purely, but the rest of his behavior did not correspond with it."[326] His supporters praised him because he "brought back to the pulpit law and gospel in proper order" (in contrast to Rabenhorst) and sincerely sought the salvation of everyone.

In contrast to the preaching style of Rabenhorst, the community found no innovations with Triebner but conformity with that which had been known and familiar to them from Boltzius. In that regard, it can be understood why the members of the community who wanted to preserve this style of teaching gathered around him, in the same way as they did with regard to the affairs of governing that they had found useful to that point. Against this background, Rabenhorst's differences with Triebner appear under a new aspect and with motives that correspond to the two theologians rather than the pure power politics and the personal, egotistical factors that up to now have been attributed to this controversy. What Muhlenberg undertook to bring into order with such great and futile effort was superficial. He was not in a position to mediate the controversies in European theology that in that epoch of American Lutheranism also were brought out to a full extent in the New World. Only in this way is explained the deep sincerity that inspired a person like Wertsch when he leveled devasting judgments over Rabenhorst[327] and the irreconcilability of the extremes in the community that went beyond personal motives. That these extremes did not already

---

324. 1C41:95 (unpaginated) = March 24, 1800 Tr. original.
325. See above, p. 197, n. 289.
326. 5B4:17, 54 = January 26, 1802 B. original.
327. 5B4:17, 236–38.

appear sooner was due to the dominant personality of Boltzius and to the personal self-effacement of Lemcke.

JOHANN ERNST BERGMANN

When it had become clear to J. A. Urlsperger that there could be no discussion of a return to Georgia by Triebner, he made the effort to find a Lutheran pastor for this territory. However, that was not at all easy, and partly for that reason he undertook a trip through Germany in September 1785. In Franconia, he even found a pastor and a teacher who accepted, but their relatives talked him out of this idea. On the way to Halle, he came across the theological candidate Christian Gottlob Müller[328] who likewise agreed and soon afterwards gave a pleasing sermon in the presence of Urlsperger and Professor Schulze, the Director of the Francke Foundations at the time. They wanted to call him to Ebenezer and then searched for a teacher,[329] who was found in Halle in Herr Probst.[330]

Also staying in the Halle Orphan House at that time was Johann Ernst Bergmann who was intended to go to Pennsylvania. He was born around 1755/1760 in Peretz near Riesa[331] and, apparently, went early to Gatterstädt in County Querfurt (Saxony-Anhalt)[332] where he grew up in rather poor circumstances.[333] His mentor here was the "President of the Higher Consistory" von Burgsdorff[334] who accepted him in the "poor house" in Eisleben[335] and also probably helped provide for his theological study which Bergmann began[336] in 1776 in Leipzig[337] where Ernesti (d. 1781) was active at the time. It seems that Bergmann afterward returned to Eisleben,[338] but he also thought later about the benefits that he had "enjoyed in the Halle Orphan House,"[339]

---

328. TK32F7, 665 = March 8, 1784 (= incorrectly; intended is 1786) Müller original; in U.'s letters, otherwise, Miller.

329. TK32F7, 434–35 = October 1, 1785 U. junior.

330. Until the time of his departure he was to teach in Eisleben.

331. Strobel garbles it as Peritzsch. Strobel, *The Salzburgers and Their Descendants*, 220.

332. 5B4:45, 142 = March 17, 1806 Bm. original.

333. 5B4:1, 1 = April 2, 1799 Bm. original.

334. A family that gave anew a great service to the Lutheran church in Georgia.

335. 5B4:1, 3.

336. Strobel, *The Salzburgers and Their Descendants*, 220.

337. 5B4:45, 142.

338. 5B3:14, 62 = August 15, (1786) Bm. original.

339. 5B3:40, 180 = August 24, 1799 Bm. original; he was not a teacher there, J *vacat*;

where, however, after the death of J. G. Knapp and Bogatzky, there was little of the original spirit of these institutions to be detected now under the Directors Gottlieb Anastasius Freylinghausen and Johann Ludwig Schulze.

After Urlsperger had recruited here for America, he went on to Dresden[340] where he discovered that Müller had been offered a position there so that he fell out of consideration for Georgia. Urlsperger now thought about Bergmann, whom he recommended getting in contact with Probst in Eisleben.[341] But then von Burgsdorf and Director Schulze, who knew both of them, intervened: under no circumstance would it be good if they were to be sent to Ebenezer together, because in such a case Probst, "following the example of Jesus, would have to be meek and humble in heart," but, unfortunately, he was just the opposite of this. When Müller, however, was not accepted in Dresden because his pietistic attitude was noticed in due time, it was planned to send Probst and Müller to Georgia but Bergmann to Philadelphia or East India.[342] Müller, however, again declined.

Now there was nothing else to do but to send Bergmann with the dangerous Probst to Ebenezer. Urlsperger wrote consolingly to Halle that he had two already ordained pastors, of whom one could be sent to Georgia to help Bergmann get along with Probst.[343] Yet just when there was joy in Halle about that, he hesitantly let it be known that the families of those two others probably would object, so there was no more discussion about them.

While Probst remained in Halle with his mother and was to go directly from there to Altona, Bergmann, in May 1786, went by way of Nuremberg to Augsburg where he probably was ordained[344] and was appointed as Ebenezer's second pastor[345] for a period of six years; the position of the first pastor was yet to be filled.[346] On August 14, 1786, they both met in Altona[347]

---

that is, not listed in the index of teachers.

340. TK32F7, 436–37 = October 21, 1785 U. junior.

341. TK32F7, 464 = December 5, 1785 U. junior.

342. TK32F7, 461–63b = February 27, 1786 U. junior.

343. TK32F7, 450–51 = April 3, 1786 U. junior.

344. Strobel gives July 19, 1783, as the ordination date; the archives give no indication of it, but the purpose of the trip to Augsburg would then not be clear. Strobel, *The Salzburgers and Their Descendants*, 220. Strobel's statement on the same page, that Bergmann came to Georgia in spring 1785, is incorrect.

345. 5B3:40, 179 = August 24, 1790 Bm. original.

346. TK32F7, 458–59 = May 1, 1786, 441 = May 19, 1786, 460 = May 29, 1786, 465–67 = May 29, 1786.

347. Because from here the next ship, not via Rotterdam-London, set sail for Georgia (TK32F7, 465–67). Triebner saw in that the intention to avoid a meeting with him in London.

where they were received very courteously by the family of Jacob Gysbert van der Smissen who had a continuing connection with the Francke Foundations and Urlsperger.[348] On August 21, 1786,[349] they set sail on the "Northern Lion" under Captain Lieshen,[350] from October 10–20 laid off of Santa Cruz at Teneriffe,[351] and landed on December 1 in Charleston, South Carolina,[352] from where they reached Ebenezer on December 20, 1786.[353]

Probst soon vanished, and Bergmann, as a new arrival, was ill for a long time with fever.[354] Although the shattered circumstances that he found did not instill courage in him, he nevertheless married, in or shortly before October 1787,[355] Catharina Herb from Savannah, "a quiet, good natured person who should be someone very compatible for him in every respect but who has little or no wealth."[356] They had four children: Johann Ernst,[357] Christoph Friedrich (his father's successor),[358] Johanna Catharina,[359] and Maria Elisabeth.[360] After Bergmann's last letter found in Halle from March 17, 1806, nothing more is heard.[361] He died on February 25, 1824.[362]

348. 5B3:16, 70 = August 20, 1786 Probst original; 5B4:16 = April 15, 1802 van der Smissen original signature in another hand.

349. 5B3:17, 73 = August 21, 1786 Bm. original.

350. 5B3:14 = August 15, 1786 Bm. original; 5B4:17, 54 = January 26, 1802 Bm. original.

351. 5B3:19, 79 = October 13, 1786 Bm. original. Gilbert, "Early History of the Lutheran Church in Georgia," 171; according to Strobel, incorrectly as 1785. Strobel, *The Salzburgers and Their Descendants*, 220; 5B3:20, 87 = October 22, 1786.

352. 5B3:21, 89 = December 6, 1786 Probst original.

353. 5B3:22, 93 = January 16, 1787 Probst original. See also p. 203, n.344.

354. In the first two years, he was sick for 1¼ years (5B3:37, 164 = December 9, 1788 Bm. original).

355. 5B3:35, 148 = May 22, 1788 Tr. original.

356. 5B3:36, 161 = July 23, 1788 Tr. original.

357. He was his first son (contrary to Strobel, *The Salzburgers and Their Descendants*, 226): born November 7, 1790, died August 17, 1793 (5B4:3, 20 = October 7, 1799 Bm. original; 5B4:34, 100 = February 7, 1804 Bm. original).

358. 5B4:34, 100. Born January 7, 1793. Hazelius, *History of the American Lutheran Church*, 236. He died on March 26, 1832. Strobel, *The Salzburgers and Their Descendants*, 265. Hazelius, gives the date as March 25. Hazelius, *History of the American Lutheran Church*, 238).

359. 5B4:40, 112 = December 3, 1804 Bm. original). Born prior to 1799 (5B4:3, 20 = October 7, 1799 Bm. original).

360. Born after Johanna Catharina, died August 26, 1805 (5B4:45, 139 = March 17, 1806 Bm. original).

361. 5B4:45. [On the additional letters that subsequently have been found, see p. 7, n.28.]

362. Gilbert, "Early History of the Lutheran Church in Georgia," 172–73; Strobel,

With Bergmann the third theological direction in the history of Georgia's Lutheran communities, something of decisive significance for the communities, makes its entry. Bergmann was an intellectually very astute person; if he had remained in Germany and had not been sent off to that faraway coast, he could very well have become a scholar. It was therefore a requirement for him to stay in close contact with the few learned people of his vicinity. Those were almost exclusively the pastors of the Presbyterians, Baptists, and Methodists who mostly lived in Savannah.[363] Soon, Bergmann went even farther: "Now also Christian English preachers, when it is desired, can preach on weekdays in the Ebenezer Church. The people always have objected that they were not of our faith. This absurd prejudice has so far hindered so much good." And he, the pastor of a community that had been founded by Salzburger emigrants, interestingly reported about a monk named "John Baptist Longinotti from St. Bernhard's mountain in Switzerland from the order of the Brothers Hospitallers who gathered collections for his cloister and in doing so also passed through Ebenezer."[364]

But that this attitude of Bergmann was not the result of an insufficient theological grounding but was genuinely considered is evident from his reflections on the Lord's Supper: "One should not wish to specify the form and manner of the partaking of the body and blood of Christ. That the body of Jesus is received with the mouth and the blood of Jesus is drunk with the mouth is something that we do not read in Scripture, but certainly that one receives with the mouth the consecrated bread and the consecrated wine, which are signs of the present body and blood of Christ. How the body and blood of Christ are received is a mystery; he is received by true believers through faith, and the Savior demonstrates here a wonder of his omnipotence."[365] "Several Presbyterians asked me, why we do not break the bread and pass around the chalice as they do. It is not to be denied that if the words of 1 Corinthians 10:16 are employed that much offense would be removed. On this point, as I have seen from English theological writings, it would certainly be desirable that sorrowful division would someday cease! . . . I myself was once asked in Savannah to administer the Supper of the Lord to several Presbyterians; I broke the bread for them and gave them the chalice by hand and after the partaking admonished them to walk worthily in the Gospel of Jesus Christ."[366] "It is delightful that the Lutherans, Reformed,

---

The Salzburgers and Their Descendants, 248.
    363. 5B4:5, 186 = April 23, 1795 Bm. original.
    364. 5B4: 10, 41 = November 23, 1801 Bm. original.
    365. 5B4:5, 26 = January 14, 1800 Bm. original.
    366. 5B4:2, 10–11 = April 3, 1799 Bm. original.

Moravian Brethren, and Mennonites get along so well in Germany, since all true believers agree on the main points."[367]

A "union"[368] theologian in whom there is no guile! With him, the Lutheran church of Georgia stood in the middle of the problem of all of Lutheranism at the time, not only in America. The reactions of the communities to this "unionism" are yet to be investigated in what follows.

---

367. 5B4:5, 25–26.

368. ["Unionism," theologically, was embedded in the general philosophical and cultural epoch of the time around 1800 (the Enlightenment). The main stream of Protestant theology in Germany asserted that in fundamental articles of faith, Lutheran and Reformed thinking agree and are united, while the other parts of Christian faith—including Lutheran and Reformed thinking concerning the presence of Christ in the Lord's Supper—are declared to be less relevant and belong to "doctrines of second order." Organizationally, "unionism" arose from the fact that in Germany, the royal family in Prussia belonged to the Reformed Church, while the majority of the Protestant inhabitants were Lutherans. Therefore, at the initiative of the Prussian King Friedrich Wilhelm III in 1817 (on occasion of the commemoration of Martin Luther's Ninety-Five Theses), the unification of these Protestant churches was established in his Prussian provinces: the United Evangelical Church, which continues to exist today (UEK) and constitutes, together with the United Evangelical Lutheran Church of Germany (VELKD), the Evangelical Church in Germany (EKD).]

6

The Relationship of the Communities to Other Denominations

THE MORAVIANS

WHEN SPANGENBERG LANDED WITH several companions in Savannah in spring 1735, an eventful prologue already had taken place. It concerns the fundamental relationship of the direction of Halle Pietism to Zinzendorf and has already been thoroughly depicted on the basis of the sources by G. Reichel.[1] The materials dealt with here that were not taken into account by him confirm and supplement his findings.

Although tensions had already existed for several years between Zinzendorf and the party of G. A. Francke (apart from personal motives) because of differing views on the concept of the church,[2] these were overlooked when Spangenberg was summoned from Jena to Halle around the turn of the year 1732/33, since from the beginning Halle had a high opinion of nascent Jena Pietism that was linked to Buddeus and that, in spite of the overall waning of Pietism as a whole, showed its vitality in the awakenings

---

1. Reichel, "Die Enststehung einer Zinzendorf feindlichen Partei in Halle und Wernigerode."

2. According to Zinzendorf, the presence in one church of several groups who do not completely agree in their views regarding belief is entirely possible. In Halle, and especially for Francke, only groups who fully agree in their views regarding belief can unite together in one church.

of students, though in less developed forms.³ The hope, therefore, was for a rejuvenating influence on Halle's own ossifying spiritual life.⁴ Furthermore, because of its more recent stage of development, Jena Pietism took something of a middle position between the two great schools of thought, Halle and Herrnhut, something about which Halle apparently was not precisely informed, just at the time when Spangenberg maintained a close relationship with Zinzendorf.

When this exploded to light in the same year and Spangenberg, by royal decree, had to leave Halle,⁵ Francke immediately blocked the imminent call of the two Jena candidates, Siebeth and his colleague, as pastors for Georgia since they likewise had become suspected of Moravianism. Boltzius and Gronau were chosen in place of them, a quick, but not erroneous choice.

But Zinzendorf gave no rest to the Halle faction that at this time successfully undertook to hinder Zinzendorf's influence everywhere; even the absence of Count von Stolberg-Wernigerode at the ordination of Boltzius and Gronau served this purpose, and the next of Halle's numerous actions referred to Georgia.⁶ Once again, Schwenkenfelders who sided with Zinzendorf were expelled from Silesia. He now attempted, to the consternation of Halle, to bring to Georgia those who had been expelled in 1734,⁷ and to this end worked in conjunction with London. Later, Spangenberg advanced further these negotiations on behalf of Zinzendorf's appointment.⁸

The extensive efforts of Francke, Urlsperger, and Ziegenhagen to foil this undertaking⁹ were, however, unsuccessful. They only received the assurance that the Moravians, in the event that they should come to Georgia, would settle a sufficient distance from the Salzburger Lutheran settlement, namely, on the Ogeechee River, south of Vernonburg.¹⁰ Spangenberg now bought from the Trustees fifty acres of land for every

---

3. 5A1:46.

4. According to Reichel, "Die Enststehung einer Zinzendorf feindlichen Partei in Halle und Wernigerode," 549–92.

5. So far, Reichel, "Die Enststehung einer Zinzendorf feindlichen Partei in Halle und Wernigerode," 549–92.

6. Reichel, "Die Enststehung einer Zinzendorf feindlichen Partei in Halle und Wernigerode," 549–92.

7. And several earlier years.

8. 5A1:43, 187; Jeremias Risler, *Leben August Gottlieb Spangenbergs, Bischof der evangelischen Brüderkirche* (Barby 1734), 94–95.

9. Depicted in detail by Reichel, "Die Enststehung einer Zinzendorf feindlichen Partei in Halle und Wernigerode"; see also 5A1:43, 157.

10. 5C4:65, 189.

Moravian going to Georgia, and 500 acres for Zinzendorf himself,[11] and indeed, as he professed, solely for the purpose of colonization. However, that openly contradicted what Zinzendorf programmatically announced, namely, that the main intention with the settlement of the Moravians was the mission to the Indians, and he did this even though the Trustees had made this mission dependent upon their special permission.[12] That had to cause great offense in Halle at that time because the mission to the Indians was still seen as the secondary responsibility of Boltzius and Gronau. For that reason, comprising almost the main content of Francke's first letters to Boltzius are urgent warnings and admonitions that, in the event of an actual Moravian settlement in Georgia, under no circumstance to get involved with them; that they meddle amicably everywhere and would like to attract to themselves community members, which would bring confusion and annoyance to the communities.

It was something that had to be opposed emphatically, since they already regarded silence as full consent. Moreover, the first parts of the journal were now published, and what sort of impression would arise if dissensions in the community subsequently had to be reported! The draft of the letter most concerned with this matter is almost ten quarto pages long with numerous handwritten marginal notes from Francke. Added to it is a postscript of five and one-half pages and also a page-long handwritten addendum by Francke.[13] What a stir!

Meanwhile, however, on January 17, 1735, Spangenberg was able to depart from London by ship for Georgia with nine Moravians,[14] and in spring 1735,[15] they arrived in Savannah where Mayor Causton, on the basis of the order of the Trustees, assigned to them land on the river between Ebenezer and Savannah.[16] It also did not take long for Spangenberg to come with his people to Ebenezer in order, in his own heartfelt manner, to greet Boltzius. But Boltzius confronted him rather forthrightly and adversely, referring to the incidents in Halle, which greatly assuaged Francke.[17]

There is no doubt that Spangenberg had nothing malicious in mind. However, the Moravians possessed a peculiar tendency of always coming

11. That was not very difficult because the Trustees gladly accepted settlers (5A1:46, 208–9; 5A3:4, 29). Spangenberg gave the appearance in England, so Boltzius reports, that he intended to become Anglican (5A3:5, 39).

12. 5A1:46, 218–19.

13. 5A1:46, 205–20 = February 24, 1735 Fr. draft.

14. 5C4:59.

15. Before April: 5A3:4, 29 = April 1, 1735 B. original.

16. 5A3:4, 29; Jones, *The History of Georgia* I, 198.

17. 5A3:9, 57–62 = May 17, 1735 B. original; 5A3:8 = November 19, 1735 Fr. draft.

to places where the pioneering work had already been done by others, such as, for example, in East India.[18] There was uproar and trouble everywhere from their effort to draw over the local community members to their circles. That was something Boltzius wanted to avoid.

Another case shows how right he was in that regard. On May 28, 1740, Boltzius, who was with Whitefield in Savannah, met the Moravian Hagen, someone with whom he could get along amicably. He was without theological training and wanted to go directly as a missionary to the Cherokee Indians.[19]

A few months later, Whitefield and Hagen were alienated, the reasons for which are not clear,[20] and Hagen gave the friendly advice to a young girl from Savannah named Mayer who went to school in Ebenezer, "If you do not want to come to the dear Savior, then you certainly may go to Ebenezer."[21] In this connection, it happened for the only time that Boltzius wrote to Halle with faint indignation to ask why Pastor Majer had omitted in the publication of his journals the entire dispute with Hagen with which he certainly had been much involved.[22] However, even the Moravians did not succeed in establishing lasting relationships with the Indians. To be sure, Oglethorpe had allowed a school, with the telling name "Irene," be built[23] by the Moravians[24] near the Yamacraw Indians four miles from Savannah where their chief Tomo-Chichi lived,[25] and in the beginning, there were even a few Indian children. But because after half a year there was only a single student present who also from time to time vanished, the English preacher Ingham, who directed the establishment, went to Pennsylvania where in the meantime Spangenberg had moved, in order to abscond with him to London. The Moravian family who was living in the Indian school also moved away, and the school went dormant.[26]

In the meantime, the Moravians in Germany had almost made an important proselyte: Commissioner von Reck. After his return from the

18. Lehmann, *Es begann in Tranquebar*, 128.
19. 5A9:8, 36 and 36a = journal May 29, 1740 extract.
20. 5A9:15, 58–59 = journal August 5, 1740 extract.
21. 5A10:3, 11 = May 13, 1741 B. original; 5A10:10, 30 = journal May 29, 1741 draft.
22. 5A10:51, 201 = June 14, 1743 B. copy.
23. 5A3:26, 189 = October 1, 1736 G. original; 5A3:49, 313 = March 1, 1737 B. original.
24. 5A3:26, 189 = October 1, 1736 G. original.
25. 5A3:59, 361.
26. 5A3:58, 361 = June 9, 1737 Gr. original. These attempted missions of the Moravians in Georgia are depicted in detail, following the sources of the Moravian community, by Karl Müller, *200 Jahre Brüdermission*, vol. 1: *Das erste Missionsjahrhundert*, 200–206.

first transport, he had arrived in Augsburg precisely at the departure of the second (September 24, 1734), where he could report about the journey and the settlement. On his return journey to Halle that took place in the first half of October he visited on his own the Moravian settlements Ebersdorf and Herrnhut, over which he naturally was greatly impressed; they seemed, after all, to be of the same character with the Halle institutions. He even negotiated with Zinzendorf over an eventual transport of Moravians which he would undertake as commissioner.[27] But after notice of it was taken, with the expected outrage, upon his arrival in Halle, they hurried to expel these plans from him again.[28]

But the Trustees had accepted additional Moravians, and when the third Salzburger transport under Commissioner von Reck on board the "London Merchant" (Captain Joseph Cornish) went to Georgia at the end of 1735/beginning of 1736, the ship the "Simonds" sailed with it (Captain John Thomas, Commissioner Captain Hermsdorf).[29] On it, along with Oglethorpe, the Wesley brothers, and their colleagues Ingham and Delamotte, were also twenty-seven Moravians and their Bishop David Nitschmann and Pastor Peter Böhler.[30] On February 5, 1736,[31] both ships landed on Tybee Island, and after the new Moravians had gotten settled, Spangenberg went already in the middle of March to Pennsylvania and subsequently to New York.[32] The Moravians in and around Savannah did not attract much attention; with the outbreak of the English-Spanish conflicts, they moved in 1738 and 1739 to Bethlehem and Nazareth in Pennsylvania as conscientious objectors to military service.[33]

Much later in Georgia there was again a Moravian scare. In the first days of January 1775, two Moravians landed in Savannah, among whom one was named Müller and the second was a tailor. They were supposed to work in the areas of Goshen and Abercorn where the plantations of Boltzius and Gronau lay. Since Boltzius and Gronau had not been able to cultivate

---

27. 5A1:45, 200.

28. Reichel, "Die Enststehung einer Zinzendorf feindlichen Partei in Halle und Wernigerode," 549–92.

29. Strobel, *The Salzburgers and Their Descendants*, 75.

30. Jacobs, *A History of the Evangelical Lutheran Church in the United States*, 169–70.

31. 5D2 = journal February 7, 1736; 5A3:5, 38; 5A3:8, 50.

32. Spangenberg was still in Georgia on January 8, 1736 (5A3:18 128). On September 1, 1736, his new residence was known in Halle (5A3:22, 155). He departed on March 15. Risler, *Leben August Gottlieb Spangenbergs*, 131–32; Hamilton, *A History of the Unitas Fratrum*, 440; 5A3:27, 202.

33. Jones, *The History of Georgia* I, 199. Müller, *200 Jahre Brüdermission* I, 204–6, 210–13, treats these matters extensively.

them due to a manpower shortage, they had been sold to an Englander in Savannah who sold them in turn to Mr. Knox in London. This gentleman had in mind to start up a profitable undertaking here with numerous slaves and several overseers. In order to conduct mission work among them, the Moravians were appointed. However, nothing became of the establishment. Soon, the slaves, the missionaries, and the fears of the Lutherans disappeared.[34]

THE METHODISTS

The beginnings of the Lutheran church in Georgia are very tightly bound with the development of Methodism. What the archival material treated here expresses about that has already been investigated and analyzed with care by Martin Schmidt,[35] so that the following is mentioned only in brief because of the comprehensiveness of the entire picture.

As mentioned above, arriving in Georgia at the same time with the third immigrant transport for Ebenezer was also the Anglican John Wesley,[36] who was designated as the successor of Samuel Quincy, the second Anglican pastor of Georgia, with whom his supervisory board, the SPG, was not very pleased.[37] Wesley came with his brother Charles "fresh from Lincoln College, Oxford,"[38] where he belonged to that circle of students that strove for an internalization of Anglican piety. For that reason, the faith convictions of the Moravians on his ship during the voyage had made a great impression on him.[39] He now intended to become a missionary to the Indians,[40] but in keeping with Oglethorpe's wish, he remained in Savannah with the Europeans to whom he dedicated himself with zeal.[41]

---

34. TK32F1b, 91 = journal January 7, 1775 M, 109 = journal January 17, 1775 M, 144 = journal February 2, 1775 M.

35. Schmidt, *John Wesleys Bekehrung*, and *John Wesley I; Der junge Wesley*. However, after his work in the Halle archives, there was a reassignment of the call numbers for the material, making his source information unverifiable.

36. 5D2 = journal April 15, 1736.

37. UN March 20, 1735; Jones, *The History of Georgia* I, 203 and 446.

38. Jacobs, *A History of the Evangelical Lutheran Church in the United States*, 169. For Quincy, see Pennington, "The Reverend Samuel Quincy, S.P.G Missionary," 157–65.

39. Jacobs, *A History of the Evangelical Lutheran Church in the United States*, 171.

40. 5A3:29, 208.

41. Cooper, *The Story of Georgia* I, 274.

On June 16, 1737,[42] he visited Ebenezer and showed great interest in the Halle hymns that the community sang and impressed him greatly.[43]

It was very important for Francke and Ziegenhagen that Boltzius establish a good relationship with Wesley.[44] They also got along very well, as long as no mention was made of episcopal ordination which Wesley held as necessary and saw to be grounded in the Church Fathers of the first three centuries. For that reason, he viewed the Moravians as like-minded comrades,[45] something that considerably distanced Boltzius from him.[46] Also, Wesley's custom of baptism by immersion aroused alienation not only in Savannah but also in Ebenezer.[47] Furthermore, Wesley had peculiar personal habits.[48] He slept on the ground, only on a blanket, did not undress, did not wear any stockings and therefore wore his pants down to the shoes, and ate his food without salt and shortening. Also living together with him was an equally strange man of noble descent,[49] Charles Delamotte,[50] who had come with him to Georgia and taught school in Savannah.[51] However, he was dismissed in 1738, went back again to Europe after a stay in Pennsylvania,[52] and was in London in the beginning of December.[53]

During Wesley's time in Savannah occurred the episode with Sophia Hopkey,[54] the niece of the mayor, Causton, who lived with Causton as his foster daughter.[55] Wesley's relationship with her has been depicted and judged in the literature in various ways. In the archival material, it is presented as follows. Wesley had considered marrying her, but Delamotte and the Moravians advised against it. But all of a sudden, the young woman was

42. 5D3 = journal June16, 1737.

43. 5D3 = journal June 28–29, 1737.

44. 5A3:25, 179–80. Fr. draft; 5A3:42, 296 Z.

45. They likewise traced their series of bishops in a direct line to the apostles. Schmidt, *John Wesley* I, 121.

46. 5A3:66, 413–14 = July 29, 1737 B. copy; 5A3:57, 357–58.

47. 5D3, 6 = journal (-UN) January 13, 1737.

48. Following a vow he made during the voyage.

49. 5A3:58, 362. He was the son of a London merchant. Schmidt, *Der junge Wesley*, 29.

50. Jones, *The History of Georgia* I, 207. Also spelled Delamoth, De la Motte (5A7:23), Delamothe (5A3:57, 358 = July 29, 1737 B. original). Boltzius got along better with him than with Wesley.

51. 5A3:58, 362.

52. 5A7:25, 102 = January 15, 1739 Fr. draft; 5D4 = journal May 16, 1738.

53. 5A7:23, 94 = December 18, 1738 Z. copy.

54. Cooper, *The Story of Georgia* I, 271 has Sophie Hopkins; Schmidt refers to her as Sophia Christiana Hopkey. Schmidt, *John Wesley* I, 172.

55. 5A3:56, 347 = August 29, 1737 G. copy.

married to the clerk Williamson[56] by Chiffelle in Purrysburg. Consequently, Wesley fell into a mighty rage, did not allow her to communion, and discovered his sympathy with all of those who were set against Causton and had been "aggrieved" by him. Williamson and Causton saw the exclusion from communion as libel and demanded 1000 pounds as satisfaction,[57] which Wesley, naturally, did not pay, whereupon his wanted poster was fastened to a tree in Savannah, as was usual with thieves and the like.[58]

As the forum for his defense, Wesley chose the prayer hour. In order to bring the matter to an end, a hearing date was set, but before then, Wesley absconded by night (December 2, 1737) on a boat to Purrysburg and from there, by way of Charleston, to London.[59]

Georgia's Lutheran pastors formed closer and friendlier relationships with George Whitefield. He had come to Georgia for the first time on May 7, 1738,[60] visited Ebenezer, and while doing so found Boltzius' pronounced affection: "He is an upright man who is zealous for the honor of the Savior and our devoted friend in the Lord."[61] In a letter preserved in the original, Whitefield acknowledged: "Their little orphan house pleased me extremely," and he was inspired by it likewise to bring such an institution to life.[62]

In the fall of the same year, he had returned to London for ordination, since up until this time he had only been a deacon.[63] Here, he developed his preaching activity for which he is known, about which Ziegenhagen made the judgment: "It would be desired that Herr Whitefield had remained in proper order after his last return from Georgia and had not caused the pulpit to be denied to him everywhere, as it seems to me, through an immature craving for conversion, and, since he does not wish to yield, but preaches in public places, streets, and fields under open sky and, as a result, occasions a great crowd of common people and disorder, he thereby causes more and more trouble and still will not let himself be counseled."[64] Through his

---

56. Lecky, incorrectly "Wilkinson." Lecky, *Geschichte Englands im achtzehnten Jarhundert*, II, 598.

57. Ellis Merton Coulter, "When John Wesley Preached in Georgia," 340–44.

58. 5A3:56, 347 = August 29, 1737 G. copy.

59. 5A7:9 = January 20, 1738; 5A3:26, 189 = October 1, 1736; 5D3 = journal January 15, 1737.

60. Cooper, *The Story of Georgia* I, 275.

61. 5A7:21, 85 = August 26, 1738 B. original.

62. 5A7:19, 82 = undated (according to 5A7:26, 110 in January 1739) Whitefield original (!).

63. 5A7:21, 85.

64. Z. original, notation to letter 5A7:46, 193–94 = March 17, 1739 B. original.

preaching, he brought in considerable collections that he intended mainly for his projected orphanage but from which Ebenezer also profited.[65]

By way of Philadelphia and Charleston he arrived again in Savannah on January 11, 1740.[66] Boltzius was greatly taken not only by the contributions for the construction of a church in Ebenezer but also by Whitefield's preaching, which he could conduct in German and in English.[67] In the area near Vernonburg, Whitefield soon erected his orphanage[68] for which he had at disposal such means that it looked "like a princely castle."[69] He named it Bethesda and had available as director of the forty children the schoolteacher and caretaker James Habersham[70] as well as the preacher Mr. Barber.[71]

In this orphanage, as already mentioned, Gronau sought healing from his illness. Boltzius engaged in regular correspondence with Whitefield, even if at greater intervals, and even in his last years of life, he reported to Europe what "the dear Herr Whitefield, who so far has been so blessed in his office" had written to him.[72]

THE REFORMED

From what has been discussed it has become clear that an essential factor in the relationship of Georgia's Lutheran communities to other denominations were the personal connections of the clergy among each other. In the case of Georgia, that is quite understandable since the clergy there represented almost the only people with an academic background among the genuinely unsophisticated population, and the pastors of the individual denominations did not, as was the case in Europe, have a numerous cohort of colleagues at their side.

But with the interconfessional connections of the community members, another element played a role: language. For the Lutherans, groups such as the Anglicans, Baptists, Methodists, and others for a long time were synonymous with the English. The Reformed, however, apart from the French

65. See p. 85.
66. 5A7:66, 287 = May 4, 1740 Fr. draft; UN January 16, 1740.
67. 5A7:66, 287; Cooper, *The Story of Georgia* I, 275.
68. 5D7 = journal March 1, 1741.
69. UN June 29, 1742. Detailed depiction: Corry, "The Houses of Colonial Georgia," 188–89.
70. UN October 13, 1739; 5D7, 65 = journal February 13, 1741; 5A10:19, 69 = May 13, 1742 B. original.
71. 5D7 = journal March 1, 1741; 5D8, 346 = journal July 3, 1741.
72. 5B2:66, 236 = September 30, 1763 B. original.

speaking Swiss of Purrysburg, were German speaking, and, consequently, it was in this case a matter of the actual relationships between the denominations with all their pros and cons. Even when the settlers had been in Georgia only for a short time, as a rule, they paid attention to the difference between the two directions and kept, with the faithfulness of emigrants, to that which they had brought from the homeland. Yet when the Lutherans, such as in Savannah, Vernonburg, or Acton where especially many Reformed from the Palatinate lived, had available no regular Lutheran preaching but when the only German preaching offered to them was Reformed, then they attended these, even if only to remain true to their Germanness. The inverse was the case with Purrysburg. Here, there was a French Reformed preacher, so that the German Reformed went to hear the German Lutheran sermons when a Lutheran pastor visited them. Moreover, in the person of Pastor Zübli, Georgia's Reformed had a learned, eloquent leader who was happy to travel, so that the Lutherans in and around Savannah found themselves in that special situation that has been described and even contributed to Zübli's salary.

The close relationships between these two denominations had the result that in Ebenezer there never was any mention of the Lutheran confession, since one was Lutheran without mentioning it; yet from time to time it was brought to mind. An intended marriage most often provided the occasion for it, as is apparent from the following account of Boltzius: "A young Salzburger was with me in Savannah to discuss marrying a woman there with herself and her parents. This family is Reformed, and the Salzburger agreed above all that the daughter, whom he wanted to take as his wife, would have to promise before God and witnesses, to confess the Evangelical-Lutheran religion, otherwise he would not enter into such a marriage. The daughter and parents are well acquainted with us and know what we teach from God's Word, but they nonetheless did not want to agree to this point but to remain with their old faith, and therefore nothing became of the marriage."[73]

Just how much the fact that Zübli spoke German overshadowed his Reformed confessional identity in the eyes of the communities is indicated by the circumstance that he, of all of Georgia's pastors, worked most closely together with the Lutheran pastors, continuously purchased the medicines from Halle, and buried Rabenhorst. Later, as a consequence of Bergmann's indifferent attitude, Reformed influence penetrated unhindered into the community, and his son Christoph Friedrich even decided to convert entirely to the Reformed confession.[74]

---

73. 5D6, 31 = journal July 31, 1739.

74. Detailed explanation of these connections is in Strobel, *The Salzburgers and Their Descendants*, chapter XII.

7

The Lutheran Confessional Identity of the Communities

AT THE END OF the time period considered here, the Lutheran church in Georgia reached a low point that already indicated its dissolution. The economically unfavorable situation of the Lutheran settlements, the external destruction of the War of Independence, the internal devastation of the pastors' controversy, and the too-lengthy retention of the German language in the worship services are the reasons agreed upon for it by the research to date,[1] and they retain their validity. Nevertheless, on the basis of recently accessible material, an in-depth view of the matter is emerging that certainly does not nullify those factors but shows them to be superficial and ascribed to a common cause.

That being said, it has become clear that the situation of the Lutheran settlements with regard to the quality of the soil was extremely unfavorable. However, that even the "second generation" of those who emigrated because of their faith were prepared to bring sizeable offerings when it was a matter of maintaining their worship services is demonstrated by the considerable number of those who turned up again at the old settlements after the war.[2] With that, the destruction of the war turns out to be less decisive for the decline of the settlements. With their return from the areas of combat the

---

1. "A spirit of indifference in the Lutheran church" was also stated by Strobel but not acknowledged as the essential reason for the decline of the communities. Strobel, *The Salzburgers and Their Descendants*, 231.

2. 5B4:2, 10 = April 3, 1799 Bm. original.

settlers further showed that it was still possible to see in the deplorable pastors' controversy a human failure and not a failure of the faith to which they clung. Here, it would have been the responsibility of the new pastor to confirm to them that the validity of the Word of God is not affected by things of that sort and to give back to them the familiar preaching of an unequivocal, active Christianity. Yet it obviously was not sufficient for the communities that Bergmann opposed "deistic tendencies,"[3] admonished in his sermons "for a true change of heart and mind,"[4] and, in contrast to Rabenhorst, placed value again on church discipline.[5]

Methodism, which also was strongly represented in Georgia, experienced in those years (1797–1805) its second "Great Revival,"[6] the effects of which by no means remained limited to this denomination but caused the piety of Methodists as well as Baptists to become more decisive, warmer, and markedly missionary. Only the Lutheran communities were not reached by them, even though Bergmann had accurate information about them.[7] He proceeded differently. Despite the protests of the communities, he opened Jerusalem Church to the preachers of other denominations, publicly administered communion to the Presbyterians, proclaimed the agreement of various Protestant denominations in the "main doctrines," and in doing so blurred the boundaries with them.

To be sure, the doctrine regarding the fundamental articles of the first and second order had been represented in the Lutheran communities from the beginning; however, Boltzius had, as indicated, always heeded the boundary from other denominations.[8] But now this boundary fell away, and indifference was preached to the communities regarding the particular confession,[9] since the poor soil and the progressive difficulty caused by preaching in the German language became the primary factors that promoted a migration of numerous community members into more agriculturally

---

3. Strobel, *The Salzburgers and Their Descendants*, 238–39.
4. 5B4:1, 3 = April 2, 1799 Bm. original.
5. 5B4:2, 10.
6. Cleveland, *The Great Revival in the West, 1797–1805*.
7. See his correspondence with the Methodist bishop Francis Asbury. Strobel, *The Salzburgers and Their Descendants*, 235–36.
8. The investigation of the state of affairs on the basis of the sources contradicts the garbled judgment of Gräbner: "The Methodist preacher Whitefield stood higher in the eyes of these Ebenezer preachers than such an orthodox Lutheran" as Wilhelm Christoph Berkenmeyer. Gräbner, *Geschichte der Lutherischen Kirche in America*, part I, 152. This sentence was published in 1892 in St. Louis, Missouri, and does not take into account the theological relationships of the time being depicted. On Berkenmeyer, see, Qualben, *The Lutheran Church in Colonial America*, 149, 193–96.
9. 5B4:20, 66 = April 8, 1802 Bm. original.

favorable areas or to denominations that offered to them preaching they could understand or that had more vital piety. Strobel, and the literature that depends on him, places particular emphasis in this connection on the language problem,[10] one that in the entire history of American Lutheranism played a serious, often consequential role.

There is no doubt that this aspect is to be considered also in Georgia. However, in churches that were conscious of their confession this threat to their existence did not lead to such extreme consequences as it did in Georgia. That is shown not only by the Lutheran Church-Missouri Synod. In the early history of the Lutheran church in Georgia, an example is to be observed of the fate of a church that no longer is conscious of its confession and is content with general, Christian-Protestant ideas. It is robbed of its spiritual uniqueness and thereby also risks organizational disintegration. A lively awareness of the confession—without confessionalism—proves itself as necessary for a church's existence.

One, single letter, discovered between extensive, unpaginated, unarranged bills and inheritance records of the Halle archives pronounces the rediscovery of Georgia's Lutheran church to its name and attests that in the ground of that dark phase of its history, the Lutheran faith had remained preserved. The letter is an original from the hand of the son of the 1824 deceased pastor J. E. Bergmann, who was the successor of his father in Ebenezer. In the letter, after decades of silence,[11] he turned once again to Halle in 1828 in a financial matter and reported: "The German had been on a decline during the latter years of my late reverend Father's ministrations. . . . I feel happy however in observing that an undiminished adherence to the doctrines of the great father of the Reformation still continues to be evinced—though we may regret the almost indispensable necessity of substit<uting> another language—yet we feel constrained to bear in <good?> remembrance the names as well as the sentiments <of> our venerated German ancestors. The first Lutheran Synod was held in my Church in November of the preceding year—which afforded general satisfaction."[12]

10. For example, Strobel, *The Salzburgers and Their Descendants*, 235–36; Hazelius, *A History of the American Lutheran Church*, 154.

11. 5E5, letter September 15, 1828, Halle to Bm. junior

12. 5E5, letter May 12, 1828 C. H. Bergmann original (strangely, not C. F. Bm.; but there is no question of there being another one). The mention of "Synod" evidently has to do with a larger meeting of congregations in which the connection with the Synod of South Carolina was officially confirmed. The occasion for the letter was the question about the interest of the legacy of Herr von Degenfeld-Schönburg founded and to be used since 1751 "for the assistance of the Salzburger emigrants in the West Indies" (5E5, letter September 15, 1828, Halle to Bm. junior draft).

The instrument of this renewed consciousness had been Pastor Dr. Bachman from South Carolina. After a phase of especially crass domination by Rationalism (John Caspar Velthusen) and the founding of a synod in North Carolina (1803) without mention of the word "Lutheran,"[13] consideration was once again given to the Augsburg Confession after the Reformation celebration of 1817,[14] and in 1824, an actual Evangelical Lutheran Synod of South Carolina and Adjacent States was founded.[15] When in this year Pastor Bergmann senior died, Bachman went to Georgia, reorganized the Lutheran congregation in Savannah,[16] and had a discussion with Christoph Friedrich Bergmann who, as the last letter of his father to Halle reports, was to be raised Methodist[17] and now was a Presbyterian minister in the area around Ebenezer. The impression of Bachman's personality had the effect of leading the young Bergmann back to the Lutheran confession, and in November 1824, he could be ordained by the Evangelical Lutheran Synod of South Carolina.[18] Soon, the gift of the recovered confession also became effective in the communities in that it led to the gathering and reformulation of the Lutheran church in Georgia—the church, whose first members had been men and women who had left their homeland on account of their faith and whose descendants, in 1860,[19] founded a self-standing Lutheran Synod.

---

13. In Salisbury, North Carolina.

14. Wentz, *A Basic History of Lutheranism in America*, 69–70, 74, 95.

15. Strobel, *The Salzburgers and Their Descendants*, 252; Wentz, *A Basic History of Lutheranism in America*, 71.

16. Strobel, *The Salzburgers and Their Descendants*, 240, 252.

17. 5B4:45, 142 = March 17, 1806 Bm. original. According to Hazelius, Bachman's visit took place still during the lifetime of the elder Bergmann. Hazelius, *A History of the American Lutheran Church*, 230–31.

18. Strobel, *The Salzburgers and Their Descendants*, 251–52. He was a member of its "Board of Directors" and, until 1830, "Secretary of the Synod." Hazelius, *A History of the American Lutheran Church*, 231–32.

19. Wentz, *A Basic History of Lutheranism in America*, 109.

Appendix I

Text of Ebenezer's First Church Constitution[1]

WITH THE APPROVAL OF the vestrymen, or of those church elders elected according to the law, the following is made known to the Christian community.

1. Sound reason, Holy Scripture, and experience teach that no community with its institutions and establishments can persist and good order be preserved for the promotion of its true welfare unless such men are elected by the community as elders who have the competence and authority to provide for the maintenance, good provisioning, and salutary order of the entire community. Thus, the important admonition is read in 1 Corinthians 14 in the last verse, "Let all things be done honorably and orderly (or according to order, good arrangement, and decency), and so that it might occur, as the holy apostle indicates in the preceding 12th chapter in the 28th verse, that God, as a God of order, had appointed in his community, purchased with a precious price, not only apostles, prophets, and ministers but also helpers and rulers, that is, such gifted and grace-filled men who, with counsel and assistance in keeping with the requirements and ordinance of the community, were to contribute everything possible for the good governance and maintenance of the entire community. It is something made known

---

1. TK32F11, 1043 a.b.c.–1064. This is the first independent church constitution of Ebenezer, drawn up in Georgia by Pastor Boltzius. It is not simply a duplication of an earlier order given by the European church institutions in London and Halle but is in line with the earlier order and includes significant passages from it.

from the Word of God that even in the church of God in the Old Testament there had been appointed at the time of Moses such men for the sake of order. Therefore it is completely in keeping with the will of God and the example not only of the first, but also all subsequent Christian communities, that also among us, just as already in previous years, therefore also lately, such church elders or assistants and rulers are unanimously elected from the entire community who, according to the law of the English Church, shall promote the best interests of this our parish.

Because, however, our congregation does not actually belong to the English Church, and, consequently, cannot be under English Church law in every matter but must make its own arrangements for the promotion of worship and edification, it is necessary that members of our community give to the aforementioned church elders, in keeping with the example of the Evangelical Lutheran congregation in London (not to mention others), a special authority to bear responsibility for the preservation of our congregation, its institutions, and facilities, because it would be too heavy, indeed impossible, for the ministers to bear the burden alone.

2. Now if these elected and authorized men are to promote the existence and welfare of the congregation with their counsel and assistance, or if they should be able to maintain and preserve it with its institutions and facilities, but [since] such things cannot be promoted without means, it naturally follows that they also, in keeping with the example of the aforementioned Evangelical Lutheran congregation in London, indeed with all other well-equipped Christian congregations, will be made capable of doing so by its members. Because the government, or the English Church constitution, contributes nothing to this [1043b], and, due to the very difficult times and the great poverty in our German fatherland, hardly anything as significant as what occurred in the past can be expected from our dear benefactors from Germany for the maintenance of our church and school establishments as well as for the aid of the poor and sick, necessity requires, that is, the honor of God and our spiritual welfare, that the members of the community bind themselves to each other in love and from year to year to contribute and donate as much in money as is and will be required for the support of the schoolteachers, the maintenance of the church and school buildings, as well as for the parsonage. Such people who are members of the community and wish to have part in the spiritual benefactions and privileges of the community will, it is hoped, also

be willing to help bear the burdens and expenses of the congregation and gladly contribute and assist with the maintenance of its aforementioned establishments and institutions. But those who are not willing to bear these burdens and do not render their obligatory duty out of gratitude will thereby exclude themselves and their dependents from the congregation and its spiritual benefactions, which certainly would not be for their good. "God loveth a cheerful giver;" "he which soweth bountifully shall also reap bountifully."

3. Those who are now members of this our Evangelical congregation, and who might be willing to contribute and donate as much as might be required from time to time as according to the estimate and determination of the duly appointed church elders for the maintenance of the schoolteachers, parsonage, church, and school buildings, as well as for other necessities that occur, will please sign their names under this document and add to it their contribution. Because our dear residents, through God's gracious providence, have a great advantage and relief ahead of many other Christian congregations in that they give their ministers no salary or need to provide for their material support, it is to be hoped that they will be all the more willing to contribute for the maintenance of the above-mentioned institutions and establishments which have as their purpose the preservation of the community and their worship services; indeed, that they will be glad that they are given the opportunity to demonstrate actively their faith through love for God, His Word, for the church and school. But where there is no active love, there is also no true faith. "Show me thy faith by thy works." James 2:18.

4. What finally concerns the office and the obligation of the church elders with regard to the teachers [1043c] in church and school, to the whole community, and to the money entrusted to them, should, in conclusion, be indicated with the words from the published London German Church Order that was given to us, with several alterations due to our particular circumstances, which read as, first, they shall apply all possible diligence that the Word of God is proclaimed purely and sincerely to the Christians of our community by pious teachers and preachers, that the holy sacraments are administered according to the command and institution of our Lord Jesus Christ, and that pure doctrine is preserved and propagated to our descendants, for which purpose at least several of them, in the event that not all of them can appear, shall be present for all sermons and listen to them. Second, they shall also ensure that the schoolteachers duly receive semi-annually

the salary promised to them. Likewise, that everything else that is required on behalf of the congregation will be accomplished.[2] As for the school children, they must have paid semi-annually a modest tuition according to the ability of the parents, so that the contribution of the entire community for the defrayment of community expenses might be somewhat lightened.[3] For that reason they also shall receive semi-annually the contributions and donations of the community and enter them properly in the church register. Third, the church deacons along with the ministers shall have oversight that all sins, disgraceful conduct, and offenses are avoided or otherwise duly punished and improved. Fourth, they also shall keep a special index and record book of everything that they spend on behalf of the congregation, and also what anyone has freely pledged or promised for the support of the church, and each one, after the set time has elapsed shall submit his account to all the other church deacons. Fifth, at the end of the year and upon the relinquishment of their office and service, they shall render account to the contributing members of the community for all of the money that they have received on behalf of the congregation during their year of office so that each person may know how the money of the congregation is applied and expended so that they might be all the more willing to contribute to that end. Sixth, in the case one or another contributor might wish to see the church register for how the money was invested, they shall present it to him. There must be paid every half year some money for the school children, according to the means of the parents, so that the contribution of the entire community for the defrayment of community expenses might be somewhat lightened [1044]. Seventh, the outgoing church deacons shall be obligated always to provide assistance with counsel and action to the meeting of the deacons and the entire congregation when they are requested and cited to do so and then to appear without hesitation. Eighth, the newly appointed church deacons and those at all times who later come into office shall also be responsible for the performance and fulfillment of those things resolved and decided by their predecessors for the tranquility, peace, and wellbeing, as well as for the benefit and advantage, of the congregation. Ninth, on communion Sundays, they also shall stand at the church doors with bowls or dishes and, upon the departure of the congregation, collect and receive gifts and donations for the support of the church and the poor. It is also proper that not

2. The following is crossed out.
3. End of the cross out.

only residents contribute something for baptisms, weddings, and for the celebration of the Lord's Supper, but that, in addition, outsiders also must be exhorted to do so, since if the congregation is not preserved with its institutions, these people also cannot enjoy these aforesaid benefactions.

5. These oft-mentioned deacons, of whom annually not fewer than seven must be elected from the number, and, indeed, none other than members of our Evangelical Lutheran community, shall have full authority to promote the wellbeing of our congregation according to their best knowledge and conscience, and for that purpose to use the money entrusted to them, but in very important matters, for example, when a church is to be built, or an important repair is to be made, and so on, the entire community must be called together and their assessment and consent must be heard. In the first gathering of the community it must be agreed, among other things, whether the church elders should proceed on the Sundays when the Lord's Supper is administered with the collection and reception of the offering as intended in no. 9, or, as has been customary until now, that each person places his contribution in the appointed boxes.

Appendix II

Index of the Bibliographically Identifiable Works of the Ebenezer Church Library That Are Mentioned in the Archives

For most of the editions that are not indicated, the most likely one in each case is cited. It is not always clear from the archives whether the books were in the church library or privately owned.

- *Agenda Ecclesiastica. Oder: Forma der Handlung der H. Sacramenten / Ehe-Einsegnung und öffentlichen Gebet / Deren der Augspurgischen Confession zugethanen Kirchen / in der freyen Reichs-Stadt Augsburg. Revidiert und erneuert im Jahre Christi 1718. Daselbst gedruckt bey Johann Jacob Lotter.*

- *Das allgemeine Gebet-Buch, wie auch die Administration der H. Sacramenten, und anderer Kirchl. Ritus und Ceremonien, nach dem Gebrauch der Kirchen von England,* etc. The Hauge 1718. XLIV, 728 pages.

- Anton, Paul. *Collegium Anti-theticum universale fundamentale Nach der in den Thesibus Breithauptianis Befindlichen Ordnung der Theologischen Materien Anno 1718. und 1719. Gehalten,* etc. Halle: Orphan House, 1732. 999 pages.

- Anton, Paul. *Evangelisches Hauß-Gespräch von der Erlösung.* 3rd ed. Halle 1738. 32 + 224 pages.

- Arndt, Johann. *Vier Bücher vom Wahren Christenthum. Nebst desselben Paradis=Gärtlein.* Ed. A. H. Francke. 3rd ed. Halle: Orphan House, 1735. 694 + 268 pages.

- Arndt, Johann, *Informatorium Biblicum, oder Etliche Erinnerungs= Puncte vor Lesung der heil. Schrift.* In *Anhang zu Johann Arndts Vier Büchern vom Wahren Christenthum.* Halle: Orphan House, 1743. 227 pages.

- Arndt, John. *Of True Christianity Four Books.* Vol. II. The Epistle Dedicatory by Anthony William Boehm. London 1714. XI + 599 pages.

- Arndt, John. *The Garden of Paradise.* London 1716. XXIV + 420 pages.

- Baumgarten, Siegmund Jacob. *Theologische Bedencken erste Samlung.* Halle 1742. 368 pages.

- *Der Königl. Dänischen Missionarien aus Ost=Indien eingesandter Ausführlichen Berichten Erster Theil . . . Vom Ersten ausführlichen Bericht an bis zu dessen zwölfter Continuation mitgetheilet*, etc. Halle: Orphan House, 1735. 986 pages.

- The Bible (various editions).

- Böhme, Anton Wilhelm. *Des Sünders Elend und Trost / In einer Predigt am Palm-Sontage 1718 in der Teutschen Schloß=Capelle zu London / vorgestellet.* Wernigerode [undated]. 48 pages.

- Bogatzky, Carl Heinrich von. *Christliche Hausschule, in welcher der kleine Catechismus Lutheri deutlich erkläret . . . wird.* Part 1. Halle: Orphan House, 1755.

- Bogatzky, Carl Heinrich von. *Tägliches Haus=Buch Der Kinder Gottes, Bestehend in erbaulichen Betrachtungen und Gebeten auf alle Tage des gan(t)zen Jahres,* etc. Part 1. 2nd ed. Halle 1753. 1108 pages. (Part 2. 1st ed. Halle 1749. 1256 pages.)

- Bogatzky, Carl Heinrich von. *Güldnes Schatz=Kästlein der Kinder Gottes, deren Schatz im Himmel ist: Bestehend In auserlesenen Sprüchen der Heil. Schrift, samt beygefügten erbaulichen Anmerkungen und Reimen.* 20th ed. Halle: Orphan House, 1753.

- Breithaupt, Joachim Justus. *Theses credendorum atque agendorum fundamentales.* 5th ed. Halle 1722. 249 pages.

- *Closter=Bergische Samlung Nützlicher Materien Zur Erbauung im Wahren Christenthum.* 1st Issue. Magdeburg and Leipzig 1745. 112 pages.

- Collin, Friedrich Eberhard, ed. *Das gewaltige Eindringen ins Reich Gottes . . . Jo. Georgii Pritti*, Frankfurt am Main 1722. 456 pages.
- Francke, August Hermann. *Betrachtungen über das Hohepriesterliche Gebeth unsers Herrn und Heylandes Jesu Christi*, etc. Halle: Orphan House, 1738. 618 pages.
- Francke, August Hermann. *Buß=Predigten. Darinn Aus verschiedenen Texten H. Schrifft deutlich gezeiget wird*, etc. Parts 1 and 2. Halle 1706. 306 and 342 pages.
- Francke, August Hermann. *Christus der Kern Heiliger Schrifft, oder Einfältige Anweisung*, etc. Halle: Orphan House, 1702. 492 pages.
- Francke, August Hermann. *Christus Sacrae Scripturae Nucleus; or Christ the sum and substance of the Holy Scriptures, in the Old and New Testament*. London 1732.
- Francke, August Hermann. *Collegium pastorale über D. Joh. Ludovici Hartmanni Pastorale Evangelicum*. Halle: Orphan House, I: 1741, 782 pages, II: 1743 760 pages.
- Francke, August Hermann. *Segens=volle Fußstapfen des noch lebenden . . . Gottes*, etc. Halle: Orphan House. 1709. I–VII installments.
- Francke, August Hermann. *Glauchisches Gedenck=Büchlein, oder Einfältiger Unterricht Für die Christliche Gemeinde zu Glaucha an Halle*. Leipzig and Halle 1693. 572 pages.
- Francke, August Hermann. *Idea studiosi Theologiae, oder Abbildung eines der Theologie Beflissenen, wie derselbe sich zum Gebrauch und Dienst des HERRN, und zu allem guten Werck, gehöriger Massen bereitet*. 4th ed. Halle: Orphan House, 1728. 293 pages. 120.
- Francke, August Hermann. *Köstritzisches Denckmal oder Ermahnungs=rede*, etc. Halle: Orphan House, 1726. 59 pages.
- Francke, August Hermann. *Schriftmäßige Lebens=Regeln / Wie man so wohl bey als ausser der Gesellschaft die Liebe und Freundligkeit gegen den Nechsten . . . bewahren . . . soll*. 7th ed. Leipzig 1717. 120 pages.
- Francke, August Hermann. *Nicodemus oder Tractätlein von der Menschenfurcht*, etc. Halle: Orphan House, 1715. 252 pages.
- Francke, August Hermann. *Kurtze Sonn- und Fest-Tags-Predigten*, etc. 2nd ed. Halle: Orphan House, 1718. 576/792 pages.
- Francke, August Hermann. *Timotheus Zum Fürbilde Allen Theologiae Studiosis dargestellet*. 2nd ed. Halle 1695. 96 pages.

- Francke, August Hermann. *Kurtzer und Einfältiger Unterricht/ Wie die Kinder zur wahren Gottseligkeit / und Christlichen Klugheit anzuführen sind*, etc. Halle: Orphan House, 1702. 60 pages.
- Francke, August Hermann. *Vorbereitung auf das heilige Pfingst=Fest / den 3. Junii 1713*. Halle: Orphan House, 1715. 72 pages.
- Fresenius, Johann Philip. *Nachrichten von Herrnhutischen Sachen*. 4 vols., 8 collections. Frankfurt am Main 1745–1751.
- Fresenius, Johann Philip. *Pastoral=Sammlungen*, parts 1–8. Frankfurt am Main and Leipzig 1748–1760.
- Freylinghausen, Johann Anastasius. *Commentatio Passionis ac Mortis Domini et Servatoris nostri Jesu Christi*, etc. Halle: Orphan House, 1734. 199 pages.
- Freylinghausen, Johann Anastasius. *Compendium, oder Kurtzer Begriff der gantzen Christlichen Lehre*, etc. 7th ed. Halle: Orphan House, 1726. 153 pages.
- Freylinghausen, Johann Anastasius. *Schrifftmäßige Einleitung zu rechter Erkäntniß und heilsamen Gebrauch des Leidens und Sterbens unsers Herrn und Heilandes Jesu Christi*. 2nd ed. Halle: Orphan House, 1715. 208 pages.
- Freylinghausen, Johann Anastasius. *Geist=Reiches Gesang=Buch, den Kern Alter und Neuer Lieder . . . in sich haltend*, etc. 8th ed. Halle: Orphan House, 1714. Vol. I: 1158 pages. Vol. II: 1176 pages.
- Freylinghausen, Johann Anastasius. *Geistreiches Gesang=Buch, . . . Nach denen unter diesen Namen allhier schon edirten Gesang=Büchern eingerichtet*. 3rd ed. Halle: Orphan House, 1725. 557 pages.
- Freylinghausen, Johann Anastasius. *Ordnung des Heyls, Nebst einem Verzeichniß Der wichtigsten Kern=Sprüche H. Schrift*, etc. 3rd ed. Halle: Orphan House, 1724. 48 pages.
- Freylinghausen, Johann Anastasius. *Predigten über die Sonn- und Fest=Tages=Episteln*, etc. 2nd ed. Halle: Orphan House, 1711. 1488 pages.
- Freylinghausen, Johann Anastasius. *Predigten über die Sonn= und Festtage=Evangelis Zur Beförderung der Wahrheit, die da ist in CHRISTO JESU*. Halle 1735. 1750 pages.
- Frisch, Johann David. *Neu klingende Harfe Davids, oder Erklärung der Psalmen*. Stuttgart 1749.

Appendix II

- *Girrendes Täublein, d. i. Gebundene Seufzerlein eines mit Gott verbundenen Hertzens, wodurch dasselbe bey allen äusseren Umständen das Feuer seiner heiligen Liebe zu unterhalten suchet.* 2nd ed. Leipzig 1731.

- Götze, Johann Melchior. *Heilsame Betrachtungen des Todes und der Ewigkeit, auf alle Tage des Jahres.* 2 vols. Dresden 1767.

- *EIN Gebeth=Büchlein: THEILS Aus der Englischen Liturgie, Theils aus anderen Geistreichen Gebeth=Büchern zusammengetragen; und zum Gebrauch der Capelle IHRER KÖNIGL. HOHEIT, Printz Georgens von DÄNEMARCK, Eingerichtet.* London 1707. 168 pages.

- Großgebauer, Theophilus. *Drey Geistreiche Schrifften, I. Wächter-Stimme aus dem verwüsteten Zion. II. Praeservatio Wider die Pest der heutigen Atheisten. III. Alte Religion.* 4th ed. Leipzig 1710. 936 pages.

- Habermann, Johann. *Christliche Gebätlein . . . Auff alle Tage in der Wochen*, etc. Alten Stettin 1660. 142 pages.

- Habermann, Johann. *Tägliche Morgen= und Abend=Gebete*, etc. Leipzig 1672. 22 pages.

- Hartmannus, Joh. Ludovicus. *Pastorale Evangelium, seu Instructio plenior ministrorum verbi*, etc. Nuremberg 1697. 1496 pages.

- Henkel, Graf W. Ludwig. *Schatzkästlein, bestehend in göttlichen Verheissungen, deren Zuneignung nebst beygefügten Reimen.* Halle: Orphan House, 1745. 160.

- Hoffmann, Johann George. *Erklärung des kleinen Catechismi Lutheri nach allen Hauptstücken, wie auch in den Fragestücken*, etc. Halle: Orphan House, 1757. XLVIII, (54). 464 pages.

- Horb, Johann Heinrich. *Der gründliche Wort=Verstand Des Kleinen Cathechismi D. Martini Lutheri, Zur Erweckung Einer Inniglichen Glaubens-Freudigkeit*, etc. 2nd ed. Frankfurt am Main 1686. 237 pages.

- Joch, Johann Georg. *Die Versetzung der Gläubigen in das himmlische Wesen An dem Exempel Der . . . Frauen Judithen Dorotheen Schorchin*, etc. Erfurt (undated; 1722). 38 pages.

- Juncker, Johann. *Conspectus Chemiae theoretico-practicae in forma tabularum.* Halle 1730. 1086 pages.

- Kalckberner, Petrus. *Christliche Freundschafft und Geistliche Verwandtschafft, Zum schuldiges Ehren=Gedächtniß Zweener . . . Freunde*, etc. Magdeburg 1726. 119 pages.

Index of the Bibliographically Identifiable Works   231

- Kleinknecht, Conrad Daniel. *Zuverlässige Nachricht, Von der, durch das Blut des erwürgten Lammes theuer=erkauften Schwarzen Schaaf= und Lämmer=Heerde, Oder von den neu-bekehrten Malabarischen Christen in Ost=Indien auf der Königl. Dänischen Küsten Coromandel,* etc. Augsburg 1749. 212 pages.
- Korthold, Christian. *Pastor fidelis, sive de officio ministrorum ecclesiae.* Lemgo 1748.
- Kuse, Henning. *Die Gnade GOttes in einer Person niedrigen Standes,* etc. Halle: Orphan House, 1736. 48 pages.
- Kyburz, Abraham. *Historien, Kinder=, Bet= und Bilderbibel, mit eingedruckten Kupferstichen.* 3 parts. Augsburg 1736–42.
- Lange, Joachim. *Biblisch=Historisches Licht und Recht, Das ist, Richtige und Erbauliche Erklärung Der sämtlichen Historischen Bücher des Alten Testaments.* Halle/Leipzig 1734. 56, 494, 818 pages. 40.
- Lange, Joachim. *Die richtige Mittel=Straße, zwischen den Abwegen der Absonderung von der euserlichen Gemeinschafft der Kirchen, auch anderer Lehr= und Lebens=Irrungen, Wie auch der Bäbstischen Ketzer=Macherey . . . Nebst gründlichem Erweiß der Kinder=Tauffe,* etc. Halle 1712. 304 pages.
- Lange, Joachim Christoph. *Doct. Johann Bugenhagens oder Pomerani . . . Leben und Schrifften,* etc. Bautzen 1731. 109 pages.
- Leland, John. *Abriß der deistischen Schriften.* Vol. 1, Vol. 2, Parts 1 and 2. Hannover 1754–1756.
- Lindhammer, Johann Ludwig. *Der Von dem H. Evangelisten Luca Beschriebenen Apostel=Geschichte Ausführliche Erklärung und Anwendung.* Halle: Orphan House, 1725. 816 pages. 20.
- Luther, Martin. *Großer Katechismus* (edition unknown).
- Luther, Martin. *Kleiner Katechismus* (edition unknown).
- Mäderjan, Daniel Gottlieb. *Unterweisung zur Seligkeit.* 9th ed. Sorau 1745.
- Moller, Martin. *Soliloquia de Passione JESU CHRISTI. Wie ein jeder Christen Mensch, das Allerheyligste Leyden vnd Sterben vnsers HERRN Jesu Christi in seinem Hertzen . . . betrachten . . . sol.* Görlitz (undated).
- *Kurtze Nachricht von einigen Evangelischen Gemeinen in America, absonderlich in Pennsylvania.* 16 parts. Halle: Orphan House, 1744–1786.

- Porst, Johann. *Compendium Theologiae Viatorum & Regenitorum Practicae, oder die Göttliche Führung der Seelen*, etc. Halle: Orphan House, 1723. 1102 pages.

- Praetorius, Stephan. *Geistliche Schatzkammer, Der Gläubigen, In welcher die Lehre vom wahren Glauben, Gerechtigkeit, Seligkeit, Majestät, Herrlichkeit, Christliches Leben, und heilsamen Creutz der Kinder Gottes*, etc. Lüneburg 1699. 664 pages.

- Rambach, Johann Jacob. *Der wohl-informierte Catechet, das ist deutlicher Unterricht Wie man der Jugend . . . Den Grund der Christlichen Lehre beybringen könne*, etc. Jena 1722. 96 pages.

- Rambach, Johann Jacob. *Erbauliches Handbüchlein für Kinder, In welchem I. Die Ordnung des Heyls, II. Die Schätze des Heyls . . . enthalten sind.* 3rd ed. Leipzig 1735. 235 pages.

- Rambach, Johann Jacob. *Sammlung erbaulicher Lebens=Geschichte gottseliger Personen aus allerhand Ständen.* Berlin 1754. XL + 710 pages.

- Richter, Christian Friedrich. *Erbauliche Betrachtungen Vom Ursprung und Adel der Seelen / und von deren ietzigen elenden Beschaffenheit*, etc. Halle 1718. 422 pages.

- Richter, Christian Friedrich. *Die höchst=nöthige Erkenntniß des Menschen, sonderlich nach dem Leibe und natürlichen Leben, oder ein deutlicher Unterricht, von der Gesundheit und deren Erhaltung*, etc. 3rd ed. Leipzig 1710. 1234 pages.

- *Sammlung Auserlesener Materien zum Bau des Reiches Gottes. Der I. Beytrag.* Leipzig: Samuel Benjamin Walther, 1731.

- (Schade, Johann Caspar). *Ein Herrliches= Geschenck, oder schöne Christ= Bescherung, in einem Einfältigen Gespräch Zwischen Lehrer und Kinder Von der Geburth des liebes Jesus=Kindleins unsers Heylandes*, etc. Leipzig 1694. 42 pages. 12°.

- Schade, Johann Caspar. *Geistreiche Predigten über Die Sonn- Fest- und Feiertags-Evangelia durch das ganze Jahr*, etc. Frankfurt/Leipzig 1731. 542 pages.

- Schaitberger, Jospeh. *Neu=vermehrter Evangelischer Send-Brief, Darinnen vier und zwanzig nutzliche Büchlein enthalten, Geschrieben an die Lands=Leut in Saltzburg*, etc. Nuremberg 1733. 686 pages.

Index of the Bibliographically Identifiable Works   233

- Schmidt, Johannes. *Christliche, Gott wolgefällige Buß, Was sie sey, worinsie bestehe, von wem, wie, wo, zu welcher Zeit sie zu üben,* etc. Strassburg 1630. 658 pages.

- Schubert, Heinrich. *Zeugniß von der Gnade und Wahrheit in Christo, Abgeleget in Predigten, Welche über die ordentliche Sonn= und Fest=Tägliche Episteln,* etc. Halle: Orphan House, 1741. 886 + 736 pages.

- Schubert, Heinrich. *Zeugniß von der Gnade und Wahrheit in Christo, Abgeleget in Predigten, Welche, So wohl über die Evangelia und Episteln Gehalten,* etc. Halle: Orphan House, 1745. 424 + 1056 pages.

- Schulz, Johann Heinrich. *Theses de materia medica in usum auditorium.* Halle 1746. 490 pages.

- Scriver, Christian. *Seelen=Schatz, Darinn von der menschlichen Seelen hohen Würde, tieffen und kläglichen Sünden-fall . . . gehandelt wird.* Leipzig, Parts 1–5, 1687–92.

- Spangenberg, Johann, *Postilla / Das ist Außlegung der Episteln vnd Evangelien / auff alle Sontag vnd fürnembsten Fest,* etc. Nuremberg 1582. 191 pages.

- Spener, Philipp Jacob. *Tabulae catecheticae, quibus 5 capita catechismi minoris magni nostri Lutheri et subnexa tabula oeconomica.* 3rd ed. Frankfurt am Main 1691. 303 pages.

- Spener, Philipp Jacob. *Catechismustabellen in Frag und Antwort.* Frankfurt am Main 1725.

- Spener, Philipp Jacob. *Einfältige Erklärung der christlichen Lehre und der Ordnung des kleinen Catechismi Lutheri, in Frag und Antwort.* Halle: Orphan House, 1742.

- Spener, Philipp Jacob. *Erbauliche Evangelisch= v. Epistolische Sonntags= Andachten. Nach Anleitung der gewöhnlichen Evangelischen und Epistolischen Sonn= Fest= und Apostel=Tägen,* etc. Frankfurt am Main 1716. 928, 502, 457 pages.

- Sturm, Leonhard Christoph. *Vollständige Mühlen Baukunst Darinnen werden I. Alle Grundreguln so zu der Praxi nöthig. . .treülich angewiesen; II. Die Vortheile, die man bey Anlegung der Wasserräder alle Sorten von Machinen zutreiben in acht nehmen muß. . . . III. Was insonderheit an Korn= Graupen= Papier= Öhl= Pulfer= Säg= Steinschneide= ́Bohr= Schleiff= Sensen= Kessel= Eisendrat= Hächsel= und Dreschmühlen zuverbessern, aufrichtig entdecket.* Augsburg 1718. 35 pages. XLII tables. 4°.

- Töllner, Justinus. *Biblisches Spruch=Buch, In welchem zu finden über 1900. herrliche Sprüche und viel bekande Reim=Gebetlein*, etc. 3rd ed. Halle: Orphan House, 1709. 70, 1180 pages. 12°.

- Urlsperger, Samuel. *Der seinem JESU gleichgesinnte öffentliche Lehrer, wurde Bey der am 23sten Sonnt. Nach Trinit. 1749. . . . geschehenen Präsentation Sr. WohlErwürden. Hrn M. Ludwig-Heinrich Burry . . . der versammelten Gemeinde vorgestellet.* Augsburg undate (1749). 40 pages.

- Walch, Johann Georg. *Historische und Theologische Einleitung in die Religions=Streitigkeiten, Welche sonderlich ausser der Evangelisch=Lutherischen Kirchen entstanden.* 3rd ed. 3 vols. Jena 1733–1739.

- Wirth, Ambrosius. *Einfältige Anweisung, Für diejenige, welche der zarten, und mit dem theuren Blut Christi erkaufften Jugend, den kleinen Catechismum Lutheri beybringen sollen.* Nuremberg 1736. 704 pages.

- Wirth, Ambrosius. *Biblisches Namen!= und Buchstabir=Büchlein*, etc. Nuremberg 1690. 63 pages. (thick paper, wood cover).

- Wirth, Ambrosius. *August Hermann Franckens S. Th. Dr. Ord. & Past. Glauch. Unterricht / Wie Die Kinder zur wahren Gottseligkeit und Christlichen Klugheit anzuführen sind*, etc. Halle: Orphan House, 1705. 120 pages.

- Wirth, Ambrosius. *Das Nürnbergische Kinder=Lehr=Büchlein—Darinnen der kleine Catechismus D. Martin Luthers*, etc. Nuremberg 1729. 192 pages.

- Wudrian, Valentin. *Schola crucis & Thessera Christianismi; Das ist: Ein Ausführlicher Christlicher Vnterricht von dem lieben Creutze*, etc. 2nd ed. Hamburg 1634. 714 pages.

- Ziegenhagen, Friedrich Michael. *Kurze Erklärung des Gebets des Herrn, oder des Vater=Unsers, nebst einer Anmerkung über dasselbe.* Halle/London 1750.

- Ziegenhagen, Friedrich Michael. *Kurzer Unterricht von dem Leiden und Sterben des Erlösers der Welt.* Halle/London 1776.

- Zimmerman, Johann Liborius. *Die überschwengliche Erkenntniß JESU Christi Als ein richtiger, leichter und seliger Weg zu einer wahren und beständigen Kraft im Christenthum zu gelangen.* Halle 1731. 112 pages.

Appendix III

Index of the Letter Manuscripts of the Archives of Halle and Tübingen

Published by Urlsperger

Urlsperger, S. *Ausführliche Nachricht*, volume I.[1]

UN Page	Date	Sender	Recipient	Archive Catalog Number
1. 193	November 26, 1733	B and G	U	5C4:16, 64–66 copy
2. 194	November 26, 1733	B and G	Fr	5A1:17, 82–85 original
3. 197	November 26, 1733	G	Majer	5C4:18, 71–74
4. 199	December 29, 1733	B	Fr	5A1:24, 107–110 original
5. 200	January 6, 1734	B	Mother of B	5A1:26. 117–120 = January 16, 1734 copy
6. 205	March 20, 1734	G	Mischke	5A2:1, 1–3 copy

1. See Abbreviations Index, p. xi.

Appendix III

UN Page	Date	Sender	Recipient	Archive Catalog Number
7. 207	March 22, 1734	B	Newman	5C4:30, 95–96. extract English
8. 209	March 22, 1734	B and G	U	5C4:25, 83–84. copy
9. 210	March 22, 1734	B	Baumgarten	5A2:2, 4–7 copy
10. 212	March 22, 1734	Zwiffler	U	5C4:22, 81–82
11. 213	March 23, 1734	B	Fr	5A1:33, 147–150 copy
12. 217	May 6, 1734	B	Arnold Leipzig	5A2:6, 24–30 copy
13. 223	May 6, 1734	B	Mother of B	5A2:4, 16–18 copy
14. 224	May 6, 1734	B	Relative	5A2:5, 18–23 copy
15. 228	May 6, 1734	G	Friend	5A2:7, 31–36 copy
16. 231	May 6, 1734	G	Orphan	5A2:8, 37–40 copy
17. 236	May 9, 1734	B	Inspector Boetcher	5A2:9, 41–44 copy
18. 238	May 24, 1734	B	Wachsmann	5A2:10, 45–47 copy
19. 469	March 28, 1735	G	Fr	5A3:6, 42–43 original and 5C4:46, 120–124
20. 471	February 6, 1735	B and G	Fr	5A3:1, 1–4 original and 5C4:53, 171–175
21. 473	March 28, 1735	B and G	Fr	5A3:4, 23–30 original
22. 477	July 6, 1735	G	Fr	5A3:10, 63e. original and 5C4:47, 125–127
23. 478	September 1, 1735	B	Fr	5A3:11, 65–76 original
24. 482	September 1, 1735	G	Fr	5A3:13, 93–95 original and 5C4:45, 118–119, 140 copy
25. 484	September 1, 1735	G	Cellarius	5A3:15, 103–104 original and 5C4:52, 168–170.

Index of the Letter Manuscripts of the Archives of Halle and Tübingen 237

UN Page	Date	Sender	Recipient	Archive Catalog Number
26. 485	January 8, 1736	B and G	Fr	5A3:17, 112–115 original
27. 488	April 2, 1735	B	Cousin of B	5C4:63, 203–208
28. 492	September 1, 1735	B	Mother of B	5C4:51, 160–167
29. 906	March 11, 1736	G	-	5C4:67, 215–216
30. 907	June 19, 1736	B and G	Fr	5A3:23, 162–165
31. 917	October 1, 1736	G	Fr	5A3:26, 185–198b.
32. 923	October 6, 1736	B and G	U	5A3:31, 212–215 copy
33. 926	October 6, 1736	B	Fr	5A3:27, 199–202
34. 939	December 4, 1736	B and G	Z	5A3:45, 285–288 copy
35. 944	October 31, 1735	Riedelsperger	U	5A3:3b, 20–21
36. 945	February 6, 1735	M. Kalcher	U	5A3:3a, 17–20
37. 1096	June 9, 1737	G	Fr	5A3:58, 360–374
38. 2021	February 10, 1738	B and G	Benefactors	5C4:74, 235–238
39. 2029	February 15, 1736	B and G	Z	5A7:10, 27–28 = February 13, 1738 extract
40. 2031	May 17, 1738	B	U	5A7:17, 62–67 copy
41. 2047	November 25, 1738	Ebenezer community	U	5A7:49b, 209–213
42. 2058	November 1738	R. Kalcher	U	5A7:50a, 214–215
43. 2059	December 6, 1738	B	U	5A7:49a, 209 extract
44. 2066	March 17, 1739	B and G	U	5A7:46, 191–194
45. 2265	May 14, 1739	B	Fr	5A7:52, 219–222
46. 2281	July 4, 1739	B	Fr	5A7:57, 242–245 original
47. 2536	October 30, 1739	B and G	Fr	5A7:64a, 267–270 B. original G signature

Appendix III

UN Page	Date	Sender	Recipient	Archive Catalog Number
48. 2542	January 5, 1740	B and G	Fr	5A9:1, 1–4 original
49. 2546	February 14, 1740	B and G	Fr	5A9:2, 5–8 B original G signature
48a 663	January 5, 1740	B and G	Fr	5A9:1, 1–4 (double printing)
49a 665	February 14, 1740	B and G	Fr	5A9:2, 5–8 (double printing)
Urlsperger, S. *Ausführliche Nachricht,* etc., volume II.				
50. 669	May 29, 1740	B and G	Fr	5A9:6, 26–29 B. original G signature
51. 673	(1740)	G	Fr	5A9:7, 30–31 = May 30, 1740 original
52. 674	August 5, 1740	B	Fr	5A9:10, 443–46 original
53. 677	September 10, 1740	B and G	Fr	5A9:9, 39–42 B original G signature
54. 680	October 10, 1740	G	Fr	5A9:15, 57, 60, 63–66 original
55. 683	June 24, 1740	Ebenezer Orphanage	Fr	5A9:13, 51–52, 55.
56. 686	(1740)	Kalcher	Fr	5A9:14, 53–54 original
57. 690	February 4, 1741	G	Fr	5A9:24, 97–98, 115 original
58. 699	February 10, 1741	B	Fr	5A9:25, 99–100, 113–114 original
59. 937	June 6, 1741	B and G	Benefactors	5A10:8, 25–26 copy
60. 939	June 5, 1741	B and G	Fr	5A10:7, 21–24 B original
61. 942	June 6, 1741	Ebenezer Community	Fr	5A10:9, 27 = June 26, 1741
62. 944	July 23, 1741	B	Fr	5A10:11, 32–35 B original

Index of the Letter Manuscripts of the Archives of Halle and Tübingen   239

UN Page	Date	Sender	Recipient	Archive Catalog Number
63. 946	July 27, 1741	Thilo	Fr	5A10:25 = July 22, 1741
64. 947	October 14, 1741	B	Fr	5A10:15, 46–49 original and 4C1:36, 122
65. 950	July 25, 1741	B	Z	5A10:12, 36–39 and 4C1:36a, 123
66. 1238	January 22, 1742	G	Fr	5A10:21, 74–77 original
67. 1229	January 26, 1742	B	Fr	5A10:16, 50–53 original
68. 1231	March 13, 1742	B	Fr	5A10:17, 54–57 original
69. 1232	May 13, 1742	B	Fr	5A10:19, 67–70 original
70. 1902	March 8, 1743	G	Fr	5A10:44, 162–164 original
71. 1904	March 9, 1743	B	Fr	5A10:42, 152–155 original
72. 1906	July 21, 1743	G	Fr	5A11:2, 4–7 original
73. 1908	September 20, 1743	B and G	Fr	5A11:5, 1518 B original G signature
74. 1912	-	B and G	Fr	5A11:3, 8–11 = 1743 B original G signature
75. 1919	March 9, 1743	B and G	U	5A10:45, 165–178 = March 9 and 12, 1743
Urlsperger, S. *Ausführliche Nachricht,* etc., volume III.				
76. 18	October 29, 1744	B	U	5A11:22, 82–83 extract
77. 23	January 14, 1745	B	U	5A11:27, 111–116 B original signature in another hand
78. 192	-	Call	B	5A1:5, 34–35 = October 31, 1733 copy

UN Page	Date	Sender	Recipient	Archive Catalog Number
79. 194	-	Instructions	B	5A1:6, 36–39 copy
80. 198	-	(Call)	G	5A1 : 7 pp. 40–41 = October 31, 1733 copy
81. 199	-	Instructions	G	5A1:8. 42–44 copy
Urlsperger, S. and J. A. *Americanisches Ackerwerk*, parts 3 and 4				
82. 3/511	February 16, 1755	B	U	TK32F11, 1030–1041 original signature in another hand
83. 4/39-	September 5, 1765	B	Z	5B2:24, 96–99 copy and 25, 100–105 original

About the Author

HERMANN WINDE WAS BORN in 1935 in Elmshorn near Hamburg. He completed his Doctor of Theology dissertation at the Martin-Luther-University at Halle in 1961. Following his ordination in 1963, he served several congregations in East Germany and, beginning in 1977, as assistant to the Bishop of the Protestant diocese of Görlitz. He has lectured in churches, seminaries, and universities in the United States. He retired in 2000 in Erfurt.

Bibliography

Ahrbeck, Hans. *Über die Erziehungs- und Unterrichtsreform A. H. Franckes und ihre Grundlagen. 450 Jahre Martin-Luther-Universität Halle-Wittenberg.* Vol. II, 77–93. Halle, 1953.
Allgemeine Deutsche Biographie. Edited and published by the historische Commission bei der Königl. Akademie der Wissenschaften. 56 vols. Leipzig, 1875–1912.
Allen, W. O. B., and Edmund McClure. *Two Hundred Years: The History of the Society for Promoting Christian Knowledge, 1698-1898.* London: SPCK, 1898.
Americanisches Ackerwerk Gottes oder zuverlässige Nachrichten, den Zustand der americanisch englischen und von salzburgischen Emigranten erbauten Pflanzstadt Ebenezer in Georgien betreffend, aus dorther eingeschickten glaubwürdigen Diarien genommen, und mit Briefen der dasigen Herren Prediger noch weiter bestättiget, 5 Parts (1st–4th installments + preliminary report to the 4th installment). Edited by Samuel Urlsperger and Johann August Urlsperger. Augsburg 1754–1767.
Andrews, Charles Maclean. *The Colonial Period in American History.* 4th ed. 2 vols. New Haven: Yale University Press, 1936.
Arnold, Carl Franklin. *Die Ausrottung des Protestantismus in Salzburg unter Erzbischof Firmian und seinen Nachfolgern. Ein Beitrag zur Kirchengeschichte des achtzehnten Jahrhunderts.* 2nd half. Schriften des Vereins für Reformationsgeschichte 18/4, no. 69. Halle 1901.
——— . "Die Salzburger in Amerika. *Jahrbuch der Gesellschaft für die Geschichte des Protestantismus in Österreich* 25 (1904) 222–261.
——— . *Die Vertreibung der Salzburger Protestanten und ihre Aufnahme bei den Glaubensgenossen. Ein kulturgeschichtliches Zeitbild aus dem achtzehnten Jahrhundert.* Leipzig 1900.
Der ausführlichen Nachrichten von der Königlich=Groß=Britannischen Colonie Saltzburgischer Emigranten in America Erster Theil, etc. Edited by Samuel Urlsperger, Senior of the Evangelical Ministerium of the City of Augsburg and Pastor of the Main Church, St. Anna's. Halle: Orphan House, 1741). Part 1 + Continuations 1–5; Part 1, *Ausführliche Nachricht von den Saltzburgischen Emigranten, Die sich in America niedergelassen haben,* etc. Halle 1735. Translated and published in English as *Detailed Reports on the Salzburger Emigrants Who Settled in America.* Edited and translated by George Fenwick Jones, et al. 18 vols. Volumes 1–17, Athens, GA: University of Georgia Press, 1968–1995; vol. 18, Camden, ME: Picton Press, 1995.
Bancroft, George. *History of the United States of America from the Discovery of the Continent. In six volumes.* Rev. ed. Vol. II. Boston: Appleton, 1878.

Bibliography

Berg, J. *Die Geschichte der schwersten Prüfungszeit der evangelischen Kirche Schlesiens und der Oberlausitz.* Jauer 1857.

Beyreuther, Erich. "Neue Forschungen zur Geschichte der Deutschen Christentumsgesellschaft." *Theologische Literaturzeitung* 81 (1956) 355–58.

———. *August Hermann Francke und die Anfänge der ökumenischen Bewegung.* Leipzig: Reich, 1957.

Binder-Johnson, Hildegard. "Die Haltung der Salzburger in Georgia zur Sklaverei (1734–1750)." *Mitteilungen der Gesellschaft für Salzburger Landeskunde* 78 (1938) 183–96.

Bittinger, Lucy Forney. *The Germans in Colonial Times.* Philadelphia: Lippincott, 1901.

Bogatzky, Carl Heinrich von. *Lebenslauf, von ihmselbst beschrieben. Für die Liebhaber seiner Schriften und als Beytrag zur Geschichte der Spener'schen theologischen Schule herausgegeben.* Halle 1801.

Brandes, Karl. *Kirchengeschichte, kirchliche Statistik und religiöses Leben der Vereinigten Staaten von Nordamerika.* Vol. I. Berlin 1844.

Brandl, Alice. "Ein Besuch in Ebenezer, der ersten Siedlung der Salzburger Emigration in Georgia, U.S.A." *Mitteilungen der Gesellschaft für Salzburger Landeskunde* 66 (1926) 159–68.

Brantley, R. L. "The Salzburgers in Georgia." *Georgia Historical Quarterly* 14 (1930) 214–24.

Burckhardt, Johann Gottlieb. *Kirchen=Geschichte der Deutschen Gemeinden in London nebst historischen Beylagen und Predigten.* Tübingen 1798.

Burke, Edmund. *An Account of the European Settlements in America.* 5th ed. 2 vols. London: Dodsley, 1770.

A Catalogue of Books Relating to the Discovery and Early History of North and South America Forming a Part of the Library of E. D: Church. Compiled and Annotated by George Watson Cole. 5 vols. New York: Peter Smith, 1951.

Cleveland, Catharine Caroline. *The Great Revival in the West, 1797–1805.* Chicago: University of Chicago Press, 1916.

Cobb, Sanford Hoadley. *The Rise of Religious Liberty in America. A History.* New York: Macmillan, 1902.

Colquitt, Dolores Boisfeuillet. "Records of Ebenezer Church, Ebenezer, Ga. From original register in Manuscript Division of the Library of Congress." *Georgia Historical Quarterly* 12 (1928) 97–99, 191–93.

Cooper, Walter G. *The Story of Georgia.* 4 vols. New York: American Historical Society, 1938.

Corry, John Pitts. "The Houses of Colonial Georgia." *Georgia Historical Quarterly* 14 (1930) 181–201.

———. "Indian Affairs in Georgia, 1732–1756." PhD diss., University of Pennsylvania, 1936.

Coulter, Ellis Merton. "Mary Musgrove, 'Queen of the Creeks,' a chapter of early Georgia troubles." *Georgia Historical Quarterly* 11 (1927) 1–30.

———. "When John Wesley Preached in Georgia." *Georgia Historical Quarterly* 9 (1925) 317–51.

Cronau, Rudolf. *Drei Jahrhunderte deutschen Lebens in Amerika.* Ruhmesblätter der Deutschen in den Vereinigten Staaten. 2nd ed. Berlin: Reimer, 1924.

Dahms, Hellmuth Günther. *Geschichte der Vereinigten Staaten von Amerika.* Munich: Oldenbourg, 1953.

Daniel, Marjorie. "John Joachim Zubly—Georgia Pamphleteer of the Revolution." *Georgia Historical Quarterly* 19 (1935) 1–16.
Dictionary of American Biography. Under the auspices of the American Council of Learned Societies. Edited by Allen Johnson. 20 vols. New York: Scribner, 1929–1936.
"An Early Description of Georgia, from the Gentleman's Magazine, January 1756. Volume 26." *Georgia Historical Quarterly* 2 (1918) 22–36.
Eberhardt, Fritz. *Amerika-Literatur. Die wichtigsten seit 1900 in deutscher Sprache erschienenen Werke über Amerika*. Koehler & Volckmars Literaturführer. Vol. VII. Leipzig: Koehler & Volckmar, 1926.
Eberlein, Hellmut. *Schlesische Kirchengeschichte*. 3rd ed. Das Evangelische Schlesien. Vol. I. Edited by Gerhard Hultsch. Goslar: Verlag der Schles. Evangel. Zentralstelle, 1952.
Ehrhardt, Siegismund Justus. *Presbyterologie des Evangelischen Schlesiens, Dritten Theils Zweiter Haupt=Abschnitt, welcher die Protestantische Kirchen= und Prediger= Geschichte der Stadt und des Fürstenthums Jauer in sich begreift*. Liegnitz 1784.
The Encyclopedia Americana. 30 vols. New York: Americana Corp., 1949.
Encyclopedia Britannica: A New Survey of Universal Knowledge. 24 vols. Chicago: Encyclopedia Britannica, 1955.
Erdmannsdörffer, Bernhard. *Deutsche Geschichte vom Westfälischen Frieden bis zum Regierungsantritt Friedrich's des Großen. 1648–1740*. 2 vols. Allgemeine Geschichte in Einzeldarstellungen. Edited by Wilhelm Oncken. 3rd Hauptabtheilung, 7th Theil. Berlin: Grote, 1892.
An Exhibition Commemorating the Settlement of Georgia 1733–1948 (February 14, 1748–May 12, 1748). Edited by the Library of Congress, Washington, DC 1948.
Falke, Robert. *Lebensbilder aus dem Hause Stolberg-Wernigerode in den letzten fünfhundert Jahren 1429–1929*. Wernigerode: Harzer Graph, 1929.
Faust, Albert Bernhardt. *The German Element in the United States with Special Reference to Its Political, Moral, Social, and Educational Influence*. 2nd ed. 2 vols. New York: Steuben Society of America, 1927. German translation of the 1st ed. (1909): *Das Deutschtum in den Vereinigten Staaten*. 2 vols. Leipzig: Teubner, 1912.
Förstemann, Ernst Wilhelm. *Graf Christian Ernst zu Stolberg-Wernigerode*. Hannover, 1868.
Geißler, Anton Gotthard. *Als Der Wohl=Ehrwürdiger und Wohlgelehrte HERR George Geißler, Treu=fleißiger Pastor in Thommendorff Dom. Misericordias Domini A. 1737. Sein Jubilaeum semi-seculare Ministerii feyerte, wollte Einige Nachricht von der Thommendorfischen Kirche und deren Lehrern . . . zum Drucke befördern*. Görlitz o. J., 1737.
Gilbert, D. M. "Early History of the Lutheran Church in Georgia." *Lutheran Quarterly* 27/2 (1897) 156–74.
Göcking, Gerhard Gottlieb Günther. *Vollkommene Emigrations-Geschichte von denen aus dem Ertz-Bissthum Saltzburg vertriebenen und größtentheils nach Preussen gegangenen Lutheranern*, etc. Vol. I: 1734. Vol. II: 1737. Frankfurt and Leipzig.
Gräbner, A. L. *Geschichte der Lutherischen Kirche in America*. Part I. St. Louis, 1892.
Grotefend, Hermann. *Taschenbuch der Zeitrechnung des deutschen Mittelalters und der Neuzeit*. 9th ed. Edited by Otto Grotefend. Hannover: Hahn, 1948.
Haas, Rudolf. *Die Pfälzer in Nordamerika*. Mannheimer Geschichtsblätter. Monatsschrift für die Geschichte, Altertums- und Volkskunde Mannheims und der Pfalz. Edited by Mannheimer Altertumsverein e.V. 27 (1926): Heft 1 (Sp. 5–13), 2 (Sp. 27–32).

Häberle, Daniel. *Pfälzische Bibliographie.* 6 vols. Die landeskundliche Literatur der Rheinpfalz. Bad Dürkheim/Speyer, 1908–1928.

Hamilton, J. Taylor. *A History of the Unitas Fratrum, or Moravian Church in the United States of America.* The American Church History Series. Vol. VIII. New York 1894.

Harden, William. "The Moravians of Georgia and Pennsylvania as Educators." *Georgia Historical Quarterly* 2 (1918) 47–56.

———. "Sir James Wright, Governor of Georgia by Royal Commission, 1760–1782." *Georgia Historical Quarterly* 2 (1918) 22–36.

———. "Rev. J. J. Zubly's Appeal to the Grand Jury, October 8, 1777." *Georgia Historical Quarterly* 1 (1917) 161.

Hauck, Albert. *Deutschland und England in ihren kirchlichen Beziehungen. Acht Vorlesungen im Oktober 1916 an der Universität Upsala gehalten.* Leipzig: Hinrichs, 1917.

Hazelius, Ernest L. *History of the American Lutheran Church, from its Commencement in the Year of Our Lord 1685, to the Year 1842.* Zanesville, OH: Edwin C. Church, 1846.

Heick, Otto William. *Amerikanische Theologie in Geschichte und Gegenwart.* Breklum: Jensens, 1954.

Hildreth, Richard. *The History of the United States of America from the Discovery of the Continent to the Organization of the Government under the Federal Constitution. In three volumes.* Vol. 2. New York: Harper, 1850.

Hilliger, Johann Gottlieb. *Beytrag zur Kirchen-Historie des Ertz-Bischofthums Saltzburg, Welcher nicht nur Die grossen Bewegungen anzeiget, so schon Anno 1528. und 63. in demselben vorgegangen.* etc. Jena, 1732.

Hofer, J. M. "The Georgia Salzburgers." *Georgia Historical Quarterly* 18 (1934) 99–117.

Hülsemann, Johann Georg. *Geschichte der Democratie in den Vereinigten Staaten von Nord-America.* Göttingen: Vandenhoeck & Ruprecht, 1823.

Humphrey, Edward Frank. *Nationalism and Religion in America 1774–1789.* Boston: Chipman Law Pub., 1924.

Jackson, Samuel Macauley, comp. *Bibliography of American Church History.* The American Church History Series, published under the auspices of the American Society of Church History. Vol. XII. New York, 1894.

Jacobs, Henry Eyster. *A History of the Evangelical Lutheran Church in the United States.* The American Church History Series. Vol. IV. New York: Christian Literature, 1893. German translation: *Geschichte der Lutherischen Kirche in Amerika auf Grund von Prof. Dr. H. E. Jacobs "History of the Evang. Luth. Church in the United States" bearbeitet von Georg J. Fritschel. 1. Teil: Geschichte der Entwicklung der Lutherischen Kirche in Amerika bis zu Mühlenbergs Tode.* Gütersloh: Bertelsmann, 1896.

Jones, Charles Colcock. *The History of Georgia.* Vol. I: *The Aboriginal and Colonial Epochs.* Vol. II: *The Revolutionary Epoch.* Boston: Houghton, Mifflin, 1883.

Die Lutherischen Kirchen in der Welt. Berlin: Lutherischen Weltbund, 1957.

Kirchen=Ordnung, Der Christlichen und der ungeänderten Augspurgischen Confession Zugethanen Gemeinde in London Welche, Durch Göttliche Verleyhung, In 1694. Jahre, Am 19. Sonntage nach dem Fest der Heiligen Dreyfaltigkeit Solenniter eingeweyhet und eingesegnet worden, In St. Mary's Savoy. No place of publication given. 1718.

Knapp, Johann Georg. *Denkmal der schuldigen Hochachtung und Liebe gestiftet dem weiland Hochwürdigen und Hochgelarten Herrn D. Gotthilf August Francken,* etc. Halle: Orphan House, 1770.

Koepp, Wilhelm. *Johann Arndt und sein "Wahres Christentum": Lutherisches Bekenntnis und Oekumene*. Aufsätze und Vorträge zur Theologie und Religionswissenschaft. Edited by Erdmann Schott and Hans Urner. Issue 7. Berlin: Evangelische Verlagsanstalt, 1959.

Koch, Eduard Emil. *Geschichte des Kirchenliedes und Kirchengesangs der christlichen, insbesondere der deutschen evangelischen Kirche*. 2nd ed. 8 vols. Stuttgart, 1852.

Kramer, Gustav. *August Hermann Francke: Ein Lebensbild*. 2 parts. Halle: Orphan House, 1880/1882.

Latourette, Kenneth Scott. *A History of the Expansion of Christianity*. 7 vols. Volume III: *Three Centuries of Advance (A.D. 1500–A.D. 1800)*. 5th ed. New York: Harper & Brothers, 1939.

Lawrence, James B. "Religious Education of the Negro in the Colony of Georgia." *Georgia Historical Quarterly* 14 (1930) 41–57.

Lecky, William Edward Hartpole. *Geschichte Englands im achtzehnten Jahrhundert*. Translated by Ferdinand Löwe. 4 vols. Leipzig: Winter, 1879–1883.

Lehmann, Arno. "Hallesche Mediziner und Medizinen am Anfang deutsch-Indischer Beziehungen." *Wissenschaftliche Zeitschrift der Martin-Luther-Universität Halle-Wittenberg, Mathematisch-naturwissenschaftliche Reihe* V, 2 (December 1955) 117–32.

———. *Es begann in Tranquebar: Die Geschichte der ersten evangelischen Kirche in Indien*. 2nd ed. Berlin: Evangelische Verlagsanstalt, 1956.

Linn, Charles A. "The Georgia Colony of the Salzburgers." PhD diss. Hartford Theological Seminary, Hartford, CT, 1931.

Mackall, Leonhard L. "The Wymberly Jones De Renne Georgia Library." *Georgia Historical Quarterly* 2 (1918) 63–86.

Mallard, John B. "Liberty County, Georgia." *Georgia Historical Quarterly* 2 (1918) 3–21.

Mann, W. J. *Heinr. Melch. Muhlenbergs Leben: Die lutherische Kirche in Amerika*. First part. Leipzig, 1893.

Mayr, Josef Karl. *Die Emigration der Salzburger Protestanten von 1731/32. Das Spiel der politischen Kräfte*. Salzburg, 1931.

McCall, Hugh. *The History of Georgia, Containing Brief Sketches of the Most Remarkable Events, up to the Present Day*. 2 vols. Savannah: Seymour & Williams, 1811/1816.

McCrady, Edward. *Slavery in the Province of South Carolina, 1670–1770*. Annual Report of the American Historical Association for the Year 1895. Washington, DC, 1896.

McKinstry, Mary Thomas. "Silk Culture in the Colony of Georgia." *Georgia Historical Quarterly* 14 (1930) 225–35.

Meynen, Emil. *Bibliographie des Deutschtums der kolonialzeitlichen Einwanderung in Nordamerika, insbesondere der Pennsylvanien-Deutschen und ihrer Nachkommen 1683–1933*. German and English. Leipzig: Harrassowitz, 1937.

Mode, Peter G. *Source Book and Bibliographical Guide for American Church History*. Menasha, WI: Banta, 1921.

Morris, John G. *Bibliotheca Lutherana: A Complete List of the Publications of all the Lutheran Ministers in the United States*. Philadelphia: Lutheran Board of Publication, 1876.

Morris, Richard B. *Encyclopedia of American History*. New York: Harper & Brothers, 1953.

Müller, Friedrich. *Müllers Großes Deutsches Ortsbuch: Vollständiges Gemeindelexikon*. 8th ed. Wuppertal-Barmen: Post- Ortsbuchverlag, 1949.

Müller, Karl. *200 Jahre Brüdermission.* Vol. 1: *Das erste Missionsjahrhundert.* Herrnhut: Verlag der Missionsbuchhandlung, 1931.

Nachrichten von den vereinigten Deutschen Evangelisch-Lutherischen Gemeinden in Nord-America, absonderlich in Pensylvanien. Mit einer Vorrede von D. Johann Ludewig Schulze. Halle: Orphan House, 1787. Neu herausgegeben mit historischen Erläuterungen und Mittheilungen aus dem Archiv der Franckeschen Stiftungen zu Halle von W. J. Mann, B. M. Schmucker, W. Germann. Vol. I. Allentown, PA, 1886.

Nebe, August. *Die Franckeschen Stiftungen und die Mission.* Geschichten und Bilder aus der Mission, no. 38. Edited by the Direktorium of the Francke Foundations. Halle: Orphan House, 1933.

Neuere Geschichte der Evangelischen Missions-Anstalten zu Bekehrung der Heiden in Ostindien. Halle: Orphan House, 1776–1804.

Neve, Juergen Ludwig. *History of the Lutheran Church in America.* 3rd ed. Edited by Willard D. Allback. Burlington, IA: German Literary Board, 1934.

Newton, Hester Walton. "The Agricultural Activities of the Salzburgers in Colonial Georgia." *Georgia Historical Quarterly* 18 (1934) 248–63.

Newton, Hester Walton. "The Industrial and Social Influences of the Salzburgers in Colonial Georgia." *Georgia Historical Quarterly* 18 (1934) 335–53.

Tappert, Theodore Gerhardt, and John Doberstein, eds. *The Journals of Henry Melchior Muhlenberg.* 3 vols. Philadelphia: Muhlenberg, 1942–1958.

"Thommendorf." *Die Heimat,* no. 41. Beilage des "Neuen Görlitzer Anzeigers," 1928, 161–63.

Otto, Gottlieb Friedrich. *Lexikon der seit dem funfzehenden Jahrhunderte verstorbenen und jetztlebenden Oberlausizischen Schriftsteller und Künstler.* Vol. 2, Part 1, "H—Layritz." Görlitz: Anton, 1802.

Panse, Karl. *Geschichte der Auswanderung der evangelischen Salzburger in Jahre 1732. Beitrag zur Kirchengeschichte nach den Quellen bearbeitet.* Leipzig: Voss, 1827.

Pascoe, Charles Frederick. *Two Hundred Years of the S. P. G.: An historical account of the Society for the Propagation of the Gospel in Foreign Parts, 1701–1900.* London 1901.

Paullin, Charles O., and John K. Wright. *Atlas of the Historical Geography of the United States.* Carnegie Institution of Washington Publication 401. Washington, DC: Carnegie Institution of Washington and the American Geographical Society of New York, 1932.

Pennington, Edgar Legare. "The Reverend Samuel Quincy, S.P.G Missionary." *Georgia Historical Quarterly* 11 (1927) 157–65.

———. "The Reverend Bartholomew Zouberbuhler." *Georgia Historical Quarterly* 18 (1934) 354–63.

Perkins, Eunice Ross. "John Joachim Zubly, Georgia's Conscientious Objector." *Georgia Historical Quarterly* 15 (1931) 313–23.

Phillips, Ulrich Bonnell. *Georgia and State Rights: A Study of the Political History of Georgia from the Revolution to the Civil War, with Particular Regard to Federal Relations.* Annual Report of the American Historical Association for the Year 1901. Vol. II. Washington, DC: American Historical Association, 1902.

Plath, Carl Heinrich Christian. *Was haben die Professoren Francke Vater und Sohn für die Mission getan?* Missionsstudien. Berlin, 1869.

Pochmann, Henry A., compiler, and Arthur R. Schultz, editor. *Bibliography of German Culture in America to 1940.* Madison: University of Wisconsin Press, 1953.

Prinzinger, A. "Die Ansiedlung der Salzburger im Staate Georgien in Nordamerika." *Mitteilungen der Gesellschaft für Salzburger Landeskunde* 22 (1882) 1–36.
Qualben, Lars P. *The Lutheran Church in Colonial America*. New York: Nelson, 1940.
Rademacher, Julius. *Predigergeschichte der Kirchenkreise Bunzlau I und II*. Stroppen 1932.
Ratzel, Friedrich. *Culturgeographie der Vereinigten Staaten von Nord-Amerika*. Vol. II. Munich: Oldenbourg, 1880.
Realencyklopädie für protestantische Theologie und Kirche. 3rd ed. 24 vols. Edited by Albert Hauck. Leipzig: Hinrichs, 1896–1913.
Reichel, Gerhard. "Die Entstehung einer Zinzendorf feindlichen Partei in Halle und Wernigerode." *Zeitschrift für Kirchengeschichte* 23 (1902) 549–92.
Die Religion in Geschichte und Gegenwart. 3rd completely rev. ed. Edited by Kurt Galling. Tübingen: Mohr/Siebeck, 1956–1965.
Renner, L. *Lebensbilder aus der Pietistenzeit: Ein Beitrag zur Geschichte und Würdigung des späteren Pietismus*. Bremen: Müller, 1886.
Richter, Martin. *Der Missionsgedanke im evangelischen Deutschland des 18. Jahrhunderts*. Missionswissenschaftliche Forschungen 6. Edited by the Deutschen Gesellschaft für Missionswissenschaft by Carl Wirbt. Leipzig: Hinrichs, 1928.
Rines, Edward Francis. *Old Historic Churches of America: Their Romantic History and Their Tradition*. New York: Macmillan, 1936.
Risler, Jeremias. *Leben August Gottlieb Spangenbergs, Bischof der evangelischen Brüderkirche*. Barby, 1794.
Ritschl, Albecht. *Geschichte des Pietismus in der lutherischen Kirche des 17. und 18. Jahrhunderts, Erste und Zweite Abtheilung*. History of Pietism. Vols. 2 and 3. Bonn: Marcus, 1884/1886.
Rouse, Ruth, and Stephen Charles Neill, eds. *A History of the Ecumenical Movement 1517–1948*. Published on Behalf of the Ecumenical Institute Château de Bossey. London: SPCK, 1954.
Rubincam, Milton. "Historical Background of the Salzburger Emigration to Georgia." *Georgia Historical Quarterly* 35 (1951) 99–115.
Schmidt, Martin. "Die Anfange der Kirchenbildung bei den Salzburgern in Georgia. Ein vergessenes Stück lutherischer Diasporageschichte." In *Lutherische Kirche in Bewegung: Festschrift für Friedrich Ulmer zum 60. Geburtstag*, edited by Gottfried Werner, 21–40. Erlangen: Martin-Luther-Verlag, 1937.
———. "Das hallische Waisenhaus und England im 18. Jahrhundert. Ein Beitrag zu dem Thema: Pietismus und Oikumene." *Theologische Zeitschrift* 7 (1951) 38–55.
———. *John Wesley*. Vol. I: *Die Zeit vom 17. Juni 1703 bis 24. Mai 1738*. Zurich: Gotthelf, 1953.
———. *John Wesleys Bekehrung*: Beiträge zur Geschichte des Methodismus 3. Verein für Geschichte des Methodismus. Bremen: Verlagshaus der Methodistenkirche, 1938.
———. *Der junge Wesley als Heidenmissionar und Missionstheologe*. Beiträge zur Missionswissenschaft und evangelischen Religionskunde 5. Gütersloh: Bertelsmann, 1955.
Selbmann, Erhard. *Die gesellschaftlichen Erscheinungsformen des Pietismus hallescher Prägung*. 450 Jahre Martin-Luther-Universität Halle-Wittenberg, vol. II, 59–76. Halle 1953.
Stäudlin, Carl Friedrich. *Kirchliche Geographie und Statistik*. Part 2. Tübingen: Cotta 1804.
Strickland, Reba Carolyn. "Building a Colonial Church." *Georgia Historical Quarterly* 17 (1933) 276–85.

———. "Religion and the State in Georgia in the Eighteenth Century." PhD diss. Columbia University, New York, 1939.
Strobel, Philip A. *The Salzburgers and Their Descendants: Being the History of a Colony of German (Lutheran) Protestants, Who Emigrated to Georgia in 1734, and Settled at Ebenezer, Twenty-five Miles above the City of Savannah*. Baltimore: Kurtz, 1855. New edition with forward, appendix, and index by Edward D. Wells. Athens, GA, 1953.
Swanton, John R. *The Indians of the Southeastern United States*. Smithsonian Institution, Bureau of American Ethnology Bulletin 137. Washington, DC, 1946.
Thiersch, Heinrich W. J. *Ursprung und Entwicklung der Colonieen in Nordamerica 1496–1776*. Augsburg: Preyss, 1880.
Tholuck, August. *Geschichte des Rationalismus: Erste Abtheilung: Geschichte des Pietismus und des ersten Stadiums der Aufklärung*. Berlin: Wiegandt & Grieben, 1865.
"Thommendorf" (unnamed). *Die Heimat*, no. 41. Beilage des "Neuen Görlitzer Anzeigers," 1928, 161–63.
Thompson, H. P. *Into All Lands: The History of the Society for the Propagation of the Gospel in Foreign Parts 1701–1950*. London: SPCK, 1951.
Triebner, Christoph Friedrich. *Die Beschaffenheit eines Menschen vor, in, und nach seiner Bekehrung*, etc. Greiz, undated (1764?).
Urlsperger, Samuel. *Einige wenige Umstände von den Personalien Tit. Herrn Samuel Urlspergers, Eines Evangelischen Ministerii zu Augspurg Senioris, etc*. Augsburg: Fincke, n.d. (after 1748).
Visser't Hooft, W. A. *Der Sinn des Wortes 'Oekumenuisch': Eine Vorlesung*. Stuttgart: Evangelische Verlagswerk, 1954.
Voigt, A. G. "John Wesley and the Salzburgers." *Lutheran Quarterly* 27 (1897) 370–76.
Vollständiges Orts-Lexikon der Vereinigten Staaten von Nordamerika. Bibliographisches Institut Hildburghausen, 1852.
Wentz, Abdel Ross. *A Basic History of Lutheranism in America*. Philadelphia: Muhlenberg, 1955.
Wilson, Caroline Price. "The Swan of Huss." *Georgia Historical Quarterly* 13 (1929) 372–91.
Winter, Eduard. *Halle als Ausgangspunkt der deutschen Russlandkunde im 18. Jahrhundert*. Deutsche Akademie der Wissenschaften zu Berlin. Veröffentlichungen des Instituts für Slawistik, no. 2. Edited by H. H. Bielfeldt. Berlin: Akademie, 1953.
Wischan, F. *Kurze Geschichte der deutschen evangl.-luther. Gemeinden in und um Philadelphia und der lutherischen Synoden Amerikas*. Die lutherische Kirche in Amerika, part 2. Leipzig, 1892.
Wissler, Clark. *The American Indian: An Introduction to the Anthropology of the New World*. 2nd ed. New York: Oxford University Press, 1922.
Wolf, Edmund Jacob. *The Lutherans in America: A Story of Struggle, Progress, Influence, and Marvelous Growth*. New York: Hill, 1890.
Writings on American History. Volume II/Supplementary Volume of the Annual Report of the American Historical Association. Washington, DC, 1918.
Zwiedineck-Südenhorst, H. von, *Deutsche Geschichte in Zeitraum der Gründung des preußischen Königtums*. 2 vols. Bibliothek Deutscher Geschichte 9. Stuttgart: Cotta, 1890/94.

Index of Names

Aaron (pastor in Tranquebar), 137
Adlerstein (itinerate preacher), 79, 97
Albinus, Samuel Theodor, 171
Altherr (Savannah resident), 136
Anne of Denmark, Queen, 19
Anton, Paul, 165, 174, 226
Arndt, Johann, 22, 149, 227

Bachman, John, 111, 220
Bancroft, George 3, 27
Baumgarten, Siegmund Jakob, 195–96, 200, 227, 236
Bergmann, Catharina (née Herb, wife of Johann Ernst), 204
Bergmann, Christoph Friedrich (son of Johann Ernst and Catharina), 204, 216, 219–20
Bergmann, Johann Ernst, xi, 3, 7–8, 56, 61, 81–84, 88, 97–98, 111, 113–14, 116, 123, 125–27, 129–31, 134, 146–47, 161–62, 178–79, 191, 193, 199, 202–6, 216, 218–20
Bergmann, Johann Ernst II (son of Johann Ernst and Catharina), 204
Bergmann, Johanna Catharina (daughter of Johann Ernst and Catharina), 204
Bergmann, Maria Elisabeth (daughter of Johann Ernst and Catharina), 204
Bernhardt, Christian Eberhard, 81, 97
Biddenbach, Matthaus, 68

Bishop (English servant), 142
Bogatzky, Carl Heinrich von, 192, 195, 201, 203, 227, 244
Böhler, Peter, 32, 106, 211
Böhme, Anton Wilhelm, 137, 174, 227
Boltzius, Catharina (sister of Johann Martin), 163–64
Boltzius, Catharina Maria (daughter of Johann Martin and Gertraud), 170–71, 173
Boltzius, Christiana Elisabeth (daughter of Johann Martin and Gertraud), 171
Boltzius, Elisabeth (née Panse, grandmother of Johann Martin, wife of Johann)
Boltzius, Eva Rosina (née Müller, mother of Johann Martin, wife of Martin), 164
Boltzius, Gertraud (née Kraher, wife of Johann Martin), 170, 173
Boltzius, Gotthilf Israel (son of Johann Martin and Gertraud), 170–73
Boltzius, Henriette (daughter of Gotthilf Israel), 173
Boltzius, Johann (grandfather of Johann Martin), 163
Boltzius, Johann Martin, xi, 2, 4–5, 7–11, 22–25, 27–38, 40–64, 66, 69, 71–72, 84–85, 88–90, 92–94, 96, 98–100, 102, 105–9, 113, 117–19, 121, 124–28, 130–33, 135–36, 138, 140, 142–44, 148–52, 155–59, 161

Index of Names

Boltzius, Johann Martin (cont.), 163–82, 184, 186–91, 193–96, 198, 201–2, 208–11, 213–16, 218, 221
Boltzius, Maria Elisabeth (sister of Johann Martin), 163
Boltzius, Martin (father of Johann Martin), 163–64
Boltzius, Samuel Leberecht (son of Johann Martin and Gertraud), 170–71
Boltzius, Sigismund (infant brother of Johann Martin), 164
Borbeck (Porbeck), General Friedrich von, 200
Boynd, D., 170
Brahm, Johann Gerhard Wilhelm von, 53, 58–59, 61, 150
Bray, Nicholas, 15
Breithaupt, Joachim Justus, 137, 165, 174–75, 182–83, 226–27
Brunnholz, Peter, 104
Burckhardt, Johann Gottlieb, 23
Bürckmann (pastor in Nuremberg), 198
Burgsdorf, Christoph Gottlob von, 82, 164–65, 202–3

Campbell, Colonel (British) Archibald, 75–6
Candler, Allen Daniel, 5
Causton, Thomas, 29–30, 34–37, 39–40, 92, 209, 213–14
Cellarius, Ludwig Johann, 30, 236
Charles II, King, 14
Charlotte Christine, Princess of Braunschweig-Wolfenbüttel, 164
Chiffelle, Henri, 106, 214
Christian Ernst, Duke (Stolberg-Wernigerode), 168–69, 188
Christian VI, King of Denmark, 169
Chur (notary in Schwäbisch-Hall), 184
Clarke, (British Brigadier General), 78
Clauder (godfather of Christian Israel Gronau), 180
Cooper, Walter G., 5, 244
Coram, Captain Thomas, 24

Cornish, Captain Joseph ("London Merchant"), 211
Crailsheim, Baron von, 183

D'Estaing, Count, 76
Daser, Frederick Augustine, 97, 109–10
Dasher(Daescher), John Martin I, 162
Dasher, John Martin II, 162
Davis, Jenking, 67–68, 74–76, 78, 80, 96, 160
Davis, Raymond E., 151
Delamotte, Charles, 32, 211, 213,
Dietrich, Archbishop Wolf, 16
Dobler, Johann, 95
Driessler, Johann Ulrich, xi, 47, 100–2, 114, 128, 138, 145–46, 181, 183–87

Ernesti, Johann August, 197, 202
Ernst, Gottlieb, 147

Fabricius, Sebastian Andreas, 7, 82
Faust, Albert Bernhardt, 4, 245
Ferdinand III of Bohemia, 166
Firmian, Archbishop Leopold Anton Freiherr von, 17
Fisher, George, 146–47
Flörl, Johann, 56, 68, 70, 72, 74, 113, 118
Francke, August Hermann, 2, 18, 137, 164–65, 174, 176–77, 183, 190, 195, 197, 228–29
Francke, Gotthilf August, xi, 2, 7, 9–11, 22, 29, 31, 44–46, 48, 51, 60, 62, 93, 117, 119–21, 143, 149, 152, 157–59, 161, 168, 170–73, 175, 180, 182–89, 192, 195, 197–98, 200–2, 207–9, 213
Frey (Fry), Captain Tobias ("Purysburg"), 10, 24
Freylinghausen, Gottlieb Anastasius, 79, 192, 203
Freylinghausen, Johann Anastasius, 137, 148, 168, 229
Fritz, W. Richard, 151

Gardner, 146
Geiger, Lucas, 143

George II, King, 14–15
George of Denmark, Prince, 19
Gerock, Johann Siegfried, 55
Gerresheim, Friedrich, 78, 96
Giese, Adam Ludwig, 169
Gnann (Genan), Jacob, 80
Gnann, Georg, 77
Goebels (Hessian major), 77
Gräbner, A. L., 4, 12, 177, 246
Grammer, Cristoffer, 80
Gronau, Anna Margaretha (née Lange, mother of Israel Christian), 179
Gronau, Catharina (daughter of Israel Christian and Catharine), 181
Gronau, Catharine (née Kraher, wife of Israel Christian, later wife of Lemcke), 170, 180, 181, 189
Gronau, Friderica Maria (daughter of Israel Christian and Catharine, later married Friedrich Triebner), 72–73, 182, 189, 199
Gronau, Hanna Elisabeth (daughter of Israel Christian and Catharine, later married Johann Caspar Wertsch), 162, 181–82, 189
Gronau, Heinrich (father of Israel Christian), 179
Gronau, Israel Christian, xi, 5, 8–9, 22, 26–28, 33–34, 37, 39, 41, 43, 45–47, 52, 59, 61, 86, 93, 98, 105–6, 109, 118, 126–27, 142–43, 155, 162, 167–68, 170, 173, 178–183, 186–87, 190, 208–9, 211, 215
Gruber, Peter, 41
Gschwandel, Thomas, 26, 41

Habersham, James, 50, 115, 215
Hahn, Friedrich Christian, 167
Hahnbaum, Johann Severin, 109
Hamilton, Henry, 142
Hamilton, Regina Charlotte, 142
Hangleiter, Johannes, 80
Hazelius, Ernest L., 4, 24, 173, 190, 204, 220, 246
Heck, Caspar, 80
Heckin (school mistress), 144
Heinzelmann, Israel, 63, 67

Helffenstein family, 107
Helffenstein, Friederica, 159
Helmuth, Justus Henry Christian, 150, 198
Herb, Catharina. *See* Bergmann, Catharina (Herb)
Hermsdorf, Commissioner (with third Salzburger transport)
Heron, Colonel (commander at Fort Frederica), 102
Herson, Hergen, 162, 189
Herson, Hanna (née Wertsch), 162
Herzog, Martin, 242
Holtzendorff, Johann, 103, 106
Holzendorff, John, 75
Hopkey, Sophie (Sophia), 213
Hoppe, Ernst Gottlieb (husband of Maria Rabenhorst), 191
Hoppe, Maria (née Rabenhorst), 191
Horton, Major (commander at Fort Frederica), 101, 188
Hudson, Christopher, 162 (second husband of Hanna Wertsch Herson)

Ingham, Benjamin, 32, 210–11

Jackson (US Army colonel), 77
Jacobs, Henry Eyster, 4, 16, 246
Jenys, Paul, 26
Jones, Charles Colcock, 4
Jones, George Fenwick, viii, 2
Juncker, Johann, 157, 230

Kalcher, Margaretha, 152, 237
Kalcher, Ruprecht, 41, 141, 151–53, 237
Karl Ludwig of the Palatinate, 16
Kieffer, Ephraim, 105
Kieffer, Theobold, 104–6, 118
Kleiminger (pastoral candidate for Ebenezer), 198
Knapp, Johann Georg, 200–1, 203, 246
Knoblach, Major General Hans von, 77, 200
Kocher, Johann Georg, 143, 161
Kogler, Captain John, 83
Kogler, George, 86

Korte, Friedrich, 164
Kraft, Anna. *See* Rabenhorst, Anna Kraft
Kraft, David, 53, 193
Krämer, Christoph, 68, 74
Krause (Salzburger), 141
Krauss, Samuel, 68, 80
Krauss (Krauß), Captain, 55, 171

Lackner, Martin, 143, 161
Lange, Andreas (father of Anna Margaretha Gronau), 179
Lau, Samuel, 169, 188
Lemcke, A. C. (brother of Hermann Heinrich), 187
Lemcke, Catharine. *See* Gronau, Catharine
Lemcke, Hermann Heinrich, xi, 9, 52, 54, 56–58, 62–64, 73, 88, 95, 101, 108, 113, 121, 126–27, 143, 171–72, 178, 181, 187–191, 193, 198, 202
Lemcke, Johanna (daughter of Hermann Heinrich and Catharine), 189
Lemcke, Timotheus (son of Hermann Heinrich and Catharine), 138, 144, 150, 160, 189
Liberkühn (pastoral candidate for Ebenezer), 167
Lieshen, Captain ("Northern Lion"), 204
Lindner, Captain (justice of the peace in Purrysburg), 107
Longinotti, John Baptist, 205
Louis XIV of France, 15–16
Luther, Martin, 24–25, 62, 106, 126, 135, 145, 147, 206

MacGillivray (McGillivray), Alexander, 61
MacCay, Charles, 77
Mack, Jacob, 69
Mackentach (McIntosh[?], English Captain), 34
Mäderjan, Daniel Gottlieb, 165–66, 177, 232
Majer, Johann August, 11, 166–67, 184, 192, 210, 235

Martin, Governor John, 78
Martin, Johann Nikolaus, 110
Martyn, Benjamin, 3, 40, 42
Mauer (pastoral candidate for Ebenezer), 197
Maulsby, Barnabas, 77
Mauritius, Inspector (Halle Orphan House), 192
Mayer, Johann Ludwig, 50, 118, 142, 159, 161, 181, 189, 190, 193
McKinstry, Mary Thomas, 49, 247
Mealy, Stephen Albion, 98
Miechel, Johannes, 80
Miller, Stephan, 69
Mosheim, Johann Lorenz von, 22, 176
Muhlenberg, Friedrich August Conrad, 88
Muhlenberg, Henry Melchior, xi, 2, 4, 8–9, 12, 43–44, 46, 63, 67–73, 79–81, 88, 91, 96, 105, 109–10, 115–16, 119, 121–22, 125, 127–28, 177, 184, 194–96, 201
Müller (Moravian tailor), 211
Müller, Christian Gottlob (pastoral candidate for Ebenezer), 202–3
Müller, Johann, 164–65
Müller, Paul, 68
Müllern, Johann Gottfried von, 42
Münch, Chrétien von, 48, 171
Musgrove, Mary, 60, 101

Nebe, Johann Friedrich, 61, 248
Neidlinger, Ulrich, 49, 68, 71, 73, 144
Neumann, Mrs. (sister of Christian Rabenhorst), 191
Newman, Henry, 21, 31, 42, 236
Nitschmann, David, 32, 211

Oglethorpe, James Edward, 10, 15, 25–29, 31–33, 35–40, 43–44, 60, 93, 99–100, 107, 113, 117–18, 156–57, 184–86, 210–12
Ortmann, Christoph, 23–24, 28, 33, 142
Ortmann, Juliana, 23–24, 28

Paine, Thomas, 146
Pasche, Friedrich Wilhelm, 7, 73, 109
Paulitsch, Johann Martin, 144

Paulus, Johann, 68
Penninger (itinerate preacher), 78, 97
Peter the Great, 164
Petrovich, Alexei, 164
Platho (Prussian ambassador in Regensburg), 144
Polasky (Pulaski), Count Casimir, 76
Porbeck. *See* Borbeck
Porst, Johann, 137, 164, 232
Prevost, General Augustine, 76, 199
Probst, Johann Gotthilf, 81–82, 110, 116, 146, 151, 173, 202–4
Purry, Jean Pierre, 29, 39, 103, 106, 108

Quarme, Captain Walther ("Judith"), 188

Rabenhorst, Anna (Kraft, widow of David Kraft; with of Christian), 53, 58, 193–94
Rabenhorst, Christian, xi, 11, 51, 56–58, 62, 64, 73–74, 96, 110, 114, 116–17, 121, 123, 127–28, 143, 173, 189–96, 200–16, 218
  dispute with Triebner, 43, 57–58, 62–73, 88, 109, 115, 127–28, 201
Rabenhorst, Christian I (father of Christian), 191
Rabenhorst, (mother of Christian, née Oldemann), 191–96
Rahn, Mattheus, 146
Räll, Chancellor Hieronymus Christian von, 17
Reck, Philipp Georg von, 2, 10, 21–22, 25–29, 31–33, 37–39, 175–76, 210–11
Reiter (Reuter), Simon, 65
Reitz, Court Chaplain, 197–98
Riedelsperger (Salzburger in Ebenezer), 153, 237
Rowlathon, Captain ("Catharine Sloep"), 186
Rudolf, Carl, 99

Schach (pastoral candidate for Frederica), 184
Schaitberger, Joseph, 16, 232

Schiele, Georg, 77
Schmidt, Johann Friedrich, 198
Schmidt, Martin, 212, 233
Schmucker, Samuel Simon, 150
Schnelle (great-grandfather of Israel Christian Gronau), 179
Schöner, Daniel, 44
Schönmannsgruber (resident of Purrysburg), 103, 106
Schuhmacher (pastoral candidate and traveling chaplain), 22, 130
Schubtrein, Joseph, 68, 72
Schulius (Moravian teacher in Purrysburg), 106
Schultze (pastor in Tulpehocken), 80
Schultze, Johann Christian, 44–45
Schulze, Johann Ludwig, 202–3
Schwarz (merchant in Schwäbisch Hall), 184
Schweiger, Georg, 34–35, 155
Schweighoffer (widow in Ebenezer), 152
Schwer (pastoral candidate for Ebenezer), 197
Semler, Johann Salomo, 200
Seydelitz, Johann August, 169
Shubtrein, Nicolaus, 80
Siebeth, Stephan Carl (pastoral candidate for Ebenezer), 167, 208
Smissen, Jacob Gysbert van der, 204
Sophie Charlotte von Stolberg-Wernigerode, 168
Spangenberg, August Gottlieb von, 46, 60, 167, 207–11, 233
Steber, Caspar, 45
Steiner, Christian, 68, 75
Steiner, David, 72
Steiner, Ruprecht, 89, 141
Stephens, William, 46, 81
Stevens, William Bacon, 4
Stirk, Colonel (British) John, 74
Streit, Christian, 73, 109–10
Streit, L., 109
Strobel, Philip A., vii, 4–6, 8, 12, 18, 25, 27, 51, 68, 81, 119–22, 131, 167, 202–4, 216–17, 219, 250.

Tappert, Theodore, 8, 248

Theus (painter, brother of Christian), 91
Theus, Christian, 91
Thilo, Christian Ernst, 10, 106, 143, 156–59, 171–72, 177, 189, 239
Thomas, Captain John ("London Merchant"), 32, 211
Tomo-Chichi, 26, 210
Treutlen, Johann Adam, 1, 63–64, 67–68, 72, 74–75, 116, 140, 144, 194
Triebner, Christoph Friedrich II (son of Christoph and Friderica), 199–200
Triebner, Christoph Friedrich, xi, 3, 62–64, 73–80, 115–16, 122, 128, 147, 162, 173, 181–82, 189, 191, 194–203
  dispute with Rabenhorst, 43, 57–58, 62–73, 88, 109, 115, 127–28, 201
Triebner, Friderica Maria (née Gronau). See Gronau, Friderica Maria
Triebner, Timotheus, Traugott (son of Christoph and Friderica), 199
Tuskenovi (Yamacraw military leader), 26

Unselt (teacher in Purrysburg), 106
Urlsperger, Johann August, 7, 9, 79–82, 85, 116, 196–97, 202–4
Urlsperger, Samuel, xi, 2, 4, 7–12, 18–22, 26–27, 30, 42–43, 48–49, 51, 53, 56–58, 62–64, 73, 90, 114–16, 119–22, 130, 140, 149–50, 152, 160, 167–68, 172, 175, 177–78, 185, 187–89, 191, 193, 196–98, 201, 208, 234–35, 238–40, 243, 250

Vat, Jean (Johann), 10, 28–30, 32, 34–36, 38, 84, 117
Vigera, Johann Friedrich, 42, 152, 185

Waldhaur, Jacob Caspar, 68, 72, 74, 80, 96

Wayne, General Anthony, 77
Weisiger, Daniel, 44–46
Wertsch, Hanna(h) (daughter of Johann Caspar and Hanna Elisabeth Gronau, widow of Hergen Herson, widow of Christopher Hudson, widow of Johann Martin Dasher II), 162, 199, 200
Wertsch, Hanna Gronau. See Gronau, Hanna Elisabeth
Wertsch, Johann Caspar, 66, 68–69, 71–73, 88, 114, 143, 161–62, 181–82, 201
Wesley, Charles, 32, 100, 211–12
Wesley, John, 32, 100, 176, 211–14
Whitefield, George, 85, 91, 100, 106, 151, 181, 210, 214–15, 218
Williams, Captain Robert, 50
Wilson, Caroline Price, 5, 250
Wolf, Edmund Jacob, 4, 250
Wolff, Christian, 195, 200
Wright, James (Royal Governor), 70

Zachariae, Carl Heinrich, 169
Ziegenhagen, Friedrich Michael, xi, 7, 9, 19–20, 30–31, 39, 42, 46, 48, 51, 62–63, 66, 73, 91, 121, 136, 144, 156–57, 159, 172–73, 182, 184, 197–98, 208, 213–14, 234
Ziegler, Werner, 169
Zinzendorf, Nikolaus Ludwig von, 9, 46, 165, 167–68, 185, 207–9, 211
Zittrauer, Ernst,, 75
Zoberbiller (Zuberbühler, Reformed pastor in Purrysburg) 106–7
Zuberbühler, Bartholomäus, 51, 95, 101, 107, 114, 188
Zübli, Ambrosius, 104
Zübli, David, 78, 94, 104
Zübli, Johann Joachim, 94–96, 99, 102, 104, 113, 194, 216
Zwiffler, Andreas, 10, 26–27, 33, 155–57, 236
Zwiffler, Anna Regina, 156

Index of Subjects

Anglican (Episcopalian) Church, 1, 87, 93–94, 101, 114–15, 119, 127, 130, 140, 196, 209, 212, 215
Book of Common Prayer, 106, 130
Archival sources, 6–13
Augsburg Agenda, 124–25
Augsburg Church Worship Book, 130
Augsburg Confession, 3, 115, 119–20 168, 220
Apology of, 168

Baptist Church, 125, 146–47, 205, 215, 218
Battle of Bloody Marsh, 44
Bethesda (orphanage founded by George Whitefield), 151, 181, 215

Calendar
    Gregorian, 24
    Julian ("old calendar"), 24, 29
"Catherine Sloep" (ship), 186
"Commerce" (ship), 200
Congregational life,
    financial support, 122–23
    forms of, 112–16
    worship and spiritual life, 123–40
    confirmation instruction, 147–49
Counter Reformation, 16, 18, 139

East India Mission. *See* Halle-Danish East India Mission
Ebenezer, viii–ix, xi, 2, 4, 6–7, 11, 24, 26–61, 78, 99, 102–10, 116–17, 154–62, 177–83, 186, 189, 191–94, 197–205, 209–10, 212–16, 218–20
charter of incorporation, 81, 113
church building in Ebenezer and related communities, 84–92
church constitution/church order, 112–17, 119–23, 221–25
Commemoration and Thanksgiving festival in, 88–89, 131
decline of the settlements, 78–84
economic activity in, 43, 48–51, 56, 153
establishment of, 26–29
Jerusalem Church, 63, 65, 71–72, 76, 84, 87–92, 114, 124, 126–28, 141, 173, 218
judiciary in, 83, 118
library, 149–51, 226–34
"New" Ebenezer, 33–34, 36, 43, 84, 104, 141, 155–56
"Old" Ebenezer, 11, 33–34, 36, 43, 56, 84, 155–56, 163, 166, 170–72,
orphanage in, 85, 103, 118, 141–42, 151–54, 158, 162, 176–77, 183
Rabenhorst–Triebner dispute, 61–74, 88, 115
relocation of, 10, 34–35, 37–38
Revolutionary War and, 74–78, 88, 146–47
school in, 83–84, 98, 107, 123, 140–44, 146, 189
worship in, 123–40

Index of Subjects

Enlightenment, 174, 197, 206
Evangelical Church in Germany (EKD), 206

Fort Frederica, 99–100
Francke Foundations (*see also* Halle Orphan House), viii, xi, 6–7, 12, 22, 44, 49, 79, 90, 95, 116, 151, 154, 161, 164–69, 172, 180, 182, 192, 197, 200, 202, 204, 211
   Collegium Musicum, 166
   girls' school, 180
   Latin school, 172, 192
Freylinghausen hymnbook (*Geistreiches Gesangbuch*), 134, 138–39

German Court Chapel at St. James (London), 19, 62, 114, 124–25, 129–30

Halle-Danish East India Mission, 9, 19, 137, 160, 203, 210
Halle Orphan House, 7, 29, 62, 85, 116, 137, 139, 143, 145, 151–52, 157–58, 160, 166, 168–70, 174, 177, 184, 187, 190–92, 195, 197, 200, 202, 210, 219–21
   medicines from, 95, 116, 144, 154–55, 206
Health care, 154–60
Hessians, 76–77, 200

Indians, 26–27, 32, 48, 59–61, 84, 209–10, 212
   Cherokee, 61, 101, 210
   Creek, 59–61
   Nottaweg, 61
   Uchee (Yuchi), 31, 59
   Yamacraw, 26, 210
   wars with, 60

Jesuits (Society of Jesus), 60
"Judith"/"Loyal Judith" (ship), 42, 188

"London Merchant" (ship), 32, 211
Lutheran Church-Missouri Synod, 219

Mennonites, 206
Methodists/Methodist Church, 205, 212–15, 218, 220
Moravians/Moravian Brethren, 10, 32, 106, 156, 176, 206–13

"Northern Lion" (ship), 204

Palatines, 25, 94, 96, 99, 102, 108
Peace of Westphalia, 15–16, 166
Pietism, 2, 134, 150, 174, 197, 201, 207
   Halle, vii, 134, 138–39, 149–50, 165, 174, 177
   Jena, 207–8
   Silesian, 166, 177
Presbyterian Church/Presbyterians (*see also* Reformed Church), 95, 97, 125, 205, 218, 220
Princeton College, 95
"Purisburg" ("Purysburg," ship), 23

Quakers (Society of Friends), 45

Reformed Church (*see also* Presbyterian Church/Presbyterians), 16, 28, 42, 91, 93–96, 98–100, 102–4, 106–8, 144, 150, 159, 187, 205–6, 215–16
Revolutionary War (*see also* Ebenezer, Revolutionary War in), 4, 19, 61, 73–79, 81, 88, 98, 110, 113, 115, 123, 126, 146, 151, 155, 199–200, 217
Romanticism, 3

St. Anna's Church (Augsburg), 19, 193
St. John's Church (Charleston), 109
St. Mary's Church in the Savoy (London), 18, 23, 29, 200
St. Paul's Church (Halberstadt), 180
St. Ulrich's Church (Halle), 11, 166, 172, 192
Salt League (*Salzbund*), 18
Salzburgers, 2, 16–25, 28–34, 38, 42, 46, 136–37, 143, 166–68, 170
   expulsions, 16–18
   emigration edict, 17

Index of Subjects 259

discord with Swabians in Ebenezer, 56
in East Prussia, 137, 180
in Lithuania, 180
transports of. *See* Transports, Salzburger
Sericulture, 43, 49, 141, 153
"Simonds" (ship), 32, 211
Slavery/slaves, 48, 50–52, 56, 68, 72, 95, 162, 194, 200, 212
Smalcald Articles, 168
Society for Promoting Christian Knowledge (SPCK), 8, 15, 18–23, 31, 42, 45, 56, 62–63, 70, 80, 114–16, 122, 156, 160, 188, 197
Society for the Propagation of the Gospel in Foreign Parts (SPG), 15, 212
South Carolina Synod and Adjacent States, 219–20
Spanish, 44, 99
conflicts with, vii, 42–44, 61, 84, 99, 211
Stamp Act, 61–62, 105, 144, 196
Swiss immigrants, 100, 103, 106–7, 215–16

Transports
Salzburger,
first, 21–25, 44, 50, 60, 88–89, 108, 130–31, 135, 155, 170
second, 25, 28, 45, 152
third, 33, 100, 211
fourth, 25, 42, 185
Swabian, 87–88, 191
first, 52–53
second, 53–54, 193
third, 55–56, 63, 171
Thirty Years War, 15–18, 139
Treaty of Asiento, 14
Trustees (in Ebenezer), 63–64, 70, 81, 83, 97, 119, 158
Trustees for Establishing the Colony of Georgia in America, 3, 8, 14–15, 19–21, 23, 28–31, 33–35, 37, 39–43, 48, 50, 52–53, 56, 60, 91, 94–98, 100, 108, 114, 118, 121, 155, 157, 159, 167–68, 184, 187, 208–9, 211

United Evangelical Lutheran Church of Germany (VELKD), 206

War of Independence. *See* Revolutionary War

Zion Church, 63, 71, 87, 89–92, 105, 117–18, 126, 134–35, 141–43, 194
Zion plantation, 63, 67, 91, 93, 105, 126, 141–43

Index of Places

Abercorn, 26, 28, 40, 54–55, 90, 113, 117, 211
Acton, 92, 95, 99, 113, 216
  worship services in, 127
Alsace, 16
Altona, 203
Amelia Township (Orangeburg, SC District), 95
Ansbach, 161, 184
Appenzell, 103, 106–8
Augsburg, 2, 7,18–19, 21–22, 29, 31–32, 42, 46, 64, 68, 115–16, 119, 137, 160, 172, 185, 192–93, 198, 203, 211
Augusta, 77, 162

Bavaria, 25
Berlin, 6, 103, 164–65, 191
Bethany, 26, 53–54, 56, 58, 64, 67, 70–1, 77, 90, 117, 123, 141–42, 144
  school in, 141
  worship services in, 70, 127
Bethlehem (PA), 211
"Blue Bluff," 53
Blumberg, 191
Bohemia, 166
Brandenburg, 31, 164
Bunzlau, 165–66

Canstatt, 42
Charleston, 8, 25–26, 28, 38, 46, 48, 58, 68–69, 73, 91, 95–98, 102, 108–11, 171, 204, 214–15
Copenhagen, 169

Crailsheim, 183

Daber (Eastern Pomerania), 191
Diemetz, 11
Dover, 21, 23–24, 130
Dresden, 82, 203
Düsseldorf, 185

Easton (Pennsylvania), 109
Ebenezer, *See* Subject Index, Ebenezer
Ebenezer Creek, 27, 31, 33, 53
Effingham County, 6, 83
Eisleben, 202–3
Etzdorf, 200

Fischbeck, 187–88
Franconia, 202
Frederica, 36–37, 44, 47–48, 86–87, 91, 95, 99–102, 108, 113, 115–17, 124, 183–86, 188
  worship in, 101, 127–28
  school in, 140, 145–46

Gatterstädt, 202
Germantown (PA), 45, 104, 110
Gibralter, 15
Goshen, 54, 56, 67, 74, 77–78, 90, 92, 117, 194, 211
  worship in, 127
  school in, 144
Gosport, 188
Greiz, 197–98, 201
Gröningen, 184
Guben, 164

Index of Places

Forst, 163–65

Halberstadt, 180
Halifax (SC), 150
Halle, vii, 7–8, 11, 19, 32, 44, 59, 82,
    92, 100, 115, 119, 121, 129,
    13–16, 151, 155, 157, 162, 165–
    66, 168, 171–78, 180, 183–84,
    186–88, 192, 201–4, 207–9
    University of, vii, 164–65, 180, 182,
    195, 200, 211
Hanau, 144
Heilbronn, 185
Hungary, 155
    Austria-Hungary, 18

Ilsenburg, 169

Jena, 207–8
Josephstown, 54–55, 90, 113

Köpenick, 164
Kroppenstedt, 179–80

Leipzig, 197, 200, 202
Leppehne, 164
Lindau, 42
Lithuania, 164, 180
London, vii, 2, 7, 16, 18–21, 23, 29,
    31–32, 36, 39, 42, 46, 53, 62,
    73, 94, 107, 109, 114, 118, 120,
    124–25, 129–30, 137, 144, 157,
    160, 162, 167, 171, 178, 186,
    188, 198, 200, 203, 208–10,
    212–14, 221–23
Lorraine, 16
Lübben (Lower Lusatia), 165
Lusatia (Lower), 163, 165

Mainz, 185
Mannheim, 185
Maryland, 96
Mecklenburg, 191, 193
Memmingen, 21, 42, 143, 159

Nassau (Bahamas), 200
Nazareth (PA), 211
Neuchatel, 103

New Hanover (PA), 44, 110
New Providence (Bahamas), 162, 200
New Windsor (SC), 107–8, 150
New York, 44–45, 48–49, 200, 211
Nova Scotia, 200
Nuremberg, 198, 203

Obergreiz, 197
Orangeburg (SC), 94–95, 108, 150

Pagenköpp, 191
Palatinate, 16, 53, 92, 98, 216
Pallachocolas (SC) 107, 150
Pennsylvania, 2, 12, 16, 25, 42, 44–48,
    55, 67, 80, 96, 103–4, 106,
    109–10, 144, 156, 171–73, 184,
    198, 202, 210–11, 213
Peretz, 202
Philadelphia, 44–46, 67, 156, 203, 215
Pommerania (Eastern), 192
Port Royal (SC), 42, 46
Pössneck, 197
Prussia, 137, 180, 205
Purrysburg, 34, 43, 78, 86, 94, 103–8,
    142, 146, 152, 155, 214, 216

Querfurt, 202

"Red Bluff," 33
Regensburg, 32, 53, 144
Riesa, 202
Rosswein, 200
Rotterdam, 2, 22–24, 29, 32, 107,
    168–69, 185–86, 188, 203
Rowan County (NC), 81

Salzburg, territory/archbishopric, vii,
    1, 16, 133
Santa Cruz (Teneriffe), 204
Savannah, 25, 27, 29–30, 32, 34–38,
    42–43, 46, 48, 50–56, 59–61,
    66, 69–71, 73, 75–79, 81–82,
    86–87, 92, 100–1, 104–5, 107–
    8, 114–15, 117–18, 145–46,
    150–51, 171, 188, 199, 204–7,
    209–16,
    Lutheran church in, 92–99, 109,
    113, 127–28, 134, 136, 181

Savannah River, 14, 25, 27, 31–33, 40–41, 50, 55, 75, 77, 103–4, 107, 160, 199
Savannahtown (SC), 107, 150
Saxe-Gothe (SC), 91, 150
Saxony, 32, 165, 179, 200, 202
Schaumburg, 187
Schwäbish Hall, 184–86
Schwarzach, 17
Silesia, 25, 152, 165–66, 192, 208
St. Augustine (FL), 79, 199–200
St. Gallen, 94, 104, 136
St. Simons Island (GA), 99
Spain, 14–15
  war with, 43, 76
Stargard, 191–92
Swabia, 16, 25, 109

Teneriffe, 204
Thommendorf, 151, 165–66, 177
Thuringia, 197

Tranquebar, 2, 19, 137, 154, 198
TübingenUniversity of, 6–8, 144, 235
Tulpehocken (PA), 80
Tybee Island, 32, 36, 55, 193, 199, 211

Vernonburg, 92, 94–95, 98–99, 113, 117, 175, 208, 215–16
  worship services in, 127
Virginia, 61, 96, 110

Wernigerode, 168, 188
West Indies, 48, 60, 160, 219
"White Bluff," 98
Württemberg, 16, 19, 25, 49, 52, 81, 97, 100, 109, 183, 197

Yorkshire, 146

Zweibrücken, 98

www.ingramcontent.com/pod-product-compliance
Lightning Source LLC
Chambersburg PA
CBHW071247230426
43668CB00011B/1630